An Elementary Treatise on the
INTEGRAL CALCULUS

Containing Applications to Plane Cur Curves and Surfaces,
With Numerous Examples

BENJAMIN WILLIAMSON M.A., F.R.S

Fellow of Trinity College,
and Professor of Natural Philosophy in the
University of Dublin

MAXWELL PRESS

Chennai   Trichy   New Delhi

MAXWELL PRESS

This edition has been published in india by arrangement with Carson Books, UK

ISBN 978-93-91270-54-4   Maxwell Press

All rights reserved   No. 44, Nallathambi Street,
Triplicane, Chennai 600 005

MJP 1150   © Publishers, 2022

Publisher :   C. Janarthanan

Publisher's Note

The legacy of a country is in its varied cultural heritage, historical literature, developments in the field of economy and science. The top nations in the world are competing in the field of science, economy and literature. This vast legacy has to be conserved and documented so that it can be bestowed to the future generation. The knowledge of this legacy is slowly getting perished in the present generation due to lack of documentation.

Keeping this in mind, the concern with retrospective acquiring of rare books has been accented recently by the burgeoning reprint industry. Maxwell Press is gratified to retrieve the rare collections with a view to bring back those books that were landmarks in their time.

In this effort, a series of rare books would be republished under the banner, "Maxwell Press". The books in the reprint series have been carefully selected for their contemporary usefulness as well as their historical importance within the intellectual. We reconstruct the book with slight enhancements made for better presentation, without affecting the contents of the original edition.

Most of the works selected for republishing covers a huge range of subjects, from history to anthropology. We believe this reprint edition will be a service to the numerous researchers and practitioners active in this fascinating field. We allow readers to experience the wonder of peering into a scholarly work of the highest order and seminal significance.

Maxwell Press

PREFACE.

THIS book has been written as a companion volume to my Treatise on the Differential Calculus, and in its construction I have endeavoured to carry out the same general plan on which that book was composed. I have, accordingly, studied simplicity so far as was consistent with rigour of demonstration, and have tried to make the subject as attractive to the beginner as the nature of the Calculus would permit.

I have, as far as possible, confined my attention to the general principles of Integration, and have endeavoured to arrange the successive portions of the subject in the order best suited for the Student.

I have paid considerable attention to the geometrical applications of the Calculus, and have introduced a number of the leading fundamental properties of the more important curves and surfaces, so far as they are connected with the Integral Calculus. This has led me to give many remarkable results, such as Steiner's general theorems on the connexion of pedals and roulettes, Amsler's Planimeter, Kempe's theorem, Landen's theorems on the rectification of the hyperbola, Genocchi's theorem on the rectification of the Cartesian oval, and others which have not been usually included in text-books on the Integral Calculus.

A Chapter has been devoted to the discussion of Integrals of Inertia. For the methods adopted, and a great part of the details in this Chapter, I am indebted to the kindness of Professor Townsend. My friend, Professor Crofton, of Woolwich, has laid me under very deep obligations by contributing a Chapter on Mean Value and Probability. I am glad to be able to lay this Chapter before the Student, as an introduction to this branch of the subject by a Mathematician whose original and admirable Papers, in the *Philosophical Transactions*, 1868-69, and elsewhere, have so largely contributed to the recent extension of this important application of the Integral Calculus.

In this Edition a short Chapter on Multiple Integration has been introduced, which I hope will be found a useful addition to the Book.

Trinity College,
April, 1884.

TABLE OF CONTENTS.

CHAPTER I.

ELEMENTARY FORMS OF INTEGRATION.

CHAPTER II.

INTEGRATION OF RATIONAL FRACTIONS.

CHAPTER III.

INTEGRATION BY SUCCESSIVE REDUCTION.

CHAPTER IV.

INTEGRATION BY RATIONALIZATION.

CHAPTER V.

MISCELLANEOUS EXAMPLES OF INTEGRATION.

Contents.

CHAPTER VI.

DEFINITE INTEGRALS.

CHAPTER VII.

AREAS OF PLANE CURVES.

---

* This theorem was communicated by Frullani to Plana in 1821, and published afterwards in *Mem. del Soc. Ital.*, 1828.

CHAPTER VIII.

LENGTHS OF CURVES.

CHAPTER IX.

VOLUMES AND SURFACES OF SOLIDS.

CHAPTER X.

INTEGRALS OF INERTIA.

Contents.

CHAPTER XI.

MULTIPLE INTEGRALS.

CHAPTER XII.

ON MEAN VALUE AND PROBABILITY.

Contents.

The beginner is recommended to omit the following portions on the *first* reading :—Arts. 46, 49, 50, 72–76, 79–81, 89, 96–125, 132, 140, 142–147, 149, 158–167, 178, 180, 182, 189–193, Chapters x., xi., xii.

INTEGRAL CALCULUS.

CHAPTER I.

ELEMENTARY FORMS OF INTEGRATION.

1. **Integration.**—The Integral Calculus is the inverse of the Differential. In the more simple case to which this treatise is principally limited, the object of the Integral Calculus is to *find a function of a single variable when its differential is known.*

Let the differential be represented by $F(x)\,dx$, then *the function whose differential is $F(x)\,dx$ is called its integral,* and is represented by the notation

$$\int F(x)\,dx.$$

Thus, since in the notation of the Differential Calculus we have

$$df(x) = f'(x)\,dx,$$

the integral of $f'(x)\,dx$ is denoted by $f(x)$; i.e.

$$\int f'(x)\,dx = f(x).$$

Moreover, as $f(x)$ and $f(x) + C$ (where C is any arbitrary quantity that does not vary with x) have the same differential, it follows, that to find the *general* form of the integral of $f'(x)\,dx$ it is necessary to add an arbitrary constant to $f(x)$; hence we obtain, as the general expression for the integral in question,

$$\int f'(x)\,dx = f(x) + C. \tag{1}$$

[1]

In the subsequent integrals the constant C will be omitted, as it can always be supplied when necessary. In the applications of the Integral Calculus the value of the *constant is determined in each case by the data of the problem*, as will be more fully explained subsequently.

The process of finding the *primitive function* or the *integral* of any given differential is called *integration*.

The expression $F(x)\, dx$ under the sign of integration is called an *element* of the integral; it is also, in the limit, the increment of the primitive function when x is changed into $x + dx$ (Diff. Calc., Art. 7); accordingly, the process of integration may be regarded as the finding the *sum** of an infinite number of such elements.

We shall postpone the consideration of Integration from this point of view, and shall commence with the treatment of Integration regarded as being the inverse of Differentiation.

2. **Elementary Integrals.**—A very slight acquaintance with the Differential Calculus will at once suggest the integrals of many differentials. We commence with the simplest cases, *an arbitrary constant being in all cases understood.*

On referring to the elementary forms of differentiation established in Chapter I. Diff. Calc. we may write down at once the following integrals :—

$$\int x^m\, dx = \frac{x^{m+1}}{m+1}. \qquad \int \frac{dx}{x^m} = \frac{-1}{(m-1)x^{m-1}}. \qquad (a)$$

$$\int \frac{dx}{x} = \log(x). \qquad\qquad (b)$$

$$\int \sin mx\, dx = -\frac{\cos mx}{m}, \qquad \int \cos mx\, dx = \frac{\sin mx}{m}. \qquad (c)$$

$$\int \frac{dx}{\cos^2 x} = \tan x, \qquad \int \frac{dx}{\sin^2 x} = -\cot x. \qquad (d)$$

---

* It was in this aspect that the process of integration was treated by Leibnitz, the symbol of integration $\int$ being regarded as the initial letter of the word *sum*, in the same way as the symbol of differentiation d is the initial letter in the word *difference*.

$$\int \frac{dx}{\sqrt{a^2 - x^2}} = \sin^{-1}\frac{x}{a}. \tag{e}$$

$$\int \frac{dx}{a^2 + x^2} = \frac{1}{a}\tan^{-1}\frac{x}{a}. \tag{f}$$

$$\int e^x\,dx = e^x, \qquad \int a^x\,dx = \frac{a^x}{\log a}. \tag{g}$$

These, together with two or three additional forms which shall be afterwards supplied, are called the *fundamental** or *elementary* integrals, to which all other forms,† that admit of integration in a finite number of terms, are ultimately reducible.

Many integrals are immediately reducible to one or other of these forms: a few simple examples are given for exercise.

EXAMPLES.

1. $\displaystyle\int \frac{dx}{x^2}.$ *Ans.* $-\dfrac{1}{x}.$

2. $\displaystyle\int \frac{dx}{\sqrt{x}}.$,, $2\sqrt{x}.$

3. $\displaystyle\int \tan x\,dx.$,, $-\log(\cos x).$

4. $\displaystyle\int \frac{x^{n-1}\,dx}{a + bx^n}.$,, $\dfrac{1}{nb}\log(a + bx^n).$

5. $\displaystyle\int \frac{x\,dx}{\sqrt{1 - x^2}}.$,, $-\sqrt{1 - x^2}.$

6. $\displaystyle\int \frac{dx}{a + bx^2}.$,, $\dfrac{1}{\sqrt{ab}}\tan^{-1}\left(x\sqrt{\dfrac{b}{a}}\right).$

7. $\displaystyle\int \frac{\sin\theta\,d\theta}{\cos^2\theta}.$,, $\sec\theta.$

8. $\displaystyle\int e^{ax}\,dx.$,, $\dfrac{1}{a}e^{ax}.$

---

* The fundamental integrals are denoted in this chapter by the letters a, b, c, &c.; the other formulæ by numerals 1, 2, 3, &c.

† By integrable forms are here understood those contained in the elementary portion of the Integral Calculus as involving the ordinary transcendental functions only, and excluding what are styled Elliptic and Hyper-Elliptic functions.

[1 a]

9. $\displaystyle\int \frac{dx}{x^{\frac{4}{3}}}.$ *Ans.* $-\dfrac{3}{x^{\frac{1}{3}}}.$

10. $\displaystyle\int \frac{dx}{x^{\frac{n-1}{n}}}.$,, $n x^{\frac{1}{n}}.$

11. $\displaystyle\int \frac{dx}{x - a}.$,, $\log (x - a).$

3. Integral of a Sum.—It follows immediately from Art. 12, Diff. Calc., that the integral of the sum of any number of differentials is the sum of the integrals of each taken separately.   For example—

$$\int (A x^m + B x^n + C x^r + \&\text{c.})\, dx = A \int x^m\, dx + B \int x^n\, dx + C \int x^r\, dx + \&\text{c.}$$

$$= \frac{A x^{m+1}}{m + 1} + \frac{B x^{n+1}}{n + 1} + \frac{C x^{r+1}}{r + 1} + \&\text{c.} \qquad (2)$$

Hence we can write down immediately the integral of any function which is reducible to a finite number of terms consisting of powers of x multiplied by constant coefficients.

Again, to find the integrals of $\cos^2 x\, dx$ and $\sin^2 x\, dx$; here

$$\int \cos^2 x\, dx = \int \frac{1 + \cos 2x}{2}\, dx = \frac{x}{2} + \frac{\sin 2x}{4}, \qquad (3)$$

$$\int \sin^2 x\, dx = \int \frac{1 - \cos 2x}{2}\, dx = \frac{x}{2} - \frac{\sin 2x}{4}. \qquad (4)$$

A few examples are added for practice.

EXAMPLES.

1. $\displaystyle\int \frac{(1 - x^2)^2\, dx}{x}.$ *Ans.* $\log x - x^2 + \dfrac{x^4}{4}.$

2. $\displaystyle\int \frac{(x - 2)\, dx}{x \sqrt{x}}.$,, $2\sqrt{x} + \dfrac{4}{\sqrt{x}}.$

3. $\displaystyle\int \tan^2 x\, dx = \int (\sec^2 x - 1)\, dx.$,, $\tan x - x.$

4. $\int \cos mx \cos nx\, dx.$ *Ans.* $\dfrac{\sin(m+n)x}{2(m+n)} + \dfrac{\sin(m-n)x}{2(m-n)}.$

5. $\int \sin mx \sin nx\, dx.$,, $\dfrac{\sin(m-n)x}{2(m-n)} - \dfrac{\sin(m+n)x}{2(m+n)}.$

6. $\int \sqrt{\dfrac{a+x}{a-x}}\, dx.$,, $a \sin^{-1}\dfrac{x}{a} - \sqrt{a^2 - x^2}.$

Multiply the numerator and denominator by $\sqrt{a+x}$.

7. $\int x \sqrt{x+a}\, dx.$ *Ans.* $\dfrac{2}{5}(x+a)^{\frac{5}{2}} - \dfrac{2}{3} a (x+a)^{\frac{3}{2}}.$

8. $\dfrac{dx}{\sqrt{x+a} + \sqrt{x}}.$,, $\dfrac{2}{3a}\left((x+a)^{\frac{3}{2}} - x^{\frac{3}{2}}\right).$

Multiply the numerator and denominator by the complementary surd

$$\sqrt{x+a} - \sqrt{x}.$$

9. $\int \dfrac{a+bx}{a'+b'x}\, dx.$ *Ans.* $\dfrac{bx}{b'} + \dfrac{ab' - ba'}{b'^2} \log(a' + b'x).$

Here $\qquad \dfrac{a+bx}{a'+b'x} = \dfrac{b}{b'} + \dfrac{ab' - ba'}{b'(a' + b'x)}.$

4. **Integration by Substitution.**—The integration of many expressions is immediately reducible to the elementary forms in Art. 2, by the substitution of a new variable.

For example, to integrate $(a + bx)^n\, dx$, we substitute z for $a + bx$; then $dz = bdx$, and

$$\int (a+bx)^n\, dx = \int \frac{z^n\, dz}{b} = \frac{z^{n+1}}{(n+1)b} = \frac{(a+bx)^{n+1}}{(n+1)b}.$$

Again, to find

$$\int \frac{x^2\, dx}{(a+bx)^n},$$

we substitute z for $a + bx$, as before, when the integral becomes

$$\frac{1}{b^3} \int \frac{(z-a)^2\, dz}{z^n},$$

or $\qquad -\dfrac{1}{b}\left\{\dfrac{1}{(n-3)z^{n-3}} - \dfrac{2a}{(n-2)z^{n-2}} + \dfrac{a^2}{(n-1)z^{n-1}}\right\}.$

On replacing z by $a + bx$ the required integral can be expressed in terms of x.

The more general integral

$$\int \frac{x^m\, dx}{(a + bx)^n},$$

where m is any positive integer, by a like substitution becomes

$$\frac{1}{b^{m+1}} \int \frac{(z - a)^m\, dz}{z^n}.$$

Expanding by the binomial theorem and integrating each term separately the required integral can be immediately obtained.

Again, to find

$$\int \frac{dx}{x^m\, (a + bx)^n},$$

we substitute z for $\dfrac{a}{x} + b$, and it becomes

$$-\frac{1}{a^{m+n-1}} \int \frac{(z - b)^{m+n-2}\, dz}{z^n},$$

which is integrable, as before, whenever $m + n$ is a positive integer greater than unity.

Thus, for example, we have

$$\int \frac{dx}{x\, (a + bx)} = \frac{1}{a} \log \left(\frac{x}{a + bx} \right).$$

It may be observed that all fractional expressions in which the numerator is the differential of the denominator can be immediately integrated.

For we obviously have, from (b),

$$\int \frac{f'(x)\, dx}{f(x)} = \log f(x). \tag{5}$$

EXAMPLES.

1. $\displaystyle\int \dfrac{\sin x\, dx}{a + b \cos x}.$ *Ans.* $-\dfrac{\log (a + b \cos x)}{b}.$

2. $\displaystyle\int \dfrac{x^3\, dx}{\sqrt{a^8 - x^8}}.$,, $\dfrac{1}{4} \sin^{-1}\left(\dfrac{x}{a}\right)^4.$

3. $\displaystyle\int \log x\, \dfrac{dx}{x}.$,, $\dfrac{1}{2}(\log x)^2.$

4. $\displaystyle\int \dfrac{dx}{x \log x}.$,, $\log (\log x).$

5. $\displaystyle\int \dfrac{x^2\, dx}{(a + bx)^3}.$,, $\dfrac{\log (a + bx)}{b^3} + \dfrac{3a^2 + 4abx}{2b^3 (a + bx)^2}.$

6. $\displaystyle\int \dfrac{dx}{x^2 (a + bx)^2}.$,, $\dfrac{2b}{a^3} \log \dfrac{a + bx}{x} - \dfrac{a + 2bx}{a^2 x\, (a + bx)}.$

7. $\displaystyle\int \dfrac{x\, dx}{(a + bx)^{\frac{1}{2}}}.$,, $\dfrac{2 (a + bx)^{\frac{3}{2}}}{3 b^2} - \dfrac{2a (a + bx)^{\frac{1}{2}}}{b^2}.$

8. $\displaystyle\int \dfrac{x\, dx}{(a + bx)^{\frac{1}{3}}}.$,, $\dfrac{3 (a + bx)^{\frac{5}{3}}}{5 b^2} - \dfrac{3a (a + bx)^{\frac{2}{3}}}{2 b^2}.$

9. $\displaystyle\int \dfrac{dx}{x \sqrt{2ax - a^2}}.$,, $\dfrac{2}{a} \tan^{-1} \sqrt{\dfrac{2x - a}{a}}.$

Assume $2ax - a^2 = z^2$, then $a\, dx = z\, dz$, and the transformed integral is

$$\int \dfrac{2\, dz}{a^2 + z^2}.$$

5. **Integration of** $\dfrac{dx}{x^2 - a^2}.$

Since $\dfrac{1}{x^2 - a^2} = \dfrac{1}{2a}\left\{\dfrac{1}{x - a} - \dfrac{1}{x + a}\right\},$

we get $\displaystyle\int \dfrac{dx}{x^2 - a^2} = \dfrac{1}{2a} \log \dfrac{x - a}{x + a}.$ (h)

This is to be regarded as another fundamental formula additional to those contained in Art. 2.

In like manner, since

$$\frac{1}{(x - a)(x - \beta)} = \frac{1}{a - \beta}\left\{\frac{1}{x - a} - \frac{1}{x - \beta}\right\},$$

we have
$$\int \frac{dx}{(x - a)(x - \beta)} = \frac{1}{a - \beta} \log \frac{x - a}{x - \beta}. \tag{6}$$

EXAMPLES.

1. $\displaystyle\int \frac{dx}{x^2 - 9}.$ *Ans.* $\dfrac{1}{6} \log \dfrac{x - 3}{x + 3}.$

2. $\displaystyle\int \frac{dx}{(x + 2)(x - 3)}.$,, $\dfrac{1}{5} \log \dfrac{x - 3}{x + 2}.$

3. $\displaystyle\int \frac{dx}{x^2 + 9x + 20}.$,, $\log \dfrac{x + 4}{x + 5}.$

4. $\displaystyle\int \frac{dx}{x^2 - 3}.$,, $\dfrac{1}{2\sqrt{3}} \log \dfrac{x - \sqrt{3}}{x + \sqrt{3}}.$

6. Integration of $\quad \dfrac{dx}{a + 2bx + cx^2}.$

This may be written in the form

$$\frac{cdx}{(cx + b)^2 + ac - b^2};$$

or, substituting z for $cx + b$,

$$\frac{dz}{z^2 + ac - b^2}.$$

This is of the form (f) or (h) according as $ac - b^2$ is positive or negative.

Hence, if $ac > b^2$ we have

$$\int \frac{dx}{a + 2bx + cx^2} = \frac{1}{\sqrt{ac - b^2}} \tan^{-1} \frac{cx + b}{\sqrt{ac - b^2}}. \tag{7}$$

If $ac < b^2$,

$$\int \frac{dx}{a + 2bx + cx^2} = \frac{1}{2\sqrt{b^2 - ac}} \log \frac{cx + b - \sqrt{b^2 - ac}}{cx + b + \sqrt{b^2 - ac}}. \qquad (8)$$

This latter form can be also immediately obtained from (6).

In the particular case when $ac = b^2$, the value of the integral is

$$\frac{-1}{cx + b}.$$

7. **Integration of** $\dfrac{(p + qx)\,dx}{a + 2bx + cx^2}$.

This can at once be written in the form

$$\frac{q}{c} \frac{(b + cx)\,dx}{a + 2bx + cx^2} + \frac{pc - qb}{c} \frac{dx}{a + 2bx + cx^2}.$$

The integral of the first term is evidently

$$\frac{q}{2c} \log (a + 2bx + cx^2),$$

while the integral of the second is obtained by the preceding Article.

For example, let it be proposed to integrate

$$\frac{(x \cos \theta - 1)\,dx}{x^2 - 2x \cos \theta + 1}.$$

The expression becomes in this case

$$\frac{\cos \theta\,(x - \cos \theta)\,dx}{x^2 - 2x \cos \theta + 1} - \frac{\sin^2 \theta\,dx}{(x - \cos \theta)^2 + \sin^2 \theta};$$

hence

$$\int \frac{(x \cos \theta - 1)\,dx}{x^2 - 2x \cos \theta + 1} = \frac{\cos \theta}{2} \log (x^2 - 2x \cos \theta + 1)$$

$$- \sin \theta \tan^{-1} \frac{x - \cos \theta}{\sin \theta}. \qquad (9)$$

When the roots of $a + 2bx + cx^2$ are real, it will be found simpler to integrate the expression by its decomposition into partial fractions. A general discussion of this method will be given in the next chapter.

EXAMPLES.

1. $\displaystyle\int \frac{dx}{1 + x + x^2}.$ *Ans.* $\dfrac{2}{\sqrt{3}} \tan^{-1}\left(\dfrac{2x + 1}{\sqrt{3}}\right).$

2. $\displaystyle\int \frac{dx}{1 + x - x^2}.$ " $\dfrac{1}{\sqrt{5}} \log\left(\dfrac{2x - 1 + \sqrt{5}}{2x - 1 - \sqrt{5}}\right).$

3. $\displaystyle\int \frac{dx}{x^2 + x - 12}.$ " $\dfrac{1}{7} \log\left(\dfrac{x - 3}{x + 4}\right).$

4. $\displaystyle\int \frac{dx}{x^2 + 4x + 5}.$ " $\tan^{-1}(x + 2).$

5. $\displaystyle\int \frac{dx}{5x^2 + 4x + 8}.$ " $\dfrac{1}{6} \tan^{-1} \dfrac{5x + 2}{6}.$

6. $\displaystyle\int \frac{x^2\, dx}{1 - x^6}.$ " $\dfrac{1}{6} \log\left(\dfrac{1 + x^3}{1 - x^3}\right).$

7. $\displaystyle\int \frac{x^3 dx}{x^8 - x^4 - 6}.$ " $\dfrac{1}{20} \log\left(\dfrac{x^4 - 3}{x^4 + 2}\right).$

8. $\displaystyle\int \frac{dx}{1 - 2x + 2x^2}.$ " $\tan^{-1}(2x - 1).$

8. Exponential Value for sin θ and cos θ.—By comparing the fundamental formulæ (f) and (h) the well-known exponential forms for $\sin \theta$ and $\cos \theta$ can be immediately deduced, as follows:

Substitute $z\sqrt{-1}$ for x in both sides of the equation

$$\int \frac{dx}{1 - x^2} = \frac{1}{2} \log\left(\frac{1 + x}{1 - x}\right) + const.;$$

and we get

$$\int \frac{dz}{1 + z^2} = \frac{1}{2\sqrt{-1}} \log\left(\frac{1 + z\sqrt{-1}}{1 - z\sqrt{-1}}\right) + const.;$$

or, by (f), $\tan^{-1}z = \dfrac{1}{2\sqrt{-1}} \log\left(\dfrac{1 + z\sqrt{-1}}{1 - z\sqrt{-1}}\right) + const.$

Now, let $z = \tan\theta$, and this becomes

$$\theta = \frac{1}{2\sqrt{-1}} \log\left(\frac{1 + \sqrt{-1}\,\tan\theta}{1 - \sqrt{-1}\,\tan\theta}\right) + const.$$

When $\theta = 0$, this reduces to $0 = const.$

Hence $e^{2\theta\sqrt{-1}} = \dfrac{\cos\theta + \sqrt{-1}\,\sin\theta}{\cos\theta - \sqrt{-1}\,\sin\theta} = (\cos\theta + \sqrt{-1}\,\sin\theta)^2,$

or $e^{\theta\sqrt{-1}} = \cos\theta + \sqrt{-1}\,\sin\theta,$

$$e^{-\theta\sqrt{-1}} = \cos\theta - \sqrt{-1}\,\sin\theta.$$

9. **Integration of** $\dfrac{dx}{\sqrt{x^2 \pm a^2}}.$

Assume* $\sqrt{x^2 \pm a^2} = z - x,$

then we get $\pm a^2 = z^2 - 2xz,$

hence $(z - x)\,dz = z\,dx,$ or $\dfrac{dx}{z - x} = \dfrac{dz}{z};$

$$\therefore \quad \int \frac{dx}{\sqrt{x^2 \pm a^2}} = \int \frac{dz}{z} = \log z = \log\left(x + \sqrt{x^2 \pm a^2}\right). \qquad (i)$$

This is to be regarded as another fundamental form.

By aid of this and of form (e) it is evident that all expressions of the shape

$$\frac{dx}{\sqrt{a + 2bx + cx^2}}$$

---

* The student will better understand the propriety of this assumption after reading a subsequent chapter, in which a general transformation, of which the above is a particular case, will be given.

can be immediately integrated; a, b, c, being any constants, positive or negative.

The preceding integration evidently depends on formula (i), or (e), according as the coefficient of x^2 is positive or negative.

Thus, we have

$$\int \frac{dx}{\sqrt{a + 2bx + cx^2}} = \frac{1}{\sqrt{c}} \log\left(cx + b + \sqrt{c(a + 2bx + cx^2)}\right), \quad (10)$$

$$\int \frac{dx}{\sqrt{a + 2bx - cx^2}} = \frac{1}{\sqrt{c}} \sin^{-1}\left(\frac{cx - b}{\sqrt{ac + b^2}}\right), \quad (11)$$

c being regarded as positive in both integrals.

When the factors in the quadratic $a + 2bx + cx^2$ are real, and given, the preceding integral can be exhibited in a simpler form by the method of the two next Articles.

10. **Integration of** $\dfrac{dx}{\sqrt{(x - a)(x - \beta)}}$.

Assume $\qquad x - a = z^2$, then $dx = 2zdz$;

$$\therefore \frac{dx}{\sqrt{x - a}} = 2dz;$$

hence $\qquad \dfrac{dx}{\sqrt{(x - a)(x - \beta)}} = \dfrac{2dz}{\sqrt{z^2 + a - \beta}};$

$$\therefore \int \frac{dx}{\sqrt{(x - a)(x - \beta)}} = 2 \int \frac{dz}{\sqrt{z^2 + a - \beta}}$$

$$= 2 \log\left(z + \sqrt{z^2 + a - \beta}\right), \text{ by } (i),$$

or $\qquad \displaystyle\int \frac{dx}{\sqrt{(x - a)(x - \beta)}} = 2 \log\left(\sqrt{x - a} + \sqrt{x - \beta}\right). \quad (12)$

11. **Integration of** $\dfrac{dx}{\sqrt{(x-a)(\beta-x)}}$.

As before, assume $x - a = z^2$, and we get

$$\frac{dx}{\sqrt{(x-a)(\beta-x)}} = \frac{2\,dz}{\sqrt{\beta - a - z^2}}.$$

Hence, by (e),

$$\int \frac{dx}{\sqrt{(x-a)(\beta-x)}} = 2\sin^{-1}\sqrt{\frac{x-a}{\beta-a}}. \qquad (13)$$

Otherwise, thus :

assume $\qquad x = a\cos^2\theta + \beta\sin^2\theta,$

then $\qquad \beta - x = (\beta-a)\cos^2\theta, \quad x - a = (\beta-a)\sin^2\theta,$

and $\qquad dx = 2(\beta-a)\sin\theta\cos\theta\,d\theta\,;$

hence $\qquad \dfrac{dx}{\sqrt{(x-a)(\beta-x)}} = 2\,d\theta\,;$

$$\therefore \int \frac{dx}{\sqrt{(x-a)(\beta-x)}} = 2\theta = 2\sin^{-1}\sqrt{\frac{x-a}{\beta-a}}.$$

12. Again, as in Art. 7, the expression

$$\frac{(p+qx)\,dx}{\sqrt{a+2bx+cx^2}}$$

can be transformed into

$$\frac{q}{c}\frac{(b+cx)\,dx}{\sqrt{a+2bx+cx^2}} + \frac{pc-qb}{c}\frac{dx}{\sqrt{a+2bx+cx^2}},$$

and is, accordingly, immediately integrable by aid of the preceding formulæ.

EXAMPLES.

1. $\displaystyle\int \frac{dx}{\sqrt{x^2 - ax}}.$ *Ans.* $2 \log (\sqrt{x} + \sqrt{x - a}).$

2. $\displaystyle\int \frac{dx}{\sqrt{ax - x^2}}.$,, $\sin^{-1} \sqrt{\dfrac{x}{a}}.$

3. $\displaystyle\int \frac{dx}{\sqrt{3x - x^2 - 2}}.$,, $2 \sin^{-1} \sqrt{x - 1}.$

4. $\displaystyle\int \frac{dx}{\sqrt{1 + x + x^2}}.$,, $\log (2x + 1 + 2\sqrt{1 + x + x^2}).$

5. $\displaystyle\int \sqrt{\frac{x + a}{x + b}}\, dx = \sqrt{(x + a)(x + b)} + (a - b) \log (\sqrt{x + a} + \sqrt{x + b}).$

Multiply the numerator and denominator by $\sqrt{x + a}.$

6. $\displaystyle\int \frac{dx}{\sqrt{1 - x - x^2}}.$ *Ans.* $\sin^{-1} \dfrac{2x + 1}{\sqrt{5}}.$

7. $\displaystyle\int \frac{dx}{\sqrt{(a + bx)(a' - b'x)}}.$,, $\dfrac{2}{\sqrt{bb'}} \sin^{-1} \sqrt{\dfrac{b'(a + bx)}{ab' + ba'}}.$

8. Show, as in Art. 8, by comparing the fundamental formulæ (e) and (i), that

$$\cos \theta + \sqrt{-1} \sin \theta = e^{\theta\sqrt{-1}}.$$

13. **Integration of** $\displaystyle \frac{dx}{(x - p)\sqrt{a + 2bx + cx^2}}.$

Let $x - p = \dfrac{1}{z}$, then

$$\frac{dx}{x - p} = -\frac{dz}{z} \quad \text{and} \quad x = \frac{1 + pz}{z}.$$

$$\therefore \int \frac{dx}{(x - p)\sqrt{a + 2bx + cx^2}} = \int \frac{-dz}{\sqrt{az^2 + 2bz(1 + pz) + c(1 + pz)^2}}$$

$$= -\int \frac{dz}{\sqrt{a' + 2b'z + c'z^2}};$$

where $a' = c, \quad b' = b + cp, \quad c' = a + 2bp + cp^2.$

The integral consequently is reducible to (10), or (11), according as c' is positive or negative.

EXAMPLES.

1. $\displaystyle\int \frac{dx}{x\sqrt{x^2 - a^2}}.$ *Ans.* $\dfrac{1}{a} \cos^{-1}\left(\dfrac{a}{x}\right).$

2. $\displaystyle\int \frac{dx}{x\sqrt{x^2 + 1}}.$,, $\log\left(\dfrac{\sqrt{1 + x^2} - 1}{x}\right).$

3. $\displaystyle\int \frac{dx}{(1 + x)\sqrt{1 - x^2}}.$,, $-\sqrt{\dfrac{1 - x}{1 + x}}.$

4. $\displaystyle\int \frac{dx}{x\sqrt{a + 2bx + cx^2}}.$ *Ans.* $\dfrac{1}{\sqrt{a}} \log\left(\dfrac{x}{a + bx + \sqrt{a}\sqrt{a + 2bx + cx^2}}\right).$

5. $\displaystyle\int \frac{dx}{x\sqrt{cx^2 + 2bx - a}}.$ *Ans.* $\dfrac{1}{\sqrt{a}} \sin^{-1}\left(\dfrac{bx - a}{x\sqrt{ac + b^2}}\right).$

6. $\displaystyle\int \frac{dx}{(1 + x)\sqrt{1 + 2x - x^2}}.$,, $\dfrac{1}{\sqrt{2}} \sin^{-1}\left(\dfrac{x\sqrt{2}}{1 + x}\right).$

7. $\displaystyle\int \frac{dx}{(1 + x)\sqrt{1 + x - x^2}}.$,, $\sin^{-1}\left(\dfrac{1 + 3x}{(1 + x)\sqrt{5}}\right).$

14. The transformation adopted in the last Article is one of frequent application in Integration. It is, accordingly, worthy of the student's notice that when we change x into $\dfrac{1}{z}$ we have $\dfrac{dx}{x} = -\dfrac{dz}{z}$; and, in general, if $x^n = \dfrac{1}{z}$, $\dfrac{dx}{x} = -\dfrac{dz}{nz}$.

These results follow immediately from *logarithmic* differentiation, and often furnish a clue as to when an Integration is facilitated by such a transformation.

For example, let us take the integral

$$\int \frac{dx}{x(a + bx^n)}.$$

Here, the substitution of $\dfrac{1}{z}$ for x^n gives

$$-\frac{1}{n}\int \frac{dz}{az + b}.$$

The value of which is obviously

$$-\frac{1}{na}\log\,(az\,+\,b),\ \text{or}\ \frac{1}{na}\log\left(\frac{x^n}{a\,+\,bx^n}\right).$$

Again, to integrate

$$\frac{dx}{x\sqrt{ax^n\,+\,b}},$$

assume $x^n = \dfrac{1}{z^2}$, and the transformed integral is

$$-\frac{2}{n}\int\frac{dz}{\sqrt{a\,+\,bz^2}}.$$

This is found by (e) or (i) according as b is positive or negative.

15. **Integration of** $\quad\dfrac{dx}{(a\,+\,cx^2)^{\frac{3}{2}}}.$

Let $x = \dfrac{1}{z}$ and the expression becomes

$$-\frac{zdz}{(az^2\,+\,c)^{\frac{3}{2}}};$$

the integral of this is evidently

$$\frac{1}{a\,(az^2\,+\,c)^{\frac{1}{2}}},\ \text{or}\ \frac{x}{a\,(a\,+\,cx^2)^{\frac{1}{2}}}.$$

Hence $\qquad\displaystyle\int\frac{dx}{(a\,+\,cx^2)^{\frac{3}{2}}}=\frac{x}{a\,(a\,+\,cx^2)^{\frac{1}{2}}}.$ $\qquad\qquad$ (14)

16. **To find the integral of**

$$\frac{dx}{(a\,+\,2bx\,+\,cx^2)^{\frac{3}{2}}}.$$

This can be written in the form

$$\frac{c^{\frac{3}{2}}\,dx}{\{ac\,-\,b^2\,+\,(cx\,+\,b)^2\}^{\frac{3}{2}}},$$

which is reduced to the preceding on making $cx + b = z$.

Hence, we get

$$\int \frac{dx}{(a + 2bx + cx^2)^{\frac{3}{2}}} = \frac{b + cx}{(ac - b^2)(a + 2bx + cx^2)^{\frac{1}{2}}}. \qquad (15)$$

Again, if we substitute $\dfrac{1}{z}$ for x,

$$\frac{xdx}{(a + 2bx + cx^2)^{\frac{3}{2}}} \text{ becomes } \frac{-dz}{(az^2 + 2bz + c)^{\frac{3}{2}}},$$

and, accordingly, we have

$$\int \frac{xdx}{(a + 2bx + cx^2)^{\frac{3}{2}}} = -\frac{a + bx}{(ac - b^2)(a + 2bx + cx^2)^{\frac{1}{2}}}.$$

Combining these two results, we get

$$\int \frac{(p + qx)\,dx}{(a + 2bx + cx^2)^{\frac{3}{2}}} = \frac{bp - aq + (cp - bq)\,x}{(ac - b^2)(a + 2bx + cx^2)^{\frac{1}{2}}}. \qquad (16)$$

17. Integration of $\dfrac{d\theta}{\sin\theta}$ **and** $\dfrac{d\theta}{\cos\theta}$.

It will be shown in a subsequent chapter that the integration of a numerous class of expressions is reducible either to that of $\dfrac{d\theta}{\sin\theta}$, or of $\dfrac{d\theta}{\cos\theta}$: we accordingly propose to investigate their values here. For this purpose we shall first find the integral of $\dfrac{d\theta}{\sin\theta \cos\theta}$.

Here $\dfrac{d\theta}{\sin\theta \cos\theta} = \dfrac{\dfrac{d\theta}{\cos^2\theta}}{\tan\theta} = \dfrac{d(\tan\theta)}{\tan\theta}$;

consequently $\displaystyle\int \frac{d\theta}{\sin\theta \cos\theta} = \log(\tan\theta). \qquad (17)$

[2]

Next, to find the integral of

$$\frac{d\theta}{\sin \theta}.$$

This can be written in the form

$$\frac{d\theta}{2 \sin\dfrac{\theta}{2} \cos\dfrac{\theta}{2}},$$

and, by the preceding, we have

$$\int \frac{d\theta}{\sin \theta} = \log \left(\tan \frac{\theta}{2} \right). \tag{18}$$

Again, to determine the integral of $\dfrac{d\theta}{\cos \theta}$ we substitute $\dfrac{\pi}{2} - \phi$ for θ, and the expression becomes $\dfrac{-\,d\phi}{\sin \phi}$: the integral of this, by (18), is

$$- \log \left(\tan \frac{\phi}{2} \right), \text{ or } \log \left(\cot \frac{\phi}{2} \right), \text{ or } \log \left\{ \cot \left(\frac{\pi}{4} - \frac{\theta}{2} \right) \right\}.$$

Accordingly, we have

$$\int \frac{d\theta}{\cos \theta} = \log \left\{ \cot \left(\frac{\pi}{4} - \frac{\theta}{2} \right) \right\} = \log \left\{ \tan \left(\frac{\pi}{4} + \frac{\theta}{2} \right) \right\}. \tag{19}$$

This integral can also be easily obtained otherwise, as follows :—

$$\int \frac{d\theta}{\cos \theta} = \int \frac{\cos \theta \, d\theta}{\cos^2 \theta} = \int \frac{d(\sin \theta)}{\cos^2 \theta}.$$

Let $\sin \theta = x$, and the integral becomes

$$\int \frac{dx}{1 - x^2} = \frac{1}{2} \log \left(\frac{1 + x}{1 - x} \right) = \frac{1}{2} \log \left(\frac{1 + \sin \theta}{1 - \sin \theta} \right).$$

The student will find no difficulty in identifying this result with that contained in (19).

18. Integration of $\dfrac{d\theta}{a + b \cos \theta}$.

This can be immediately written in the form

$$\frac{d\theta}{(a + b) \cos^2 \dfrac{\theta}{2} + (a - b) \sin^2 \dfrac{\theta}{2}},$$

or

$$\frac{\sec^2 \dfrac{\theta}{2}\, d\theta}{a + b + (a - b) \tan^2 \dfrac{\theta}{2}} :$$

on substituting z for $\tan \dfrac{\theta}{2}$ this becomes

$$\frac{2dz}{a + b + (a - b) z^2}.$$

Consequently, by Ex. 6, Art. 2, we get

(1) when $a > b$,

$$\int \frac{d\theta}{a + b \cos \theta} = \frac{2}{\sqrt{a^2 - b^2}} \tan^{-1} \left\{ \sqrt{\frac{a - b}{a + b}} \, \tan \frac{\theta}{2} \right\}. \qquad (20)$$

(2) when $a < b$, by formula (h),

$$\int \frac{d\theta}{a + b \cos \theta} = \frac{1}{\sqrt{b^2 - a^2}} \log \left\{ \frac{\sqrt{b + a} + \sqrt{b - a} \, \tan \dfrac{\theta}{2}}{\sqrt{b + a} - \sqrt{b - a} \, \tan \dfrac{\theta}{2}} \right\}. (21)$$

If we assume $a = b \cos a$, we deduce immediately from the latter integral

$$\int \frac{d\theta}{\cos a + \cos \theta} = \frac{1}{\sin a} \log \left\{ \frac{\cos \dfrac{a - \theta}{2}}{\cos \dfrac{a + \theta}{2}} \right\}.$$

The integral in (20) can be transformed into

$$\int \frac{d\theta}{a + b \cos \theta} = \frac{1}{\sqrt{a^2 - b^2}} \cos^{-1} \left\{ \frac{b + a \cos \theta}{a + b \cos \theta} \right\}.$$

$$[2 \, a]$$

In a subsequent chapter a more general class of integrals which depend on the preceding will be discussed.

19. **Methods of Integration.**—The reduction of the integration of functions to one or other of the fundamental formulæ is usually effected by one of the following methods:—

(1). Transformation by the introduction of a new variable.
(2). Integration by parts.
(3). Integration by rationalization.
(4). Successive reduction.
(5). Decomposition into partial fractions.

Two or more of these methods can often be combined with advantage. It may also be observed that these different methods are not essentially distinct: thus the method of rationalization is a case of the first method, as it is always effected by the substitution of a new variable.

We proceed to illustrate these processes by a few elementary examples, reserving their fuller treatment for subsequent consideration.

20. **Integration by Transformation.**—Examples of this method have been already given in Arts. 4, 10, &c. One or two more cases are here added.

Ex. 1. To find the integral of $\sin^2 x \cos^3 x\, dx$.

Let $\sin x = y$, and the transformed integral is

$$\int y^2 (1 - y^2)\, dy = \int y^2\, dy - \int y^4\, dy = \frac{y^3}{3} - \frac{y^5}{5} = \frac{\sin^3 x}{3} - \frac{\sin^5 x}{5}.$$

Ex. 2.
$$\int \frac{e^x\, dx}{1 + e^{2x}}.$$

Let $e^x = y$, and we get

$$\int \frac{dy}{1 + y^2} = \tan^{-1} y = \tan^{-1}(e^x).$$

21. **Integration by Parts.**—We have seen in Art. 13, Diff. Calc., that

$$d(uv) = u\,dv + v\,du\,;$$

hence we get

$$uv = \int u\,dv + \int v\,du,$$

or
$$\int u\,dv = uv - \int v\,du. \tag{22}$$

Consequently the integration of an expression of the form udv can always be made to depend on that of the expression vdu.

The advantage of this method will be best exhibited by applying it to a few elementary cases.

Ex. 1.
$$\int \sin^{-1} x \, dx = x \sin^{-1} x - \int \frac{x \, dx}{\sqrt{1 - x^2}}$$

$$= x \sin^{-1} x + \sqrt{1 - x^2}.$$

Ex. 2.
$$\int x \log x \, dx.$$

Let
$$u = \log x, \; v = \frac{x^2}{2}, \text{ and we get}$$

$$\int x \log x \, dx = \frac{x^2 \log x}{2} - \frac{1}{2} \int x^2 \frac{dx}{x} = \frac{x^2}{2} \left(\log x - \frac{1}{2} \right).$$

Ex. 3.
$$\int e^{ax} x \, dx.$$

Let
$$x = u, \frac{e^{ax}}{a} = v, \text{ then}$$

$$\int x e^{ax} \, dx = \frac{x e^{ax}}{a} - \int \frac{e^{ax}}{a} \, dx = \frac{e^{ax}}{a} \left(x - \frac{1}{a} \right).$$

Ex. 4.
$$\int e^{ax} \sin mx \, dx.$$

Let
$$\sin mx = u, \; \frac{e^{ax}}{a} = v, \text{ then}$$

$$\int e^{ax} \sin mx \, dx = \frac{e^{ax} \sin mx}{a} - \frac{m}{a} \int e^{ax} \cos mx \, dx.$$

Similarly,
$$\int e^{ax} \cos mx \, dx = \frac{e^{ax} \cos mx}{a} + \frac{m}{a} \int e^{ax} \sin mx \, dx.$$

Substituting, and solving for $\int e^{ax} \sin mx\, dx$, we obtain

$$\int e^{ax} \sin mx\, dx = \frac{e^{ax}\,(a \sin mx - m \cos mx)}{a^2 + m^2}. \tag{23}$$

In like manner we get

$$\int e^{ax} \cos mx\, dx = \frac{e^{ax}\,(a \cos mx + m \sin mx)}{a^2 + m^2}. \tag{24}$$

Ex. 5. $\qquad\qquad \displaystyle\int \sqrt{a^2 + x^2}\, dx.$

Let $\qquad\qquad \sqrt{a^2 + x^2} = u,$ then

$$\int \sqrt{a^2 + x^2}\, dx = x\sqrt{a^2 + x^2} - \int \frac{x^2\, dx}{\sqrt{a^2 + x^2}};$$

also $\quad \displaystyle\int \sqrt{a^2 + x^2}\, dx = a^2 \int \frac{dx}{\sqrt{a^2 + x^2}} + \int \frac{x^2\, dx}{\sqrt{a^2 + x^2}}.$

Hence, by addition, and dividing by 2,

$$\int \sqrt{a^2 + x^2}\, dx = \frac{x\sqrt{a^2 + x^2}}{2} + \frac{a^2}{2} \log\left(x + \sqrt{a^2 + x^2}\right). \tag{25}$$

Ex. 6. $\qquad\qquad \displaystyle\int \log\left(x + \sqrt{x^2 \pm a^2}\right) dx.$

Here $\quad \displaystyle\int \log\left(x + \sqrt{x^2 \pm a^2}\right) dx = x \log\left(x + \sqrt{x^2 \pm a^2}\right).$

$$- \frac{x\, dx}{\sqrt{x^2 \pm a^2}}$$

$$= x \log\left(x + \sqrt{x^2 \pm a^2}\right) - \sqrt{x^2 \pm a^2}. \tag{26}$$

EXAMPLES.

1. $\displaystyle\int x^n \log x \, dx.$ *Ans.* $\dfrac{x^{n+1}}{n+1}\left(\log x - \dfrac{1}{n+1}\right).$

2. $\displaystyle\int \tan^{-1} x \, dx.$ „ $x \tan^{-1} x - \dfrac{1}{2}\log(1+x^2).$

3. $\displaystyle\int x \tan^2 x \, dx.$ „ $x \tan x + \log(\cos x) - \dfrac{x^2}{2}.$

4. $\displaystyle\int \dfrac{\sin^{-1} x \, dx}{(1-x^2)^{\frac{3}{2}}}.$ „ $\dfrac{x \sin^{-1} x}{\sqrt{1-x^2}} + \dfrac{1}{2}\log(1-x^2).$

Let $x = \sin y$, and the integral becomes

$$\int dy\,\frac{y}{\cos^2 y} = \int y\, d(\tan y) = y \tan y + \log(\cos y).$$

5. $\displaystyle\int e^x x^2 \, dx.$ „ $e^x(x^2 - 2x + 2).$

22. Integration by Rationalization.—By a proper assumption of a new variable we can, in many cases, change an irrational expression into a rational one, and thus integrate it. An instance of this method has been given in Art. 8.

The simplest case is where the quantity under the radical sign is of the form $a + bx$: such expressions admit of being easily integrated.

For example, let the expression be of the form

$$\frac{x^n \, dx}{(a + bx)^{\frac{1}{2}}},$$

where n is a positive integer. Suppose $a + bx = z^2$, then

$$dx = \frac{2z\,dz}{b}, \text{ and } x = \frac{z^2 - a}{b}:$$

making these substitutions, the expression becomes

$$\frac{2\,(z^2 - a)^n \, dz}{b^{n+1}}.$$

Expanding by the Binomial Theorem and integrating the terms separately, the required integral can be immediately found. It is also evident that the expression $\dfrac{x^n\, dx}{(a + bx)^{\frac{p}{q}}}$ can be integrated by a similar substitution.

23. Integration of $\dfrac{x^{2m+1}\, dx}{(a + cx^2)^{\frac{1}{2}}}$,

where m is a positive integer.

Let $a + cx^2 = z^2$; then $x\, dx = \dfrac{z\, dz}{c}$, $x^2 = \dfrac{z^2 - a}{c}$; and the transformed expression is

$$\frac{(z^2 - a)^m\, dz}{c^{m+1}}.$$

This can be integrated as before. It can be easily seen that the expression $\dfrac{x^{2m+1}\, dx}{(a + cx^2)^{\frac{r}{2}}}$ is immediately integrable by the same substitution.

A considerable number of integrals will be found to be reducible to this form : a few examples are given for illustration.

EXAMPLES.

1. $\displaystyle\int \frac{x^3\, dx}{\sqrt{1 - x^2}}.$ *Ans.* $\dfrac{(1 - x^2)^{\frac{3}{2}}}{3} - (1 - x^2)^{\frac{1}{2}}.$

2. $\displaystyle\int \frac{x^5\, dx}{\sqrt{1 + x^2}}.$,, $\dfrac{z^5}{5} - \dfrac{2z^3}{3} + z$; where $z = \sqrt{1 + x^2}.$

3. $\displaystyle\int \frac{x^3\, dx}{(a + cx^2)^{\frac{5}{2}}}.$,, $\dfrac{-(2a + 3cx^2)}{3c^2 (a + cx^2)^{\frac{3}{2}}}.$

24. It is easily seen that the more general expression

$$\frac{f(x^2)\, x\, dx}{\sqrt{a^2 + cx^2}},$$

where $f(x^2)$ is a rational algebraic function, can be rationalized by the same transformation.

Again, if we make $x = \dfrac{1}{z}$ the expression

$$\frac{dx}{x^n (a + cx^2)^{\frac{1}{2}}}$$

transforms into

$$\frac{z^{n-1}\, dz}{(az^2 + c)^{\frac{1}{2}}};$$

and is reducible to the preceding form when n is an *even positive* integer.

Hence, in this case, the expression can be easily integrated by the substitution $(a + cx^2)^{\frac{1}{2}} = xy$.

It will be subsequently seen that the integrals discussed in this and the preceding Articles are cases of a more general form, which is integrable by a similar transformation.

EXAMPLES.

1. $\displaystyle\int \frac{dx}{x^4 (x^2 - 1)^{\frac{1}{2}}}$.   *Ans.* $\dfrac{\sqrt{x^2 - 1}}{3x^3} (2x^2 + 1)$.

2. $\displaystyle\int \frac{dx}{x^6 (1 + x^2)^{\frac{1}{2}}}$.   ,, $-\dfrac{(x^2 + 1)^{\frac{1}{2}}}{15x} \left\{ 8 - \dfrac{4}{x^2} + \dfrac{3}{x^4} \right\}$.

25. **Integration of** $\dfrac{dx}{(A + Cx^2)(a' + cx^2)^{\frac{1}{2}}}$.

As in the preceding Article, let $(a + cx^2)^{\frac{1}{2}} = xz$, or $a + cx^2 = x^2 z^2$: then, if we differentiate and divide by $2x$, we shall have

$$c\,dx = z^2 dx + xz\, dz, \quad \text{or } \frac{dx}{xz} = \frac{dz}{c - z^2},$$

$$\therefore \frac{dx}{(a + cx^2)^{\frac{1}{2}}} = \frac{dz}{c - z^2}; \qquad (27)$$

and the transformed expression evidently is

$$\frac{dz}{(Ac' - Ca) - Az^2}.$$

This is reducible to the fundamental formula (h), or (f), according as $\dfrac{Ac - Ca}{A}$ is positive or negative.

Hence, (1) if $\dfrac{Ac - Ca}{A} > 0$, the integral is easily seen to be

$$\frac{1}{2\sqrt{A(Ac - Ca)}} \log\left(\frac{\sqrt{A(a + cx^2)} + x\sqrt{Ac - Ca}}{\sqrt{A(a + cx^2)} - x\sqrt{Ac - Ca}}\right). \quad (28)$$

(2). If $\dfrac{Ac - Ca}{A} < 0$, the value of the integral is

$$\frac{1}{\sqrt{A(Ca - Ac)}} \tan^{-1} \frac{x\sqrt{Ca - Ac}}{\sqrt{A(a + cx^2)}}. \quad (29)$$

EXAMPLES.

1. $\displaystyle\int \frac{dx}{(1 + x^2)(1 - x^2)^{\frac{1}{2}}}.$ $\quad Ans.\ \dfrac{1}{\sqrt{2}} \tan^{-1}\left(\dfrac{x\sqrt{2}}{\sqrt{1 - x^2}}\right).$

2. $\displaystyle\int \frac{dx}{(3 + 4x^2)(4 - 3x^2)^{\frac{1}{2}}}.$ $\quad ,,\ \dfrac{1}{5\sqrt{3}} \tan^{-1}\left(\dfrac{5x}{\sqrt{12 - 9x^2}}\right).$

3. $\displaystyle\int \frac{dx}{(4 - 3x^2)(3 + 4x^2)^{\frac{1}{2}}}.$ $\quad ,,\ \dfrac{1}{20} \log \dfrac{2\sqrt{3 + 4x^2} + 5x}{2\sqrt{3 + 4x^2} - 5x}.$

26. Rationalization by Trigonometrical Transformation.—It can be easily seen, as in Art. 6, that the irrational expression $\sqrt{a + 2bx + cx^2}$ can be always transformed into one or other of the following shapes:

$$(1)\ (a^2 - z^2)^{\frac{1}{2}}, \quad (2)\ (a^2 + z^2)^{\frac{1}{2}}, \quad (3)\ (z^2 - a^2)^{\frac{1}{2}};$$

neglecting a constant multiplier in each case.

Accordingly, any algebraic expression in x which contains one, and but one, surd of a quadratic form, is capable of being rationalized by a trigonometrical transformation: the first of the forms, by making $z = a \sin \theta$; the second, by $z = a \tan \theta$; and the third, by $z = a \sec \theta$.

For, (1) when $z = a \sin \theta$, we have $(a^2 - z^2)^{\frac{1}{2}} = a \cos \theta$, and $dz = a \cos \theta \, d\theta$.

(2). When $z = a \tan \theta$, ... $(a^2 + z^2)^{\frac{1}{2}} = a \sec \theta$, and $dz = \dfrac{a \, d\theta}{\cos^2 \theta}$.

(3). When $z = a \sec \theta$, ... $(z^2 - a^2)^{\frac{1}{2}} = a \tan \theta$, and $dz = a \tan \theta \sec \theta \, d\theta$.

A number of integrations can be performed by aid of one or other of these transformations.   In a subsequent place this class of transformations will be again considered.   For the present we shall merely illustrate the method by a few examples.

EXAMPLES.

$$\int \frac{dx}{x^2 \left(1 + x^2\right)^{\frac{1}{2}}}.$$

Let $x = \tan \theta$, and the integral becomes

$$\int \frac{\cos \theta \, d\theta}{\sin^2 \theta} = \int \frac{d(\sin \theta)}{\sin^2 \theta} = - \frac{1}{\sin \theta} = - \frac{\sqrt{1 + x^2}}{x}.$$

2.
$$\int \frac{dx}{\left(a^2 - x^2\right)^{\frac{3}{2}}}.$$

Let $x = a \sin \theta$, and we get

$$\frac{1}{a^2} \int \frac{d\theta}{\cos^2 \theta} = \frac{\tan \theta}{a^2} = \frac{x}{a^2 \sqrt{a^2 - x^2}}.$$

This has been integrated by another transformation in Art. 15.

$$\int \frac{dx}{x^3 \left(x^2 - 1\right)^{\frac{1}{2}}}.$$

Let $x = \sec \theta$, and the integral becomes

$$\int \cos^2 \theta \, d\theta \; ; \; \text{or, by (3) Art. 3,} \; \frac{\sin \theta \cos \theta}{2} + \frac{\theta}{2} :$$

accordingly, the value of the integral in question is

$$\frac{\sqrt{x^2 - 1}}{2x^2} + \frac{1}{2} \sec^{-1} x.$$

$$\int \frac{e^{a\tan^{-1}x}\,dx}{(1+x^2)^{\frac{3}{2}}}.$$

Let $x = \tan\theta$, and we get

$$\int \cos\theta\, e^{a\theta}\, d\theta\,; \quad\text{or by (23),}\quad \frac{e^{a\theta}\,(a\cos\theta + \sin\theta)}{1+a^2}.$$

Hence

$$\int \frac{dx\, e^{a\tan^{-1}x}}{(1+x^2)^{\frac{3}{2}}} = \frac{(a+x)\, e^{a\tan^{-1}x}}{(1+a^2)\,(1+x^2)^{\frac{1}{2}}}.$$

$$\int dx\, \sin^{-1}\left(\frac{x}{a+x}\right)^{\frac{1}{2}}.$$

Let $\dfrac{x}{a+x} = \sin^2\theta$, or $x = a\tan^2\theta$, and the integral becomes

$$a\int \theta\, d(\tan^2\theta), \quad\text{or}\quad a\int \theta\, d(\sec^2\theta): \quad (\text{since } \sec^2\theta = 1 + \tan^2\theta).$$

Integrating by parts, we have

$$\int \theta\, d\,(\sec^2\theta) = \theta\sec^2\theta - \int \sec^2\theta\, d\theta = \theta\sec^2\theta - \tan\theta:$$

hence the value of the proposed integral is

$$(a+x)\tan^{-1}\left(\frac{x}{a}\right)^{\frac{1}{2}} - (ax)^{\frac{1}{2}}.$$

It may be observed that the fundamental formulæ (e) and (f) can be at once obtained by aid of the transformations of this Article.

27. **Remarks on Integration.**—The student must not, however, take for granted that whenever one or other of the preceding transformations is applicable, it furnishes the simplest method of integration. We have, in Arts. 9 and 13, already met with integrals of the class here discussed, and have treated them by other substitutions: all that can be stated is, that the method given in the preceding Article will often be found the most simple and useful. The most suitable transformation in each case can only be arrived at after considerable practice and familiarity with the results introduced by such transformations.

By employing different methods we often obtain integrals of the same expression which appear at first sight not to agree. On examination, however, it will always be found that they only differ by some constant; otherwise, they could not have the same differential.

28. **Higher Transcendental Functions.**—Whenever the expression under the radical sign contains powers of x beyond the second, the integral cannot, unless in exceptional cases, be reduced to any of the fundamental formulæ; and consequently cannot be represented in finite terms of x, or of the ordinary transcendental functions : i. e. logarithmic, exponential, trigonometrical, or circular functions. Accordingly, the investigation of such integrals necessitates the introduction of higher classes of transcendental functions.

Thus the integration of irrational functions of x, in which the expression under the square root is of the third or fourth degree in x, depends on a higher class of transcendentals called Elliptic Functions.

29. The method of integration by successive reduction is reserved for a subsequent place. The integration of rational fractions by the method of decomposition into partial fractions will be considered in the next chapter.

30. **Observations on Fundamental Forms.**—From what has been already stated, the sign of integration ($\int$) may be regarded in the light of a question : i. e. the meaning of the expression $\int F(x)\,dx$ is the same as asking what function of x has $F(x)$ for its first derived. *The answer to this question can only be derived from our previous knowledge of the differential coefficients of the different classes of functions, as obtained by the aid of the Differential Calculus.* The number of fundamental formulæ of integration must therefore, ultimately, be the same as the number of independent kinds of functions in Algebra and Trigonometry. These may be briefly classed as follows :—

(1). Ordinary powers and roots, such as x^m, $x^{\frac{p}{q}}$, &c.
(2). Exponentials, a^x, &c., and their inverse functions; viz., Logarithms.
(3). Trigonometric functions, $\sin x$, $\tan x$, &c., and their inverse functions; $\sin^{-1}x$, $\tan^{-1}x$, &c.

This classification may assist the student towards understanding why an expression, in order to be capable of integration in a finite form, in terms of x and the ordinary transcendental functions, must be reducible by transformation to one or other of the fundamental formulæ given in this chapter. He will also soon find that the classes of integrals which are so reducible are very limited, and that the large majority of expressions can only be integrated by the aid of infinite series.

The student must not expect to understand at once the *reason* for each transformation which he finds given: as he, however, gains familiarity with the subject he will find that most of the elementary integrations which can be performed group themselves under a few heads; and that the proper transformations are in general simple, not numerous, and usually not difficult to arrive at. He must often be prepared to abandon the transformations which seemed at first sight the most suitable: such failures are not, however, to be considered as waste of time, for it is by the application of such processes only that the student is enabled gradually to arrive at the general principles according to which integrals may be classified.

Many expressions will be found to admit of integration in two or more different ways. Such modes of arriving at the same results mutually throw light on each other, and will be found an instructive exercise for the beginner.

(31.· **Definite Integrals.**—We now proceed to a brief consideration of the *process of integration regarded as a summation*, reserving a more complete discussion for a subsequent chapter.

If we suppose any magnitude, u, to vary continuously by successive increments, commencing with a value a, and terminating with a value β, its total increment is obviously represented by $\beta - a$. But this total increment is equal to the sum of its partial increments; and this holds, however small we consider each increment to be.

This result is denoted in the case of finite increments by the equation

$$\sum_{a}^{\beta} (\Delta u) = \beta - a;$$

and in the case of infinitely small increments, by

$$\int_{a}^{\beta} du = \beta - a; \qquad\qquad (30)$$

in which β and a are called the *limits of integration :* the former being the *superior* and the latter the *inferior* limit.

Now, suppose u to be a function of another variable, x, represented by the equation

$$u = f(x):$$

then, if when $x = a$, u becomes a, and when $x = b$, u becomes β, we have

$$a = f(a), \quad \beta = f(b).$$

Moreover, in the limit, we have

$$du = f'(x)\,dx,$$

neglecting* infinitely small quantities of the second order (See Diff. Calc., Art. 7).

Hence, formula (30) becomes

$$\int_a^b f'(x)\,dx = f(b) - f(a) ; \qquad (31)$$

in which b and a are styled the *superior* and the *inferior* limits of x, respectively.

It should be observed that the expression $\int_a^b f'(x)\,dx$, represents here the *limit* of the sum denoted by $\sum\limits_a^b (f'(x)\,\Delta x)$, when Δx is regarded as evanescent.

In the preceding we assume that each element $f'(x)\,dx$ is infinitely small for all values of x between the limits of integration a and b; and also that the limits, a and b, are both finite.

A general investigation of these exceptional cases will be found in a subsequent chapter: meanwhile it may be stated, reserving these exceptions, that whenever $f(x)$, i.e. the integral of $f'(x)\,dx$, can be found, the value of the definite integral $\int_b^a f'(x)\,dx$ is obtained by substituting each limit separately

---

* In a subsequent chapter on Definite Integrals a rigorous demonstration will be found of the property here assumed, namely that the sum of these quantities of the second order becomes evanescent in the limit, and consequently may be neglected. Compare also Art. 39, *Diff. Calc.*

instead of x in $f(x)$, and subtracting the value for the lower limit from that for the upper.

A few easy examples are added for illustration.

EXAMPLES.

1. $\displaystyle\int_0^1 x^n\, dx.$ *Ans.* $\dfrac{1}{n+1}.$

2. $\displaystyle\int_0^{\frac{\pi}{2}} \sin\theta\, d\theta.$

3. $\displaystyle\int_0^a \dfrac{dx}{a^2 + x^2}.$ „ $\dfrac{\pi}{4a}.$

4. $\displaystyle\int_0^{\frac{\pi}{2}} \sin^2 x\, dx.$ „ $\dfrac{\pi}{4}.$

5. $\displaystyle\int_0^{\frac{\pi}{4}} \sin^2 x\, dx.$ „ $\dfrac{\pi}{8} - \dfrac{1}{4}.$

6. $\displaystyle\int_0^{\pi} \sin^2 x\, dx.$ „ $\dfrac{\pi}{2}.$

7. $\displaystyle\int_1^4 \dfrac{dx}{x^{\frac{3}{2}}}.$

8. $\displaystyle\int_0^1 \dfrac{dx}{1 + x + x^2}.$ „ $\dfrac{\pi}{3\sqrt{3}}.$

9. $\displaystyle\int_0^{\frac{\pi}{2}} \cos^5 x\, dx.$ „ $\dfrac{2\cdot 4}{3\cdot 5}.$

10. $\displaystyle\int_2^3 \dfrac{x\, dx}{1 + x^2}.$ „ $\dfrac{1}{2}\log 2.$

11. $\displaystyle\int_a^{\beta} \dfrac{dx}{\sqrt{(x-a)(\beta - x)}}.$ „ $\pi.$

See Art. 11.

12. $\displaystyle\int_0^{\frac{\pi}{2}} x \sin x\, dx.$ „   1.

13. $\displaystyle\int_0^{\pi} \dfrac{dx}{a + b\cos\theta},$ where $a > b.$ „ $\dfrac{\pi}{\sqrt{a^2 - b^2}}.$

14. $\displaystyle\int_0^{\pi} \dfrac{dx}{1 - 2a\cos x + a^2}.$ „ $\dfrac{\pi}{1 - a^2}.$

32. Change of Limits.—It should be observed that it is not necessary that the increment dx should be regarded as positive, for we may regard x as decreasing by successive stages, as well as increasing.

Accordingly we have

$$\int_b^a f'(x)\, dx = f(a) - f(b) = -\int_a^b f'(x)\, dx. \qquad (32)$$

That is, *the interchange of the limits is equivalent to a change of sign of the definite integral.*

Also, it is obvious that

$$\int_a^c \phi(x)dx = \int_b^c \phi(x)dx + \int_a^b \phi(x)dx\,;$$

and so on.

Again, if we assume x to be any function of a new variable z, so that $\phi(x)dx$ becomes $\psi(z)dz$, we obviously have

$$\int_{x_0}^X \phi(x)\, dx = \int_{z_0}^Z \psi(z)dz, \qquad (33)$$

where Z and z_0 are the values which z assumes when X and x_0 are substituted for x, respectively.

For example, if $x = a \tan z$, the expression $\dfrac{dx}{(a^2 + x^2)^{\frac{3}{2}}}$ becomes $\dfrac{\cos z\, dz}{a^2}$; and if the limits of x be o and a, those of z are o and $\dfrac{\pi}{4}$. Consequently

$$\int_0^a \frac{dx}{(a^2 + x^2)^{\frac{3}{2}}} = \frac{1}{a^2}\int_0^{\frac{\pi}{4}} \cos z\, dz = \frac{1}{a^2\sqrt{2}}.$$

Also, if we substitute $a - z$ for x, we have

$$\int_0^a \phi(x)dx = -\int_a^0 \phi(a - z)dz = \int_0^a \phi(a - z)dz.$$

Since neither x nor z occurs in the result, this equation may evidently be written in the form

$$\int_0^a \phi(x)\,dx = \int_0^a \phi(a-x)\,dx. \tag{34}$$

For example, let $\phi(x) = \sin^n x$, then $\phi\left(\dfrac{\pi}{2} - x\right) = \cos^n x$, and we have

$$\int_0^{\frac{\pi}{2}} \sin^n x\,dx = \int_0^{\frac{\pi}{2}} \cos^n x\,dx.$$

And, in general, for any function,

$$\int_0^{\frac{\pi}{2}} f(\sin x)\,dx = \int_0^{\frac{\pi}{2}} f(\cos x)\,dx. \tag{35}$$

33. **Values of** $\displaystyle\int_0^\pi \sin mx \sin nx\,dx,$ **and** $\displaystyle\int_0^\pi \cos mx \cos nx\,dx.$ Since

$$2 \sin mx \sin nx = \cos(m-n)\,x - \cos(m+n)\,x,$$

and

$$2 \cos mx \cos nx = \cos(m-n)\,x + \cos(m+n)\,x,$$

we have

$$\int \sin mx \sin nx\,dx = \frac{\sin(m-n)\,x}{2(m-n)} - \frac{\sin(m+n)\,x}{2(m+n)},$$

and

$$\int \cos mx \cos nx\,dx = \frac{\sin(m-n)\,x}{2(m-n)} + \frac{\sin(m+n)\,x}{2(m+n)}.$$

Hence, when m and n are unequal integers, we have

$$\int_0^\pi \sin mx \sin nx\,dx = 0, \text{ and } \int_0^\pi \cos mx \cos nx\,dx = 0. \tag{36}$$

When $m = n$, we have

$$\int \sin^2 nx\,dx = \int \frac{1 - \cos 2nx}{2}\,dx = \frac{x}{2} - \frac{\sin 2nx}{4n},$$

$$\therefore \int_0^\pi \sin^2 nx\,dx = \frac{\pi}{2}, \text{ when } n \text{ is an integer.}$$

In like manner, with the same condition, we have

$$\int_0^\pi \cos^2 nx\, dx = \frac{\pi}{2}. \tag{37}$$

Again, to find the value of

$$\int_a^\beta \sqrt{(x-a)(\beta-x)}\, dx.$$

Assume, as in Art. 11, $x = a\cos^2\theta + \beta\sin^2\theta$; then, when $\theta = 0$, we have $x = a$; and when $\theta = \dfrac{\pi}{2}$, $x = \beta$.

Hence, as in the article referred to, we have

$$\int_a^\beta \sqrt{(x-a)(\beta-x)}\, dx = 2(\beta-a)^2 \int_0^{\frac{\pi}{2}} \sin^2\theta \cos^2\theta\, d\theta.$$

Also $2\displaystyle\int_0^{\frac{\pi}{2}} \sin^2\theta \cos^2\theta\, d\theta = \tfrac{1}{2}\int_0^{\frac{\pi}{2}} \sin^2 2\theta\, d\theta$

$$= \tfrac{1}{4}\int_0^\pi \sin^2\phi\, d\phi = \frac{\pi}{8};$$

$$\therefore \int_a^\beta \sqrt{(x-a)(\beta-x)}\, dx = \frac{\pi}{8}(\beta-a)^2. \tag{38}$$

EXAMPLES.

1. $\displaystyle\int \frac{(1 + \cos x)\, dx}{(x + \sin x)^3}$ *Ans.* $-\dfrac{1}{2}\dfrac{1}{(x + \sin x)^2}$.

2. $\displaystyle\int x \sin x \, dx$.   ,, $\sin x - x \cos x$.

3. $\displaystyle\int \frac{1 - x}{1 + x}\, dx$.   ,, $2 \log (1 + x) - x$.

4. $\displaystyle\int (a + bx^n)^m x^{n-1}\, dx$.   ,, $\dfrac{(a + bx^n)^{m+1}}{n(m + 1)b}$.

5. $\displaystyle\int \frac{x^2 dx}{(a^3 + x^3)^{\frac{3}{2}}}$.   ,, $-\dfrac{2}{3}\dfrac{1}{(a^3 + x^3)^{\frac{1}{2}}}$.

6. $\displaystyle\int \frac{dx}{(1 + x^2)\tan^{-1} x}$.   ,, $\log (\tan^{-1} x)$.

7. $\displaystyle\int \frac{dx}{\sqrt{5 + 4x - x^2}}$.   ,, $2 \sin^{-1}\sqrt{\dfrac{x + 1}{6}}$.

8. $\displaystyle\int \frac{x^2 dx}{x^6 + x^3 - 2}$.   ,, $\dfrac{1}{9} \log \left(\dfrac{x^3 - 1}{x^3 + 2}\right)$.

9. $\displaystyle\int \frac{dx}{a^2 \cos^2 x + b^2 \sin^2 x}$.   ,, $\dfrac{1}{ab} \tan^{-1} \left(\dfrac{b}{a} \tan x\right)$.

10. $\displaystyle\int \frac{\tan x \, dx}{a + b \tan^2 x}$.   ,, $\dfrac{1}{2(b - a)} \log (a \cos^2 x + b \sin^2 x)$.

11. $\displaystyle\int \frac{\cos (\log x)\, dx}{x}$.   ,, $\sin (\log x)$.

12. Show that the integral of $\dfrac{dx}{x}$ can be obtained from that of $x^m dx$.

Write the integral of $x^m dx$ in the form $\dfrac{x^{m+1} - a^{m+1}}{m + 1}$; and, by the method of indeterminate forms, **Ex. 5, Ch. iv. Diff. Calc.**, it can easily be seen that the true value of the fraction when $m + 1 = 0$ is $\log \left(\dfrac{x}{a}\right)$, or $\log x$, omitting the arbitrary constant.

13. $\displaystyle\int e^{ax} \sin mx \cos nx \, dx$.

This is immediately reducible to the integral given in formula (23).

14. $\displaystyle\int \frac{dx}{5 + 4 \sin x}$.   *Ans.* $\dfrac{2}{3} \tan^{-1} \left(\dfrac{4 + 5 \tan \frac{x}{2}}{3}\right)$.

15. $\displaystyle\int \frac{x\, e^{a\tan^{-1}x}\, dx}{(1+x^2)^{\frac{3}{2}}}.$ *Ans.* $\dfrac{e^{a\tan^{-1}x}(ax-1)}{(1+a^2)(1+x^2)^{\frac{1}{2}}}.$

16. $\displaystyle\int x(a+x)^{\frac{1}{3}}\, dx.$ „ $\dfrac{3(a+x)^{\frac{4}{3}}(4x-3a)}{4\cdot 7}.$

17. $\displaystyle\int \frac{x^3\, dx}{(a+bx^2)^{\frac{3}{2}}}.$ „ $\dfrac{2a+bx^2}{b^2(a+bx^2)^{\frac{1}{2}}}.$

Let $a + bx^2 = z^2$.

18. $\displaystyle\int \frac{(p + q\cos x)\, dx}{a + b\cos x}.$

This is equivalent to

$$\int \frac{q\, dx}{b} + \frac{pb - qa}{b}\int \frac{dx}{a + b\cos x},$$

and accordingly can be integrated by Art. 18.

19. $\displaystyle\int \frac{x e^x\, dx}{(1 + x)^2}.$ *Ans.* $\dfrac{e^x}{1+x}.$

20. $\displaystyle\int \frac{x\, dx}{1 + x^4}.$ „ $\dfrac{1}{2}\tan^{-1}(x^2).$

21. $\displaystyle\int \frac{x^2\, dx}{(a + bx^2)^{\frac{5}{2}}}.$ „ $\dfrac{x^3}{3a(a+bx^2)^{\frac{3}{2}}}.$

22. $\displaystyle\int \frac{dx}{x\sqrt{x^3 + 1}}.$ „ $\dfrac{1}{3}\log\left(\dfrac{\sqrt{1+x^3}-1}{\sqrt{1+x^3}+1}\right).$

Let $x^3 + 1 = z^2$.

23. $\displaystyle\int \frac{dx}{x\sqrt{x^n + 1}}.$ „ $\dfrac{1}{n}\log\left(\dfrac{\sqrt{1+x^n}-1}{\sqrt{1+x^n}+1}\right).$

24. Integrate $\qquad \dfrac{d\theta}{a + b\cos\theta}$

by aid of the assumption $\qquad x = \dfrac{b + a\cos\theta}{a + b\cos\theta}.$

The expression transforms into

$$\frac{dx}{\sqrt{(a^2 - b^2)(1 - x^2)}}:$$

accordingly, when $a > b$, its integral is $\dfrac{1}{\sqrt{a^2 - b^2}}\sin^{-1}x$; and when $a < b$, it is

$\dfrac{1}{\sqrt{b^2 - a^2}}\log(x + \sqrt{x^2 - 1})$, &c.

25. Deduce Gregory's expansion for $\tan^{-1} x$ from formula (f).
When $x < 1$, we have

$$\frac{1}{1 + x^2} = 1 - x^2 + x^4 - x^6 + \&\text{c.} \; ;$$

$$\therefore \; \tan^{-1} x = \int \frac{dx}{1 + x^2} = x - \frac{x^3}{3} + \frac{x^5}{5} - \frac{x^7}{7} + \&\text{c.}$$

No constant is added since $\tan^{-1} x$ vanishes with x.

26. Deduce in a similar manner the expansions of $\log (1 + x)$, and $\sin^{-1} x$.

27. Find the integral of $\dfrac{d\theta}{a + b \cos \theta + c \sin \theta}$.

This can be reduced to the form in Art. 18, by assuming $\dfrac{b}{c} = \cot a$, &c.

28. $\displaystyle\int \frac{dx}{(a + bx) \sqrt{1 + x^2}}$.

$$\text{\textit{Ans.}} \quad \frac{1}{\sqrt{a^2 + b^2}} \log \left\{ \frac{a + bx}{b - ax + \sqrt{(a^2 + b^2)(1 + x^2)}} \right\}.$$

This can be integrated either by the method of Art. 13 or by that of Art. 23.

29. $\displaystyle\int \frac{dx}{x\sqrt{x^n - 1}}$.   *Ans.* $\dfrac{2}{n} \sec^{-1}\left(x^{\frac{n}{2}} \right)$.

30. $\displaystyle\int_0^{\frac{\pi}{4}} \frac{\sin x \, dx}{\cos x}$.   , $\dfrac{1}{2} \log 2$.

31. $\displaystyle\int_0^{\frac{\pi}{4}} \frac{dx}{\cos x}$.   ,, $\log \left(1 + \sqrt{2} \right)$.

32. $\displaystyle\int_0^2 \frac{dx}{(4 + 3x^2)^{\frac{3}{2}}}$.   , $\dfrac{1}{8}$.

33. $\displaystyle\int_0^a \sqrt{a^2 - x^2} \, dx$.   , $\dfrac{\pi a^2}{4}$.

34. $\displaystyle\int_0^{2a} x \operatorname{versin}^{-1}\left(\frac{x}{a} \right) dx$.   ,, $\dfrac{5 \pi a^2}{4}$.

35. $\displaystyle\int_0^{\frac{\pi}{2}} \frac{dx}{4 + 5 \sin x}$.   ,, $\dfrac{1}{3} \log 2$.

36. $\displaystyle\int_0^{\frac{\pi}{2}} \frac{dx}{5 + 4 \sin x}$.   ,, $\dfrac{2}{3} \tan^{-1}\left(\frac{1}{3} \right)$.

CHAPTER II.

INTEGRATION OF RATIONAL FRACTIONS.

34. Rational Fractions.—A fraction whose numerator and denominator are both rational and algebraic functions of a variable is called a rational fraction.

Let the expression in question be of the form

$$\frac{ax^m + bx^{m-1} + cx^{m-2} + \&c.}{a'x^n + b'x^{n-1} + c'x^{n-2} + \&c.},$$

in which m and n are positive integers, and $a, b, \ldots a', b', \ldots$ are constants.

In the first place, if the degree of the numerator be greater than, or equal to, that of the denominator, by division we can obtain a quotient, together with a new fraction in which the numerator is of a lower degree than the denominator: the former part can be immediately integrated by Art. 3. The integration of the latter part in general comes under the method of Partial Fractions.

35. Elementary Applications.—Before proceeding to the general process of integration of rational fractions, we propose to consider a few elementary examples, which will lead up to, and indicate in what the general method really consists.

We commence with the form already considered in Art. 7 ; in which, denoting by a_1 and a_2 the roots of the denominator, the expression to be integrated may be represented by

$$\frac{(p + qx)\,dx}{(x - a_1)(x - a_2)}.$$

Assume

$$\frac{p + qx}{(x - a_1)(x - a_2)} = \frac{A_1}{x - a_1} + \frac{A_2}{x - a_2}.$$

Multiplying by $(x - a_1)(x - a_2)$ we get

$$p + qx = - (A_1 a_2 + A_2 a_1) + (A_1 + A_2) x.$$

Hence, we get for the determination of A_1 and A_2 the equations

$$p = - A_1 a_2 - A_2 a_1, \quad q = A_1 + A_2 ;$$

whence we obtain

$$A_1 = \frac{p + q a_1}{a_1 - a_2}, \qquad A_2 = - \frac{p + q a_2}{a_1 - a_2}.$$

Consequently

$$\int \frac{(p + qx)\, dx}{(x - a_1)(x - a_2)} = \frac{p + q a_1}{a_1 - a_2} \int \frac{dx}{x - a_1} - \frac{p + q a_2}{a_1 - a_2} \int \frac{dx}{x - a_2}$$

$$= \frac{1}{a_1 - a_2} \left\{ (p + q a_1) \log (x - a_1) - (p + q a_2) \log (x - a_2) \right\}.$$

In like manner

$$\frac{p + qx^2}{(x^2 - a_1)(x^2 - a_2)} = \frac{A_1}{x^2 - a_1} + \frac{A_1}{x^2 - a_2},$$

where A_1 and A_2 have the same values as above; hence

$$\int \frac{(p + qx^2)\, dx}{(x^2 - a_1)(x^2 - a_2)} = \frac{p + q a_1}{a_1 - a_2} \int \frac{dx}{x^2 - a_1} - \frac{p + q a_2}{a_1 - a_2} \int \frac{dx}{x^2 - a_2}.$$

But each of the latter integrals is of one or other of the fundamental forms (f) and (h) of Chapter I.; hence the proposed expression can be always integrated.

Again, let it be proposed to integrate an expression of the form

$$\frac{(p + qx + rx^2)\, dx}{(x - a_1)(x - a_2)(x - a_3)}.$$

We assume

$$\frac{p + qx + rx^2}{(x - a_1)(x - a_2)(x - a_3)} = \frac{A_1}{x - a_1} + \frac{A_2}{x - a_2} + \frac{A_3}{x - a_3} ;$$

then clearing from fractions, and identifying both sides by equating the coefficients of x^2, of x, and the part independent of x, at both sides, we obtain three equations of the first degree in A_1, A_2, A_3, which can be readily solved by ordinary algebra; thus determining the values of A_1, A_2, A_3 in terms of the given constants.

By this means we get

$$\int \frac{(p + qx + rx^2)\,dx}{(x - a_1)(x - a_2)(x - a_3)} = A_1 \int \frac{dx}{x - a_1} + A_2 \int \frac{dx}{x - a_2} + A_3 \int \frac{dx}{x - a_3}$$

$$= A_1 \log (x - a_1) + A_2 \log (x - a_2) + A_3 \log (x - a_3).$$

We shall illustrate these results by a few simple examples.

EXAMPLES.

1. $\displaystyle\int \frac{(x - 1)\,dx}{(x - 3)(x + 2)}.$
   $\qquad Ans.\ \dfrac{2}{5} \log (x - 3) + \dfrac{3}{5} \log (x + 2).$

2. $\displaystyle\int \frac{x\,dx}{x^2 + 2x - 3}.$
   $\qquad ,,\ \dfrac{3}{4} \log (x + 3) + \dfrac{1}{4} \log (x - 1).$

3. $\displaystyle\int \frac{dx}{x^4 - 1}.$
   $\qquad ,,\ \dfrac{1}{4} \log \dfrac{x - 1}{x + 1} - \dfrac{1}{2} \tan^{-1} x.$

4. $\displaystyle\int \frac{dx}{x^4 + 5x^2 + 4}.$
   $\qquad ,,\ \dfrac{1}{3} \tan^{-1} x - \dfrac{1}{6} \tan^{-1} \dfrac{x}{2}.$

5. $\displaystyle\int \frac{x\,dx}{x^4 - 1}.$
   $\qquad ,,\ \dfrac{1}{4} \log \dfrac{x^2 - 1}{x^2 + 1}.$

6. $\displaystyle\int \frac{(3x^2 - 2)\,dx}{x^4 - 3x^2 - 4}.$
   $\qquad ,,\ \dfrac{1}{2} \log \left(\dfrac{x^2 - 2}{x^2 + 2} \right) + \tan^{-1} x.$

7. $\displaystyle\int \frac{(x^3 + x - 1)\,dx}{x^3 + x^2 - 6x}.$
   $\qquad ,,\ \dfrac{1}{6} \log x + \dfrac{1}{2} \log (x - 2) + \dfrac{1}{3} \log (x + 3).$

Here the denominator is equal to $x(x - 2)(x + 3)$; and we have

$$\frac{x^2 + x - 1}{x(x - 2)(x + 3)} = \frac{A_1}{x} + \frac{A_2}{x - 2} + \frac{A_3}{x + 3};$$

hence $\quad x^3 + x - 1 = A_1(x^2 + x - 6) + A_2 x(x + 3) + A_3 x(x - 2)$;

$\therefore$ the equations for determining A_1, A_2 and A_3 are

$$A_1 + A_2 + A_3 = 1, \qquad A_1 + 3A_2 - 2A_3 = 1, \qquad 6A_1 = 1,$$

whence we get

$$A_1 = \frac{1}{6}, \qquad A_2 = \frac{1}{2}, \qquad A_3 = \frac{1}{3}.$$

8. $\quad \displaystyle\int \frac{(2x^3 + 2x^2 + 4x + 1)\,dx}{x^2 + x + 1}.$ *Ans.* $x^2 + \log(x^2 + x + 1)$.

We now proceed to the consideration of the general method, and, as it is based on the decomposition of partial fractions, we begin with the latter process.

36. **Partial Fractions.**—The method of decomposition of a fraction into its partial fractions is usually given in treatises on Algebra; as, however, the process is intimately connected with the integration of a large class of expressions, a short space is devoted to its consideration here.

For brevity, we shall denote the fraction under consideration by $\dfrac{f(x)}{\phi(x)}$.

Let a_1, a_2, a_3, . . . a_n denote the roots of $\phi(x)$; then

$$\phi(x) = (x - a_1)(x - a_2)(x - a_3) \ldots (x - a_n). \qquad (1)$$

There are four cases to be considered, according as we have roots, (1) real and unequal; (2) real and equal; (3) imaginary and unequal; (4) imaginary and equal.

We proceed to discuss each class separately

37. **Real and Unequal Roots.**—In this case we may assume

$$\frac{f(x)}{\phi(x)} = \frac{A_1}{x - a_1} + \frac{A_2}{x - a_2} + \frac{A_3}{x - a_3} + \ldots + \frac{A_n}{x - a_n}, \qquad (2)$$

where A_1, A_2, ... A_n are independent of x. For, if the equation be cleared from fractions by multiplying by $\phi(x)$, on equating the coefficients of like powers of x on both sides we obtain n equations for the determination of the n constants A_1, A_2, . . . A_n.

Moreover, since these equations contain A_1, A_2, &c., only in the first degree, they can always be solved : however, since the equations are often too complicated for ready solution, the following method is usually more expeditious :—

The question (2), when cleared from fractions, gives

$$f(x) = A_1(x - a_2)(x - a_3) \ldots (x - a_n) + A_2(x - a_1)(x - a_3) \ldots (x - a_n)$$

$$+ \text{&c.} + A_n(x - a_1)(x - a_2) \ldots (x - a_{n-1}) ;$$

and since, by hypothesis, both sides of this equation are identical for all values of x, we may substitute a_1 for x throughout; this gives

$$f(a_1) = A_1(a_1 - a_2)(a_1 - a_3) \ldots (a_1 - a_n),$$

or
$$A_1 = \frac{f(a_1)}{\phi'(a_1)}.$$

In like manner, we have

$$A_2 = \frac{f(a_2)}{\phi'(a_2)}, \quad A_3 = \frac{f(a_3)}{\phi'(a_3)}, \ldots A_n = \frac{f(a_n)}{\phi'(a_n)}. \tag{3}$$

Hence, when all the roots are unequal, we have

$$\frac{f(x)}{\phi(x)} = \frac{f(a_1)}{\phi'(a_1)} \frac{1}{x - a_1} + \frac{f(a_2)}{\phi'(a_2)} \frac{1}{x - a_2} + \text{&c.} + \frac{f(a_n)}{\phi'(a_n)} \frac{1}{x - a_n}. \tag{4}$$

Accordingly, in this case

$$\int \frac{f(x)}{\phi(x)} dx = \frac{f(a_1)}{\phi'(a_1)} \log(x - a_1) + \frac{f(a_2)}{\phi'(a_2)} \log(x - a_2) + \text{&c.}$$

$$+ \frac{f(a_n)}{\phi'(a_n)} \log(x - a_n). \tag{5}$$

The preceding investigation shows that to any root (a), which is *not a multiple root*, corresponds a single term in the integral, viz.

$$\frac{f(a)}{\phi'(a)} \log(x - a) ;$$

one which can always be found, whether the remaining roots are known or not; and whether they are real or imaginary.

38. **Case where Numerator is of higher Degree than Denominator.**—It should also be observed that even when the degree of x in the numerator is greater than, or equal to, that in the denominator, the partial fraction corresponding to any root (a) in the denominator is still of the form found above.

For let

$$\frac{f(x)}{\phi(x)} = Q + \frac{R}{\phi(x)},$$

where Q and R denote the quotient and remainder, and let $\dfrac{A}{x-a}$ be the partial fraction of $\dfrac{R}{\phi(x)}$ corresponding to a single root a; then, by multiplying by $\phi(x)$ and substituting a instead of x, it is easily seen, as before, that we get

$$A = \frac{f(a)}{\phi'(a)}.$$

For, example, let it be proposed to integrate the expression

$$\frac{x^5\, dx}{x^3 - 2x^2 - 5x + 6}.$$

Here the factors of the denominator are easily seen to be

$$x - 1, \quad x + 2, \text{ and } x - 3\,;$$

accordingly, we may assume

$$\frac{x^5}{x^3 - 2x^2 - 5x + 6} = x^2 + ax + \beta + \frac{A}{x-1} + \frac{B}{x+2} + \frac{C}{x-3}.$$

To find a and β, we equate the coefficients of x^4 and x^3 to zero, after clearing from fractions: this gives, immediately, $a = 2$, and $\beta = 9$.

Again, since $\phi(x) = x^3 - 2x^2 - 5x + 6$, we have

$$\phi'(x) = 3x^2 - 4x - 5.$$

Accordingly, substituting $1, -2$, and 3, successively for x in the fraction

$$\frac{x^5}{3x^2 - 4x - 5},$$

we get

$$A = -\frac{1}{6}, \quad B = -\frac{32}{15}, \quad C = \frac{243}{10};$$

and hence

$$\frac{x^5}{x^3 - 2x^2 - 5x + 6} = x^2 + 2x + 9 - \frac{1}{6(x-1)} - \frac{32}{15(x+2)} + \frac{243}{10(x-3)};$$

$$\therefore \int \frac{x^5\,dx}{x^3 - 2x^2 - 5x + 6} = \frac{x^3}{3} + x^2 + 9x - \frac{\log(x-1)}{6}$$

$$- \frac{32}{15}\log(x+2) + \frac{243}{10}\log(x-3).$$

39. **Case of Even Powers.**—If the numerator and denominator contain x in even powers only, the process can generally be simplified; for, on substituting z for x^2, the fraction becomes of the form

$$\frac{f(z)}{\phi(z)}.$$

Accordingly, whenever the roots of $\phi(z)$ are *real and unequal*, the fraction can be decomposed into partial fractions, and to any root (a) corresponds a fraction of the form

$$\frac{f(a)}{\phi'(a)} \frac{1}{z - a}.$$

The corresponding term in the integral of

$$\frac{f(x^2)}{\phi(x^2)}\,dx$$

is obviously represented by

$$\frac{f(a)}{\phi'(a)} \int \frac{dx}{x^2 - a}.$$

This is of the form (f) or (h), according as a is a positive or negative root.

The case of imaginary roots in $\phi(z)$ will be considered in a subsequent part of the chapter.

It may be observed that the integrals treated of in Art. 5 are simple cases of the method of partial fractions discussed in this Article.

EXAMPLES.

$$\int \frac{(2x + 3)\, dx}{x^3 + x^2 - 2x}.$$

Here the factors of the denominator evidently are x, $x - 1$, and $x + 2$; we accordingly assume

$$\frac{2x + 3}{x^3 + x^2 - 2x} = \frac{A}{x} + \frac{B}{x - 1} + \frac{C}{x + 2}.$$

Again, as $\phi(x) = x^3 + x^2 - 2x$, we have $\phi'(x) = 3x^2 + 2x - 2$;

$$\therefore \frac{f(x)}{\phi'(x)} = \frac{2x + 3}{3x^2 + 2x - 2}.$$

Hence, by (3) we have

$$A = -\frac{3}{2}, \qquad B = \frac{5}{3}, \qquad C = -\frac{1}{6};$$

consequently

$$\int \frac{(2x + 3)\, dx}{x^3 + x^2 - 2x} = -\frac{3}{2} \log x + \frac{5}{3} \log (x - 1) - \frac{1}{6} \log (x + 2).$$

$$2.\qquad \int \frac{dx}{(x^2 + a^2)(x^2 + b^2)}.$$

Here

$$\frac{1}{(x^2 + a^2)(x^2 + b^2)} = \frac{1}{a^2 - b^2} \left(\frac{1}{x^2 + b^2} - \frac{1}{x^2 + a^2} \right);$$

hence the value of the required integral is

$$\frac{1}{(a^2 - b^2)} \left\{ \frac{1}{b} \tan^{-1} \left(\frac{x}{b} \right) - \frac{1}{a} \tan^{-1} \left(\frac{x}{a} \right) \right\}.$$

$$\int \frac{x\, dx}{(x^2 + a)(x^2 + b)}.$$

Substitute z for x^2 and the transformed integral is

$$\int \frac{1}{2} \frac{dz}{(z + a)(z + b)}.$$

Consequently the value of the required integral is

$$\frac{1}{2(a - b)} \log \left(\frac{x^2 + b}{x^2 + a}\right).$$

4. $\displaystyle\int \frac{(3x^2 - 1)\,dx}{x^2 - 3x + 2}.$ *Ans.* $3x + 11 \log(x - 2) - 2 \log(x - 1).$

5. $\displaystyle\int \frac{(x^2 - 3)\,dx}{x^3 - 7x + 6}.$,, $\dfrac{1}{2} \log(x - 1) + \dfrac{1}{5}\log(x - 2) + \dfrac{3}{10} \log(x + 3).$

6. $\displaystyle\int \frac{(2x + 1)\,dx}{x(x + 1)(x + 2)}.$,, $\dfrac{1}{2} \log x + \log(x + 1) - \dfrac{3}{2} \log(x + 2).$

7. $\displaystyle\int \frac{x^2\,dx}{x^4 - x^2 - 12}.$,, $\dfrac{\sqrt{3}}{7} \tan^{-1}\left(\dfrac{x}{\sqrt{3}}\right) + \dfrac{1}{7} \log\left(\dfrac{x - 2}{x + 2}\right).$

8. $\displaystyle\int \frac{dx\,(a' + b'x^n)}{x^{n+1}(a + bx^n)}.$

Let $x^n = \dfrac{1}{z}.$

40. **Multiple Real Roots.**—Suppose $\phi(x)$ has r roots each equal to a, then the fraction can be written in the shape

$$\frac{f(x)}{(x - a)^r \psi(x)}.$$

In this case we may assume

$$\frac{f(x)}{(x - a)^r \psi(x)} = \frac{M_1}{(x - a)^r} + \frac{M_2}{(x - a)^{r-1}} + \ldots + \frac{M_r}{x - a} + \frac{P}{\psi(x)},$$

where the last term arises from the remaining roots.

For, when the expression is cleared from fractions, it is readily seen that, on equating the coefficients of like powers at both sides, we have as many equations as there are unknown quantities, and accordingly the assumption is a legitimate one.

In order to determine the coefficients, M_1, M_2, &c. .... M_r, clear from fractions, and we get

$$f(x) = M_1\psi(x) + M_2(x-a)\psi(x) + M_3(x-a)^2\psi(x) + \&c. \ldots \quad (6)$$

This gives, when a is substituted for x,

$$f(a) = M_1\psi(a), \text{ or } M_1 = \frac{f(a)}{\psi(a)}. \quad (7)$$

Next, differentiate with respect to x, and substitute a instead of x in the resulting equation, and we get

$$f'(a) = M_1\psi'(a) + M_2\psi(a) ; \quad (8)$$

which determines M_2.

By a second differentiation, M_3 can be determined; and so on.

It can be readily seen, that the series of equations thus arrived at may be written as follows—

$$f(a) = M_1\psi(a),$$
$$f'(a) = M_1\psi'(a) + \mathrm{I} \cdot M_2\psi(a),$$
$$f''(a) = M_1\psi''(a) + 2 \cdot M_2\psi'(a) + \mathrm{I} \cdot 2 \cdot M_3\psi(a),$$
$$f'''(a) = M_1\psi'''(a) + 3 \cdot M_2\psi''(a) + 2 \cdot 3 \cdot M_3\psi'(a) + \mathrm{I} \cdot 2 \cdot 3 \cdot M_4\psi(a),$$
$$f^{iv}(a) = M_1\psi^{iv}(a) + 4 \cdot M_2\psi'''(a) + 3 \cdot 4 \cdot M_3\psi''(a) + 2 \cdot 3 \cdot 4 \cdot M_4\psi'(a)$$
$$+ \mathrm{I} \cdot 2 \cdot 3 \cdot 4 \cdot M_5\psi(a),$$

in which the law of formation is obvious, and the coefficients can be obtained in succession.

The corresponding part of the integral of

$$\frac{f(x)\,dx}{(x-a)^r\psi(x)}$$

evidently is

$$M_r \log (x-a) - \frac{M_{r-1}}{x-a} - \frac{\mathrm{I}}{2}\frac{M_{r-2}}{(x-a)^2} - \cdots - \frac{M_1}{(r-\mathrm{I})(x-a)^{r-1}}. \quad (9)$$

If $\phi(x)$ have a second set of multiple roots, the corresponding terms in the integral can be obtained in like manner.

41. **Imaginary Roots.**—The results arrived at in Art. 37 apply to the case of imaginary, as well as to real roots; however, as the corresponding partial fractions appear in this case under an imaginary form, it is desirable to show that conjugate imaginaries give rise to groups in which the coefficients are all real.

Suppose $a + b\sqrt{-1}$ and $a - b\sqrt{-1}$ to be a pair of conjugate roots in the equation $\phi(x) = 0$; then the corresponding quadratic factor is

$(x-a)^2 + b^2$; which may be written in the form $x^2 + px + q$.

We accordingly assume

$$\phi(x) = (x^2 + px + q)\psi(x),$$

and hence

$$\frac{f(x)}{\phi(x)} = \frac{Lx + M}{x^2 + px + q} + \frac{P}{Q};$$

where $\dfrac{P}{Q}$ represents the portion arising from the remaining

roots, and $\dfrac{Lx + M}{x^2 + px + q}$ is the part arising from the roots

$a \pm b\sqrt{-1}$.

Multiplying by $\phi(x)$ we get

$$f(x) = (Lx + M)\,\psi(x) + (x^2 + px + q)\frac{P}{Q}\,\psi(x). \qquad (10)$$

If in this, $-(px + q)$ be substituted for x^2, the last term disappears; and by repeating the same substitution in the equation

$$f(x) = \psi(x)(Lx + M),$$

it ultimately reduces to a simple equation in x: on identifying both sides of this equation, we can determine the values of L and M.

42. In many cases we can determine the coefficients L, M more expeditiously, either by equating coefficients directly, or else by determining the other partial fractions first, and subtracting their sum from the given fraction.

It will also be found that the determination of many

integrals of this class can be much simplified by a transformation to a new variable, or by some other suitable expedient.

Some elementary examples are added for the purpose of illustration.

Examples.

$$\int \frac{x\,dx}{(1+x)(1+x^2)}.$$

Assume

$$\frac{x}{(1+x)(1+x^2)} = \frac{A}{1+x} + \frac{Lx+M}{1+x^2}:$$

clearing from fractions, this becomes

$$x = A(1+x^2) + (Lx+M)(1+x).$$

Equate the coefficients, and we get

$$L + A = 0, \qquad L + M = 1, \qquad A + M = 0.$$

Hence

$$L = \frac{1}{2}, \qquad M = \frac{1}{2}, \qquad A = -\frac{1}{2};$$

and accordingly

$$\frac{x}{(1+x)(1+x^2)} = -\frac{1}{2}\frac{1}{1+x} + \frac{1}{2}\frac{1+x}{1+x^2},$$

$$\therefore \int \frac{x\,dx}{(1+x)(1+x^2)} = \frac{1}{4}\log\left|\frac{1+x^2}{(1+x)^2}\right| + \frac{1}{2}\tan^{-1}x.$$

2.
$$\int \frac{dx}{1+x^3}.$$

Let

$$\frac{1}{1+x^3} = \frac{A}{1+x} + \frac{Lx+M}{1-x+x^2};$$

consequently, $A = \frac{1}{3}$, by formula (3).   Substituting and clearing from fractions we have

$$3 = 1 - x + x^2 + 3(Lx+M)(1+x);$$

hence, dividing by $1+x$, we have

$$2 - x = 3(Lx+M).$$

Consequently

$$\int \frac{dx}{1 + x^3} = \frac{1}{3}\int \frac{dv}{1 + x} + \frac{1}{3}\int \frac{(2 - x)\,dx}{1 - x + x^2}$$

$$= \frac{1}{3}\log\,(1 + x) - \frac{1}{6}\log\,(1 - x + x^2) + \frac{1}{\sqrt{3}}\tan^{-1}\left(\frac{2x - 1}{\sqrt{3}}\right).$$

3. $\displaystyle\int \frac{dx}{1 - x^3}.$ $\quad Ans.\ \dfrac{1}{6}\log\left(\dfrac{1 + x + x^2}{1 - 2x + x^2}\right) + \dfrac{1}{\sqrt{3}}\tan^{-1}\left(\dfrac{2x + 1}{\sqrt{3}}\right).$

This can be got from the last by changing the sign of x.

4. $$\int \frac{dx}{1 - x^6}.$$

In this case we have

$$\frac{1}{1 - x^6} = \frac{1}{2}\left(\frac{1}{1 - x^3} + \frac{1}{1 + x^3}\right).$$

5. $\displaystyle\int \frac{x^7\,dx}{x^{12} - 1}.$ $\quad Ans.\ \dfrac{1}{24}\log\left\{\dfrac{(x^4 - 1)^2}{x^8 + x^4 + 1}\right\} + \dfrac{1}{4\sqrt{3}}\tan^{-1}\left\{\dfrac{2x^4 + 1}{\sqrt{3}}\right\}.$

Let $x^4 = z$, and the integral becomes

$$\frac{1}{4}\int \frac{z\,dz}{z^3 - 1}.$$

6. $$\int \frac{x^2\,dx}{(x - 1)^2(x^2 + 1)}.$$

Assume

$$\frac{x^2}{(x - 1)^2(x^2 + 1)} = \frac{A}{(x - 1)^2} + \frac{B}{x - 1} + \frac{Lx + M}{1 + x^2}.$$

To find L and M, clear from fractions, and by Art. 41 the values of L and M are found by making $x^2 = -1$ in the following equation:

$$x^2 = (Lx + M)(x - 1)^2.$$

This gives immediately $L = -\dfrac{1}{2}$, $M = 0$.

Again, by Art. 40, we get immediately $A = \dfrac{1}{2}$.

To find B, make $x = 0$ in both sides of our identity, and we get

$$0 = A - B + M; \quad \therefore B = A = \frac{1}{2}.$$

$$[4\,a]$$

Finally

$$\frac{x^2}{(x-1)^2(x^2+1)} = \frac{1}{2}\frac{1}{(x-1)^2} + \frac{1}{2}\frac{1}{x-1} - \frac{1}{2}\frac{x}{1+x^2};$$

$$\therefore \int \frac{x^2\,dx}{(x-1)^2(x^2+1)} = -\frac{1}{2}\frac{1}{x-1} + \frac{1}{2}\log(x-1) - \frac{1}{4}\log(x^2+1).$$

$$\int \frac{dx}{x^8 + x^7 - x^4 - x^3}.$$

Here the denominator is easily seen to be $x^3(x-1)(x+1)^2(x^2+1)$, and the expression becomes

$$\int \frac{dx}{x^3(x-1)(x+1)^2(x^2+1)}.$$

Assume $x = \dfrac{1}{z}$, and the transformed expression is evidently

$$\int \frac{z^6\,dz}{(z-1)(z+1)^2(z^2+1)}.$$

The quotient is easily seen to be $z - 1$; and, by the method of Art. 38, we may assume

$$\frac{z^6}{(z-1)(z+1)^2(z^2+1)} = z - 1 + \frac{A}{z-1} + \frac{B}{(z+1)^2} + \frac{C}{z+1} + \frac{Lz+M}{z^2+1}.$$

Hence (Arts. 37, 40), we have

$$A = \frac{1}{8}; \quad B = -\frac{1}{4}.$$

Next, L and M are found by making $z^2 = -1$, in the equation

$$z^6 = (Lz+M)(z-1)(z+1)^2;$$

$$\therefore 1 = 2(Lz+M)(z+1) = 2\{Lz^2 + (L+M)z + M\},$$

which gives

$$L + M = 0, \quad L - M = -\frac{1}{2};$$

$$\therefore M = \frac{1}{4}, \quad L = -\frac{1}{4}.$$

In order to find the remaining coefficient C, we make $z = 0$, when we get

$$0 = -1 - A + B + C + M; \quad \therefore C = \frac{9}{8}.$$

hence we have

$$\frac{z^6}{(z-1)(z+1)^2(z^2+1)} = z - 1 + \frac{1}{8(z-1)} - \frac{1}{4(z+1)^2} + \frac{9}{8(z+1)} - \frac{z-1}{4(z^2+1)};$$

$$\therefore \int \frac{z^6\,dz}{(z-1)(z+1)^2(z^2+1)} = \frac{z^2}{2} - z + \frac{1}{8}\log(z-1) + \frac{1}{4(z+1)}$$

$$+ \frac{9}{8}\log(z+1) - \frac{1}{8}\log(z^2+1) + \frac{1}{4}\tan^{-1}z.$$

Hence

$$\int \frac{dx}{x^8 + x^7 - x^4 - x^3} = \frac{1}{2x^2} - \frac{1}{x} + \frac{x}{4(x+1)} + \frac{1}{8}\log\frac{1-x^2}{1+x^2} + \log\frac{x+1}{x} + \frac{1}{4}\tan^{-1}\frac{1}{x}$$

8. $\displaystyle\int \frac{(3x+1)\,dx}{(x-1)^2(x+3)}.$ *Ans.* $\displaystyle \frac{1}{2}\log\frac{x-1}{x+3} - \frac{1}{x-1}.$

43. **Multiple Imaginary Roots.**—To complete the discussion of the decomposition of the fraction $\dfrac{f(x)}{\phi(x)}$, suppose the denominator $\phi(x)$ to contain r pairs of equal and imaginary roots, i. e. let the denominator contain a factor of the form $\{(x-a)^2 + b^2\}^r$; and suppose $\phi(x) = \{(x-a)^2 + b^2\}^r\,\phi_1(x)$

In this case we assume

$$\frac{f(x)}{\{(x-a)^2 + b^2\}^r\,\phi_1(x)} = \frac{L_1 x + M_1}{\{(x-a)^2 + b^2\}^r} + \frac{L_2 x + M_2}{\{(x-a)^2 + b^2\}^{r-1}}$$

$$+ \ldots + \frac{L_r x + M_r}{(x-a)^2 + b^2} + \frac{P}{\phi_1(x)};$$

the remaining partial fractions being obtained from the other roots.

There is no difficulty in seeing that we shall still have as many equations as unknown quantities, L_1, M_1, L_2, M_2, $\ldots$ when the coefficients of like powers of x are equated on both sides.

To determine L_1, M_1, L_2, &c.; let the factor $(x-a)^2 + b^2$ be represented by X, and multiply up by X^r, when we get

$$\frac{f(x)}{\phi_1(x)} = L_1 x + M_1 + (L_2 x + M_2)X + \text{&c.} + (L_r x + M_r)X^{r-1} + \frac{PX^r}{\phi_1(x)}. \quad (11)$$

The coefficients L_1 and M_1 are determined as in Art. 41. To find L_2 and M_2; differentiate with respect to x, and substitute $a + b\sqrt{-1}$ for x in the result, when it becomes

$$\frac{d}{dx}\left[\frac{f(x)}{\phi_1(x)}\right]_0 = L_1 + 2(x_0 - a)(L_2 x_0 + M_2),$$

where $x_0 = a + b\sqrt{-1}$.

Hence, equating real and imaginary parts, we get two equations for the determination of L_2 and M_2. By a second differentiation, L_3 and M_3 can be determined, and so on.

It is unnecessary to go into further detail, as sufficient has been stated to show that the decomposition into partial fractions is possible in all cases, when the roots of $\phi(x) = 0$ are known.

The practical application is often simplified by transformation to a new variable.

44. The preceding investigation shows that the integration of rational fractions is in all cases reducible to that of one or more fractions of the following forms:

$$\frac{dx}{x - a}, \quad \frac{dx}{(x - a)^r}, \quad \frac{(A + B)dx}{(x - a)^2 + b^2}, \quad \frac{(Lx + M)dx}{\{(x - a)^2 + b^2\}^r}.$$

The methods of integrating the first three forms have been given already. We proceed to show the mode of dealing with the last.

45. In the first place it can be divided into two others,

$$\frac{L(x - a)dx}{\{(x - a)^2 + b^2\}^r} + \frac{(La + M)dx}{\{(x - a^2) + b^2\}^r}.$$

The integral of the first part is evidently

$$\frac{-L}{2(r - 1)\{(x - a)^2 + b^2\}^{r-1}}.$$

To determine the integral of the other part, we substitute z for $x - a$, and, omitting the constant coefficient, it becomes

$$\int \frac{dz}{(z^2 + b^2)^r}.$$

Again

$$\int \frac{dz}{(z^2 + b^2)^r} = \frac{1}{b^2} \int \frac{(z^2 + b^2 - z^2)\,dz}{(z^2 + b^2)^r} = \frac{1}{b^2} \int \frac{dz}{(z^2 + b^2)^{r-1}} - \frac{1}{b^2} \int \frac{z^2\,dz}{(z^2 + b^2)^r}.$$

But we get by integration by parts

$$\int \frac{z^2\,dz}{(z^2 + b^2)^r} = \int z \cdot \frac{z\,dz}{(z^2 + b^2)^r} = - \frac{1}{2(r-1)} \int z\,d\left(\frac{1}{(z^2 + b^2)^{r-1}}\right)$$

$$= - \frac{z}{2(r-1)(z^2 + b^2)^{r-1}} + \frac{1}{2(r-1)} \int \frac{dz}{(z^2 + b^2)^{r-1}}.$$

Substituting in the preceding, we obtain

$$\int \frac{dz}{(z^2 + b^2)^r} = \frac{2r-3}{2(r-1)b^2} \int \frac{dz}{(z^2 + b^2)^{r-1}} + \frac{z}{2(r-1)b^2\,(z^2 + b^2)^{r-1}}. \qquad (12)$$

This formula reduces the integral to another of the same shape, in which the exponent r is replaced by $r-1$. By successive repetitions of this formula the integral can be reduced to depend on that of $\dfrac{dz}{(z^2 + b^2)}$.

The preceding is a case of the method of integration by *successive reduction*, referred to in Art. 19. Other examples of this method will be found in the next Chapter.

The preceding integral can often be found more expeditiously by the following transformation:—Substitute $b \tan \theta$ for z, and the expression $\dfrac{dz}{(z^2 + b^2)^r}$ becomes, obviously,

$$\frac{1}{b^{2r-1}} \int \cos^{2r-2}\theta\,d\theta.$$

The discussion of this class of integrals will be found in the next Chapter.

46. We shall next return to the integration of $\dfrac{f(x^2)dx}{\phi(x^2)}$, which has been already considered in Art. 39 in the case

where the roots of $\phi(z)$ are real. To a pair of imaginary roots, $a \pm b\sqrt{-1}$, corresponds a partial fraction of the form

$$\frac{(Ax^2 + B)\, dx}{(x^2 - a)^2 + b^2}, \quad \text{or} \quad \frac{(Ax^2 + B)\, dx}{x^4 - 2ax^2 + c^2},$$

where $c^2 = a^2 + b^2$.

In order to integrate this, we assume $a = c \cos 2\phi$, when the fraction becomes

$$\frac{(Ax^2 + B)\, dx}{x^4 - 2x^2 c \cos 2\phi + c^2}.$$

The quadratic factors of the denominator are easily seen to be

$$x^2 - 2x\sqrt{c} \cos \phi + c, \text{ and } x^2 + 2x\sqrt{c} \cos \phi + c.$$

Accordingly we assume

$$\frac{Ax^2 + B}{x^4 - 2x^2 c \cos 2\phi + c^2} = \frac{Lx + M}{x^2 - 2x\sqrt{c} \cos \phi + c} + \frac{L'x + M'}{x^2 + 2x\sqrt{c} \cos \phi + c}.$$

hence it can be seen without difficulty that

$$L = -L' = \frac{Ac - B}{4\, c^{\frac{3}{2}} \cos \phi}, \quad M = M' = \frac{B}{2c},$$

and after a few easy transformations, we find

$$\int \frac{(Ax^2 + B)\, dx}{x^4 - 2x^2 c \cos 2\phi + c^2} = \frac{Ac - B}{8 \cos \phi\, c^{\frac{3}{2}}} \log \left(\frac{x^2 - 2x\sqrt{c} \cos \phi + c}{x^2 + 2x\sqrt{c} \cos \phi + c} \right)$$

$$+ \frac{Ac + B}{4 \sin \phi\, c^{\frac{3}{2}}} \tan^{-1} \left(\frac{2x\sqrt{c} \sin \phi}{c - x^2} \right).$$

47. **Integration of** $\dfrac{dx}{(x - a)^m (x - b)^n}$.

This expression can be easily transformed into a shape

which is immediately integrable, by the following substitution :—

Assume $x - a = (x - b)\,z$; then

$$x = \frac{a - bz}{1 - z}\;;\;\; \therefore\; x - a = \frac{(a - b)\,z}{1 - z},\;\; x - b = \frac{a - b}{1 - z},\;\; dx = \frac{(a - b)\,dz}{(1 - z)^2}\;;$$

and the expression transforms into

$$\frac{(1 - z)^{m+n-2}\,dz}{(a - b)^{m+n-1}\,z^m}.$$

Expand the numerator by the Binomial Theorem, and the integral can be immediately obtained. (Compare Art. 4.)

For example, take the integral

$$\frac{dx}{(x - a)^2(x - b)^3}.$$

Here the transformed expression is

$$\int \frac{(1 - z)^3\,dz}{(a - b)^4\,z^2},$$

or

$$\frac{1}{(a - b)^4}\int\left(\frac{1}{z^2} - \frac{3}{z} + 3 - z\right)dz = \frac{-1}{(a - b)^4}\left\{\frac{z^2}{2} - 3z + 3\,\log z + \frac{1}{z}\right\}.$$

Substituting $\dfrac{x - a}{x - b}$ for z, the integral can be expressed in terms of x.

48. Integration of $\dfrac{x^{2m+1}\,dx}{(a + cx^2)^n}$.

where m and n are integers.

Let $a + cx^2 = z$, and the expression becomes

$$\frac{(z - a)^m\,dz}{2\,c^{m+1}\,z^n}\;;$$

a form which is immediately integrable by aid of the Binomial Theorem.

It is evident that the expression is made integrable by the same transformation when n is either a fractional or a negative index.

It may be also observed that the more general expression $\dfrac{f(x^2)\,x\,dx}{(a + cx^2)^n}$ can be integrated by the same transformation, where $f(x^2)$ denotes an integral algebraic function of x^2.

EXAMPLES.

1. $\displaystyle\int \frac{x^5\,dx}{(a^2 - x^2)^2}.$ *Ans.* $\dfrac{a^4}{2(a^2 - x^2)} + \dfrac{x^2}{2} + a^2 \log(a^2 - x^2).$

2. $\displaystyle\int \frac{x^3\,dx}{(a + cx^2)^4}.$,, $-\dfrac{1}{4c^2(a + cx^2)^2} + \dfrac{a}{6c^2(a + cx^2)^3}.$

3. $\displaystyle\int \frac{x^5\,dx}{(1 + x^2)^3}.$,, $\dfrac{1}{x^2 + 1} - \dfrac{1}{4(x^2 + 1)^2} + \dfrac{1}{2}\log(x^2 + 1).$

49. Integration of $\dfrac{dx}{x^n - 1}$,

where n is a positive integer.

Suppose a an imaginary root of $x^n - 1 = 0$, then it is evident that a^{-1} is the conjugate root: also, by (3), the partial fraction corresponding to the root a is

$$\frac{1}{na^{n-1}(x - a)}, \quad \text{or} \quad \frac{a}{n(x - a)}.$$

If to this the fraction arising from the root a^{-1} be added, we get

$$\frac{1}{n}\left\{\frac{a}{x - a} + \frac{a^{-1}}{x - a^{-1}}\right\}, \quad \text{or} \quad \frac{1}{n}\left\{\frac{x(a + a^{-1}) - 2}{x^2 - (a + a^{-1})x + 1}\right\}.$$

But, by the theory of equations, a is of the form

$$\cos\frac{2k\pi}{n} + \sqrt{-1}\,\sin\frac{2k\pi}{n},$$

where k is any integer;

$$\therefore \ a + a^{-1} = 2 \cos \frac{2k\pi}{n}.$$

Hence, if θ be substituted for $\dfrac{2k\pi}{n}$, the preceding fraction becomes

$$\frac{2}{n} \cdot \frac{x \cos \theta - 1}{x^2 - 2x \cos \theta + 1}.$$

The integral of this, by Art. 7, is

$$\frac{\cos \theta}{n} \log (1 - 2x \cos \theta + x^2) - \frac{2 \sin \theta}{n} \tan^{-1} \left(\frac{x - \cos \theta}{\sin \theta} \right).$$

There are two cases to be considered, according as n is even or odd.

(1). Let $n = 2r$: in this case the equation $x^{2r} - 1 = 0$ has two real roots, viz., $+ 1$ and $- 1$; and it is easily seen that

$$\int \frac{dx}{x^{2r} - 1} = \frac{1}{2r} \log \frac{x - 1}{x + 1} + \frac{1}{2r} \Sigma \cos \frac{k\pi}{r} \log \left(1 - 2x \cos \frac{k\pi}{r} + x^2 \right)$$

$$- \frac{1}{r} \Sigma \sin \frac{k\pi}{r} \tan^{-1} \left(\frac{x - \cos \dfrac{k\pi}{r}}{\sin \dfrac{k\pi}{r}} \right), \qquad (13)$$

where the summation represented by Σ extends to all integer values of k from 1 to $r - 1$.

(2). Let $n = 2r + 1$, we obtain

$$\int \frac{dx}{x^{2r+1} - 1} = \frac{\log (x - 1)}{2r + 1} + \frac{1}{2r + 1} \Sigma \cos \frac{2k\pi}{2r + 1} \log \left(1 - 2x \cos \frac{2k\pi}{2r + 1} + x^2 \right)$$

$$- \frac{2}{2r + 1} \Sigma \sin \frac{2k\pi}{2r + 1} \tan^{-1} \left(\frac{x - \cos \dfrac{2k\pi}{2r + 1}}{\sin \dfrac{2k\pi}{2r + 1}} \right), \qquad (14)$$

where the summation represented by Σ extends to all integer values of k from 1 up to r.

50. Integration of $\dfrac{x^{m-1}dx}{x^n - 1}$**, where** m **is less than** $n + 1$.

As before, let a be a root, and the corresponding partial fraction is $\dfrac{a^{m-1}}{na^{n-1}(x - a)}$ or $\dfrac{a^m}{n(x - a)}$; hence the partial fraction arising from the conjugate roots, a and a^{-1}, is

$$\frac{1}{n}\left(\frac{a^m}{x - a} + \frac{a^{-m}}{x - a^{-1}}\right) = \frac{1}{n}\cdot\frac{x\left(a^m + a^{-m}\right) - \left(a^{m-1} + a^{-(m-1)}\right)}{x^2 - \left(a + a^{-1}\right)x + 1}.$$

$$= \frac{2}{n}\frac{x\cos m\theta - \cos(m - 1)\theta}{x^2 - 2x\cos\theta + 1},$$

where θ is of the same form as before.

The corresponding term in the proposed integral is easily seen, by Art. 7, to be

$$\frac{1}{n}\left\{\cos m\theta \log\left(x^2 - 2x\cos\theta + 1\right) - 2\sin m\theta \tan^{-1}\frac{x - \cos\theta}{\sin\theta}\right\}. \quad (15)$$

By giving to k all values from 1 to $\dfrac{n}{2} - 1$, when n is even, and from 1 to $\dfrac{n - 1}{2}$ when n is odd, the integral required can be written down as in the preceding Article.

EXAMPLES.

1. $\displaystyle\int \frac{dx}{x^2 + 6x + 8}.$ *Ans.* $\dfrac{1}{2}\log\left(\dfrac{x+2}{x+4}\right).$

2. $\displaystyle\int \frac{3x\,dx}{x^2 - x - 2}.$,, $2\log(x-2) + \log(x+1).$

3. $\displaystyle\int \frac{(A + Bx^2)dx}{x(a + bx^2)}.$,, $\dfrac{A}{a}\log x + \dfrac{Ba - Ab}{2ab}\log(a + bx^2).$

4. $\displaystyle\int \frac{x^2 dx}{x^4 + x^2 - 2}.$,, $\dfrac{1}{6}\log\dfrac{x-1}{x+1} + \dfrac{\sqrt{2}}{3}\tan^{-1}\left(\dfrac{x}{\sqrt{2}}\right).$

5. $\displaystyle\int \frac{dx}{x^4 + 1}.$,, $\dfrac{1}{4\sqrt{2}}\log\dfrac{x^2 + x\sqrt{2} + 1}{x^2 - x\sqrt{2} + 1} + \dfrac{1}{2\sqrt{2}}\tan^{-1}\left(\dfrac{x\sqrt{2}}{1 - x^2}\right).$

6. $\displaystyle\int \frac{(2x - 5)dx}{(x + 3)(x + 1)^2}.$,, $\dfrac{7}{2(x+1)} + \dfrac{11}{4}\log\left(\dfrac{x+1}{x+3}\right).$

7. $\displaystyle\int \frac{dx}{x(a + bx^2)^2}.$,, $\dfrac{1}{2a(a+bx^2)} + \dfrac{1}{2a^2}\log\left(\dfrac{x^2}{a + bx^2}\right).$

8. $\displaystyle\int \frac{dx}{x(a + bx^n)^2}.$,, $\dfrac{1}{na^2}\log\left(\dfrac{x^n}{a + bx^n}\right) + \dfrac{1}{na(a + bx^n)}.$

9. $\displaystyle\int \frac{dx}{x(a + bx^n)^r}.$

Let $a + bx^n = x^n z$, and the transformed expression is $-\dfrac{(z - b)^{r-1}dz}{na^r z^r}.$

10. $\displaystyle\int \frac{x\,dx}{x^3 + x^2 + x + 1}.$ *Ans.* $\dfrac{1}{4}\log(x^2 + 1) - \dfrac{1}{2}\log(x + 1) + \dfrac{1}{2}\tan^{-1}x.$

11. $\displaystyle\int \frac{dx}{x^4 + 4x^3 + 5x^2 + 4x + 4}.$,, $\dfrac{2}{25}\log\dfrac{(x+2)^2}{x^2 + 1} + \dfrac{3}{25}\tan^{-1}x - \dfrac{1}{5(x+2)}.$

12. Apply the method of Art. 47 to the integration of $\dfrac{dx}{(1 - x^2)^n}.$

The transformed expression is $-\dfrac{(1 + z)^{2n-2}dz}{2^{2n-1}z^n}.$

13. $\displaystyle\int \frac{x^2 dx}{(1 - x^2)^3}.$ *Ans.* $\dfrac{1}{8}\dfrac{x(1 + x^2)}{(1 - x^2)^2} - \dfrac{1}{16}\log\dfrac{1 + x}{1 - x}.$

14. Prove that

$$\int \frac{dx}{x^n (1 - x)^m} \text{ transforms into } -\int \frac{(1 + z)^{m+n-2}\, dz}{z^m},$$

if we make $x = \dfrac{1}{1 + z}$.

15. $\displaystyle\int \frac{dx}{\sin x\,(a + b \cos x)}.$ *Ans.* $\dfrac{1}{a + b} \log \sin \dfrac{x}{2} - \dfrac{1}{a - b} \log \cos \dfrac{x}{2}$

$$+ \frac{b}{a^2 - b^2} \log (a + b \cos x).$$

Multiply by $\sin x$, substitute u for $\cos x$, and the integral becomes

$$\int \frac{-\,du}{(1 - u^2)(a + bu)}.$$

16. $\displaystyle\int \frac{dx}{3 \sin x + \sin 2x}.$ *Ans.* $\dfrac{1}{5} \log \sin \dfrac{x}{2} - \log \cos \dfrac{x}{2} + \dfrac{2}{5} \log (3 + 2 \cos x).$

17. $\displaystyle\int \frac{(1 - x^2)\, dx}{x\,(1 + x^2 + x^4)}.$,, $\dfrac{\sqrt{3}}{2} \tan^{-1} \left(\dfrac{2 + x^2}{x^2 \sqrt{3}} \right) - \dfrac{1}{4} \log \left(\dfrac{x^4 + x^2 + 1}{x^4} \right).$

Let $x^2 = \dfrac{1}{z}$, &c.

18. Prove that

$$\int \frac{dx}{1 + x^{2n}} = -\frac{1}{2n} \Sigma \cos \frac{(2k - 1)\pi}{2n} \log \left(1 - 2x \cos \frac{(2k - 1)\pi}{2n} + x^2 \right)$$

$$+ \frac{1}{n} \Sigma \sin \frac{(2k - 1)\pi}{2n} \cdot \tan^{-1} \left\{ \frac{x - \cos \dfrac{(2k - 1)\pi}{2n}}{\sin \dfrac{(2k - 1)\pi}{2n}} \right\};$$

where k extends through all integer values from 1 to n, inclusive.

19. $\displaystyle\int \frac{dx}{1 + x^{2n+1}} = \frac{\log (1 + x)}{2n + 1} - \frac{1}{2n + 1} \Sigma \cos \frac{(2k - 1)\pi}{2n + 1} \log \left(1 - 2x \cos \frac{(2k - 1)\pi}{2n + 1} + x^2 \right)$

$$+ \frac{2}{2n + 1} \Sigma \sin \frac{(2k - 1)\pi}{2n + 1} \tan^{-1} \left\{ \frac{x - \cos \dfrac{(2k - 1)\pi}{2n + 1}}{\sin \dfrac{(2k - 1)\pi}{2n + 1}} \right\},$$

where k assumes all integer values from 1 to n inclusive.

CHAPTER III.

INTEGRATION BY SUCCESSIVE REDUCTION.

51. **Cases in which** $\sin^m \theta \cos^n \theta\, d\theta$ **is immediately Integrable.**—We shall commence this Chapter* with the discussion of the integral

$$\int \sin^m \theta \, \cos^n \theta \, d\theta \, ;$$

to which form it will be seen that a number of other expressions are readily reducible.

In the first place it is easily seen that whenever *either m or n is an odd positive integer* the expression $\sin^m \theta \cos^n \theta\, d\theta$ can be immediately integrated.

For, if $n = 2r + 1$, the integral becomes

$$\int \sin^m \theta \, \cos^{2r+1} \theta \, d\theta, \ \text{or,} \ \int \sin^m \theta \, (\cos^2 \theta)^r \, d(\sin \theta).$$

If we assume $x = \sin \theta$, the integral transforms into

$$\int x^m (1 - x^2)^r \, dx \, ; \tag{1}$$

and as, by hypothesis, r is a positive integer, $(1 - x^2)^r$ can be expanded by the Binomial Theorem in a finite number of terms, each of which can be integrated separately. In like manner, if the index of $\sin \theta$ be an odd integer, we assume $x = \cos \theta$, &c.

A few examples are added for the purpose of making the student familiar with this principle.

---

* It may be observed that a large number of the integrals discussed in this Chapter do not require the method of Successive Reduction: however, since other integrals of the same form require this method, it was not considered advisable to separate the discussion into distinct Chapters.

EXAMPLES.

1. $\displaystyle\int \sin^3\theta\, d\theta.$ *Ans.* $\dfrac{\cos^3\theta}{3} - \cos\theta.$

2. $\displaystyle\int \cos^5\theta\, d\theta.$,, $\sin\theta - \dfrac{2}{3}\sin^3\theta + \dfrac{\sin^5\theta}{5}.$

3. $\displaystyle\int \sin^3\theta \cos^7\theta\, d\theta.$,, $\dfrac{\cos^{10}\theta}{10} - \dfrac{\cos^8\theta}{8}.$

4. $\displaystyle\int \dfrac{\sin^5\theta\, d\theta}{\cos^2\theta}.$,, $\dfrac{1}{\cos\theta} + 2\cos\theta - \dfrac{\cos^3\theta}{3}.$

5. $\displaystyle\int \sqrt{\sin\theta}\,\cos^3\theta\, d\theta.$,, $\dfrac{2\sin^{\frac{3}{2}}\theta}{3} - \dfrac{2\sin^{\frac{7}{2}}\theta}{7}.$

6. $\displaystyle\int \dfrac{\sin^3\theta\, d\theta}{\sqrt{\cos\theta}}.$,, $\dfrac{2\cos^{\frac{5}{2}}\theta}{5} - 2\cos^{\frac{1}{2}}\theta.$

7. $\displaystyle\int \dfrac{\cos^3\theta\, d\theta}{\sin^{\frac{5}{2}}\theta}.$,, $3\sin^{\frac{1}{2}}\theta - \dfrac{3}{7}\sin^{\frac{7}{3}}\theta.$

52. Again, whenever $m + n$ *is an even negative integer* the expression $\sin^m\theta \cos^n\theta\, d\theta$ can be readily integrated.

For if we assume $x = \tan\theta$, we have

$$\cos\theta = \frac{1}{\sqrt{1 + x^2}}, \quad \sin\theta = \frac{x}{\sqrt{1 + x^2}}, \text{ and } d\theta = \frac{dx}{1 + x^2},$$

and the expression transforms into

$$\frac{x^m\, dx}{\left(1 + x^2\right)^{\frac{m+n}{2}+1}}.$$

Hence, if $m + n = -2r$, this becomes

$$x^m\left(1 + x^2\right)^{r-1} dx,$$

a form which is immediately integrable.

Take, for example, $\quad \displaystyle\int \frac{\sin^2\theta\, d\theta}{\cos^6\theta}.$

Let $x = \tan\theta$, and we get

$$\int x^2\,(1 + x^2)\, dx, \text{ or } \frac{\tan^3\theta}{3} + \frac{\tan^5\theta}{5}.$$

Next, to find $\quad \displaystyle\int \frac{d\theta}{\sin\theta \cos^5\theta}.$

Making the same substitution, we obtain

$$\int \frac{(1 + x^2)^2 dx}{x}.$$

Hence, the value of the proposed integral is

$$\frac{\tan^4\theta}{4} + \tan^2\theta + \log\,(\tan\theta).$$

Again, to find $\displaystyle\int \frac{d\theta}{\sin^{\frac{3}{2}}\theta \cos^{\frac{5}{2}}\theta}.$

Here the transformed expression is $\dfrac{(1 + x^2)\, dx}{x^{\frac{3}{2}}}$, and accordingly the value of the proposed integral is

$$\frac{2}{3}\tan^{\frac{3}{2}}\theta - \frac{2}{\tan^{\frac{1}{2}}\theta}.$$

In many cases it is more convenient to assume $x = \cot\theta$. For example, to find $\displaystyle\int \frac{d\theta}{\sin^4\theta}.$

Since $\quad d(\cot\theta) = -\dfrac{d\theta}{\sin^2\theta}$, if $\cot\theta = x$, the transformed integral is

$$-\int (1 + x^2)\, dx, \text{ or } -\cot\theta - \frac{\cot^3\theta}{3}.$$

The following examples are added for illustration :—

[5]

EXAMPLES.

1. $\displaystyle\int \frac{\sin^3\theta\, d\theta}{\cos^5\theta}.$ *Ans.* $\dfrac{\tan^4\theta}{4}.$

2. $\displaystyle\int \frac{d\theta}{\cos^6\theta}.$,, $\tan\theta + \dfrac{2\tan^3\theta}{3} + \dfrac{\tan^5\theta}{5}.$

3. $\displaystyle\int \frac{d\theta}{\sin\theta\,\cos^3\theta}$,, $\dfrac{\tan^2\theta}{2} + \log(\tan\theta).$

4. $\displaystyle\int \frac{\sin^{\frac{1}{2}}\theta\, d\theta}{\cos^{\frac{5}{2}}\theta}.$,, $\dfrac{2}{3}\tan^{\frac{3}{2}}\theta.$

5. $\displaystyle\int \frac{d\theta}{\sin^4\theta\,\cos^4\theta}.$,, $-8\cot 2\theta - \dfrac{8}{3}\cot^3 2\theta.$

6. $\displaystyle\int \frac{d\theta}{\sin^{\frac{1}{2}}\theta\,\cos^{\frac{7}{2}}\theta}.$,, $2\tan^{\frac{1}{2}}\theta\left(1 + \dfrac{\tan^2\theta}{5}\right).$

When neither of the preceding methods is applicable, the integration of the expression $\sin^m\theta\,\cos^n\theta\, d\theta$ can be obtained only by aid of successive reduction.

We proceed to establish the formulæ of reduction suitable to this case.

53. **Formulæ of Reduction for** $\sin^m\theta\,\cos^n\theta\, d\theta.$

$$\int \sin^m\theta\,\cos^n\theta\, d\theta = \int \cos^{n-1}\theta\,\sin^m\theta\, d(\sin\theta):$$

consequently, if we assume

$$u = \cos^{n-1}\theta, \quad v = \frac{\sin^{m+1}\theta}{m+1},$$

the formula for integration by parts (Art. 21) gives

$$\int \sin^m\theta\,\cos^n\theta\, d\theta = \frac{\cos^{n-1}\theta\,\sin^{m+1}\theta}{m+1} + \frac{n-1}{m+1}\int \sin^{m+2}\theta\,\cos^{n-2}\theta\, d\theta. \quad (2)$$

In like manner, if the integral be written in the form

$$- \int \sin^{m-1}\theta \, \cos^n\theta \, d\,(\cos\theta),$$

we obtain

$$\int \sin^m\theta \, \cos^n\theta \, d\theta = \frac{m-1}{n+1} \int \sin^{m-2}\theta \, \cos^{n+2}\theta \, d\theta - \frac{\sin^{m-1}\theta \cos^{n+1}\theta}{n+1}. \quad (3)$$

It may be observed that this latter formula can be derived from (2) by substituting $\frac{\pi}{2} - \phi$ for θ, and interchanging the letters m and n in it.

54. **Case of one Positive and one Negative Index.** —The results in (2) and (3) hold whether m or n be positive or negative; accordingly, let one of them be negative (n suppose), and on changing n into $-n$, formula (3) becomes

$$\int \frac{\sin^m\theta}{\cos^n\theta} \, d\theta = \frac{\sin^{m-1}\theta}{(n-1)\cos^{n-1}\theta} - \frac{m-1}{n-1} \int \frac{\sin^{m-2}\theta}{\cos^{n-2}\theta} \, d\theta, \quad (A)$$

in which m and n are supposed to have positive* signs.

By this formula the integral of $\dfrac{\sin^m\theta}{\cos^n\theta} \, d\theta$ is made to depend on another in which the indices of $\sin\theta$ and $\cos\theta$ are each diminished by two. The same method is applicable to the new integral, and so on.

If m be an odd integer, the expression is integrable immediately by Art. 51. If m be even, and n even and greater than m, the method of Art. 52 is applicable; if $m = n$, the expression becomes $\int \tan^m\theta \, d\theta$, which will be treated subsequently; if $n < m$, the integral reduces to that of $\sin^{m-n}\theta \, d\theta$.

Again, if n be odd, and $> m$, the integral reduces to $\int \dfrac{d\theta}{\cos^{n-m}\theta}$;

[5 a]

and if $n < m$, it reduces to $\int \dfrac{\sin^{m-n+1}\theta\, d\theta}{\cos\theta}$. The mode of finding these latter integrals will be considered subsequently.

Again, if the index of $\sin\theta$ be negative, we get, by changing the sign of m in (2),

$$\int \frac{\cos^n\theta}{\sin^m\theta}\, d\theta = -\frac{\cos^{n-1}\theta}{(m-1)\sin^{m-1}\theta} - \frac{n-1}{m-1}\int \frac{\cos^{n-2}\theta}{\sin^{m-2}\theta}\, d\theta. \qquad (B,$$

We shall next consider the case where the indices are both positive.

55. Indices both Positive.—If $\sin^m\theta\,(1-\cos^2\theta)$ be written instead of $\sin^{m+2}\theta$ in formula (2), it becomes

$$\int \sin^m\theta\,\cos^n\theta\, d\theta = \frac{\cos^{n-1}\theta\,\sin^{m+1}\theta}{m+1}$$

$$+ \frac{n-1}{m+1}\int \sin^m\theta\,(\cos^{n-2}\theta - \cos^n\theta)\, d\theta = \frac{\cos^{n-1}\theta\,\sin^{m+1}\theta}{m+1}$$

$$+ \frac{n-1}{m+1}\int \sin^m\theta\,\cos^{n-2}\theta\, d\theta - \frac{n-1}{m+1}\int \sin^m\theta\,\cos^n\theta\, d\theta:$$

hence, transposing the latter integral to the other side, and dividing by $\dfrac{m+n}{m+1}$, we get

$$\int \sin^m\theta\,\cos^n\theta\, d\theta = \frac{\cos^{n-1}\theta\,\sin^{m+1}\theta}{m+n} + \frac{n-1}{m+n}\int \sin^m\theta\,\cos^{n-2}\theta\, d\theta. \qquad (C)$$

In like manner, from (3), we get

$$\int \sin^m\theta\,\cos^n\theta\, d\theta = \frac{m-1}{m+n}\int \sin^{m-2}\theta\,\cos^n\theta\, d\theta - \frac{\sin^{m-1}\theta\,\cos^{n+1}\theta}{m+n}. \qquad (D)$$

By aid of these formulæ the integral of $\sin^m\theta\,\cos^n\theta\, d\theta$ is made to depend on another in which the index of either $\sin\theta$, or of $\cos\theta$, is reduced by two. By successive application of these formulæ the complete integral can always be found when the indices are *integers*.

56. Formulæ of Reduction for $\sin^n \theta \, d\theta$ **and** $\cos^n \theta \, d\theta$. These integrals are evidently cases of the general formulæ (C) and (D); however, they are so frequently employed that we give the formulæ of reduction separately in their case,

$$\int \cos^n \theta \, d\theta = \frac{\sin \theta \, \cos^{n-1} \theta}{n} + \frac{n - 1}{n} \int \cos^{n-2} \theta \, d\theta. \qquad (4)$$

$$\int \sin^n \theta \, d\theta = -\frac{\cos \theta \, \sin^{n-1} \theta}{n} + \frac{n - 1}{n} \int \sin^{n-2} \theta \, d\theta. \qquad (5)$$

The former gives, when n is even,

$$\int \cos^n \theta \, d\theta = \frac{\sin \theta}{n} \left(\cos^{n-1} \theta + \frac{n - 1}{n - 2} \cos^{n-3} \theta \right.$$
$$\left. + \frac{(n - 1)(n - 3)}{(n - 2)(n - 4)} \cos^{n-5} \theta + \&\text{c.} \right)$$
$$+ \frac{(n - 1)(n - 3)(n - 5) \dots 1}{n \, (n - 2)(n - 4) \dots 2} \theta. \qquad (6)$$

A similar expression is readily obtained for the latter integral.

EXAMPLES.

1. $\int \sin^4 \theta \, d\theta.$ *Ans.* $-\dfrac{\sin \theta \, \cos \theta}{4} \left(\sin^2 \theta + \dfrac{3}{2} \right) + \dfrac{3}{8} \theta.$

2. $\int \cos^2 \theta \, \sin^4 \theta \, d\theta.$,, $\dfrac{\sin \theta \, \cos \theta}{2} \left(\dfrac{\sin^4 \theta}{3} - \dfrac{\sin^2 \theta}{12} - \dfrac{1}{8} \right) + \dfrac{\theta}{16}.$

3. $\int \cos^6 \theta \, d\theta.$,, $\dfrac{\sin \theta \, \cos^3 \theta}{6} \left(\cos^2 \theta + \dfrac{5}{4} \right) + \dfrac{5}{16} \left(\sin \theta \cos \theta + \theta \right).$

57. Indices both Negative.—It remains to consider the case where the indices of $\sin \theta$ and $\cos \theta$ are both negative.

Writing $-m$ and $-n$ instead of m and n, in formula (C), it becomes

$$\int \frac{d\theta}{\sin^m \theta \, \cos^n \theta} = \frac{-1}{(m + n) \cos^{n+1} \theta \, \sin^{m-1} \theta} + \frac{n + 1}{m + n} \int \frac{d\theta}{\sin^m \theta \, \cos^{n+2} \theta};$$

or, transposing and multiplying by $\dfrac{m + n}{n + 1}$,

$$\int \frac{d\theta}{\sin^m\theta \cos^{n+2}\theta} = \frac{1}{(n + 1)\cos^{n+1}\theta \sin^{m-1}\theta} + \frac{m + n}{n + 1}\int \frac{d\theta}{\sin^m\theta \cos^n\theta}.$$

Again, if we substitute n for $n + 2$ in this, it becomes

$$\int \frac{d\theta}{\sin^m\theta \cos^n\theta} = \frac{1}{(n - 1)\cos^{n-1}\theta \sin^{m-1}\theta}$$

$$+ \frac{m + n - 2}{n - 1}\int \frac{d\theta}{\sin^m\theta \cos^{n-2}\theta}. \qquad (E)$$

Making a like transformation* in formula (D), it becomes

$$\int \frac{d\theta}{\sin^m\theta \cos^n\theta} = \frac{-1}{(m - 1)\sin^{m-1}\theta \cos^{n-1}\theta}$$

$$+ \frac{m + n - 2}{m - 1}\int \frac{d\theta}{\sin^{m-2}\theta \cos^n\theta}. \qquad (F)$$

In each of these, one of the indices is reduced by two degrees, and consequently, by successive applications of the formulæ, the integrals are reducible ultimately to those of one or other of the forms $\dfrac{d\theta}{\cos\theta}$ or $\dfrac{d\theta}{\sin\theta}$: these have been already integrated in Art. 17.

The formulæ of reduction for $\dfrac{d\theta}{\sin^n\theta}$ and $\dfrac{d\theta}{\cos^n\theta}$ are so important that they are added independently, as follows :—

---

* It may be observed that formulæ (B), (D), and (F) can be immediately obtained from (A), (C), and (E), by interchanging the letters m and n, and substituting $\dfrac{\pi}{2} - \phi$ instead of θ. For, in this case, $\sin\theta$, $\cos\theta$, and $d\theta$, transform into $\cos\phi$, $\sin\phi$, and $- d\phi$, respectively.

$$\int \frac{d\theta}{\cos^n \theta} = \frac{\sin \theta}{(n-1)\cos^{n-1}\theta} + \frac{n-2}{n-1}\int \frac{d\theta}{\cos^{n-2}\theta}. \qquad (7)$$

$$\int \frac{d\theta}{\sin^n \theta} = \frac{-\cos \theta}{(n-1)\sin^{n-1}\theta} + \frac{n-2}{n-1}\int \frac{d\theta}{\sin^{n-2}\theta}. \qquad (8)$$

It may be here observed that, since $\sin^2\theta + \cos^2\theta = 1$, we have immediately

$$\int \frac{d\theta}{\sin^m \theta \cos^n \theta} = \int \frac{d\theta}{\sin^{m-2}\theta \cos^n \theta} + \int \frac{d\theta}{\sin^m \theta \cos^{n-2}\theta}; \qquad (9)$$

and a similar process is applicable to the latter integrals. This method is often useful in elementary cases.

EXAMPLES.

1. $$\int \frac{d\theta}{\sin \theta \cos^2 \theta} = \int \frac{\sin \theta\, d\theta}{\cos^2 \theta} + \int \frac{d\theta}{\sin \theta} = \frac{1}{\cos \theta} + \log \tan \frac{\theta}{2}.$$

2. $$\int \frac{d\theta}{\sin \theta \cos^4 \theta} = \int \frac{\sin \theta\, d\theta}{\cos^4 \theta} + \int \frac{d\theta}{\sin \theta \cos^2 \theta},$$

and is accordingly immediately integrated by the last.

3. $$\int \frac{d\theta}{\sin^3 \theta}. \qquad\qquad Ans.\ -\frac{\cos \theta}{2\sin^2 \theta} + \frac{1}{2}\log \tan \frac{\theta}{2}.$$

4. $$\int \frac{d\theta}{\sin^3 \theta \cos^2 \theta}. \qquad\qquad ,,\ \ \frac{1}{\cos \theta} - \frac{\cos \theta}{2\sin^2 \theta} + \frac{3}{2}\log \tan \frac{\theta}{2}.$$

58. **Application of Method of Differentiation.—** The formulæ of reduction given in the preceding Articles can also be readily arrived at by direct differentiation.

Thus, for example, we have

$$\frac{d}{d\theta}\left(\frac{\sin^m \theta}{\cos^n \theta}\right) = \frac{m\sin^{m-1}\theta}{\cos^{n-1}\theta} + \frac{n\,\sin^{m+1}\theta}{\cos^{n+1}\theta};$$

and, consequently,

$$\int \frac{\sin^{m+1}\theta}{\cos^{n+1}\theta}\, d\theta = \frac{1}{n}\frac{\sin^m \theta}{\cos^n \theta} - \frac{m}{n}\int \frac{\sin^{m-1}\theta}{\cos^{n-1}\theta}\, d\theta.$$

This result is easily identified with formula (A).

Again,

$$\frac{d}{d\theta}\left(\sin^m\theta\,\cos^n\theta\right) = m\sin^{m-1}\theta\,\cos^{n+1}\theta - n\sin^{m+1}\theta\,\cos^{n-1}\theta.$$

If we substitute for $\cos^{n+1}\theta$ its equivalent $\cos^{n-1}\theta\,(1-\sin^2\theta)$, we get

$$\frac{d}{d\theta}\left(\sin^m\theta\,\cos^n\theta\right) = m\sin^{m-1}\theta\,\cos^{n-1}\theta - (m+n)\sin^{m+1}\theta\,\cos^{n-1}\theta\,;$$

hence we get

$$\int\sin^{m+1}\theta\,\cos^{n-1}\theta\,d\theta = -\frac{\sin^m\theta\,\cos^n\theta}{m+n} + \frac{m}{m+n}\int\sin^{m-1}\theta\,\cos^{n-1}\theta\,d\theta,$$

a result easily identified with (D).

The other formulæ of reduction can be readily obtained in like manner.

59. **Integration of** $\tan^n\theta\,d\theta$ **and** $\dfrac{d\theta}{\tan^n\theta}$.

These integrals may be regarded as cases of the preceding : they can, however, be arrived at in a simpler manner, as follows :—

Since $\tan^2\theta = \sec^2\theta - 1$, we have

$$\int\tan^n\theta\,d\theta = \int\tan^{n-2}\theta\,(\sec^2\theta - 1)\,d\theta = \int\tan^{n-2}\theta\,d\,(\tan\theta)$$

$$-\int\tan^{n-2}\theta\,d\theta = \frac{\tan^{n-1}\theta}{n-1} - \int\tan^{n-2}\theta\,d\theta. \quad (10)$$

By aid of this formula we have, at once,

$$\int\tan^n\theta\,d\theta = \frac{\tan^{n-1}\theta}{n-1} - \frac{\tan^{n-3}\theta}{n-3} + \frac{\tan^{n-5}\theta}{n-5} - \&c. \quad (11)$$

(1.) If $n = 2r + 1$, the last term is easily seen to be $(-1)^{r+1}\log(\cos\theta)$.

(2.) If $n = 2r$, the two last terms may be represented by $(-1)^{r+1}(\tan\theta - \theta)$.

In a similar manner we have

$$\int \frac{d\theta}{\tan^n\theta} = \int \frac{\sec^2\theta\, d\theta}{\tan^n\theta} - \int \frac{d\theta}{\tan^{n-2}\theta} = \frac{-1}{(n-1)\tan^{n-1}\theta} - \int \frac{d\theta}{\tan^{n-2}\theta}. \quad (12)$$

EXAMPLES.

1. $\int \tan^4\theta\, d\theta.$ *Ans.* $\dfrac{\tan^3\theta}{3} - \tan\theta + \theta.$

2. $\int \dfrac{d\theta}{\tan^3\theta}.$,, $-\dfrac{1}{2\tan^2\theta} - \log(\sin\theta).$

3. $\int \dfrac{d\theta}{\tan^5\theta}.$,, $\dfrac{-1}{4\tan^4\theta} + \dfrac{1}{2\tan^2\theta} + \log(\sin\theta).$

4. $\int \cot^4\theta\, d\theta.$,, $-\dfrac{\cot^3\theta}{3} + \cot\theta + \theta.$

60. **Trigonometrical Transformations.**—Many elementary integrations are immediately reducible to one or other of the preceding formulæ of reduction by aid of the transformations given in Art. 26. For example, if we assume $x = a\tan\theta$, the expression $\dfrac{x^m\, dx}{(a^2 + x^2)^{\frac{n}{2}}}$ transforms into $\sin^m\theta \cos^{n-m-2}\theta\, d\theta$ (neglecting a constant multiplier).

In like manner, the substitution of $a\sin\theta$ for x transforms the expression $\dfrac{x^m\, dx}{(a^2 - x^2)^{\frac{n}{2}}}$ into $\dfrac{a^{m-n+1}\sin^m\theta\, d\theta}{\cos^{n-1}\theta}$: and, if $x = a\sec\theta$, the expression $\dfrac{x^m\, dx}{(x^2 - a^2)^{\frac{n}{2}}}$ transforms into $\dfrac{\cos^{n-m-2}\theta\, d\theta}{\sin^{n-1}\theta}$ (neglecting the constant multiplier).

A similar transformation may be applied in other cases. For example, to find the integral of $\dfrac{x^n\, dx}{(2ax - x^2)^{\frac{1}{2}}}$;

let $x = 2a\sin^2\theta$, then $dx = 4a\sin\theta\cos\theta\, d\theta$,

and the transformed integral is

$$2^{n+1}\, a^n \int \sin^{2n}\theta\, d\theta :$$

accordingly the formula of reduction is the same as that in (5) ;

EXAMPLES.

1. $\displaystyle\int \frac{x^4 dx}{(1 - x^2)^{\frac{1}{2}}}.$ *Ans.* $\dfrac{1\cdot 3}{2\cdot 4}\sin^{-1}x - \dfrac{x\sqrt{1 - x^2}}{8}(3 + 2x^2).$

2. $\displaystyle\int \frac{dx}{x^3 \sqrt{1 - x^2}}.$ „ $\dfrac{1}{2}\log\dfrac{1 - \sqrt{1 - x^2}}{x} - \dfrac{\sqrt{1 - x^2}}{2x^2}.$

3. $\displaystyle\int \frac{dx}{(a^2 + x^2)^{\frac{5}{2}}}.$ „ $\dfrac{x}{a^4(a^2 + x^2)^{\frac{1}{2}}} - \dfrac{x^3}{3a^4(a^2 + x^2)^{\frac{3}{2}}}.$

4. $\displaystyle\int \frac{x^4 dx}{(a^2 + x^2)^2}.$ „ $\dfrac{-x^3}{2(a^2 + x^2)} + \dfrac{3}{2}\left(x - a\tan^{-1}\dfrac{x}{a}\right).$

5. $\displaystyle\int \frac{x^2 dx}{(2ax - x^2)^{\frac{1}{2}}}.$ „ $-(2ax - x^2)^{\frac{1}{2}}\left(\dfrac{x}{2} + \dfrac{3a}{2}\right) + 3a^2\sin^{-1}\sqrt{\dfrac{x}{2a}}.$

The integrals considered in this Article admit also of a more direct treatment. We shall commence with the following:—

61. Cases in which $\dfrac{x^m dx}{(a + cx^2)^{\frac{n}{2}}}$ is immediately integrable.

We have seen, in Art. 48, that the proposed expression is integrable immediately when m is an *odd positive integer*.

Again, when m is an even integer, if we assume $a + cx^2 = x^2 z^2$, the transformed expresssion is

$$\frac{-(z^2 - c)^{\frac{n - m - 3}{2}}\, dz}{a^{\frac{n - m - 1}{2}}\, z^{n-1}}.$$

This is immediately integrable when $n - m - 1$ is even and positive, i.e. when m is either an *even negative integer*, or an *even positive integer, less than $n - 1$.*

For example, $\dfrac{dx}{(a + cx^2)^{\frac{n}{2}}}$ becomes $-\dfrac{(z^2 - c)^{\frac{n-3}{2}}\, dz}{a^{\frac{n-1}{2}}\, z^{n-1}},$ and

accordingly is always integrable by this transformation, since n is an odd integer, by hypothesis.

EXAMPLES.

1. $\displaystyle\int \frac{dx}{(a + cx^2)^{\frac{5}{2}}}.$ $\qquad$ *Ans.* $\displaystyle \frac{x}{a^2 (a + cx^2)^{\frac{1}{2}}} \left\{ 1 - \frac{cx^2}{3 (a + cx^2)} \right\}.$

2. $\displaystyle\int \frac{x^2 dx}{(a + cx^2)^{\frac{7}{2}}}.$ $\qquad$ " $\displaystyle \frac{x^3}{a^2 (a + cx^2)^{\frac{3}{2}}} \left\{ \frac{1}{3} - \frac{cx^2}{5 (a + cx^2)} \right\}.$

3. $\displaystyle\int \frac{x^3 dx}{(a^2 + x^2)^{\frac{5}{2}}}.$ $\qquad$ " $\displaystyle \frac{- (2a^2 + 3x^2)}{3 (a^2 + x^2)^{\frac{3}{2}}}.$

4. $\displaystyle\int \frac{dx}{x^4 (a + cx^2)^{\frac{7}{2}}}.$

The differentials considered in this Article are cases of a more general class called binomial differentials.

62. **Binomial Differentials.**—Expressions of the form

$$x^m (a + bx^n)^p \, dx,$$

in which m, n, p denote any numbers, positive, negative, or fractional, are called Binomial Differentials.

Such expressions can be immediately integrated in two cases, which we proceed to determine by transformations analogous to those adopted in the preceding Article:—

(1). Let $a + bx^n = z$; then $x = \left(\dfrac{z - a}{b} \right)^{\frac{1}{n}}$,

and $\qquad dx = \dfrac{1}{nb} \left(\dfrac{z - a}{b} \right)^{\frac{1}{n} - 1} dz$;

hence $\qquad x^m (a + bx^n)^p dx = \dfrac{(z - a)^{\frac{m+1}{n} - 1} z^p \, dz}{n \, b^{\frac{m+1}{n}}}.$

Consequently, whenever $\dfrac{m + 1}{n}$ is a *positive integer*, the transformed expression is immediately integrable after expansion by the Binomial Theorem.

(2). Again, if we substitute $\dfrac{1}{y}$ for x, the differential becomes

$$- y^{-np-m-2}(ay^n + b)^p \, dy.$$

This is immediately integrable, as in the preceding case, whenever $\dfrac{-(np+m+1)}{n}$ is a positive integer; i. e. when $\dfrac{m+1}{n} + p$ is a *negative integer*. In this latter case the integration is effected by the substitution of z for $ax^{-n} + b$.

EXAMPLES.

1. $\displaystyle\int \frac{x^5 \, dx}{(1 + x^3)^{\frac{1}{2}}}.$ 　　　　　　　　　$Ans.\ \dfrac{2 (1 + x^3)^{\frac{1}{2}} (x^3 - 2)}{9}.$

2. $\displaystyle\int \frac{dx}{(1 + x^3)^{\frac{4}{3}}}.$ 　　　　　　　　　　$,,\ \ \dfrac{x}{(1 + x^3)^{\frac{1}{3}}}.$

3. $\displaystyle\int \frac{dx}{x^2 (1 + x^4)^{\frac{3}{4}}}.$ 　　　　　　　　$,,\ \ -\dfrac{(1 + x^4)^{\frac{1}{4}}}{x}.$

4. $\displaystyle\int \frac{dx}{x^{\frac{1}{2}} (1 + x^2)^{\frac{5}{4}}}.$ 　　　　　　　　$,,\ \ \dfrac{2x^{\frac{1}{2}}}{(1 + x^2)^{\frac{1}{4}}}.$

When neither of the preceding processes is applicable, the expression, if p be a fractional index, is, in general, incapable of integration in a finite number of terms. Before proceeding with this investigation we shall discuss a few simple forms of integration by reduction, involving transcendental functions.

63. **Reduction of** $\displaystyle\int e^{mx} x^n \, dx,$

where n is an integer.

Integrating by parts, we have

$$\int x^n e^{mx} \, dx = \frac{x^n e^{mx}}{m} - \frac{n}{m} \int x^{n-1} e^{mx} \, dx. \qquad (13)$$

By successive applications of this formula the integral is made to depend on $\displaystyle\int e^{mx} \, dx$, i. e. on $\dfrac{e^{mx}}{m}$.

Again, to find $\int \dfrac{e^{mx}}{x^n} dx$.

Assuming $u = e^{mx}$, $v = \dfrac{-1}{(n-1)x^{n-1}}$, and integrating by parts, we have

$$\int \frac{e^{mx}\,dx}{x^n} = \frac{-e^{mx}}{(n-1)x^{n-1}} + \frac{m}{n-1}\int \frac{e^{mx}\,dx}{x^{n-1}}. \tag{14}$$

By means of this the integral is reduced to depend on

$$\int \frac{e^{mx}\,dx}{x}.$$

The value of this integral cannot be obtained in a finite form; it however may be exhibited in the shape of an infinite series; for, expanding e^{mx} and integrating each term separately, we have

$$\int \frac{e^{mx}\,dx}{x} = \log x + \frac{mx}{1} + \frac{m^2 x^2}{1\,.\,2^2} + \frac{m^3 x^3}{1\,.\,2\,.\,3^2} + \&c. \tag{15}$$

The integral of $a^x x^n\, dx$ is immediately reducible to the preceding, since $a^x = e^{x \log a}$. Consequently, by the substitution of $\log a$ for m in (13) and (14), we obtain the formulæ of reduction for

$$\int a^x x^n\, dx \text{ and } \int \frac{a^x}{x^n} dx.$$

In like manner we have immediately

$$\int e^{-x} x^n\, dx = -e^{-x} x^n + n \int e^{-x} x^{n-1}\, dx. \tag{16}$$

64. Reduction of $\int x^m (\log x)^n dx$.

Let $y = \log x$, and the integral reduces to that discussed in the last Article.

The formula of reduction is

$$\int x^m (\log x)^n\, dx = \frac{x^{m+1}(\log x)^n}{m+1} - \frac{n}{m+1}\int x^m (\log x)^{n-1}\, dx. \tag{17}$$

Examples.

1. $\int x^3 e^{ax}\, dx.$
       Ans. $\dfrac{e^{ax}}{a}\left\{x^3 - \dfrac{3}{a}x^2 + \dfrac{3\cdot 2}{a^2}x - \dfrac{3\cdot 2\cdot 1}{a^3}\right\}.$

2. $\int x^3 (\log x)^2\, dx.$
       ,, $\dfrac{x^4}{4}\left\{(\log x)^2 - \dfrac{\log x}{2} + \dfrac{1}{8}\right\}.$

    $\int \dfrac{e^x\, dx}{x^4}.$
       ,, $-\dfrac{e^x}{3}\left\{\dfrac{1}{x^3} + \dfrac{1}{2x^2} + \dfrac{1}{2x}\right\} + \dfrac{1}{3\cdot 2\cdot 1}\int \dfrac{e^x\, dx}{x}.$

65. Reduction of $\int x^n \cos ax\, dx.$

Here $\displaystyle\int x^n \cos ax\, dx = \frac{x^n \sin ax}{a} - \frac{n}{a}\int x^{n-1} \sin ax\, dx\,;$
again

$$\int x^{n-1} \sin ax\, dx = -\frac{x^{n-1}\cos ax}{a} + \frac{n-1}{a}\int x^{n-2} \cos ax\, dx,$$

hence

$$\int x^n \cos ax\, dx = \frac{x^{n-1}(ax \sin ax + n \cos ax)}{a^2} - \frac{n(n-1)}{a^2}\int x^{n-2} \cos ax\, dx.$$

The formula of reduction for $x^n \sin ax\, dx$ can be obtained in like manner.

Again, if we substitute y for $\sin^{-1} x$, the integral

$$\int (\sin^{-1}x)^n\, dx$$

transforms into

$$\int y^n \cos y\, dy,$$

and accordingly its value can be found by the preceding formula.

Examples.

1. $\int x^3 \cos x\, dx.$ *Ans.* $x^3 \sin x + 3x^2 \cos x - 3\cdot 2\cdot x \sin x - 3\cdot 2\cdot 1\cdot \cos x.$

2. $\int x^4 \sin x\, dx.$

Ans. $-x^4 \cos x + 4x^3 \sin x + 4\cdot 3\cdot x^2 \cos x - 4\cdot 3\cdot 2\cdot x \sin x - 4\cdot 3\cdot 2\cdot 1\cdot \cos x.$

66. Reduction of $\int e^{ax} \cos^n x\, dx.$

Integrating by parts, we get

$$\int e^{ax} \cos^n x\, dx = \frac{\cos^n x \, e^{ax}}{a} + \frac{n}{a}\int e^{ax} \cos^{n-1}x \sin x\, dx.$$

Again,

$$\int e^{ax} \cos^{n-1}x \sin x\, dx$$

$$= \frac{e^{ax} \cos^{n-1}x \sin x}{a} - \frac{1}{a}\int e^{ax} \left\{\cos^n x - (n-1)\cos^{n-2}x \sin^2 x\right\} dx$$

$$= \frac{e^{ax} \cos^{n-1}x \sin x}{a} + \frac{(n-1)}{a}\int e^{ax} \cos^{n-2}x\, dx - \frac{n}{a}\int e^{ax} \cos^n x\, dx :$$

substituting, and solving for $\int e^{ax} \cos^n x\, dx$, we get

$$\int e^{ax} \cos^n x\, dx = \frac{e^{ax} \cos^{n-1}x \, (a \cos x + n \sin x)}{a^2 + n^2}$$

$$+ \frac{n(n-1)}{a^2 + n^2}\int e^{ax} \cos^{n-2} x\, dx. \tag{18}$$

The form of reduction for $e^{ax} \sin^n x\, dx$ can be obtained in like manner.

67. Reduction of $\int \cos^m x \sin nx\, dx.$

Integrating by parts, we get

$$\int \cos^m x \sin nx\, dx = - \frac{\cos^m x \cos nx}{n} - \frac{m}{n}\int \cos^{m-1}x \cos nx \sin x\, dx :$$

replacing $\cos nx \sin x$ by $\sin nx \cos x - \sin(n-1)x$, after one or two simple transformations we get

$$\int \cos^m x \sin nx\, dx = - \frac{\cos^m x \cos nx}{m + n}$$

$$+ \frac{m}{m + n}\int \cos^{m-1}x \sin(n-1)x\, dx. \tag{19}$$

The mode of reduction for $\cos^m x \cos nx\, dx$, $\sin^m x \cos nx\, dx$, and $\sin^m x \sin nx\, dx$ can be easily found in like manner.

EXAMPLES.

1. $\int e^{ax} \sin^2 x \, dx.$ *Ans.* $\dfrac{e^{ax} \sin x}{4 + a^2}(a \sin x - 2 \cos x) + \dfrac{2 e^{ax}}{a(4 + a^2)}.$

2. $\int \cos^2 x \sin 4x \, dx.$ „ $-\dfrac{\cos^2 x \cos 4x}{6} - \dfrac{\cos x \cdot \cos 3x}{12} - \dfrac{\cos 2x}{24}.$

3. $\int e^{-x} \cos^2 x \, dx.$ „ $-\dfrac{e^{-x}}{5}(\cos^2 x - \sin 2x + 2).$

68. Reduction by Differentiation.—We shall now return to the discussion of the integrals already considered in Arts. 60 and 61 ; and commence with the reduction of the expression $\dfrac{x^m \, dx}{(a + cx^2)^{\frac{1}{2}}}$. This, as well as other formulæ of reduction of the same type, is best investigated by the aid of a previous differentiation.

Thus we have

$$\frac{d}{dx}\left\{ x^{m-1}(a + cx^2)^{\frac{1}{2}} \right\} = (m - 1)\, x^{m-2}(a + cx^2)^{\frac{1}{2}} + \frac{cx^m}{(a + cx^2)^{\frac{1}{2}}}$$

$$= \frac{(m - 1)\, x^{m-2}(a + cx^2) + cx^m}{(a + cx^2)^{\frac{1}{2}}}$$

$$= \frac{(m - 1)\, a x^{m-2}}{(a + cx^2)^{\frac{1}{2}}} + \frac{mc\, x^m}{(a + cx^2)^{\frac{1}{2}}};$$

hence, transposing and integrating, we obtain

$$\int \frac{x^m \, dx}{(a + cx^2)^{\frac{1}{2}}} = \frac{x^{m-1}(a + cx^2)^{\frac{1}{2}}}{mc} - \frac{(m - 1)\, a}{mc}\int \frac{x^{m-2} \, dx}{(a + cx^2)^{\frac{1}{2}}}. \tag{20}$$

By this formula the integral is reduced to one or more dimensions ; and by repetition of the same process the expression can be always integrated when m is a positive integer.

The formula (20) evidently holds whether m be positive

or negative; accordingly, if we change m into $-(m-2)$, we obtain, after transposing and dividing,

$$\int \frac{dx}{x^m (a + cx^2)^{\frac{1}{2}}} = -\frac{(a + cx^2)^{\frac{1}{2}}}{(m-1) a x^{m-1}} - \frac{(m-2) c}{(m-1) a} \int \frac{dx}{x^{m-2} (a + cx^2)^{\frac{1}{2}}}. \quad (21)$$

69. **More generally, we have**

$$\frac{d}{dx} \left\{ x^{m-1} (a + cx^2)^n \right\} = (m-1) x^{m-2} (a + cx^2)^n + 2nc x^m (a + cx^2)^{n-1}$$

$$= (a + cx^2)^{n-1} \left\{ (m-1) a x^{m-2} + (m + 2n - 1) c x^m \right\}.$$

Hence

$$\int x^m (a + cx^2)^{n-1} dx = \frac{x^{m-1} (a + cx^2)^n}{(m + 2n - 1) c}$$

$$- \frac{(m-1) a}{(m + 2n - 1) c} \int x^{m-2} (a + cx^2)^{n-1} dx. \quad (22)$$

Consequently, when m is positive the integral can be reduced to one lower by two degrees. If m be negative, the formula can be transformed as in the preceding Article, and the integration reduced two degrees.

We next proceed to consider the case where n is negative.

70. **Reduction of** $\int \dfrac{x^m \, dx}{(a + cx^2)^n}$,

m and n being both positive.

Here $$\int \frac{x^m \, dx}{(a + cx^2)^n} = \int x^{m-1} \frac{x \, dx}{(a + cx^2)^n}.$$

Let $x^{m-1} = u$, and $$\int \frac{x \, dx}{(a + cx^2)^n} = v,$$

or $$\frac{-1}{2 (n-1) c (a + cx^2)^{n-1}} = v,$$

and we get

$$\int \frac{x^m \, dx}{(a + cx^2)^n} = \frac{-x^{m-1}}{2 (n-1) c (a + cx^2)^{n-1}} + \frac{m-1}{2 (n-1) c} \int \frac{x^{m-2} \, dx}{(a + cx^2)^{n-1}}. \quad (23)$$

[6]

By successive applications of this form the integral admits of being reduced to another of a simpler shape. We are not able, however, to find the complete integral by this formula, unless when n is either an integer, or is of the form $\frac{r}{2}$, where r is an integer.

71. Reduction of $\displaystyle\int \frac{x^m\,dx}{(a + 2bx + cx^2)^{\frac{1}{2}}}.$

By differentiation, we have

$$\frac{d}{dx}\left\{x^{m-1}(a + 2bx + cx^2)^{\frac{1}{2}}\right\} = (m - 1)\,x^{m-2}\,(a + 2bx + cx^2)^{\frac{1}{2}}$$

$$+ \frac{x^{m-1}(b + cx)}{(a + 2bx + cx^2)^{\frac{1}{2}}} = \frac{(m - 1)\,ax^{m-2} + (2m - 1)\,bx^{m-1} + mcx^m}{(a + 2bx + cx^2)^{\frac{1}{2}}} ;$$

hence

$$\int \frac{x^m\,dx}{(a + 2bx + cx^2)^{\frac{1}{2}}} = \frac{x^{m-1}(a + 2bx + cx^2)^{\frac{1}{2}}}{mc}$$

$$- \frac{(2m - 1)\,b}{mc}\int \frac{x^{m-1}\,dx}{(a + 2bx + cx^2)^{\frac{1}{2}}} - \frac{(m - 1)\,a}{mc}\int \frac{x^{m-2}\,dx}{(a + 2bx + cx^2)^{\frac{1}{2}}}. \quad (24)$$

This furnishes the formula of reduction for this case: by successive applications of it the integral depends ultimately on those of

$$\frac{x\,dx}{(a + 2bx + cx^2)^{\frac{1}{2}}} \quad \text{and} \quad \frac{dx}{(a + 2bx + cx^2)^{\frac{1}{2}}}.$$

These have been determined already in Arts. 9 and 12.

Again, the integral of $\dfrac{dx}{x^m\,(a + 2bx + cx^2)^{\frac{1}{2}}}$ can be reduced to the preceding form by making $x = \dfrac{1}{z}$.

72. The more general integral

$$\int \frac{x^m\,dx}{(a + 2bx + cx^2)^{n}}$$

admits of being treated in like manner.

For if $a + 2bx + cx^2$ be represented by T, we have, by differentiation,

$$\frac{d}{dx}\left(\frac{x^{m-1}}{T^{n-1}}\right) = \frac{(m-1)x^{m-2}}{T^{n-1}} - \frac{2(n-1)x^{m-1}(b+cx)}{T^n}$$

$$= \frac{(m-1)x^{m-2}(a+2bx+cx^2) - 2(n-1)x^{m-1}(b+cx)}{T^n}$$

$$= \frac{(m-1)ax^{m-2}}{T^n} + \frac{2b(m-n)x^{m-1}}{T^n} - \frac{(2n-m-1)cx^m}{T^n}.$$

Hence, we get the formula of reduction

$$\int \frac{x^m\, dx}{T^n} = \frac{-x^{m-1}}{(2n-m-1)c\, T^{n-1}} + \frac{2(m-n)b}{(2n-m-1)c}\int \frac{x^{m-1}\, dx}{T^n}$$

$$+ \frac{(m-1)a}{(2n-m-1)c}\int \frac{x^{m-2}\, dx}{T^n}. \quad (25)$$

By aid of this, the integral of $\dfrac{x^m\, dx}{T^n}$, when m is a positive integer, is made to depend on those of $\dfrac{x\, dx}{T^n}$ and $\dfrac{dx}{T^n}$. Again, it is easily seen that the integral of $\dfrac{x\, dx}{T^n}$ is reduced to that of $\dfrac{dx}{T^n}$, for

$$\int \frac{x\, dx}{T^n} = \frac{1}{c}\int \frac{(b+cx)\, dx}{T^n} - \frac{b}{c}\int \frac{dx}{T^n}$$

$$= \frac{-1}{2(n-1)c\, T^{n-1}} - \frac{b}{c}\int \frac{dx}{T^n}. \quad (26)$$

$$[\mathbf{6\,a}]$$

73. Reduction of $\displaystyle\int \frac{dx}{(a + 2bx + cx^2)^n}.$

In order to reduce $\displaystyle\int \frac{dx}{T^n}$, we have

$$\frac{d}{dx}\left(\frac{b+cx}{T^n}\right) = \frac{c}{T^n} - \frac{2n(b+cx)^2}{T^{n+1}}$$

$$= \frac{c}{T^n} + \frac{2n(ac - b^2)}{T^{n+1}} - \frac{2nc}{T^n} = \frac{2n(ac - b^2)}{T^{n+1}} - \frac{(2n-1)c}{T^n}.$$

Hence

$$\int \frac{dx}{T^{n+1}} = \frac{b + cx}{2n(ac - b^2)\, T^n} + \frac{(2n-1)c}{2n(ac - b^2)}\int \frac{dx}{T^n}. \qquad (27)$$

By aid of this formula of reduction the integral of $\dfrac{dx}{T^n}$ can be found whenever n is an integer, or when it is of the form $\dfrac{r}{2}$ (r being an integer).

74. Reduction of $\displaystyle\int \frac{dx}{(a + b\cos x)^n},$

when n is a positive integer.

Let $U = a + b\cos x$, then $\dfrac{dU}{dx} = -b\sin x$, $\cos x = \dfrac{U - a}{b}$.

Again, by differentiation, we have

$$\frac{d}{dx}\left\{\frac{\sin x}{U^{n-1}}\right\} = \frac{\cos x}{U^{n-1}} + \frac{(n-1)b\sin^2 x}{U^n}$$

$$= \frac{\cos x}{U^{n-1}} + \frac{(n-1)b}{U^n} - \frac{(n-1)b\cos^2 x}{U^n};$$

substitute $\dfrac{U - a}{b}$ for $\cos x$ in the numerators of these fractions, and we get

$$\frac{d}{dx}\left\{\frac{\sin x}{U^{n-1}}\right\} = \frac{1}{bU^{n-2}} - \frac{a}{bU^{n-1}} + \frac{(n-1)b}{U^n} - \frac{n-1}{bU^{n-2}} + \frac{2(n-1)a}{bU^{n-1}}$$

$$- \frac{(n-1)a^2}{bU^n} = \frac{-(n-2)}{bU^{n-2}} + \frac{(2n-3)a}{bU^{n-1}} - \frac{(n-1)(a^2 - b^2)}{bU^n}.$$

Hence, transposing and integrating, we get

$$\int \frac{dx}{U^n} = \frac{-\,b \sin x}{(n-1)(a^2-b^2)\,U^{n-1}} + \frac{(2n-3)\,a}{(n-1)(a^2-b^2)} \int \frac{dx}{U^{n-1}}$$

$$- \frac{n-2}{(n-1)(a^2-b^2)} \int \frac{dx}{U^{n-2}}. \qquad (28)$$

By this formula the proposed integral can be reduced to depend on

$$\int \frac{dx}{a + b \cos x},$$

the value of which has been found in Art. 18.

75. The integral considered in the last Article can also be found by aid of a transformation, whenever a is greater than b, as follows :—

$$\frac{dx}{(a + b \cos x)^n} = \frac{dx}{\left\{(a+b) \cos^2 \dfrac{x}{2} + (a-b) \sin^2 \dfrac{x}{2}\right\}^n}$$

$$= \frac{dx}{\left(A \cos^2 \dfrac{x}{2} + B \sin^2 \dfrac{x}{2}\right)^n} = \frac{\left(1 + \tan^2 \dfrac{x}{2}\right)^n dx}{\left(A + B \tan^2 \dfrac{x}{2}\right)^n}.$$

(where $A = a + b,\ B = a - b$).

Next, assume $\tan \dfrac{x}{2} = \sqrt{\dfrac{A}{B}} \tan \phi$, then

$$\left(1 + \tan^2 \frac{x}{2}\right) dx = 2 \sqrt{\frac{A}{B}} (1 + \tan^2 \phi)\, d\phi :$$

and we get

$$\frac{\left(1 + \tan^2\dfrac{x}{2}\right)^n dx}{\left(A + B\tan^2\dfrac{x}{2}\right)^n} = 2\sqrt{\frac{A}{B}}\,\frac{\left(1 + \dfrac{A}{B}\tan^2\phi\right)^{n-1} d\phi}{A^n \sec^{2n-2}\phi}$$

$$= \frac{2(B\cos^2\phi + A\sin^2\phi)^{n-1} d\phi}{(AB)^{n-\frac{1}{2}}}.$$

Hence, replacing A and B by $a + b$ and $a - b$, we get

$$\int \frac{dx}{(a + b\cos x)^n} = 2\int \frac{(a - b\cos 2\phi)^{n-1} d\phi}{(a^2 - b^2)^{n-\frac{1}{2}}}. \tag{29}$$

When n is a positive integer, the integral at the right-hand side can be found by expanding $(a - b\cos 2\phi)^{n-1}$, and integrating each term separately by formula (4).

Again, if in (28) we make $b = a\cos a$, and $2\phi = y$, we obtain

$$\int \frac{dx}{(1 + \cos a\cos x)^n} = \frac{1}{\sin^{2n-1} a}\int (1 - \cos a\cos y)^{n-1} dy, \tag{30}$$

where $\tan\dfrac{y}{2} = \tan\dfrac{a}{2}\tan\dfrac{x}{2}$.

Hence, if we take 0 and $\dfrac{\pi}{2}$ as limits for x, we have

$$\int_0^{\frac{\pi}{2}} \frac{dx}{(1 + \cos a\cos x)^n} = \frac{1}{\sin^{2n-1} a}\int_0^{\frac{a}{2}} (1 - \cos a\cos y)^{n-1} dy.$$

76. **Integration of** $\dfrac{f(x)\,dx}{\phi(x)\sqrt{a + 2bx + cx^2}}$.

We shall conclude this Chapter with the discussion of the above form, where $f(x)$ and $\phi(x)$ are supposed rational algebraic functions of x.

If $f(x)$ be of higher dimensions than $\phi(x)$, the fraction may be written in the form

$$\frac{f(x)}{\phi(x)} = Q + \frac{R}{\phi(x)}.$$

Again, since Q is of the form $p + qx + rx^2 + \&c.$, the integration of $\dfrac{Q\,dx}{\sqrt{a+2bx+cx^2}}$ can be found by the method of Art. 71.

The fraction $\dfrac{R}{\phi(x)}$ can be decomposed by the method of partial fractions (Chap. II.). To any root a, which is not a multiple root, corresponds a term of the form $\dfrac{A}{x-a}$, and the corresponding term in the expression under discussion is

$$\frac{A\,dx}{(x-a)\sqrt{a+2bx+cx^2}}.$$

The method of integration of this has been given in Art. 13. Next, to a multiple root correspond terms of the form

$$\frac{B\,dx}{(x-a)^r\sqrt{a+2bx+cx^2}}.$$

This is reducible to the form of Art. 71 on making $x - a = \dfrac{1}{z}$. Again, to a pair of imaginary roots corresponds an expression of the form

$$\frac{(lx+m)\,dx}{\{(x-a)^2+\beta^2\}\sqrt{a+2bx+cx^2}}.$$

If z be substituted for $x - a$, the transformed expression may be written

$$\frac{(Lz+M)\,dz}{(z^2+\beta^2)\sqrt{A+2Bz+Cz^2}},$$

where L, M, A, B, C, are constants.

To integrate this form; assume* $z = \beta \tan(\theta + \gamma)$, where

---

* For this simple method of determining the integral in question I am indebted to Mr. Cathcart.

θ is a new variable, and γ an arbitrary constant, and the transformed expression is

$$\frac{\{L\beta \sin (\theta + \gamma) + M \cos (\theta + \gamma)\}d\theta}{\beta \sqrt{A \cos^2 (\theta + \gamma) + 2B\beta \cos (\theta + \gamma) \sin (\theta + \gamma) + C\beta^2 \sin^2 (\theta + \gamma)}}.$$

Again, the expression under the square root is easily transformed into

$$\tfrac{1}{2}\{A + C\beta^2 + (A - C\beta^2) \cos 2 (\theta + \gamma) + 2B\beta \sin 2 (\theta + \gamma)\}$$

$$= \tfrac{1}{2}\left[A + C\beta^2 + \cos 2\theta \{(A - C\beta^2) \cos 2\gamma + 2B\beta \sin 2\gamma\} \right.$$

$$\left. + \sin 2\theta \{2B\beta \cos 2\gamma - (A - C\beta^2) \sin 2\gamma\} \right].$$

Moreover, since γ is perfectly arbitrary, it may be assumed so as to satisfy the equation

$$2B\beta \cos 2\gamma - (A - C\beta^2) \sin 2\gamma = 0, \text{ or } \tan 2\gamma = \frac{2B\beta}{A - C\beta^2}:$$

and consequently the proposed expression is reducible to the form

$$\frac{(L' \cos \theta + M' \sin \theta)d\theta}{\sqrt{P + Q \cos 2\theta}}$$

(in which L', M', P and Q are constants), or

$$\frac{L'd (\sin \theta)}{\sqrt{P + Q - 2Q \sin^2 \theta}} - \frac{M'd (\cos \theta)}{\sqrt{P - Q + 2Q \cos^2 \theta}},$$

each of which is immediately integrable.

EXAMPLES.

1. $\displaystyle\int \cos^3\theta \sin 2\theta\, d\theta.$ *Ans.* $-\dfrac{2}{5}\cos^5\theta.$

2. $\displaystyle\int \sin^2\theta \cos^3\theta\, d\theta.$,, $\dfrac{\sin^3\theta}{3} - \dfrac{\sin^5\theta}{5}.$

3. $\displaystyle\int \sin^5\theta \cos^5\theta\, d\theta.$,, $-\dfrac{1}{64}\left\{\cos 2\theta - \dfrac{2}{3}\cos^3 2\theta + \dfrac{1}{5}\cos^5 2\theta\right\}.$

4. $\displaystyle\int \dfrac{\cos^4\theta\, d\theta}{\sin\theta}.$,, $\dfrac{\cos^3\theta}{3} + \cos\theta + \log\left(\tan\dfrac{\theta}{2}\right).$

5. $\displaystyle\int \dfrac{\cos^4\theta\, d\theta}{\sin^3\theta}.$,, $\left(\cos^3\theta - \dfrac{3}{2}\cos\theta\right)\dfrac{1}{\sin^2\theta} - \dfrac{3}{2}\log\tan\left(\dfrac{\theta}{2}\right).$

6. $\displaystyle\int \dfrac{dx}{(1+x^2)^{\frac{7}{2}}}.$,, $\left(\dfrac{4\cdot 2}{5\cdot 3}x^4 + \dfrac{4}{3}x^2 + 1\right)\dfrac{x}{(1+x^2)^{\frac{5}{2}}}.$

7. $\displaystyle\int x^{2n-1}(a + bx^n)^p\, dx.$,, $\dfrac{(a + bx^n)^{p+1}\{(p+1)bx^n - a\}}{n(p+1)(p+2)b^2}.$

8. $\displaystyle\int e^{-x}\cos^3 x\, dx.$,, $\dfrac{e^{-x}}{10}\left\{3(\sin x - \cos x) + \cos^2 x\,(3\sin x - \cos x)\right\}.$

9. If $\displaystyle\int \dfrac{d\theta}{\sin^m\theta\,\cos^n\theta} = \dfrac{A}{\sin^{m-1}\theta\,\cos^{n-1}\theta} + B\int \dfrac{d\theta}{\sin^{m-2}\theta\,\cos^n\theta},$

determine the values of A and B by differentiation.

10. $\displaystyle\int \dfrac{(x^2 - a^2)dx}{(x^2 + a^2)^3}.$

11. $\displaystyle\int \dfrac{\sin^2\theta\, d\theta}{(1 + \cos\theta)^2}.$ *Ans.* $2\tan\dfrac{\theta}{2} - \theta.$

12. Prove that the integral $\displaystyle\int \dfrac{\sin^m\theta\, d\theta}{(1 + \cos\theta)^n}$ transforms into $2^{m-n+1}\displaystyle\int \dfrac{\sin^m\phi\, d\phi}{\cos^{2n-m}\phi},$ where $\theta = 2\phi.$

13. $\displaystyle\int \frac{dx}{(a + b \cos x)^2}.$

$$Ans. \quad \frac{- b \sin x}{(a^2 - b^2)(a + b \cos x)} + \frac{2a}{(a^2 - b^2)^{\frac{3}{2}}} \tan^{-1} \left\{ \left(\frac{a - b}{a + b} \right)^{\frac{1}{2}} \tan \frac{x}{2} \right\}.$$

14. $\displaystyle\int \frac{\cos \theta \, d\theta}{(5 + 4 \cos \theta)^2}.$ $Ans. \quad \dfrac{5}{9} \cdot \dfrac{\sin \theta}{5 + 4 \cos \theta} - \dfrac{8}{27} \tan^{-1} \left(\dfrac{\tan \frac{\theta}{2}}{3} \right).$

15. $\displaystyle\int (\sin^{-1} x)^4 \, dx = x \left\{ (\sin^{-1} x)^4 - 4 . 3 . (\sin^{-1} x)^2 + 4 . 3 . 2 . 1 \right\}$

$$+ 4\sqrt{1 - x^2} \, \sin^{-1} x \left\{ (\sin^{-1} x)^2 - 3 . 2 \right\}.$$

16. Prove by Art. 74, that any expression of the form $\dfrac{f(\cos x) \, dx}{(a + b \cos x)^n}$ is capable of being integrated when $f(\cos x)$ consists of integral powers of $\cos x$.

17. Show, in like manner, that the expression

$$\frac{f(\cos x, \sin x) dx}{(a + b \cos x)^n}$$

can be integrated when $f(\cos x \sin x)$ consists only of integral powers of $\cos x$ and $\sin x$.

18. If $\displaystyle\int \frac{(A + Bx + Cx^2) \, dx}{(a + \beta x)(a + bx + cx^2)} = P \log (a + \beta x) + Q \log (a + bx + cx^2),$

$$+ R \int \frac{dx}{a + bx + cx^2},$$

find the values of P, Q, and R.

19. $\displaystyle\int \frac{d\theta}{(a \cos^2 \theta + b \sin^2 \theta)^2}.$ $Ans. \quad \dfrac{(a + b) \phi}{2 (ab)^{\frac{3}{2}}} - \dfrac{(a - b) \sin 2\phi}{4 (ab)^{\frac{3}{2}}},$

where $\tan \phi = \sqrt{\dfrac{b}{a}} \tan \theta.$

20. Find the values of n for which $\displaystyle\int \frac{x^n \, dx}{\sqrt{a^{2n} - x^{2n}}}$ is integrable in finite terms.

21. Prove that

$$\int_0^\pi \frac{dx}{(1 + \cos a \cos x)^n} = \frac{1}{\sin^{2n-1} a} \int_0^\pi (1 - \cos a \cos y)^{n-1} dy.$$

CHAPTER IV.

INTEGRATION BY RATIONALIZATION.

77. Integration of Monomials.—If an algebraic expression contain fractional powers of the variable x it can evidently be rendered rational by assuming $x = z^n$, where n is the least common multiple of the denominators of the several fractional powers. By this means the integration of such expressions is reduced to that of rational functions.

For example, to find

$$\int \frac{(1 + x^{\frac{3}{4}})\,dx}{1 + x^{\frac{1}{2}}}.$$

Let $x = z^4$, and the transformed expression is

$$4\int \frac{z^3 (1 + z)\,dz}{1 + z^2}.$$

Consequently the value of the integral is

$$\frac{4x^{\frac{3}{4}}}{3} + 2x^{\frac{1}{2}} - 4x^{\frac{1}{4}} + 4 \tan^{-1}(x^{\frac{1}{4}}) - 2 \log (1 + x^{\frac{1}{2}}).$$

Again, any algebraic expression containing integral powers of x along with irrational powers of an expression of the form $a + bx$ is immediately reduced to the preceding, by the substitution of z for $a + bx$.

EXAMPLES.

1. $\displaystyle \int \frac{x^3\,dx}{\sqrt{x - 1}}$ *Ans.* $\displaystyle \frac{2\sqrt{x - 1}}{5 \cdot 7} [5x^3 + 6x^2 + 8x + 16].$

2. $\displaystyle \int \frac{x\,dx}{(a + bx)^{\frac{3}{2}}}$,, $\displaystyle \frac{2}{b^2} \frac{(2a + bx)}{\sqrt{a + bx}}.$

3. $\displaystyle \int \frac{dx}{x + \sqrt{x - 1}}.$,, $\displaystyle \log (x + \sqrt{x - 1}) - \frac{2}{\sqrt{3}} \tan^{-1} \left(\frac{2\sqrt{x - 1} + 1}{\sqrt{3}} \right).$

78. Rationalization of $F(x, \sqrt{a + 2bx + cx^2})\,dx$. It has been observed (Art. 28) that the integration, in a finite form of irrational expressions containing powers of x beyond the second, is in general impossible without introducing new transcendental functions. We shall accordingly restrict our investigation to the case of an algebraic function containing a single radical of the form $\sqrt{a + 2bx + cx^2}$, where a, b, c are any constants, positive or negative.

Integrals of this form have been already treated by the method of Reduction (Art. 76). We shall discuss them here by the method of rationalization.

The expression* $\dfrac{f(x)}{\phi(x)} \dfrac{dx}{\sqrt{a + 2bx + cx^2}}$ can be made rational in several ways, which we propose to consider in order :—

(1). Assume $\qquad \sqrt{a + 2bx + cx^2} = z - x\sqrt{c}.$ $\qquad$ **(1)**

Then $a + 2bx = z^2 - 2xz\sqrt{c}$; $\therefore bdx = zdz - \sqrt{c}\,(xdz + zdx)$,

or $\qquad dx(b + z\sqrt{c}) = dz(z - x\sqrt{c}) = dz\sqrt{a + 2bx + cx^2}$;

$$\therefore \frac{dx}{\sqrt{a + 2bx + cx^2}} = \frac{dz}{b + z\sqrt{c}}. \qquad \textbf{(2)}$$

Also $\qquad\qquad x = \dfrac{z^2 - a}{2(b + z\sqrt{c})}. \qquad \textbf{(3)}$

This substitution obviously renders the proposed expression rational; and its integration is reducible to that of the class considered in Chapter II.

---

* It will be shown subsequently that the integration of all expressions of the form

$$F(x, \sqrt{a + 2bx + cx^2})\,dx$$

is reducible to that of the above when F is a rational algebraic function.

It may also be observed that, in general, the most expeditious method of integration in practice is that of successive Reduction (Arts. 71, 72, 76).

When $b = 0$, we get

$$\frac{dx}{\sqrt{a + cx^2}} = \frac{dz}{z\sqrt{c}}, \text{ and } x = \frac{z^2 - a}{2z\sqrt{c}} \text{ (see Art. 9).}$$

By aid of the preceding substitution the expression

$$\frac{dx}{(x - p)\sqrt{a + 2bx + cx^2}} \text{ (Art. 13)}$$

transforms into $\qquad \dfrac{dz}{z^2 - 2zp\sqrt{c} - a - 2pb}.$

For example, to find $\displaystyle\int \frac{dx}{(p + qx)\sqrt{1 + x^2}}.$

Here $\quad x = \dfrac{z^2 - 1}{2z}$, and $\dfrac{dx}{(p + qx)\sqrt{1 + x^2}} = \dfrac{2\,dz}{qz^2 + 2pz - q}$;

$$\therefore \int \frac{dx}{(p + qx)\sqrt{1 + x^2}} = \frac{1}{\sqrt{p^2 + q^2}} \log\left(\frac{qz + p - \sqrt{p^2 + q^2}}{qz + p + \sqrt{p^2 + q^2}}\right).$$

When the coefficient c is negative the preceding method introduces imaginaries: we proceed to other transformations in which they are avoided.

(2). Assume* $\quad \sqrt{a + 2bx + cx^2} = \sqrt{a} + xz.$ $\qquad$ (4)

Squaring both sides, we get immediately

$$2b + cx = 2z\sqrt{a} + xz^2 ;$$

$$\therefore dx(c - z^2) = 2\,dz(\sqrt{a} + xz) = 2\,dz\sqrt{a + 2bx + cx^2}.$$

Hence $\qquad \dfrac{dx}{\sqrt{a + 2bx + cx^2}} = \dfrac{2\,dz}{c - z^2}.$ $\qquad$ (5)

---

* This is reducible to the preceding, by changing x into $\dfrac{1}{y}$, and then employing the former transformation.

And
$$x = \frac{2\,(z\sqrt{a} - b)}{c - z^2}. \tag{6}$$

This substitution also evidently renders the proposed expression rational, provided a be positive.

For example, to find
$$\int \frac{dx}{x\sqrt{1 - x^2}}.$$

Assume $\sqrt{1 - x^2} = 1 - xz$, and we get
$$\int \frac{dx}{x\sqrt{1 - x^2}} = \int \frac{dz}{z} = \log z = \log\left(\frac{1 - \sqrt{1 - x^2}}{x}\right).$$

(3). Again, when the roots of $a + 2bx + cx^2$ are real, there is another method of transformation.

For, let a and β be the roots, and the radical becomes of the form
$$\sqrt{c\,(x - a)(x - \beta)}, \text{ or } \sqrt{c\,(x - a)(\beta - x)},$$

according as the coefficient of x^2 is positive or negative.

In the former case, assume $\sqrt{x - a} = z\sqrt{x - \beta}$, and we get
$$x = \frac{a - \beta z^2}{1 - z^2}; \text{ hence } x - \beta = \frac{a - \beta}{1 - z^2}; \therefore \frac{dx}{x - \beta} = \frac{2z\,dz}{1 - z^2}.$$

Accordingly
$$\frac{dx}{\sqrt{c\,(x - a)(x - \beta)}} = \frac{dx}{z\,(x - \beta)\sqrt{c}} = \frac{2}{\sqrt{c}}\frac{dz}{1 - z^2}. \tag{7}$$

In the latter case, let $\sqrt{x - a} = z\sqrt{\beta - x}$, and we get
$$x = \frac{a + \beta z^2}{1 + z^2},$$

and
$$\frac{dx}{\sqrt{c\,(x - a)(\beta - x)}} = \frac{2}{\sqrt{c}}\frac{dz}{1 + z^2}. \tag{8}$$

For example, the integral

$$\int \frac{dx}{(p + qx)\sqrt{1 - x^2}}$$

transforms into

$$\int \frac{2\,dz}{(p + q)z^2 + p - q},$$

on making $x = \dfrac{z^2 - 1}{z^2 + 1}$.

The student can compare this method of integrating the preceding example with that of Art. 13, and he will find no difficulty in identifying the results.

It may be observed that in the application of the foregoing methods it is advisable that the student should in each case select whichever method avoids the introduction of imaginaries.

Thus, as already observed, the first should be employed only when c is positive: in like manner, the second requires a to be positive; and the third, that the roots be real.

It is easily seen that when a and c are both negative, the roots must be real; for the expression

$$\sqrt{-a + 2bx - cx^2}, \text{ or } \sqrt{\frac{b^2 - ac - (cx - b)^2}{c}}$$

is imaginary for all real values of x unless $b^2 - ac$ is positive; i.e. unless the roots are real.

Accordingly, the third method is always applicable when the other two fail.

From the preceding investigation it follows that the expression

$$F(x, \sqrt{a + 2bx + cx^2})\,dx$$

can be always rationalized; F denoting a rational algebraic function of x and of $\sqrt{a + 2bx + cx^2}$.

EXAMPLES.

1. $\displaystyle\int \frac{dx}{(2+3x)\sqrt{4-x^2}}.$ *Ans.* $\dfrac{1}{4\sqrt{2}} \log \dfrac{\sqrt{4+2x}-\sqrt{2-x}}{\sqrt{4+2x}+\sqrt{2-x}}.$

2. $\displaystyle\int \frac{dx}{[(a^2+x^2)^{\frac{1}{2}}+x]^{\frac{1}{4}}}.$

Assume $z = (a^2+x^2)^{\frac{1}{2}} + x$, and we get for the value of the proposed integral

$$\frac{2}{3} z^{\frac{3}{4}} - \frac{2}{5} \frac{a^2}{z^{\frac{5}{4}}}.$$

3. $\displaystyle\int dx \sqrt{x + \sqrt{2+x^2}}.$ *Ans.* $\dfrac{2}{3} \dfrac{x^2 + x\sqrt{2+x^2} - 2}{\sqrt{x+\sqrt{2+x^2}}}.$

4. $\displaystyle\int x^m \left\{ (a^2+x^2)^{\frac{1}{2}} + x \right\}^n dx.$

Making the same assumption as in Ex. 2, the transformed expression is

$$\frac{(z^2 - a^2)^m (a^2 + z^2)\, dz}{2^{m+1} z^{m-n+2}},$$

which is immediately integrable when m is a *positive* integer.

5. $\displaystyle\int \frac{dx}{\left\{(1+x^2)^{\frac{1}{2}}-x\right\}^n}.$ *Ans.* $\dfrac{[(1+x^2)^{\frac{1}{2}}+x]^{n+1}}{2(n+1)} + \dfrac{[(1+x^2)^{\frac{1}{2}}+x]^{n-1}}{2(n-1)}.$

6. $\displaystyle\int \frac{\left\{(1+x^2)^{\frac{1}{2}}+x\right\}^n dx}{(1+x^2)^{\frac{1}{2}}}.$,, $\dfrac{1}{n}\left\{(1+x^2)^{\frac{1}{2}}+x\right\}^n.$

7. $\displaystyle\int \frac{dx}{\sqrt{a+2bx+cx^2}\left(\sqrt{a+2bx+cx^2} \pm x\sqrt{c}\right)^n}.$

Let $\sqrt{a+2bx+cx^2} \pm x\sqrt{c} = z$, then, as in Art. 78, we get

$$\frac{dx}{\sqrt{a+2bx+cx^2}} = \frac{dz}{b \pm z\sqrt{c}};$$

hence the proposed expression transforms into

$$\frac{dz}{z^n(b \pm z\sqrt{c})}; \quad \therefore \ \&c.$$

79. **General Investigation.**—The following more general investigation may be worthy of the notice of the student.

Let R denote the quadratic expression $a + 2bx + cx^2$; then, since the even powers of $\sqrt{R}$ are rational, and the odd contain $\sqrt{R}$ as a factor, any rational algebraic function of x and of $\sqrt{R}$ can evidently be reduced to the form

$$\frac{P + Q\sqrt{R}}{P' + Q'\sqrt{R}},$$

where P, Q, P', Q' are rational algebraic functions of x.

On multiplying the numerator and denominator of this fraction by the complementary surd $P' - Q'\sqrt{R}$, the denominator becomes rational, and the resulting expression may be written in the form

$$M + N\sqrt{R},$$

where M and N are rational functions.

The integration of Mdx is effected by the methods of Chapter II.

Also $$\int N\sqrt{R}\,dx = \int \frac{NR\,dx}{\sqrt{R}};$$

which is of the form

$$\int \frac{f(x)\,dx}{\phi(x)\sqrt{a + 2bx + cx^2}}.$$

Let, as before, $\sqrt{a + 2bx + cx^2} = \sqrt{c(x - a)(x - \beta)}$, and substitute $\dfrac{\lambda + 2\mu z + \nu z^2}{\lambda' + 2\mu' z + \nu' z^2}$ instead of x, when the radical becomes

$$\frac{\sqrt{c\{\lambda - a\lambda' + 2(\mu - a\mu')z + (\nu - a\nu')z^2\}\{\lambda - \beta\lambda' + 2(\mu - \beta\mu')z + (\nu - \beta\nu')z^2\}}}{\lambda' + 2\mu'z + \nu'z^2}.$$

$$(9)$$

Again, if the quadratic factors under this radical be made each a perfect square, the expression obviously becomes rational.

[7]

The simplest method of fulfilling these conditions is by reducing one factor to a constant, and the other to the term containing z^2.

Accordingly, let

$$\lambda - a\lambda' = 0, \quad \mu - a\mu' = 0, \quad \mu - \beta\mu' = 0, \quad \nu - \beta\nu' = 0;$$

or

$$\mu = 0, \quad \mu' = 0, \quad \lambda = a\lambda', \quad \nu = \beta\nu'.$$

On making these substitutions the expression (9) becomes

$$\frac{(\beta - a)z\sqrt{-c\lambda'\nu'}}{\lambda' + \nu'z^2}, \text{ while } x = \frac{a\lambda' + \beta\nu'z^2}{\lambda' + \nu'z^2}.$$

In order that $\sqrt{-c\lambda'\nu'}$ should be real, λ' and ν' must have opposite signs when c is positive, and the same sign when c is negative.

It is also easily seen that without loss* of generality we may assume $\lambda' = 1$, and $\nu' = \pm 1$.

Hence, when c is positive, we get $x = \dfrac{a - \beta z^2}{1 - z^2}$, and when c is negative, $x = \dfrac{a + \beta z^2}{1 + z^2}$.

These agree with the third transformation in the preceding Article.

More generally, when the factors in (9) are each squares, we must have

$$(\mu - a\mu')^2 - (\lambda - a\lambda')(\nu - a\nu') = 0,$$

or

$$\mu^2 - \lambda\nu + (\lambda\nu' + \nu\lambda' - 2\mu\mu')a + (\mu'^2 - \lambda'\nu')a^2 = 0, \qquad (10)$$

and a similar equation with β instead of a.

Moreover, by hypothesis, a satisfies the equation

$$a + 2ba + ca^2 = 0.$$

---

* For the substitution of y^2 for $\dfrac{\nu'z^2}{\lambda'}$ transforms

$$\frac{a\lambda' + \beta\nu'z^2}{\lambda' + \nu'z^2} \text{ into } \frac{a + \beta y^2}{1 + y^2}; \quad \therefore \text{ &c.}$$

Accordingly (10) is satisfied if we assume the constants λ, μ, &c., so as to satisfy the equations

$$\mu^2 - \lambda\nu = a, \quad \lambda'\nu + \lambda\nu' - 2\mu\mu' = 2b, \quad \mu'^2 - \lambda'\nu' = c. \qquad (11)$$

Again, solving for z from the equation

$$x(\lambda' + 2\mu'z + \nu'z^2) = \lambda + 2\mu z + \nu z^2, \qquad (12)$$

we obtain

$$(\nu - x\nu')z + \mu - x\mu' = \sqrt{\mu^2 - \lambda\nu + (\lambda\nu' + \lambda'\nu - 2\mu\mu')x + (\mu'^2 - \lambda'\nu')x^2}$$

$$= \sqrt{a + 2bx + cx^2}. \qquad (13)$$

Also, by differentiation, we get from (12),

$$(\lambda' + 2\mu'z + \nu'z^2)\,dx = 2\{\mu + \nu z - x(\mu' + \nu'z)\}\,dz$$

$$= 2\sqrt{a + 2bx + cx^2}\,dz;$$

$$\therefore \quad \frac{dx}{\sqrt{a + 2bx + cx^2}} = \frac{2dz}{\lambda' + 2\mu'z + \nu'z^2}. \qquad (14)$$

Now, since we have but three equations (11) connecting λ, μ, &c., they can be satisfied in an indefinite number of ways.

We proceed to consider the simplest cases for real transformations.

(1). Let a be positive, and we may assume $\nu = 0$, and $\mu' = 0$; this gives

$$\mu = \sqrt{a}, \quad \lambda\nu' = 2b, \quad \lambda'\nu' = -c.$$

Again, without loss of generality, we may assume $\nu' = -1$, which gives

$$\lambda = -2b, \quad \lambda' = c; \text{ whence } x = \frac{2(z\sqrt{a} - b)}{c - z^2},$$

and

$$\frac{dx}{\sqrt{a + 2bx + cx^2}} = \frac{2dz}{c - z^2}.$$

These agree with the results in (5) and (6).

$$[7\,\mathrm{a}]$$

(2). In like manner, if c be positive we may assume

$$\nu' = 0, \quad \mu = 0, \quad \text{and} \quad \nu = 1,$$

which gives

$$\mu' = \sqrt{c}, \quad \lambda = -a, \quad \text{and} \quad \lambda' = 2b;$$

$$\therefore \quad x = \frac{z^2 - a}{2(b + z\sqrt{c})}, \quad \text{and} \quad \frac{dx}{\sqrt{a + 2bx + cx^2}} = \frac{dz}{b + z\sqrt{c}};$$

as in (2) and (3).

It may be observed that since these results do not contain the roots a and β, they hold whether these roots be real or imaginary; as already shown in Art. 78.

It is easily seen that if we make $\mu = 0$, and $\mu' = 0$, we get the third transformation.

80. If the expression to be integrated be of the form

$$\frac{f(x)\,dx}{\sqrt{a + 2bx + cx^2}},$$

where $f(x)$ is a *rational algebraic* function of x, it is often more convenient to proceed as follows:—

The substitution of $z - \dfrac{b}{c}$ for x transforms the proposed

into $\qquad \dfrac{f\left(z - \dfrac{b}{c}\right)dz}{\sqrt{a' + cz^2}}$, where $a' = \dfrac{ac - b^2}{c}$.

If the even and odd powers be separated in the expansion of $f\left(z - \dfrac{b}{c}\right)$, it can plainly be written in the form

$$\phi(z^2) + z\psi(z^2),$$

and the proposed integral becomes

$$\int \frac{\phi(z^2)\,dz}{\sqrt{a' + cz^2}} + \int \frac{z\psi(z^2)\,dz}{\sqrt{a' + cz^2}}.$$

The former of these is rationalized (**Art. 24**), by making $\sqrt{a' + cz^2} = yz$, and the latter by making $\sqrt{a' + cz^2} = y$.

It may be observed that in general the expression

$$\frac{f(x^2)}{\phi(x^2)}\frac{dx}{\sqrt{a + cx^2}}$$

is also made rational by the transformation

$$\sqrt{a + cx^2} = xy.$$

81. **Case of a Recurring Biquadratic under the Radical Sign.**—As the solution of a recurring equation of the fourth degree is immediately reducible to that of a quadratic, it is natural to consider in what case an Elliptic Integral (Art. 28), in which the biquadratic under the radical sign is recurring, is reducible by the corresponding substitution.

Writing the expression in the form

$$\frac{\phi(x)\,dx}{\sqrt{a + 2bx + cx^2 + 2bx^3 + ax^4}}, \text{ or } \frac{\phi(x)\,dx}{x\sqrt{a\left(x^2 + \dfrac{1}{x^2}\right) + 2b\left(x + \dfrac{1}{x}\right) + c}},$$

and, assuming $x + \dfrac{1}{x} = z$, the radical becomes $\sqrt{az^2 + 2bz + c - 2a}$;

and also

$$\frac{dx}{x}\left(x - \frac{1}{x}\right) = dz.$$

Consequently, in order that the transformed expression should be of the required type, it is obvious that $\phi(x)$ must be reducible to the form

$$\left(x - \frac{1}{x}\right) f\left(x + \frac{1}{x}\right).$$

In this case

$$\frac{\left(x - \dfrac{1}{x}\right) f\left(x + \dfrac{1}{x}\right) dx}{\sqrt{a + 2bx + cx^2 + 2bx^3 + ax^4}}$$

transforms into

$$\frac{f(z)\,dz}{\sqrt{az^2 + 2bz + c - 2a}}.$$

In like manner, the expression

$$\frac{\left(x + \frac{1}{x}\right) f\left(x - \frac{1}{x}\right) dx}{\sqrt{a + 2bx + cx^2 - 2bx^3 + ax^4}}$$

transforms into $\dfrac{f(z)\, dz}{\sqrt{az^2 - 2bz + 2a - c}}$, by the assumption $x - \dfrac{1}{x} = z$.

When $b = 0$ the expression can in some cases be reduced by assuming either

$$x^2 + \frac{1}{x^2} \ \text{ or } \ x^2 - \frac{1}{x^2} = z.$$

EXAMPLES.

1. $\displaystyle\int \frac{(x^2 - 1)\, dx}{x\sqrt{1 + x^4}}.$ *Ans.* $\log \dfrac{1 + x^2 + \sqrt{1 + x^4}}{x}.$

2. $\displaystyle\int \frac{(x^2 + 1)\, dx}{x\sqrt{1 + x^4}}.$,, $\log \dfrac{x^2 - 1 + \sqrt{1 + x^4}}{x}.$

3. $\displaystyle\int \frac{1 - x^2}{1 + x^2}\frac{dx}{\sqrt{1 + x^4}}.$,, $\dfrac{1}{\sqrt{2}} \sin^{-1}\left(\dfrac{x\sqrt{2}}{1 + x^2}\right).$

4. $\displaystyle\int \frac{1 + x^2}{1 - x^2}\frac{dx}{\sqrt{1 + x^4}}.$,, $\dfrac{1}{\sqrt{2}} \log \dfrac{\sqrt{1 + x^4} + x\sqrt{2}}{1 - x^2}.$

This and the preceding were given by Euler (*Calc. Int.*, tom. 4): the connexion, however, of their solution with the method of recurring equations does not appear to have been pointed out by him.

5. $\displaystyle\int \frac{(x^4 - 1)\, dx}{x^2\sqrt{x^4 + x^2 + 1}}.$ *Ans.* $\dfrac{\sqrt{x^4 + x^2 + 1}}{x}.$

Let $\quad x^2 + \dfrac{1}{x^2} = z,$ &c.

6. $\displaystyle\int \frac{(x^2 - 1)\, dx}{x\sqrt{(x^2 + \alpha x + 1)(x^2 + \beta x + 1)}}.$

$\qquad\qquad$ *Ans.* $2 \log \dfrac{\sqrt{x^2 + \alpha x + 1} + \sqrt{x^2 + \beta x + 1}}{x}.$

7. $\displaystyle\int \frac{(1 - x^2)\, dx}{(1 + x^2)\sqrt{1 + x^2 + x^4}}.$ *Ans.* $\sin^{-1}\left(\dfrac{x}{1 + x^2}\right).$

8. $\displaystyle\int \frac{x\,dx}{(a+bx)^{\frac{1}{3}}}.$ *Ans.* $\displaystyle\frac{3(2bx-3a)}{10b^2}(a+bx)^{\frac{2}{3}}.$

9. $\displaystyle\int \frac{1+x^2}{1-x^2}\,\frac{dx}{\sqrt{1+x^2+x^4}}.$,, $\displaystyle\frac{1}{\sqrt{3}}\log\frac{\sqrt{1+x^2+x^4}+x\sqrt{3}}{1-x^2}.$

10. $\displaystyle\int \frac{dx}{(1+x^4)\{(1+x^4)^{\frac{1}{2}}-x^2\}^{\frac{1}{2}}}.$,, $\displaystyle\sin^{-1}\left(\frac{x}{(1+x^4)^{\frac{1}{4}}}\right).$

Assume $x=(1+x^4)^{\frac{1}{4}}\sin\theta,$ &c.

11. $\displaystyle\int \frac{dx}{(1+x^{2n})\{(1+x^{2n})^{\frac{1}{n}}-x^2\}^{\frac{1}{2}}}.$,, $\displaystyle\sin^{-1}\left(\frac{x}{(1+x^{2n})^{\frac{1}{2n}}}\right).$

12. $\displaystyle\int \frac{x\,dx}{(1+x)^{\frac{1}{2}}+(1+x)^{\frac{1}{3}}}.$

Assume $1+x=z^6.$

13. $\displaystyle\int \frac{x^2\,dx}{(1-x^4)(1+x^4)^{\frac{1}{2}}}.$

$$\text{Ans. } \frac{1}{4\sqrt{2}}\log\frac{(1+x^4)^{\frac{1}{2}}+x\sqrt{2}}{1-x^2}+\frac{1}{4\sqrt{2}}\tan^{-1}\frac{(1+x^4)^{\frac{1}{2}}}{x\sqrt{2}}.$$

14. $\displaystyle\int \frac{(1+x^4)\,dx}{(1-x^4)^{\frac{3}{2}}}.$ *Ans.* $\displaystyle\frac{x}{(1-x^4)^{\frac{1}{2}}}.$

15. $\displaystyle\int \frac{(1+x^4)^{\frac{1}{2}}\,dx}{1-x^4}.$

$$\text{Ans. } \frac{1}{2\sqrt{2}}\log\left(\frac{\sqrt{1+x^4}+x\sqrt{2}}{1-x^2}\right)+\frac{1}{2\sqrt{2}}\tan^{-1}\frac{x\sqrt{2}}{\sqrt{1+x^4}}.$$

16. $\displaystyle\int \frac{1-x^2}{1+2ax+x^2}\,\frac{dx}{\sqrt{1+2ax+2bx^2+2ax^3+x^4}}.$

17. $\displaystyle\int \frac{1-ax^2}{1+ax^2}\,\frac{dx}{\sqrt{1+2cx^2+a^2x^4}}.$

$$\text{Ans. } \frac{1}{\sqrt{2(c-a)}}\log\frac{x\sqrt{2(c-a)}+\sqrt{1+2cx^2+a^2x^4}}{1+ax^2},\text{ when } c>a.$$

$$\text{,, } \frac{1}{\sqrt{2(a-c)}}\sin^{-1}\left(\frac{x\sqrt{2(a-c)}}{1+ax^2}\right),\text{ when } a>c.$$

CHAPTER V.

MISCELLANEOUS EXAMPLES OF INTEGRATION.

82. **Integration of** $\dfrac{(A \cos x + B \sin x + C)\, dx}{a \cos x + b \sin x + c}$.

Let $a \cos x + b \sin x + c = u$, then $-a \sin x + b \cos x = \dfrac{du}{dx}$.
Next assume

$$A \cos x + B \sin x + C = \lambda u + \mu \frac{du}{dx} + \nu,$$

and, equating coefficients, we have

$$A = \lambda a + \mu b, \quad B = \lambda b - \mu a, \quad C = \lambda c + \nu.$$

Solving for λ, μ, ν, we get

$$\lambda = \frac{Aa + Bb}{a^2 + b^2}, \quad \mu = \frac{Ab - Ba}{a^2 + b^2}, \quad \nu = C - \frac{(Aa + Bb)\, c}{a^2 + b^2}.$$

Hence

$$\int \frac{(A \cos x + B \sin x + C)\, dx}{a \cos x + b \sin x + c}$$

$$= \frac{(Aa + Bb)\, x}{a^2 + b^2} + \frac{Ab - Ba}{a^2 + b^2} \log (a \cos x + b \sin x + c)$$

$$+ \frac{(a^2 + b^2)\, C - (Aa + Bb)\, c}{a^2 + b^2} \int \frac{dx}{a \cos x + b \sin x + c}.$$

The latter integral can be readily found; for, if we make $a = r \cos a$, $b = r \sin a$, we get

$$a \cos x + b \sin x = r (\cos x \cos a + \sin x \sin a) = r \cos (x - a).$$

On making $x - a = \theta$, the integral reduces to the form considered in Art. 18.

As a simple example, let us take

$$\int \frac{(A + B \tan x)\, dx}{a + b \tan x}.$$

Here
$$\frac{A + B \tan x}{a + b \tan x} = \frac{A \cos x + B \sin x}{a \cos x + b \sin x},$$

and we evidently have

$$\int \frac{(A + B \tan x)\, dx}{a + b \tan x} = \frac{(Aa + Bb)\, x}{a^2 + b^2} + \frac{Ab - Ba}{a^2 + b^2} \log\left(a \cos x + b \sin x\right).$$

83. **Integration of** $\dfrac{f(\cos x,\ \sin x)\, dx}{a \cos x + b \sin x + c}$;

where f is a rational algebraic function, not involving fractions.

As in the preceding Article, assume $x = \theta + a$, and the expression becomes of the form

$$\frac{\phi(\cos \theta,\ \sin \theta)\, d\theta}{A \cos \theta + B}.$$

Again, since $\sin^2 \theta = 1 - \cos^2 \theta$, any integral function of $\sin \theta$ and $\cos \theta$ can be transformed into another of the form

$$\phi_1(\cos \theta) + \sin \theta\ \phi_2(\cos \theta).$$

Accordingly, the proposed expression is reducible to

$$\frac{\phi_1(\cos \theta)\, d\theta}{A \cos \theta + B} + \frac{\phi_2(\cos \theta) \sin \theta\, d\theta}{A \cos \theta + B}.$$

The latter is immediately integrable, by assuming

$$A \cos \theta + B = z.$$

To integrate the former, we divide by $A \cos \theta + B$, and integrate each term separately.

84. **Integration of**

$$\frac{f(\cos x)\,dx}{(a_1 + b_1 \cos x)(a_2 + b_2 \cos x)\ldots(a_n + b_n \cos x)},$$

where f, as before, denotes a rational algebraic function.

Substitute z for $\cos x$ and decompose

$$\frac{f(z)}{(a_1 + b_1 z)(a_2 + b_2 z)\ldots(a_n + b_n z)}$$

by the method of partial fractions: then the expression to be integrated reduces to the sum of a number of terms of the form

$$\frac{dx}{A + B \cos x},$$

each of which can be immediately integrated.

EXAMPLES.

1. $\displaystyle\int \frac{dx}{\cos x\,(5 + 3 \cos x)}.$ *Ans.* $\dfrac{1}{10} \log \left(\dfrac{1 + \sin x}{1 - \sin x}\right) - \dfrac{3}{10} \tan^{-1}\left(\dfrac{\tan \frac{x}{2}}{2}\right).$

2. $\displaystyle\int \frac{dx}{\sin^2 x\,(a + b \cos x)},$ when $a > b.$

$$Ans.\quad \frac{b - a \cos x}{(a^2 - b^2)\sin x} - \frac{b^2}{(a^2 - b^2)^{\frac{3}{2}}} \cos^{-1}\left(\frac{b + a \cos x}{a + b \cos x}\right).$$

3. $\displaystyle\int \frac{dx}{\cos^2 x\,(a + b \cos x)}.$ *Ans.* $\dfrac{\tan x}{a} - \dfrac{b}{a^2} \log \tan\left(\dfrac{\pi}{4} + \dfrac{x}{2}\right) + \dfrac{b^2}{a^2}\displaystyle\int \frac{dx}{a + b \cos x}.$

85. **Integration of** $\{f(x) + f'(x)\}e^x dx.$

The expression $e^x P dx$ is immediately integrable whenever P can be divided into the sum of two functions, one of which is the derived of the other.

For, let
$$P = f(x) + f'(x),$$

then
$$\int e^x P dx = \int e^x f(x)\, dx + \int e^x f'(x)\, dx.$$

Again, integrating by parts, we have

$$\int e^x f(x)\, dx = f(x)\, e^x - \int e^x f'(x)\, dx.$$

Accordingly,

$$\int \{f(x) + f'(x)\}\, e^x\, dx = e^x f(x).$$

For instance, to find

$$\int e^x \frac{x}{(1 + x)^2}\, dx.$$

Here

$$\frac{x}{(1 + x)^2} = \frac{1}{1 + x} - \frac{1}{(1 + x)^2};$$

consequently the value of the proposed integral is $\dfrac{e^x}{1 + x}$.

EXAMPLES.

1. $\displaystyle\int e^x (\cos x + \sin x)\, dx.$ *Ans.* $e^x \sin x.$

2. $\displaystyle\int e^x \frac{1 + x \log x}{x}\, dx.$,, $e^x \log x.$

3. $\displaystyle\int e^x \frac{x^2 + 1}{(x + 1)^2}\, dx.$,, $e^x \dfrac{x - 1}{x + 1}.$

4. $\displaystyle\int e^x \left(\frac{1 - x}{1 + x^2}\right)^2 dx.$,, $\dfrac{e^x}{1 + x^2}.$

86. Differentiation under the Sign of Integration.—The integral of any expression of the form $\phi(x, a)\, dx$, where a is independent of x, is obviously a function of a as well as of x.

Suppose the integral to be denoted by $F(x, a)$, i. e. let

$$F(x, a) = \int \phi(x, a)\, dx,$$

then

$$\frac{d}{dx}\{F(x, a)\} = \phi(x, a).$$

Again, differentiating both sides with respect to a, we have, since x and a are independent,

$$\frac{d^2 \cdot F(x,\, a)}{da\, dx} = \frac{d \cdot \phi(x,\, a)}{da},$$

or (Art. 119, Diff. Calc.),

$$\frac{d}{dx}\left(\frac{d \cdot F(x,\, a)}{da}\right) = \frac{d \cdot \phi(x,\, a)}{da}.$$

Consequently, integrating with respect to x, we get

$$\frac{d \cdot F(x,\, a)}{da} = \int \frac{d \cdot \phi(x,\, a)}{da} dx,$$

$$\text{i.e. } \frac{d}{da}\int \phi(x,\, a)\, dx = \int \frac{d\phi(x,\, a)}{da}\, dx. \qquad (1)$$

In other words, if

$$u = \int \phi(x,\, a)\, dx.$$

then

$$\frac{du}{da} = \int \frac{d\phi}{da}\, dx,$$

provided a be independent of x; in which case, accordingly, it is permitted to *differentiate under the sign of integration.*

By continuing the same process of reasoning we obviously get

$$\frac{d^n u}{da^n} = \int \frac{d^n \phi(x,\, a)}{da^n}\, dx, \qquad (2)$$

where $u = \int \phi(x,\, a)\, dx$, a being independent of x.

For example, if the equation

$$\int e^{ax} dx = \frac{e^{ax}}{a}$$

be differentiated n times with respect to a, we get

$$\int x^n e^{ax}\, dx = \left(\frac{d}{da}\right)^n \left(\frac{e^{ax}}{a}\right)$$

$$= e^{ax} \left(x + \frac{d}{da}\right)^n \left(\frac{1}{a}\right).$$

(See Art. 49, Diff. Calc.).

Again, in Art. 21 we have seen that

$$\int e^{ax} \sin mx\, dx = \frac{e^{ax}\,(a \sin mx - m \cos mx)}{m^2 + a^2}.$$

Accordingly,

$$\int x^n e^{ax} \sin mx\, dx = \left(\frac{d}{da}\right)^n \left(\frac{e^{ax}\,(a \sin mx - m \cos mx)}{m^2 + a^2}\right).$$

We now proceed to consider the inverse process, namely, the method of integration under the sign of integration.

87. Integration under the Sign of Integration.— If in the last Article we suppose $\phi(x, a)$ to be the derived with respect to a of another function v, i.e. if

$$\phi(x, a) = \frac{dv}{da},$$

then $$v = \int \phi(x, a)\, da.$$

Also by the preceding Article we have

$$\frac{d}{da}\left(\int v\, dx\right) = \int \frac{dv}{da}\, dx = \int \phi(x, a)\, dx = F(x, a).$$

Hence $$\int v\, dx = \int F(x, a)\, da.$$

In other words, if

$$F(x, a) = \int \phi(x, a)\, dx,$$

then $$\int F(x,\,a)\,da = \int \left[\int \phi\,(x,\,a)\,da\right] dx. \qquad (3)$$

It may be remarked that the results established in this and in the preceding Article are chiefly of importance in connexion with definite integrals. Some examples of such application will be given in the next Chapter.

88. Integration by Infinite Series.—It has been already observed that in most cases we fail in exhibiting the integral of any proposed expression in finite terms. In such cases, however, we can often represent the integral in the form of a series containing an infinite number of terms.

An example of an integral exhibited in such a form has been given in Art. 63.

The simplest mode of seeking the integral of $f(x)dx$ in the form of an infinite series consists in expanding $f(x)$ in a series of ascending powers of x, and integrating each term separately: then if the series thus obtained be convergent, it represents the integral proposed.

It can be easily seen that if the expansion of $f(x)$ be a convergent series, that of $\int f(x)dx$ is also convergent.

For let

$$f(x) = a_0 + a_1 x + a_2 x^2 + \ldots a_n x^n + \&c.,$$

then

$$\int f(x)\,dx = a_0 x + \frac{a_1 x^2}{2} + \frac{a_2 x^3}{3} + \ldots + \frac{a_n x^{n+1}}{n+1} + \ldots$$

Now (Diff. Calc., Art. 73), the expression for $f(x)$ is convergent whenever $\dfrac{a_n x}{a_{n-1}}$ is less than unity for all values of n beyond a certain number; and the latter series is convergent provided $\dfrac{n}{n+1}\dfrac{a_n x}{a_{n-1}}$ be less than unity, under the same conditions.

Accordingly, the latter series is convergent whenever the former is so.

EXAMPLES.

1. $$\int \frac{dx}{\sqrt{1 - x^5}} = \frac{x}{1} + \frac{1}{2}\frac{x^6}{6} + \frac{1 \cdot 3}{2 \cdot 4}\frac{x^{11}}{11} + \frac{1 \cdot 3 \cdot 5}{2 \cdot 4 \cdot 6}\frac{x^{16}}{16} + \&c.$$

2. $$\int \frac{dx}{\sqrt{\sin x}} = 2\sqrt{\sin x}\left(1 + \frac{1}{2}\frac{\sin^2 x}{5} + \frac{1 \cdot 3}{2 \cdot 4}\frac{\sin^4 x}{9} + \ldots\right).$$

3. $$\int (1 + cx^n)^{\frac{p}{q}} x^{m-1} dx = x^m \left(\frac{1}{m} + \frac{pc}{q}\frac{x^n}{m+n} + \frac{p(p-q)c^2}{1 \cdot 2 \cdot q^2}\frac{x^{2n}}{m+2n} + \&c.\right).$$

89. **Expansion of** $\displaystyle\int \log\left(1 + 2\,m\cos x + m^2\right)dx.$

We shall conclude by showing that the integral

$$\int \log\left(1 + 2m\cos x + m^2\right)dx$$

can be exhibited in the form of an infinite series.

For we have

$$1 + 2m\cos x + m^2 = \left(1 + me^{x\sqrt{-1}}\right)\left(1 + me^{-x\sqrt{-1}}\right).$$

Hence

$$\log\left(1 + 2m\cos x + m^2\right) = \log\left(1 + me^{x\sqrt{-1}}\right) + \log\left(1 + me^{-x\sqrt{-1}}\right)$$

$$= m\left(e^{x\sqrt{-1}} + e^{-x\sqrt{-1}}\right) - \frac{m^2}{2}\left(e^{2x\sqrt{-1}} + e^{2x\sqrt{-1}}\right) + \&c.$$

$$= 2\left(m\cos x - \frac{m^2}{2}\cos 2x + \frac{m^3}{3}\cos 3x - \&c.\right).$$

Accordingly

$$\int \log\left(1 + 2m\cos x + m^2\right)dx = 2\left(m\sin x - m^2\frac{\sin 2x}{2^2} + m^3\frac{\sin 3x}{3^2} - \right). \quad (4)$$

This series becomes divergent when m is greater than unity. In that case, however, the corresponding series can be easily obtained.

For
$$1 + 2m\cos x + m^2 = m^2\left(1 + \frac{e^{x\sqrt{-1}}}{m}\right)\left(1 + \frac{e^{-x\sqrt{-1}}}{m}\right),$$
and accordingly
$$\log\left(1 + 2m\cos x + m^2\right) = 2\log m + 2\left(\frac{\cos x}{m} - \frac{\cos 2x}{2m^2} + \frac{\cos 3x}{3m^3} - \&c.\right).$$
Consequently, when $m > 1$, we have
$$\int\log\left(1 + 2m\cos x + m^2\right)dx = 2x\log m + 2\left(\frac{\sin x}{m} - \frac{\sin 2x}{2^2 m^2} + \frac{\sin 3x}{3^2 m^3} - \ldots\right).$$

From the above it is easily seen that the integral
$$\int\log\left(1 + a\cos x\right)dx$$
can be exhibited in the form of an infinite series when a is less than unity : for making $a = \dfrac{2m}{1 + m^2}$ we have
$$\log\left(1 + a\cos x\right) = \log\left(1 + 2m\cos x + m^2\right) - \log\left(1 + m^2\right).$$

The relation between m and a admits of being exhibited in a simple form ; for let $a = \sin a$, and we get $m = \tan\dfrac{a}{2}$.

Making this substitution in (4), we get
$$\int\log\left(1 + \sin a\cos x\right)dx = 2x\log\left(\cos\frac{a}{2}\right)$$
$$+ 2\left(\tan\frac{a}{2}\sin x - \tan^2\frac{a}{2}\frac{\sin 2x}{2^2} + \&c.\right). \tag{5}$$

EXAMPLES.

1. $\displaystyle\int \frac{(2\cos x + 3\sin x)\,dx}{3\cos x + 2\sin x}.$ *Ans.* $\dfrac{12x}{13} - \dfrac{5}{13}\log\,(3\cos x + 2\sin x).$

2. $\displaystyle\int \frac{d\theta}{1 - \sin^4\theta}.$,, $\dfrac{1}{2}\tan\theta + \dfrac{1}{2\sqrt{2}}\tan^{-1}(\tan\theta\sqrt{2}).$

3. $\displaystyle\int \frac{e^x\,(x^3 + x + 1)\,dx}{(1+x^2)^{\frac{3}{2}}}.$,, $\dfrac{e^x x}{\sqrt{1+x^2}}.$

4. $\displaystyle\int \frac{d\theta}{\sin 2\theta - \sin\theta} = \dfrac{1}{6}\log\,(1+\cos\theta) + \dfrac{1}{2}\log\,(1-\cos\theta) - \dfrac{2}{3}\log\,(1 - 2\cos\theta).$

5. $\displaystyle\int \frac{\sin\dfrac{\theta}{2}\tan\dfrac{\theta}{2}\,d\theta}{\cos\theta} = \log\left(\dfrac{1 - \sin\dfrac{\theta}{2}}{1 + \sin\dfrac{\theta}{2}}\right) + \dfrac{1}{\sqrt{2}}\log\left(\dfrac{\sqrt{2}\sin\dfrac{\theta}{2} + 1}{\sqrt{2}\sin\dfrac{\theta}{2} - 1}\right).$

6. When $x^2 < 1$, prove that

$$\int \frac{dx}{\sqrt{1+x^4}} = \frac{x}{1} - \frac{1}{2}\frac{x^5}{5} + \frac{1\,.\,3}{2\,.\,4}\frac{x^9}{9} - \frac{1\,.\,3\,.\,5}{2\,.\,4\,.\,6}\frac{x^{13}}{13} + \ldots :$$

and when $x^2 > 1$

$$\int \frac{dx}{\sqrt{1+x^4}} = -\frac{1}{x} + \frac{1}{2}\frac{1}{5x^5} - \frac{1\,.\,3}{2}\frac{1}{4}\frac{1}{9x^9} + \frac{1\,.\,3\,.\,5}{2\,.\,4\,.\,6}\frac{1}{13x^{13}} - \ldots$$

7. Prove that

$$\int \frac{e^{ax}}{b+x}\,dx = e^{-ab}\left\{\log\,(b+x) + \frac{a}{1}\frac{b+x}{1} + \frac{a^2}{1\,.\,2}\frac{(b+x)^2}{2} + \ldots\right\},$$

and determine when the series is convergent, and when divergent.

8. Prove that

$$\int \frac{e^{\lambda\omega} + e^{-\lambda\omega}}{2}\sin^\mu\omega\,d\omega = \frac{\sin^{\mu+1}\omega}{\mu+1} + \frac{\lambda^2 + 1^2}{1\,.\,2}\cdot\frac{\sin^{\mu+3}\omega}{\mu+3}$$

$$+ \frac{(\lambda^2 + 1^2)(\lambda^2 + 3^2)}{1\,.\,2\,.\,3\,.\,4}\frac{\sin^{\mu+5}\omega}{\mu+5} + \ldots$$

Substitute ω for $\sin^{-1}x$ in the expansion of $e^{\lambda\sin^{-1}x}$ (*Diff. Calc.*, Art. 87), &c.

9. $\displaystyle\int \frac{e^{\lambda\omega} - e^{-\lambda\omega}}{2}\sin^\mu\omega\,d\omega = \frac{\lambda}{1}\cdot\frac{\sin^{\mu+2}\omega}{\mu+2} + \frac{\lambda\,(\lambda^2 + 2^2)}{1\,.\,2\,.\,3}\frac{\sin^{\mu+4}\omega}{\mu+4}$

$$+ \frac{\lambda\,(\lambda^2 + 2^2)(\lambda^2 + 4^2)}{1\,.\,2\,.\,3\,.\,4\,.\,5}\frac{\sin^{\mu+6}\omega}{\mu+6} + \&\text{c}.$$

[8]

CHAPTER VI.

DEFINITE INTEGRALS.

90. **Integration regarded as Summation.**—We have in the commencement observed that the process of integration may be regarded as that of finding the limit of the sum of the series of values of a differential $f(x)\,dx$, when x varies by indefinitely small increments from any one assigned value to another.

It is in this aspect that the practical importance of integration chiefly consists. For example, in seeking the area of a curve, we conceive it divided into an indefinite number of suitable elementary areas, of which we seek to determine the sum by a process of integration. Applications of finding areas by this method will be given in the next Chapter.

We now proceed to show more fully than in Chapter I. the connexion between the process of integration regarded from this point of view and that from which we have hitherto considered it.

Suppose $\phi(x)$ to represent a function of x which is *finite and continuous* for all values of x between the limits X and x_0; suppose also that $X - x_0$ is divided into n intervals $x_1 - x_0$, $x_2 - x_1$, $x_3 - x_2$, ... $X - x_{n-1}$; then by definition (Diff. Calc., Art. 6), we have

$$\frac{\phi(x_1) - \phi(x_0)}{x_1 - x_0} = \phi'(x_0)$$

in the limit when $x_1 = x_0$; accordingly we have

$$\phi(x_1) - \phi(x_0) = (x_1 - x_0)(\phi'(x_0) + \epsilon_0),$$

where ε_0 becomes infinitely small along with $x_1 - x_0$. Hence we may write

$$\phi(x_1) - \phi(x_0) = (x_1 - x_0)\{\phi'(x_0) + \varepsilon_0\},$$

$$\phi(x_2) - \phi(x_1) = (x_2 - x_1)\{\phi'(x_1) + \varepsilon_1\},$$

$$\phi(x_3) - \phi(x_2) = (x_3 - x_2)\{\phi'(x_2) + \varepsilon_2\},$$

$$\cdot \qquad \cdot \qquad \cdot \qquad \cdot \qquad \cdot \qquad \cdot \qquad \cdot$$

$$\phi(X) - \phi(x_{n-1}) = (X - x_{n-1})\{\phi'(x_{n-1}) + \varepsilon_{n-1}\},$$

where $\varepsilon_0,\ \varepsilon_1 \ldots \varepsilon_{n-1}$ become evanescent when the intervals are taken as infinitely small.

By addition, we have

$$\phi(X) - \phi(x_0) = (x_1 - x_0)\,\phi'(x_0) + (x_2 - x_1)\,\phi'(x_1) + \ldots$$

$$+ (X - x_{n-1})\,\phi'(x_{n-1}) + (x_1 - x_0)\,\varepsilon_0 + (x_2 - x_1)\,\varepsilon_1 + \ldots + (X - x_{n-1})\,\varepsilon_{n-1}.$$

Now if η denote the greatest of the quantities $\varepsilon_0,\ \varepsilon_1, \ldots \varepsilon_{n-1}$, the latter portion of the right-hand side is evidently less than $(X - x_0)\eta$; and accordingly becomes evanescent ultimately (compare Diff. Calc., Art. 39).

Hence

$$\phi(X) - \phi(x_0) = \text{limit of } \big[(x_1 - x_0)\,\phi'(x_0) + (x_2 - x_1)\,\phi'(x_1) + \ldots$$

$$+ (X - x_{n-1})\,\phi'(x_{n-1})\big], \quad (1)$$

when n is increased indefinitely.

This result can also be written in the form

$$\phi(X) - \phi(x_0) = \Sigma\,\phi'(x)\,dx,$$

where the sign of summation Σ is supposed to extend through all values of x between the limits x_0 and X.

91. **Definite Integrals, Limits of Integration.**— The result just arrived at, as already stated in Art. 31, is written in the form

$$f(X) - f(x_0) = \int_{x_0}^{X} f'(x)\,dx, \quad (2)$$

where X is called the *superior*, and x_0 the *inferior limit* of the integral.

[**8 a**]

Again, the expression

$$\int_{x_0}^{X} \phi(x)\, dx$$

is called the *definite integral* of $\phi(x)dx$ between the limits x_0 and X, and represents the limit of the sum of the infinitely small elements $\phi(x)\, dx$, taken between the proposed limits.

From equation (1) we see that the limit of

$$(x_1 - x_0) f'(x_0) + (x_2 - x_1) f'(x_1) + \ldots + (X - x_{n-1}) f'(x_{n-1}),$$

when $x_1 - x_0,\ x_2 - x_1,\ \ldots X - x_{n-1}$ become evanescent, is got by finding the integral of $f'(x)\, dx$ (i. e. the function of which $f'(x)$ is the derived), and substituting the limits x_0, X for x in it, and subtracting the value for the lower limit from that for the upper.

If we write x instead of X in (2) we have

$$f(x) - f(x_0) = \int_{x_0}^{x} f'(x)\, dx, \qquad\qquad (3)$$

in which the upper limit* x may be regarded as variable. Again, as the lower limit x_0 may be assumed arbitrarily, $f(x_0)$ may have any value, and may be regarded as an arbitrary constant. This agrees with the results hitherto arrived at.

In contradistinction, the name *indefinite integrals* is often applied to integrals such as have been considered in the previous chapters, in which the form of the function is merely taken into account, without regard to any assigned limits.

As already observed, the definite integral of any expression between assigned limits can be at once found whenever the indefinite integral is known.

A few easy examples are added for illustration.

---

* The student should observe that in (3) the letter x which stands for the superior limit and the x in the element $f'(x)\, dx$ must be considered as being entirely distinct. The want of attention to this distinction often causes much confusion in the mind of the beginner.

EXAMPLES.

1. $\displaystyle\int_a^b x^n\,dx.$

    Ans. $\displaystyle\frac{b^{n+1}-a^{n+1}}{n+1}.$

2. $\displaystyle\int_0^{\frac{\pi}{4}}\frac{\sin\theta\,d\theta}{\cos^2\theta}.$

    ,, $\sqrt{2}-1.$

3. $\displaystyle\int_0^a\frac{dx}{\sqrt{x+a}+\sqrt{x}}.$

    ,, $\dfrac{4}{3}\sqrt{a}\left(\sqrt{2}-1\right).$

4. $\displaystyle\int_0^\infty\frac{dx}{a^2+x^2}.$

    ,, $\dfrac{\pi}{2a}.$

5. $\displaystyle\int_0^a\frac{dx}{\sqrt{a^2-x^2}}.$

    ,, $\dfrac{\pi}{2}.$

6. $\displaystyle\int_0^\infty e^{-ax}\,dx\ (a\text{ positive}).$

    ,, $\dfrac{1}{a}.$

7. $\displaystyle\int_0^1\frac{dx}{1+2x\cos\phi+x^2}.$

    ,, $\dfrac{\phi}{2\sin\phi}.$

8. $\displaystyle\int_0^\infty\frac{dx}{1+2x\cos\phi+x^2}.$

    ,, $\dfrac{\phi}{\sin\phi}.$

9. $\displaystyle\int_0^\infty e^{-ax}\sin mx\,dx.$

    ,, $\dfrac{m}{a^2+m^2}.$

10. $\displaystyle\int_0^\infty e^{-ax}\cos mx\,dx.$

    ,, $\dfrac{a}{a^2+m^2}.$

11. $\displaystyle\int_{-\infty}^{+\infty}\frac{dx}{a+2bx+cx^2}=\frac{\pi}{\sqrt{ac-b^2}},$ when $ac-b^2$ is positive.

92. To prove that

$$\int_0^1 x^{n-1}(1-x)^{m-1}\,dx=\int_0^1 x^{m-1}(1-x)^{n-1}\,dx=\frac{1\cdot2\cdot3\ldots(m-1)}{n(n+1)\ldots(n+m-1)},$$

when m and n are positive, and m is an integer.

The first relation is evident from (31), Art. 32.

Again, integrating by parts, we have

$$\int x^{n-1} (1 - x)^{m-1} dx = \frac{x^n}{n} (1 - x)^{m-1} + \frac{m-1}{n} \int x^n (1 - x)^{m-2} dx.$$

Moreover, since n and $m - 1$ are positive, the term $x^n (1 - x)^{m-1}$ vanishes for both limits ;

$$\therefore \int_0^1 x^{n-1} (1 - x)^{m-1} dx = \frac{m-1}{n} \int_0^1 x^n (1 - x)^{m-2} dx.$$

The repeated application of this formula reduces the integral to depend on $\int_0^1 x^{m+n-2} dx$, the value of which is $\dfrac{1}{m + n - 1}$.

Hence we have

$$\int_0^1 x^{n-1} (1 - x)^{m-1} dx = \frac{1 \cdot 2 \cdot 3 \cdot \ldots \cdot (m-1)}{n (n+1) \cdot \ldots \cdot (n + m - 1)}. \qquad (4)$$

This formula, combined with the equation

$$\int_0^1 x^{n-1} (1 - x)^{m-1} dx = \int_0^1 x^{m-1} (1 - x)^{n-1} dx,$$

shows that when either m or n is an integer the definite integral

$$\int_0^1 x^{n-1} (1 - x)^{m-1} dx$$

can be easily evaluated.

When m and n are both fractional, the preceding is one of the most important definite integrals in analysis.

We purpose in a subsequent part of the Chapter to give an investigation of some of its simplest properties.

EXAMPLES.

1. $\displaystyle\int_0^1 x^3 (1 - x)^{\frac{5}{2}} dx.$ $Ans.\ \dfrac{2^5}{3 \cdot 7 \cdot 11 \cdot 13}$

2. $\displaystyle\int_0^1 x^4 (1 - x)^{\frac{1}{2}} dx.$ $,,\ \dfrac{2^{13}}{5 \cdot 7 \cdot 9 \cdot 13 \cdot 17}.$

93. **Values of** $\displaystyle\int_0^{\frac{\pi}{2}} \sin^n x\, dx$ **and** $\displaystyle\int_0^{\frac{\pi}{2}} \cos^n x\, dx$.

One of the simplest and most useful applications of definite integration is to the case of the circular integrals considered in the commencement of Chapter III.

We begin with the simple case of

$$\int_0^{\frac{\pi}{2}} \sin^n x\, dx.$$

If in the equation (Art. 56)

$$\int \sin^n x\, dx = -\frac{\cos x \sin^{n-1} x}{n} + \frac{n-1}{n} \int \sin^{n-2} x\, dx$$

we take 0 and $\dfrac{\pi}{2}$ for limits, the term $\dfrac{\cos x \sin^{n-1} x}{n}$ vanishes for both limits, and we have

$$\int_0^{\frac{\pi}{2}} \sin^n x\, dx = \frac{n-1}{n} \int_0^{\frac{\pi}{2}} \sin^{n-2} x\, dx.$$

Now, if n be an integer, the definite integral can be easily obtained; its form, however, depends on whether the index n is even or odd.

(1). Suppose the index even, and represented by $2m$, then

$$\int_0^{\frac{\pi}{2}} \sin^{2m} x\, dx = \frac{2m-1}{2m} \int_0^{\frac{\pi}{2}} \sin^{2m-2} x\, dx.$$

Similarly,

$$\int_0^{\frac{\pi}{2}} \sin^{2m-2} x\, dx = \frac{2m-3}{2m-2} \int_0^{\frac{\pi}{2}} \sin^{2m-4} x\, dx;$$

and by successive application of the formula, we get

$$\int_0^{\frac{\pi}{2}} \sin^{2m} x\, dx = \frac{1 \cdot 3 \cdot 5 \cdot \ldots \cdot (2m-1)}{2 \cdot 4 \cdot 6 \cdot \ldots \cdot 2m} \cdot \frac{\pi}{2}. \tag{5}$$

(2). Suppose the index odd, and represented by $2m + 1$, then

$$\int_0^{\frac{\pi}{2}} \sin^{2m+1} x\, dx = \frac{2m}{2m + 1} \int_0^{\frac{\pi}{2}} \sin^{2m-1} x\, dx.$$

Hence, it is easily seen that

$$\int_0^{\frac{\pi}{2}} \sin^{2m+1} x\, dx = \frac{2 \cdot 4 \cdot 6 \dots 2m}{3 \cdot 5 \cdot 7 \dots (2m + 1)}. \qquad (6)$$

Again, it is evident from (31), Art. 32, that

$$\int_0^{\frac{\pi}{2}} \cos^n x\, dx = \int_0^{\frac{\pi}{2}} \sin^n x\, dx,$$

and consequently (5) and (6) hold when $\cos x$ is substituted for $\sin x$.

94. **Investigation of** $\displaystyle\int_0^{\frac{\pi}{2}} \sin^m x \cos^n x\, dx.$

From Art. 55, when m and n are positive, we have

$$\int_0^{\frac{\pi}{2}} \sin^m x \cos^n x\, dx = \frac{n - 1}{m + n} \int_0^{\frac{\pi}{2}} \sin^m x \cos^{n-2} x\, dx,$$

and

$$\int_0^{\frac{\pi}{2}} \sin^m x \cos^n x\, dx = \frac{m - 1}{m + n} \int_0^{\frac{\pi}{2}} \sin^{m-2} x \cos^n x\, dx.$$

Hence, when one of the indices is an odd integer, the value of the definite* integral is easily found.

---

* The result in this case follows also immediately from Art. 92, by making $\cos^2 x = z$; for this substitution transforms the integral into

$$\frac{1}{2} \int_0^1 (1 - z)^m z^{\frac{n-1}{2}}\, dz.$$

For, writing $2m + 1$ instead of m, we have

$$\int_0^{\frac{\pi}{2}} \sin^{2m+1} x \cos^n x \, dx = \frac{2m}{2m + n + 1} \int_0^{\frac{\pi}{2}} \sin^{2m-1} x \cos^n x \, dx.$$

Hence

$$\int_0^{\frac{\pi}{2}} \sin^{2m+1} x \cos^n x \, dx$$

$$= \frac{2m(2m - 2) \ldots \ldots 2}{(2m + n + 1)(2m + n - 1) \ldots \ldots (n + 3)} \int_0^{\frac{\pi}{2}} \sin x \cos^n x \, dx$$

$$= \frac{2 \cdot 4 \cdot 6 \ldots (2m)}{(n + 1)(n + 3) \ldots (n + 2m + 1)}. \qquad (7)$$

In like manner,

$$\int_0^{\frac{\pi}{2}} \sin^{2m} x \cos^{2n} x \, dx = \frac{2n - 1}{2(m + n)} \int_0^{\frac{\pi}{2}} \sin^{2m} x \cos^{2n-2} x \, dx.$$

Hence

$$\int_0^{\frac{\pi}{2}} \sin^{2m} x \cos^{2n} x \, dx = \frac{1 \cdot 3 \cdot 5 \ldots (2n - 1)}{(2m + 2) \ldots (2m + 2n)} \int_0^{\frac{\pi}{2}} \sin^{2m} x \, dx$$

$$= \frac{1 \cdot 3 \cdot 5 \ldots (2n-1) \cdot 1 \cdot 3 \cdot 5 \ldots (2m-1)}{2 \cdot 4 \cdot 6 \cdot \ldots \ldots \ldots (2m + 2n)} \cdot \frac{\pi}{2}, \qquad (8)$$

in which m and n are supposed both positive integers.

Many elementary definite integrals are immediately reducible to one or other of the preceding forms.

For example, on making $x = \tan \theta$, we get

$$\int_0^{\infty} \frac{dx}{(1 + x^2)^n} = \int_0^{\frac{\pi}{2}} \cos^{2n-2} \theta \, d\theta = \frac{1 \cdot 3 \cdot 5 \ldots (2n - 3)}{2 \cdot 4 \cdot 6 \ldots (2n - 2)} \cdot \frac{\pi}{2}. \qquad (9)$$

Similarly, by $x = a \sin \theta$, $\displaystyle\int_0^a x^n (a^2 - x^2)^{\frac{m}{2}} \, dx$ transforms into

$$a^{n+m+1} \int_0^{\frac{\pi}{2}} \sin^n \theta \cos^{m+1} \theta \, d\theta.$$

In like manner $\displaystyle\int_0^a (2ax - x^2)^{\frac{m}{2}} dx$,

on making $x = a\,(1 - \cos\theta)$, becomes

$$a^{m+1} \int_0^{\frac{\pi}{2}} \sin^{m+1}\theta\, d\theta.$$

The expressions for these integrals, when m and n are fractional in form, will be given in a subsequent Article.

EXAMPLES.

1. $\displaystyle\int_0^{\frac{\pi}{2}} \sin^7 x \cos^4 x \, dx.$ *Ans.* $\dfrac{4^2}{3 \cdot 5 \cdot 7 \cdot 11}.$

2. $\displaystyle\int_0^{\frac{\pi}{2}} \sin^9 x \cos^{\frac{4}{3}} x \, dx.$,, $\dfrac{5 \cdot 10 \cdot 20 \cdot 30 \cdot 40}{9 \cdot 19 \cdot 29 \cdot 39 \cdot 49}.$

3. $\displaystyle\int_0^{\frac{\pi}{2}} \sin^{2m-1} x \cos^{2n-1} x \, dx.$,, $\dfrac{1 \cdot 2 \cdot 3 \cdots (m-1)}{n \cdot (n+1) \cdots (n+m-1)}.$

4. $\displaystyle\int_0^1 (1 - x^2)^n dx.$,, $\dfrac{2 \cdot 4 \cdot 6 \cdots (2n)}{3 \cdot 5 \cdot 7 \cdots (2n+1)}.$

5. $\displaystyle\int_0^1 \frac{x^{2n} dx}{\sqrt{1 - x^2}}.$,, $\dfrac{1 \cdot 3 \cdot 5 \cdots (2n-1)}{2 \cdot 4 \cdot 6 \cdots 2n} \cdot \dfrac{\pi}{2}.$

6. $\displaystyle\int_0^1 \frac{x^{2n+1} dx}{\sqrt{1 - x^2}}.$,, $\dfrac{2 \cdot 4 \cdot 6 \cdots 2n}{3 \cdot 5 \cdot 7 \cdots (2n+1)}.$

7. Deduce Wallis's value for π by aid of the two preceding definite integrals.

8. $\displaystyle\int_0^\infty \frac{x^n dx}{(a + bx^2)^{\frac{n}{2}+1}}.$ *Ans.* $\dfrac{2 \cdot 4 \cdot 6 \cdots (n-1)}{3 \cdot 5 \cdot 7 \cdots n} \dfrac{1}{\sqrt{ab^{n+1}}},$

when n is an *odd* integer.

9. $\displaystyle\int_0^a x^3 (2ax - x^2)^{\frac{3}{2}} dx.$

95. Value of $\int_0^\infty e^{-x} x^n \, dx$**, when n is a positive integer.**
In Art. 63 we have seen that

$$\int e^{-x} x^n \, dx = - e^{-x} x^n + n \int e^{-x} x^{n-1} \, dx.$$

Again, the expression $\dfrac{x^n}{e^x}$ vanishes when $x = 0$, and also when $x = \infty$ (Diff. Calc., Art. 94, Ex. 2).

Hence
$$\int_0^\infty e^{-x} x^n \, dx = n \int_0^\infty e^{-x} x^{n-1} \, dx. \tag{10}$$

Consequently
$$\int_0^\infty e^{-x} x^n \, dx = 1 \cdot 2 \cdot 3 \ldots n. \tag{11}$$

Many other forms are immediately reducible to the preceding definite integral.

For example, if we make $x = az$ we get

$$\int_0^\infty e^{-az} z^n \, dz = \frac{1 \cdot 2 \cdot 3 \ldots n}{a^{n+1}}, \tag{12}$$

in which a is supposed to be positive.

Again, to find $\int_0^1 x^m (\log x)^n \, dx$; let $x = e^{-z}$, and the integral becomes

$$(-1)^n \int_0^\infty e^{-(m+1)z} z^n \, dz = (-1)^n \frac{1 \cdot 2 \cdot 3 \ldots n}{(m+1)^{n+1}}.$$

Since $\log x = - \log \left(\dfrac{1}{x} \right)$, this result may be written in the form

$$\int_0^1 x^m \left(\log \frac{1}{x} \right)^n \, dx = \frac{1 \cdot 2 \cdot 3 \ldots n}{(m+1)^{n+1}}. \tag{13}$$

The definite integral $\int_0^\infty e^{-x} x^{n-1}\, dx$ is sometimes known as The Second* Eulerian Integral, and is fundamental in the theory of definite integrals. Being obviously a function of n, it is denoted by the symbol $\Gamma(n)$, and is styled the Gamma-Function.

It follows from (10) that

$$\Gamma(n+1) = n\Gamma(n). \tag{14}$$

Also, when n is an integer we have

$$\Gamma(n+1) = 1 \cdot 2 \cdot 3 \ldots n. \tag{15}$$

Again, when x is less than unity, we have

$$\frac{1}{1-x} = 1 + x + x^2 + x^3 + \&c\,;$$

$$\therefore \int_0^1 \log x \cdot \frac{dx}{1-x} = \int_0^1 \log x\,(1 + x + x^2 + \ldots)\, dx$$

$$= -\left(1 + \frac{1}{2^2} + \frac{1}{3^2} + \ldots\right) = -\frac{\pi^2}{6},$$

(by a well-known result in Trigonometry).

In like manner we get

$$\int_0^1 \frac{\log x\, dx}{1+x} = -\frac{\pi^2}{12}.$$

An account of the more elementary properties of Gamma-Functions will be given at the end of this Chapter.

---

* The integral $\int_0^1 x^{m-1}(1-x)^{n-1}\, dx$, considered in Art. 92, is sometimes called the First Eulerian Integral; we shall show subsequently how it can be expressed in terms of Gamma-Functions.

EXAMPLES.

1. $\displaystyle\int_0^1 \left\{ \log\left(\frac{1}{x}\right) \right\}^n dx.$

Ans. $1 \cdot 2 \cdot 3 \ldots n.$

2. $\displaystyle\int_0^\infty a^{-x} x^n\, dx.$

,, $\displaystyle\frac{1 \cdot 2 \ldots n}{(\log a)^{n+1}}.$

3. $\displaystyle\int_0^1 \frac{\log x}{1 - x^2}\, dx.$

,, $-\dfrac{\pi^2}{8}.$

4. $\displaystyle\int_0^1 \frac{dx\,(\log x)^{2n-1}}{1 - x} = -\,1 \cdot 2 \cdot 3 \ldots (2n-1)\left[1 + \frac{1}{2^{2n}} + \frac{1}{3^{2n}} + \cdots \right].$

5. $\displaystyle\int_0^1 \frac{dx}{x} \log\left(\frac{1 + x}{1 - x}\right).$

Ans. $\dfrac{\pi^2}{4}.$

96. *If u and v be both functions of x, and if v preserve the same sign while x varies from x_0 to X, then we shall have*

$$\int_{x_0}^{X} uv\, dx = U \int_{x_0}^{X} v\, dx,$$

where U is some quantity comprised between the greatest and the least values of u, between the assigned limits.

For, let A and B be the greatest and the least values of u, and we shall have, when v is positive,

$$Av > uv > Bv;$$

when v is negative,

$$Av < uv < Bv.$$

Consequently, for all values of x between x_0 and X the expression $uv\,dx$ lies between $Av\,dx$ and $Bv\,dx$, and accordingly, if the sign of v does not change between the limits,

$$\int_{x_0}^{X} uv\,dx \text{ lies between } A \int_{x_0}^{X} v\,dx \text{ and } B \int_{x_0}^{X} v\,dx,$$

which establishes the theorem proposed.

Cor. If $f(x)$ be *finite* and continuous for all values of x between the finite limits x_0 and X, then the integral

$$\int_{x_0}^{X} f(x)dx$$

will also have a finite value.

For, let A be the greatest value of $f(x)$, and B the least, then $\int_{x_0}^{X} f(x)\, dx$ evidently lies between the quantities

$$A \int_{x_0}^{X} dx \text{ and } B \int_{x_0}^{X} dx\,;$$

$$\therefore \int_{x_0}^{X} f(x)\, dx > B(X - x_0) \text{ and } < A(X - x_0).$$

97. **Taylor's Theorem.**—The method of definite integration combined with that of integration by parts furnishes a simple proof of Taylor's series.

For, if in the equation

$$f(X + h) - f(X) = \int_{X}^{X+h} f'(x)\, dx$$

we assume $x = X + h - z$, we get $dx = -\,dz$, and also

$$\int_{X}^{X+h} f'(x)\, dx = \int_{0}^{h} f'(X + h - z)\, dz\,;$$

$$\therefore f(X + h) - f(X) = \int_{0}^{h} f'(X + h - z)\, dz.$$

Again, integrating by parts, we have

$$\int f'(X + h - z)\, dz = zf'(X + h - z) + \int zf''(X + h - z)\, dz.$$

Hence, substituting the limits, we have

$$\int_{0}^{h} f'(X + h - z)\, dz = hf'(X) + \int_{0}^{h} zf''(X + h - z)\, dz.$$

In like manner,

$$\int zf''(X + h - z)\,dz = \frac{z^2}{2}f''(X + h - z) + \int \frac{z^2}{2}f'''(X + h - z)\,dz,$$

which gives

$$\int_0^h zf''(X + h - z)\,dz = \frac{h^2}{2}f''(X) + \int_0^h \frac{z^2}{2}f'''(X + h - z)\,dz\,;$$

and so on.

Accordingly, we have finally

$$f(X + h) = f(X) + \frac{h}{1}f'(X) + \frac{h^2}{1 \cdot 2}f''(X) + \ldots + \frac{h^{n-1}}{\lfloor n-1}f^{(n-1)}(X)$$

$$+ \int_0^h f^{(n)}(X + h - z)\frac{z^{n-1}\,dz}{\lfloor n-1}. \qquad (16)$$

This is Taylor's well-known expansion.[*]

98. **Remainder in Taylor's Theorem expressed as a Definite Integral.**—Let R_n represent the remainder after n terms in Taylor's series, then by the preceding Article we have

$$R_n = \int_0^h f^{(n)}(X + h - z)\frac{z^{n-1}\,dz}{\lfloor n-1}. \qquad (17)$$

There is no difficulty in deducing Lagrange's form for the remainder from this result.

For, by Art. 96, we have

$$R_n = U\int_0^h \frac{z^{n-1}\,dz}{1 \cdot 2 \cdot 3 \ldots (n-1)} = U\frac{h^n}{1 \cdot 2 \ldots n},$$

where U lies between the greatest and least values which $f^{(n)}(X + h - z)$ assumes while z varies between o and h.

---

[*] The student will observe that it is essential for the validity of this proof (Art. 90), that the successive derived functions, $f'(x), f''(x)$, &c., should be finite and continuous for all values of x between the limits X and $X + h$. Compare Articles 54 and 75, *Diff. Calc.*

Hence, as in Art. 75, Diff. Calc. (since any value of z between o and h may be represented by $(1 - \theta) h$, where $\theta > $ o and < 1); we have

$$R_n = \frac{h^n}{1 \cdot 2 \ldots n} f^{(n)}(X + \theta h)$$

where θ is some quantity between the limits zero and unity.

99. **Bernoulli's Series.**—If we apply the method of integration by parts to the expression $f(x)dx$ we get

$$\int f(x) \, dx = xf(x) - \int xf'(x)dx \, ;$$

$$\therefore \int_0^X f(x) \, dx = Xf(X) - \int_0^X f'(x) \, x \, dx.$$

In like manner,

$$\int_0^X f'(x) \, x \, dx = \frac{X^2}{1 \cdot 2} f'(X) - \int_0^X f''(x) \, \frac{x^2 \, dx}{1 \cdot 2},$$

$$\int_0^X f''(x) \, \frac{x^2 \, dx}{1 \cdot 2} = \frac{X^3}{1 \cdot 2 \cdot 3} f''(X) - \int_0^X f'''(x) \frac{x^3 \, dx}{1 \cdot 2 \cdot 3},$$

and so on.

Hence, we get finally

$$\int_0^X f(x)dx = \frac{X}{1} f(X) - \frac{X^2}{1 \cdot 2} f'(X) + \frac{X^3}{1 \cdot 2 \cdot 3} f''(X) - \&c. \ldots (18)$$

Compare Art 66, Diff. Calc., where the result was obtained directly from Taylor's expansion.

100. **Exceptional Cases in Definite Integrals.**— In the foregoing discussion of definite integrals we have supposed that the function $f(x)$, under the sign of integration, has a finite value for all values of x between the limits. We have also supposed that the limits are finite. We purpose now to give a short discussion of the exceptional cases.* They may

---

* The complete investigation of definite integrals in these exceptional cases is due to Cauchy. For a more general discussion the student is referred to M. Moigno's *Calcul Intégral*, as also to those of M. Serret and M. Bertrand.

be classed as follows :—(1). When $f(x)$ becomes infinite at one of the limits of integration. (2). When $f(x)$ becomes infinite for one or more values of x between the limits of integration. (3). When one or both of the limits become infinite.

In these cases, the integral $\displaystyle\int_{x_0}^{X} f(x)\,dx$ may still have a finite value, or it may be infinite, or indeterminate : depending on the form of the function $f(x)$ in each particular case. The following investigation will be found to comprise the cases which usually arise.

101. **Case in which $f(x)$ becomes infinite at one of the Limits.**—Suppose that $f(x)$ is finite for all values of x between x_0 and X, but that it becomes infinite when $x = X$.

The case that most commonly arises is where $f(x)$ is of the form $\dfrac{\psi(x)\,dx}{(X-x)^n}$, in which $\psi(x)$ is finite for all values between the limits, and n is a positive index.

Let a be assumed so that $\psi(x)$ preserves the same sign between the limits a and X; then

$$\int_{x_0}^{X} \frac{\psi(x)\,dx}{(X-x)^n} = \int_{x_0}^{a} \frac{\psi(x)\,dx}{(X-x)^n} + \int_{a}^{X} \frac{\psi(x)\,dx}{(X-x)^n}.$$

The former of the integrals at the right-hand side is finite by Art. 96. The consideration of the latter resolves into two cases, according as n is less or greater than unity.

(1). Let $n < 1$, and also let A and B be the greatest and least values of $\psi(x)$ between the limits a and X : then, by Art. 96, the integral

$$\int_{a}^{X} \frac{\psi(x)\,dx}{(X-x)^n} \text{ lies between } A \int_{a}^{X} \frac{dx}{(X-x)^n} \text{ and } B \int_{a}^{X} \frac{dx}{(X-x)^n}.$$

Moreover, since $n < 1$, we have evidently

$$\int_{a}^{X} \frac{dx}{(X-x)^n} = \frac{(X-a)^{1-n}}{1-n},$$

and consequently, in this case, the proposed integral has a finite value.

[9]

(2). Let $n > 1$, and, as before, suppose A and B the greatest and least values of $\psi(x)$ between a and X; then

$$\int_a^X \frac{\psi(x)\,dx}{(X-x)^n} \text{ lies between } A\int_a^X \frac{dx}{(X-x)^n} \text{ and } B\int_a^X \frac{dx}{(X-x)^n}.$$

Again, we have

$$\int \frac{dx}{(X-x)^n} = \frac{1}{(n-1)(X-x)^{n-1}}.$$

Now $\dfrac{1}{(X-x)^{n-1}}$ becomes infinite when $x = X$, but has a finite value when $x = a$; consequently the definite integral proposed has an infinite value in this case.

When $n = 1$, $\displaystyle\int \frac{dx}{(X-x)} = -\log(X-x)$. This becomes infinite when $x = X$; and consequently in this case also the proposed integral becomes infinite.

The investigation when $f(x)$ becomes infinite for $x = x_0$ follows from the preceding by interchanging the limits.

102. **Case where $f(x)$ becomes infinite between the Limits.**—Suppose $f(x)$ becomes infinite when $x = a$, where a lies between the limits x_0 and X; then since

$$\int_{x_0}^X f(x)\,dx = \int_{x_0}^a f(x)\,dx + \int_a^X f(x)\,dx,$$

the investigation is reduced to two integrals, each of which may be treated as in the preceding Article.

Hence, if we suppose $f(x) = \dfrac{\psi(x)}{(x-a)^n}$, it follows, as in the last Article, that $\displaystyle\int_{x_0}^X f(x)\,dx$ has a finite or an infinite value according as n is *less* or *not less* than unity.

The case in which $f(x)$ becomes infinite for two or more values between the limits is treated in a similar manner.

For example, if

$$f(a_1) = \infty, \quad f(a_2) = \infty, \; \ldots \; f(a_n) = \infty,$$

where $a_1, a_2 \ldots a_n$ lie between the limits X and x_0; then

$$\int_{x_0}^{X} f(x)\, dx = \int_{x_0}^{a_1} f(x)\, dx + \int_{a_1}^{a_2} f(x)\, dx + \&\mathrm{c.} + \int_{a_n}^{X} f(x)\, dx,$$

each of which can be treated separately.

103. **Case of Infinite Limits.**—Suppose the superior limit X to be infinite, and, as in the preceding discussion, let $f(x)$ be of the form $\dfrac{\psi(x)}{(x-a)^n}$, where $\psi(x)$ is finite for all values of x.

As before, we have

$$\int_{x_0}^{X} f(x)\, dx = \int_{x_0}^{a} f(x)\, dx + \int_{a}^{X} f(x)\, dx.$$

The integral between the finite limits x_0 and a has a finite value as before. The investigation of the other integral consists again of two cases.

(1). Let $n > 1$, and let A be the greatest value of $\psi(x)$ between the limits a and ∞, then

$$\int_{a}^{\infty} \frac{\psi(x)\, dx}{(x-a)^n} \text{ is less than } A \int_{a}^{\infty} \frac{dx}{(x-a)^n}.$$

But
$$\int_{a}^{X} \frac{dx}{(x-a)^n} = \frac{1}{n-1}\left[\frac{1}{(a-a)^{n-1}} - \frac{1}{(X-a)^{n-1}}\right].$$

The latter term becomes evanescent when $X = \infty$: accordingly in this case the proposed integral has a finite value.

In like manner it is easily seen that if n be *not greater than* unity, the definite integral

$$\int_{a}^{\infty} \frac{dx}{(x-a)^n}$$

$$\lceil 9\,a \rceil$$

132

Definite Integrals.

has an infinite value ; and consequently

$$\int_a^\infty \frac{\psi(x)\,dx}{(x-a)^n}$$

is also infinite, provided $\psi(x)$ does not become evanescent for infinite values of x.

Hence, the definite integral

$$\int_{x_0}^n \frac{\psi(x)\,dx}{(x-a)^n}$$

has, in general, a finite or an infinite value according as n is greater or not greater than unity : $\psi(x)$ being supposed finite, and x_0 being greater than a.

If X become $-\infty$, a similar investigation is applicable; for on changing x into $-x$, we have

$$\int_{x_0}^X f(x)\,dx = -\int_{-x_0}^{-X} f(-x)\,dx,$$

in which the superior limit becomes ∞.

104. **Principal and General Values of a Definite Integral.**—We shall conclude this discussion with a short account of Cauchy's* method of investigation.

Suppose $f(x)$ to be infinite when $x = a$, where a lies between the limits x_0 and X; then the integral $\int_{x_0}^X f(x)\,dx$ is regarded as the limit towards which the sum

$$\int_{x_0}^{a-\mu\epsilon} f(x)\,dx + \int_{a+\nu\epsilon}^X f(x)\,dx$$

approaches when ϵ becomes evanescent; μ and ν being any arbitrary constants.

---

* This and the four following Articles have been taken, with some modifications, from Moigno's *Calcul Intégral.*

This value depends on the nature of $f(x)$, and may be finite and determinate, or infinite, or indeterminate.

If we suppose $\mu = \nu$, the limiting value of the preceding sum is called the *principal value* of the proposed integral; while that given above is called its *general* value.

For example, let us consider the integral $\displaystyle\int_{-x_0}^{X} \frac{dx}{x}$.

Here
$$\int_{-x_0}^{X} \frac{dx}{x} = \text{limit} \left[\int_{\nu\epsilon}^{X} \frac{dx}{x} + \int_{-x_0}^{-\mu\epsilon} \frac{dx}{x} \right].$$

But
$$\int_{\nu\epsilon}^{X} \frac{dx}{x} = \log\left(\frac{X}{\nu\epsilon}\right).$$

Also, making $x = -z$,

$$\int_{-x_0}^{-\mu\epsilon} \frac{dx}{x} = \int_{x_0}^{\mu\epsilon} \frac{dz}{z} = \log\left(\frac{\mu\epsilon}{x_0}\right).$$

Accordingly, the principal value of $\displaystyle\int_{-x_0}^{X} \frac{dx}{x}$ is $\log\left(\dfrac{X}{x_0}\right)$; while its general value is $\log\left(\dfrac{X}{x_0}\right) + \log\left(\dfrac{\mu}{\nu}\right)$. The latter expression is perfectly arbitrary and indeterminate.

Again, let us take $\displaystyle\int_{-x_0}^{X} \frac{dx}{x^2}$.

As before,
$$\int_{-x_0}^{X} \frac{dx}{x^2} = \text{limit} \left[\int_{\nu\epsilon}^{X} \frac{dx}{x^2} + \int_{-x_0}^{-\mu\epsilon} \frac{dx}{x^2} \right].$$

But
$$\int_{\nu\epsilon}^{X} \frac{dx}{x^2} = \frac{1}{\nu\epsilon} - \frac{1}{X}; \text{ and } \int_{-x_0}^{-\mu\epsilon} \frac{dx}{x^2} = \frac{1}{\mu\epsilon} - \frac{1}{x_0};$$

$$\therefore \int_{-x_0}^{X} \frac{dx}{x^2} = \text{limit} \left[\frac{1}{\mu\epsilon} + \frac{1}{\nu\epsilon} - \frac{1}{X} - \frac{1}{x_0} \right].$$

Consequently, both the principal and the general value of the integral are infinite in this case.

In like manner,

$$\int_{-x_0}^{X} \frac{dx}{x^3} = \text{limit of } \frac{1}{2}\left(\frac{1}{\nu^2\epsilon^2} - \frac{1}{\mu^2\epsilon^2} + \frac{1}{x_0^2} - \frac{1}{X^2}\right).$$

Hence the general value of the integral is infinite, while its principal value is $\dfrac{1}{2}\left(\dfrac{1}{x_0^2} - \dfrac{1}{X^2}\right)$.

It may be observed that the principal value of

$$\int_{-x_0}^{X} \frac{dx}{x^3} \quad \text{is equal to} \quad \int_{x_0}^{X} \frac{dx}{x^3}.$$

This holds also whenever $f(x)$ is a function of an odd order: i.e. when $f(-x) = -f(x)$.

For we have

$$\int_{-x_0}^{x_0} f(x)\,dx = \int_{0}^{x_0} f(x)\,dx + \int_{-x_0}^{0} f(x)\,dx.$$

But $\quad \displaystyle\int_{-x_0}^{0} f(x)\,dx = -\int_{x_0}^{0} f(-x)\,dx = \int_{0}^{x_0} f(-x)\,dx\ ;$

$$\therefore \int_{-x_0}^{x_0} f(x)\,dx = \int_{0}^{x_0} \{f(x) + f(-x)\}\,dx. \tag{19}$$

Accordingly, if $f(-x) = -f(x)$, we get

$$\int_{-x_0}^{x_0} f(x)\,dx = 0.$$

Again, if $f(x)$ be of an even order, i.e. if $f(-x) = f(x)$, we have

$$\int_{-x_0}^{x_0} f(x)\,dx = 2\int_{0}^{x_0} f(x)\,dx.$$

105. **Singular Definite Integral.**—The difference between the general and the principal value of the integral considered at the commencement of the preceding Article is represented by

$$\int_{a+\nu\epsilon}^{a+\mu\epsilon} f(x)\,dx,$$

in which $f(a) = \infty$, and ϵ is evanescent.

Such an integral is called by Cauchy a *singular definite integral*, in which the limits differ by an infinitely small quantity.   The preceding discussion shows that such an integral may be either *infinite* or *indeterminate*.

106. **Infinite Limits.**—If the superior limit be infinite, we regard $\int_{x_0}^{\infty} f(x)\,dx$ as the limit of $\int_{x_0}^{\frac{1}{\mu\epsilon}} f(x)\,dx$, when ϵ becomes evanescent.

Also $\int_{-\infty}^{\infty} f(x)\,dx = $ limit of $\int_{-\frac{1}{\mu\epsilon}}^{\frac{1}{\nu\epsilon}} f(x)\,dx$ when ϵ is evanescent.

In the latter case the value of the definite integral when $\mu = \nu$ is, as before, called the *principal value* of

$$\int_{-\infty}^{\infty} f(x)\,dx.$$

In this we assume that $f(x)$ does not become infinite for any real value of x.

107. **Example.**—Suppose $\dfrac{f(x)}{F(x)}$ to be a rational algebraic fraction, in which $f(x)$ is at least two degrees lower in x than $F(x)$, and suppose all the roots of $F(x) = 0$ to be imaginary, it is required to find the value of

$$\int_{-\infty}^{\infty} \frac{f(x)}{F(x)}\,dx.$$

From the foregoing conditions it follows that $\dfrac{f(x)}{F(x)}$ cannot become infinite for any real value of x: accordingly the true value of the integral is the limit of

$$\int_{-\frac{1}{\mu\epsilon}}^{\frac{1}{\nu\epsilon}} \frac{f(x)}{F(x)}\,dx$$

when ϵ vanishes.

To find this value, suppose $\dfrac{f(x)}{F(x)}$ decomposed by the method of partial fractions, and let

$$\frac{A - B\sqrt{-1}}{x - a - b\sqrt{-1}} \quad \text{and} \quad \frac{A + B\sqrt{-1}}{x - a + b\sqrt{-1}}$$

be the fractions corresponding to the pair of conjugate roots

$$a + b\sqrt{-1} \text{ and } a - b\sqrt{-1}, \text{ of } F(x) = 0;$$

then the corresponding quadratic fraction is the sum of

$$\frac{A - B\sqrt{-1}}{x - a - b\sqrt{-1}} \quad \text{and} \quad \frac{A + B\sqrt{-1}}{x - a + b\sqrt{-1}},$$

$$\text{i. e. } \frac{2A(x - a) + 2Bb}{(x - a)^2 + b^2}.$$

Again
$$\int \frac{2Bb\,dx}{(x - a)^2 + b^2} = 2B \tan^{-1}\left(\frac{x - a}{b}\right);$$

$$\therefore \int_{-\frac{1}{\mu\epsilon}}^{\frac{1}{\nu\epsilon}} \frac{2Bb\,dx}{(x - a)^2 + b^2} = 2\pi B \text{ when } \epsilon \text{ vanishes.}$$

Also
$$\int \frac{2A(x - a)\,dx}{(x - a)^2 + b^2} = A \log \{(x - a)^2 + b^2\};$$

$$\therefore \int_{-\frac{1}{\mu\epsilon}}^{\frac{1}{\nu\epsilon}} \frac{2A(x - a)\,dx}{(x - a)^2 + b^2} = A \log \left\{\frac{\mu^2 (1 - a\nu\epsilon)^2 + b^2\nu^2\epsilon^2}{\nu^2 (1 + a\mu\epsilon)^2 + b^2\mu^2\epsilon^2}\right\}$$

$$= 2A \log \frac{\mu}{\nu}, \text{ when } \epsilon = 0.$$

Hence
$$\int_{-\frac{1}{\mu\epsilon}}^{\frac{1}{\nu\epsilon}} \frac{\{2A(x-a)+2B\}\,dx}{(x-a)^2+b^2} = 2A\log\left(\frac{\mu}{\nu}\right)+2\pi B. \quad (20)$$

Now, suppose $F(x)$ to be of the degree $2n$ in x, and let the values of A and B, corresponding to the n pairs of imaginary roots, be denoted by $A_1, A_2, \ldots A_n$, and $B_1, B_2, \ldots B_n$, respectively; then we have

$$\int_{-\frac{1}{\mu\epsilon}}^{\frac{1}{\nu\epsilon}} \frac{f(x)}{F(x)}\,dx = 2\,(A_1 + A_2 + \ldots + A_n)\log\left(\frac{\mu}{\nu}\right)$$

$$+\; 2\pi\,(B_1 + B_2 + \ldots + B_n).$$

Again, since $f(x)$ is of the degree $2n-2$ at most, we have

$$A_1 + A_2 + \ldots + A_n = 0.$$

For, if we clear the equation

$$\frac{f(x)}{F(x)} = \frac{2A_1(x-a_1)+2B_1 b_1}{(x-a_1)^2+b_1{}^2} + \ldots + \frac{2A_n(x-a_n)+2B_n b_n}{(x-a_n)^2+b_n{}^2}$$

from fractions, the coefficient of x^{2n-1} at the right-hand side is evidently

$$2\,(A_1 + A_2 + \ldots + A_n)\,;$$

which must be zero, as there is no corresponding term on the other side.

Accordingly we have, in this* case,

$$\int_{-\infty}^{\infty} \frac{f(x)}{F(x)}\,dx = 2\pi\,(B_1 + B_2 + \ldots + B_n). \quad (21)$$

---

* It may be observed that when $f(x)$ is but *one* degree lower than $F(x)$, the *principal value* of $\int_{-\infty}^{\infty} \dfrac{f(x)}{F(x)}\,dx$ is still of the form given in (21).

We proceed to apply this result to an important example.

108. **Value of** $\int_0^\infty \dfrac{x^{2m}\,dx}{1 + x^{2n}}$ **when m and n are Positive Integers, and $n > m$.**

Let a be a root of $x^{2n} + 1 = 0$, and, by Art. 37, we have

$$A - B\sqrt{-1} = \frac{a^{2m}}{2n\,a^{2n-1}} = -\frac{a^{2m+1}}{2n}.$$

Again, by the theory of equations, a is of the form

$$\cos\frac{(2k + 1)\pi}{2n} + \sqrt{-1}\,\sin\frac{(2k + 1)\pi}{2n},$$

in which k is either zero or a positive integer less than n;

$$\therefore a^{2m+1} = \cos(2k + 1)\theta + \sqrt{-1}\,\sin(2k + 1)\theta,$$

where
$$\theta = \frac{(2m + 1)\pi}{2n}.$$

Hence $B = \dfrac{\sin(2k + 1)\theta}{2n}$; and accordingly we have

$$B_1 + B_2 + \ldots + B_n = \frac{1}{2n}\{\sin\theta + \sin 3\theta + \ldots + \sin(2n - 1)\theta\}.$$

To find this sum, let

$$S = \sin\theta + \sin 3\theta + \ldots + \sin(2n - 1)\theta;$$

then

$$2S\sin\theta = 2\sin^2\theta + 2\sin\theta\sin 3\theta + \ldots + 2\sin\theta\sin(2n - 1)\theta$$
$$= 1 - \cos 2\theta + \cos 2\theta - \cos 4\theta + \ldots + \cos(2n - 2)\theta - \cos 2n\theta$$
$$= 1 - \cos 2n\theta = 2\sin^2 n\theta = 2\sin^2(2m + 1)\frac{\pi}{2} = 2;$$

$$\therefore S = \frac{1}{\sin\theta} = \frac{1}{\sin\dfrac{(2m + 1)\pi}{2n}}.$$

Accordingly, we have

$$\int_{-\infty}^{\infty} \frac{x^{2m}\, dx}{1 + x^{2n}} = \frac{\pi}{n \sin \dfrac{(2m + 1)\, \pi}{2n}}.$$

Hence, by (19),

$$\int_{0}^{\infty} \frac{x^{2m}\, dx}{1 + x^{2n}} = \frac{1}{2}\int_{-\infty}^{\infty} \frac{x^{2m}\, dx}{1 + x^{2n}} = \frac{\pi}{2n} \frac{1}{\sin \dfrac{(2m + 1)\, \pi}{2n}}. \qquad (22)$$

We now proceed to consider the analogous integral $\displaystyle\int_0^\infty \frac{x^{2m}\, dx}{1 - x^{2n}}$, where m and n, as before, are positive integers, and $n > m$.

109. **Investigation of** $\displaystyle\int_0^\infty \frac{x^{2m}}{1 - x^{2n}}\, dx.$

We commence by showing that

$$\int_0^\infty \frac{dx}{1 - x^2} = 0.$$

This is easily seen as follows :

$$\int_0^\infty \frac{dx}{1 - x^2} = \int_0^1 \frac{dx}{1 - x^2} + \int_1^\infty \frac{dx}{1 - x^2}.$$

Now, transform the latter integral, by making $x = \dfrac{1}{z}$, and we get

$$\int_1^\infty \frac{dx}{1 - x^2} = \int_1^0 \frac{dz}{1 - z^2} = -\int_0^1 \frac{dz}{1 - z^2} = -\int_0^1 \frac{dx}{1 - x^2} \, ;$$

$$\therefore \int_0^\infty \frac{dx}{1 - x^2} = 0.$$

Again, proceeding to the integral

$$\int_0^\infty \frac{x^{2m}\, dx}{1 - x^{2n}},$$

we observe that $1 + x$ and $1 - x$ are the only real factors of $1 - x^{2n}$, and that the corresponding partial quadratic fraction in the decomposition of

$$\frac{x^{2m}}{1 - x^{2n}} \text{ is } \frac{1}{n(1 - x^2)}.$$

Consequently, the part of the definite integral which corresponds to the real roots disappears.

Moreover, it is easily seen that the method of Arts. 107 and 108 applies to the fractions arising from the $n - 1$ pairs of imaginary roots, and accordingly

$$\int_{-\infty}^{\infty} \frac{x^{2m}\, dx}{1 - x^{2n}} = 2\pi (B_1 + B_2 + \ldots + B_{n-1}),$$

where $B_1, B_2, \ldots B_{n-1}$ have the same signification as before.

Again, since the roots of $x^{2n} - 1 = 0$ are of the form

$$\cos \frac{k\pi}{n} \pm \sqrt{-1} \sin \frac{k\pi}{n},$$

it follows, as in Art. 108, that

$$B_1 + B_2 + \ldots + B_{n-1} = \frac{1}{2n} \left[\sin 2\theta + \sin 4\theta + \ldots + \sin 2(n - 1)\theta \right],$$

where $\qquad \theta = \dfrac{(2m + 1)\pi}{2n}$, as before.

Proceeding as in the former case, it is easily seen that

$$\sin 2\theta + \sin 4\theta + \ldots + \sin 2(n - 1)\theta$$

$$= \frac{\cos \theta - \cos(2n - 1)\theta}{2 \sin \theta} = \cot \frac{2m + 1}{2n}\, \pi.$$

Hence $\qquad \displaystyle\int_{-\infty}^{\infty} \frac{x^{2m}\, dx}{1 - x^{2n}} = \frac{\pi}{n} \cot \frac{2m + 1}{2n}\, \pi ;$

$$\therefore \int_{0}^{\infty} \frac{x^{2m}\, dx}{1 - x^{2n}} = \frac{\pi}{2n} \cot \frac{2m + 1}{2n}\, \pi. \qquad (23)$$

Again, if we transform (22) and (23) by making $x^{2n} = z$ and $a = \dfrac{2m + 1}{2n}$, we get

$$\int_0^\infty \frac{z^{a-1}\,dz}{1 + z} = \frac{\pi}{\sin a\pi}, \qquad \int_0^\infty \frac{z^{a-1}\,dz}{1 - z} = \pi \cot a\pi. \qquad (24)$$

The conditions imposed on m and n require that a should be positive and less than unity.

Moreover, since the results in (24) hold for all integer values of m and n, provided $n > m$, we assume, by the law of continuity, that they hold for all values of a, so long as it is positive and less than unity.

110. The definite integrals discussed in the two preceding Articles admit of several important transformations, of which we proceed to add a few.

For example, on making $u = z^a$ in (24), we get

$$\int_0^\infty \frac{du}{1 + u^{\frac{1}{a}}} = \frac{a\pi}{\sin a\pi}; \qquad \int_0^\infty \frac{du}{1 - u^{\frac{1}{a}}} = a\pi \cot a\pi.$$

If $\dfrac{1}{a} = r$, these become

$$\int_0^\infty \frac{du}{1 + u^r} = \frac{\pi}{r \sin \dfrac{\pi}{r}}, \qquad \int_0^\infty \frac{du}{1 - u^r} = \frac{\pi}{r} \cot \frac{\pi}{r}, \qquad (25)$$

where r is positive and greater than unity.

Again

$$\int_0^\infty \frac{x^n\,dx}{1 + x^2} = \int_0^1 \frac{x^n\,dx}{1 + x^2} + \int_1^\infty \frac{x^n\,dx}{1 + x^2}.$$

Now, if in the latter integral we make $x = \dfrac{1}{z}$, we get

$$\int_1^\infty \frac{x^n\,dx}{1 + x^2} = -\int_1^0 \frac{z^{-n}\,dz}{1 + z^2} = \int_0^1 \frac{x^{-n}\,dx}{1 + x^2};$$

$$\therefore \int_0^\infty \frac{x^n\,dx}{1 + x^2} = \int_0^1 \frac{x^n + x^{-n}}{1 + x^2}\,dx. \qquad (26)$$

Moreover, from (22), when n is less than unity, we have

$$\int_0^\infty \frac{x^n\,dx}{1 + x^2} = \frac{\pi}{2\cos\dfrac{n\pi}{2}}. \tag{27}$$

Accordingly

$$\int_0^1 \frac{x^n + x^{-n}}{x + x^{-1}}\frac{dx}{x} = \frac{\pi}{2\cos\dfrac{n\pi}{2}}. \tag{28}$$

In like manner, it is easily seen that

$$\int_0^1 \frac{x^n - x^{-n}}{x - x^{-1}}\frac{dx}{x} = \frac{\pi}{2}\tan\frac{n\pi}{2}. \tag{29}$$

It should be noted, that in these results n must be less than unity.

Again, transform (28) and (29) by making $x = e^{-\pi z}$ and $n\pi = a$, and we get

$$\int_0^\infty \frac{e^{az} + e^{-az}}{e^{\pi z} + e^{-\pi z}}\,dz = \frac{1}{2}\sec\frac{a}{2}, \quad \int_0^\infty \frac{e^{az} - e^{-az}}{e^{\pi z} - e^{-\pi z}}\,dz = \frac{1}{2}\tan\frac{a}{2}. \tag{30}$$

We add a few examples for illustration.

EXAMPLES.

1. $\displaystyle\int_0^a \frac{dx}{(a^n - x^n)^{\frac{1}{n}}}.$ *Ans.* $\dfrac{\pi}{n\sin\dfrac{\pi}{n}}.$

2. $\displaystyle\int_0^\infty \frac{dx}{(x^2 + a^2)(x^2 + b^2)}.$,, $\dfrac{\pi}{2ab\,(a + b)}.$

3. $\displaystyle\int_0^\infty \frac{dx}{1 - x^4}.$,, $\dfrac{\pi}{4}.$

4. $\displaystyle\int_0^{\frac{\pi}{2}} \tan^n\theta\,d\theta$, where n lies between $+1$ and -1.   ,, $\dfrac{\pi}{2\cos\dfrac{n\pi}{2}}.$

5. $\displaystyle\int_0^1 \frac{x^m + x^{-m}}{x^n + x^{-n}} \frac{dx}{x}$, where $n > m$.
$\qquad\qquad$ *Ans.* $\displaystyle\frac{\pi}{2n \cos \dfrac{m\pi}{2n}}.$

6. $\displaystyle\int_0^\infty \frac{(e^{ax} + e^{-ax})(e^{bx} + e^{-bx})}{e^{\pi x} + e^{-\pi x}} dx.$
$\qquad\qquad$,, $\displaystyle\frac{2\cos\dfrac{a}{2}\cos\dfrac{b}{2}}{\cos a + \cos b}.$

7. $\displaystyle\int_0^\infty \frac{(e^{ax} + e^{-ax})(e^{bx} - e^{-bx})}{e^{\pi x} - e^{-\pi x}} dx.$
$\qquad\qquad$,, $\displaystyle\frac{\sin b}{\cos a + \cos b}.$

It should be observed, that in these we must have $a + b < \pi$.

8. Hence, when $b < \pi$, prove that

$$\int_0^\infty \frac{e^{bx} + e^{-bx}}{e^{\pi x} + e^{-\pi x}} \cos ax\, dx = \frac{\left(e^{\frac{a}{2}} + e^{-\frac{a}{2}}\right)\cos\dfrac{b}{2}}{e^a + 2\cos b + e^{-a}}.$$

$$\int_0^\infty \frac{e^{bx} - e^{-bx}}{e^{\pi x} - e^{-\pi x}} \cos ax\, dx = \frac{\sin b}{e^a + 2\cos b + e^{-a}}. \;:$$

$$\int_0^\infty \frac{e^{bx} + e^{-bx}}{e^{\pi x} + e^{-\pi x}} \sin ax\, dx = \frac{1}{2}\frac{e^a - e^{-a}}{e^a + 2\cos b + e^{-a}}.$$

9. $\displaystyle\int_0^1 \frac{z^a - z^{-a}}{1 - z} dz.$
$\qquad\qquad$ *Ans.* $\pi \cot a\pi - \dfrac{1}{a}.$

III. **Differentiation of Definite Integrals.**—It is plain from Art. 86 that the method of *differentiation under the sign of integration* applies to definite as well as to indefinite integrals, provided the limits of integration are independent of the quantity with respect to which we differentiate.

On account of the importance of this principle we add an independent proof, as follows :—

Suppose u to denote the definite integral in question, i.e. let

$$u = \int_a^b \phi(x,\, a)\, dx,$$

where a and b are independent of a.

To find $\dfrac{du}{da}$ let Δu denote the change in u arising from the change Δa in a; then, since the limits are unaltered,

$$\Delta u = \int_a^b \{\phi(x,\, a + \Delta a) - \phi(x,\, a)\}\, dx;$$

$$\therefore \frac{\Delta u}{\Delta a} = \int_a^b \frac{\phi(x,\, a + \Delta a) - \phi(x,\, a)}{\Delta a}\, dx.$$

Hence, on passing to the limit,* we have

$$\frac{du}{da} = \int_a^b \frac{d\phi(x,\, a)}{da}\, dx.$$

Also, if we differentiate n times in succession, we obviously have

$$\frac{d^n u}{da^n} = \int_a^b \frac{d^n \phi(x,\, a)}{da^n}\, dx.$$

The importance of this method will be best exhibited by a few elementary examples.

112. **Integrals deduced by Differentiation.**—If the equation

$$\int_0^\infty e^{-ax}\, dx = \frac{1}{a}$$

be differentiated n times with respect to a, we get

$$\int_0^\infty x^n e^{-ax}\, dx = \frac{1 \cdot 2 \cdot 3 \ldots n}{a^{n+1}},$$

as in Art. 95.

Again, from the equation

$$\int_0^\infty \frac{dx}{x^2 + a} = \frac{\pi}{2} \frac{1}{a^{\frac{1}{2}}},$$

we get, after n differentiations with respect to a,

$$\int_0^\infty \frac{dx}{(x^2 + a)^{n+1}} = \frac{\pi}{2} \frac{1 \cdot 3 \cdot 5 \ldots (2n - 1)}{2 \cdot 4 \cdot 6 \ldots \quad 2n} \frac{1}{a^{n+\frac{1}{2}}};$$

which agrees with Art. 94.

---

* For exceptions to this general result the student is referred to Bertrand's *Calcul Intégral*, p. 181.

Again, if we take o and ∞ for limits in the integrals (23) and (24) of Art. 21, we get

$$\int_0^\infty e^{-ax} \cos mx\, dx = \frac{a}{a^2+m^2}, \qquad \int_0^\infty e^{-ax} \sin mx\, dx = \frac{m}{a^2+m^2}. \qquad (31)$$

Now, differentiate each of these n times with respect to a, and we get

$$\int_0^\infty e^{-ax} x^n \cos mx\, dx = (-1)^n \left(\frac{d}{da}\right)^n \left(\frac{a}{a^2+m^2}\right)$$

$$= \frac{\lfloor n \cdot \cos(n+1)\theta}{(a^2+m^2)^{\frac{n+1}{2}}},$$

$$\int_0^\infty e^{-ax} x^n \sin mx\, dx = \frac{\lfloor n \cdot \sin(n+1)\theta}{(a^2+m^2)^{\frac{n+1}{2}}}, \qquad (32)$$

where $m = a \tan \theta$.   (See Ex. 17, 18, Diff. Calc., pp. 58, 59.)
  Next, from (24) we have

$$\int_0^\infty \frac{x^{a-1}\, dx}{1-x} = \pi \cot a\pi.$$

Accordingly, if we differentiate with respect to a, we have

$$\int_0^\infty \frac{x^{a-1} \log x\, dx}{1-x} = -\frac{\pi^2}{\sin^2 a\pi}.$$

Again, if the equation

$$\int_0^1 y^{n-1}\, dy = \frac{1}{n}$$

be transformed, by making $y = \dfrac{bx}{a+bx}$, it evidently gives

$$\int_0^\infty \frac{x^{n-1}\, dx}{(a+bx)^{n-1}} = \frac{1}{na\, b^n}.$$

[10]

Now, differentiating with respect to a, we have

$$\int_0^\infty \frac{x^{n-1}\,dx}{(a+bx)^{n+2}} = \frac{1}{n(n+1)a^2 b^n}.$$

If we proceed to differentiate $m-1$ times with regard to a, we have

$$\int_0^\infty \frac{x^{n-1}\,dx}{(a+bx)^{m+n}} = \frac{1\,.\,2\,.\,3\,\ldots\,(m-1)}{n\,.\,(n+1)(n+2)\,\ldots\,(n+m-1)} \cdot \frac{1}{a^m b^n}.$$

113. By aid of the preceding method the determination of a definite integral can often be reduced to a known integral. We shall illustrate this statement by one or two examples.

Ex. 1. To find

$$\int_0^\pi \frac{\log\left(1 + \sin a \cos x\right)}{\cos x}\,dx.$$

Denote the definite integral by u, and differentiate with respect to a; then

$$\frac{du}{da} = \int_0^\pi \frac{\cos a\,dx}{1 + \sin a \cos x} = \pi \text{ (by Art. 18).}$$

Hence, we get

$$\int_0^\pi \frac{dx\,\log\left(1 + \sin a \cos x\right)}{\cos x} = \pi a.$$

No constant is added since the integral evidently vanishes along with a.

Ex. 2. $$u = \int_0^\infty \frac{e^{-ax} \sin mx}{x}\,dx.$$

In this case

$$\frac{du}{dm} = \int_0^\infty e^{-ax} \cos mx\,dx = \frac{a}{a^2 + m^2};$$

$$\therefore u = a\int \frac{dm}{a^2 + m^2} = \tan^{-1}\left(\frac{m}{a}\right).$$

No constant is added since u vanishes with m.

Ex. 3. Next suppose

$$u = \int_0^\infty \frac{\log\left(1 + a^2 x^2\right)}{1 + b^2 x^2}\, dx.$$

Here
$$\frac{du}{da} = \int_0^\infty \frac{2 a x^2\, dx}{\left(1 + a^2 x^2\right)\left(1 + b^2 x^2\right)}$$

$$= \frac{1}{a^2 - b^2}\left[\int_0^\infty \frac{2a\, dx}{1 + b^2 x^2} - \int_0^\infty \frac{2a\, dx}{1 + a^2 x^2}\right]$$

$$= \frac{1}{a^2 - b^2}\left(\frac{a}{b} - 1\right)\pi = \frac{\pi}{b(a + b)};$$

$$\therefore\ u = \frac{\pi}{b}\int \frac{da}{a + b} = \frac{\pi}{b}\log\left(a + b\right) + \text{const.}$$

To determine the constant: let $a = 0$, and we obviously have $u = 0$.

Consequently, the constant is $-\dfrac{\pi}{b}\log b$;

$$\therefore \int_0^\infty \frac{\log\left(1 + a^2 x^2\right)}{1 + b^2 x^2}\, dx = \frac{\pi}{b}\log\left(\frac{a + b}{b}\right).$$

The method adopted in this Article is plainly equivalent to a process of integration under the sign of integration. Before proceeding to this method we shall consider the case of differentiation when the limits a and b are functions of the quantity with respect to which we differentiate.

114. **Differentiation where the Limits are Variable.**—Let the indefinite integral of the expression $\phi(x, a)dx$ be denoted by $F(x, a)$; then, by Art. 91, we have

$$u = \int_a^b \phi(x, a)\, dx = F(b, a) - F(a, a);$$

$$\therefore \frac{du}{db} = \frac{d \cdot F(b, a)}{db} = \phi(b, a),$$

$$[\mathbf{10\,a}]$$

and
$$\frac{du}{dx} = -\frac{dF(a,\,a)}{da} = -\phi(a,\,a).$$

Again, taking the total differential coefficient of u regarding a and b as functions of a, we have

$$\frac{du}{da} = \int_a^b \frac{d\phi(x,\,a)}{da}\,dx + \frac{du}{db}\frac{db}{da} + \frac{du}{da}\frac{da}{da}$$

$$= \int_a^b \frac{d\phi(x,\,a)}{da}\,dx + \phi(b,\,a)\frac{db}{da} - \phi(a,\,a)\frac{da}{da}. \quad (33)$$

By repeating this process, the values of $\dfrac{d^2u}{da^2}$, $\dfrac{d^3u}{da^3}$, &c., can be obtained, if required.

115. **Integration under the Sign of Integration.—** Returning to the equation

$$u = \int_a^b \phi(x,\,a)dx,$$

where the limits are independent of a, it is obvious, as in Art. 87, that

$$\int u\,da = \int_a^b \left[\int \phi(x,\,a)\,da\right]dx,$$

provided a be taken between the same limits in both cases.

If we denote the limits of a by a_0 and a_1, we get

$$\int_{a_0}^{a_1} u\,da = \int_a^b\left[\int_{a_0}^{a_1} \phi(x,\,a)\,da\right]dx,$$

or
$$\int_{a_0}^{a_1}\left[\int_a^b \phi(x,\,a)\,dx\right]da = \int_a^b\left[\int_{a_0}^{a_1} \phi(x,\,a)\,da\right]dx. \quad (34)$$

This result is easily written in the form

$$\int_{a_0}^{a_1}\int_a^b \phi(x,\,a)dx\,da = \int_a^b\int_{a_0}^{a_1} \phi(x,\,a)\,da\,dx. \quad (35)$$

These expressions are called *double definite integrals,* as involving successive integrations with respect to two variables, taken between limits.

It may be observed that the expression

$$\int_{a_0}^{a_1}\int_{a}^{b} \phi(x,\ a)\,dx\,da$$

is here taken as an abbreviation of

$$\int_{a_0}^{a_1}\left[\int_{a}^{b} \phi(x,\ a)\,dx\right]da,$$

in which the definite integral between the brackets is supposed to be first determined, and the result afterwards integrated with respect to a, between the limits a_0 and a_1.

The principle* established above may be otherwise stated, thus: *In the determination of the integral of the expression*

$$\phi(x,\ a)\,dx\,da$$

between the respective limits x_0, x_1, and a_0, a_1, we may effect the integrations in either order, provided the limits of x and a are independent of each other.

In a subsequent chapter the geometrical interpretation of this, as well as of a more general theorem, will be given.

We now proceed to illustrate the importance of this method by a few examples.

116. **Applications of Integration under the Sign $\int$.**

Ex. 1. From the equation

$$\int_{0}^{1} x^{a-1}\,dx = \frac{1}{a}$$

we get

$$\int_{0}^{1}\int_{a_0}^{a_1} x^{a-1}\,da\,dx = \int_{a_0}^{a_1}\frac{da}{a} = \log\left(\frac{a_1}{a_0}\right).$$

---

* It should be noted that this principle fails whenever $\phi(x,\ a)$, or either of its integrals with respect to a, or to x, becomes infinite for any values of x and a contained between the limits of integration. The student will find that the examples here given are exempt from such failure.

Hence

$$\int_0^1 \frac{x^{a_1-1} - x^{a_0-1}}{\log x}\, dx = \log\left(\frac{a_1}{a_0}\right).$$

Again, if we make $x = e^{-z}$ in this equation, we get

$$\int_0^\infty \frac{e^{-a_1 z} - e^{-a_0 z}}{z}\, dz = \log\left(\frac{a_0}{a_1}\right).$$

Ex. 2. We have already seen that

$$\int_0^\infty e^{-ax} \cos mx\, dx = \frac{a}{a^2 + m^2}.$$

Hence

$$\int_0^\infty \int\left[\int_{a_0}^{a_1} e^{-ax}\, da\right] \cos mx\, dx = \int_{a_0}^{a_1} \frac{a\, da}{a^2 + m^2}$$

$$= \frac{1}{2} \log\left(\frac{a_1^2 + m^2}{a_0^2 + m^2}\right),$$

or

$$\int_0^\infty \frac{e^{-a_1 x} - e^{-a_0 x}}{x} \cos mx\, dx = \frac{1}{2} \log\left(\frac{a_1^2 + m^2}{a_0^2 + m^2}\right).$$

Ex. 3. Again, from the equation

$$\int_0^\infty e^{-ax} \sin mx\, dx = \frac{m}{a^2 + m^2},$$

we get

$$\int_0^\infty \int_{a_0}^{a_1} e^{-ax} \sin mx\, da\, dx = \int_{a_0}^{a_1} \frac{m\, da}{a^2 + m^2};$$

$$\therefore \int_0^\infty \frac{e^{-a_0 x} - e^{-a_1 x}}{x} \sin mx\, dx = \tan^{-1}\left(\frac{a_1}{m}\right) - \tan^{-1}\left(\frac{a_0}{m}\right).$$

Compare Ex. 2, Art. 113.

If we make $a_0 = 0$ and $a_1 = \infty$ in the latter result, we obtain

$$\int_0^\infty \frac{\sin mx}{x}\, dx = \frac{\pi}{2}.$$

$$\textit{Value of} \int_0^\infty e^{-x^2} dx.$$

Ex. 4. To find the value of

$$\int_0^\infty e^{-x^2}\, dx.$$

Denoting the proposed integral by k, and substituting ax for x, we obviously have

$$\int_0^\infty e^{-a^2 x^2}\, a\, dx = k;$$

$$\therefore \int_0^\infty e^{-a^2(1+x^2)} a\, dx = k e^{-a^2}.$$

Hence

$$\int_0^\infty \int_0^\infty e^{-a^2(1+x^2)} a\, da\, dx = k \int_0^\infty e^{-a^2} da = k^2.$$

But

$$\int_0^\infty e^{-a^2(1+x^2)} a\, da = \frac{1}{2}\frac{1}{1+x^2};$$

$$\therefore \frac{1}{2}\int_0^\infty \frac{dx}{1+x^2} = k^2; \quad \therefore \frac{\pi}{4} = k^2.$$

Hence

$$\int_0^\infty e^{-x^2} dx = k = \frac{1}{2}\sqrt{\pi}. \tag{36}$$

This definite integral is of considerable importance, and several others are readily deduced from it.

117. For example, to find

$$\text{(A)} \qquad u = \int_0^\infty e^{-x^2 - \frac{a^2}{x^2}} dx.$$

Here

$$\frac{du}{da} = -2\int_0^\infty e^{-x^2 - \frac{a^2}{x^2}} a\, \frac{dx}{x^2}.$$

Again, let $z = \dfrac{a}{x}$, and we get

$$\int_0^\infty e^{-x^2-\frac{a^2}{x^2}}\frac{a\,dx}{x^2} = \int_0^\infty e^{-z^2-\frac{a^2}{z^2}}dz = u \; ;$$

$$\therefore \frac{du}{da} = -\,2u \; ; \text{ hence } u = Ce^{-2a}.$$

To determine C, let $a = 0$, and, by the preceding example, u becomes $\dfrac{\sqrt{\pi}}{2}$.

Consequently

$$\int_0^\infty e^{-x^2-\frac{a^2}{x^2}}dx = \frac{\sqrt{\pi}}{2}e^{-2a}. \tag{37}$$

Again, to find

$$(B) \qquad u = \int_0^\infty e^{-a^2x^2}\cos 2bx\,dx.$$

Here

$$\frac{du}{db} = -\,2\int_0^\infty e^{-a^2x^2}\cos 2bx\,x\,dx.$$

But, integrating by parts, we have

$$2\int e^{-a^2x^2}\sin 2bx\,x\,dx = -\frac{e^{-a^2x^2}\sin 2bx}{a^2} + \frac{2b}{a^2}\int e^{-a^2x^2}\cos 2bx\,dx \; ;$$

$$\therefore \int_0^\infty e^{-a^2x^2}\sin 2bx\,x\,dx = \frac{2b}{a^2}\int_0^\infty e^{-a^2x^2}\cos 2bx\,dx.$$

Hence

$$\frac{du}{db} = -\frac{2bu}{a^2}, \text{ or } \frac{du}{u} = -\frac{2b\,db}{a^2}.$$

Hence

$$u = Ce^{-\frac{b^2}{a^2}};$$

Also, when $b = 0$, u becomes $\dfrac{\sqrt{\pi}}{2a}$;

$$\therefore \int_0^\infty e^{-a^2x^2}\cos 2bx\,dx = \frac{\sqrt{\pi}}{2a}e^{-\frac{b^2}{a^2}}. \tag{38}$$

Again, if we differentiate n times, with respect to a, the equation

$$\int_0^\infty e^{-ax^2}dx = \frac{\sqrt{\pi}}{2\sqrt{a}},$$

and afterwards make $a = 1$, we get

$$(\text{C}) \qquad \int_0^\infty e^{-x^2}x^{2n}\,dx = \frac{1 \cdot 3 \cdot 5 \dots (2n-1)}{2^{n+1}}\,\sqrt{\pi}.$$

Next, to find

$$(\text{D}) \qquad \int_0^\infty \frac{\cos mx\,dx}{1 + x^2}.$$

We obviously have

$$2\int_0^\infty a\,e^{-a^2(1+x^2)}da = \frac{1}{1 + x^2};$$

$$\therefore\ 2\int_0^\infty\int_0^\infty a\,e^{-a^2(1+x^2)}\cos mx\,dx\,da = \int_0^\infty \frac{\cos mx\,dx}{1 + x^2}.$$

But, by (38), we have

$$2\int_0^\infty e^{-a^2x^2}\cos mx\,dx = \frac{\sqrt{\pi}}{a}\,e^{-\frac{m^2}{4a^2}};$$

$$\therefore\ \sqrt{\pi}\int_0^\infty e^{-a^2-\frac{m^2}{4a^2}}da = \int_0^\infty \frac{\cos mx\,dx}{1 + x^2}.$$

Hence, by (37), we have

$$\int_0^\infty \frac{\cos mx\,dx}{1 + x^2} = \frac{\pi}{2}e^{-m}. \tag{39}$$

Again, differentiating with respect to m, we obtain

$$\int_0^\infty \frac{x\sin mx\,dx}{1 + x^2} = \frac{\pi}{2}e^{-m}. \tag{40}$$

EXAMPLES.

1. $\displaystyle\int_0^\infty \frac{e^{-ax} + e^{-a x}}{e^{\pi x} - e^{-\pi x}}\, x\, dx.$ *Ans.* $\dfrac{1}{4}\sec^2\dfrac{a}{2}.$

2. $\displaystyle\int_2^1 \frac{x^{a-1} + x^{-a}}{1 + x}\frac{dx}{x}.$,, $\log\left(\tan\dfrac{a\pi}{2}\right),$

when $a > 0$ and < 1.

3. $\displaystyle\int_0^1 \frac{z^a + z^{-a} - 2}{1 - z}\frac{dz}{\log z}.$,, $\log\left(\dfrac{a\pi}{\sin a\pi}\right).$

4. $\displaystyle\int_0^{\frac{\pi}{2}} \log\left(1 + \cos\theta\cos x\right)\frac{dx}{\cos x}.$,, $\dfrac{1}{2}\left(\dfrac{\pi^2}{4} - \theta^2\right).$

5. $\displaystyle\int_0^\infty \cos x \log\left(\frac{x^2 + \beta^2}{x^2 + a^2}\right) dx.$,, $\pi\left(e^{-a} - e^{-\beta}\right).$

6. $\displaystyle\int_0^\infty \frac{z^r \log z\, dz}{1 + z^2}.$,, $\dfrac{\pi^2}{4}\dfrac{\sin\dfrac{r\pi}{2}}{\cos^2\dfrac{r\pi}{2}}.$

7. $\displaystyle\int_0^\infty \frac{\sin a\theta\, d\theta}{e^{\pi\theta} - e^{-\pi\theta}}.$,, $\dfrac{1}{4}\dfrac{e^a - 1}{e^a + 1}.$

118. The values of some important definite integrals can be easily deduced from formula (31), Art. 32.

For example,* to find

$$\int_0^{\frac{\pi}{2}} \log\left(\sin\theta\right) d\theta.$$

Here $\displaystyle\int_0^{\frac{\pi}{2}} \log\left(\sin\theta\right) d\theta = \int_0^{\frac{\pi}{2}} \log\left(\cos\theta\right) d\theta.$

Hence, denoting either integral by u, we have

$$2u = \int_0^{\frac{\pi}{2}} \{\log\left(\sin\theta\right) + \log\left(\cos\theta\right)\}\, d\theta$$

---

* These examples are taken from a Paper, signed "H. G.," in the *Cambridge Mathematical Journal*, Vol. 3.

$$= \int_0^{\frac{\pi}{2}} \log (\sin 2\theta) d\theta - \frac{\pi}{2} \log 2.$$

Again, if $z = 2\theta$, we have

$$\int_0^{\frac{\pi}{2}} \log (\sin 2\theta) d\theta = \frac{1}{2} \int_0^{\pi} \log (\sin z) dz$$

$$= \frac{1}{2} \int_0^{\frac{\pi}{2}} \log (\sin z) dz + \frac{1}{2} \int_{\frac{\pi}{2}}^{\pi} \log (\sin z) dz ;$$

but, since $\sin (\pi - z) = \sin z$,

$$\int_{\frac{\pi}{2}}^{\pi} \log (\sin z) dz = \int_0^{\frac{\pi}{2}} \log (\sin z) dz.$$

Consequently

$$\int_0^{\frac{\pi}{2}} \log (\sin 2\theta) d\theta = \int_0^{\frac{\pi}{2}} \log (\sin \theta) d\theta ;$$

$$\therefore \int_0^{\frac{\pi}{2}} \log (\sin \theta) d\theta = - \frac{\pi}{2} \log (2). \tag{41}$$

Again, to find

$$\int_0^{\pi} \theta \log (\sin \theta) d\theta.$$

Here

$$\int_0^{\pi} \theta \log (\sin \theta) d\theta = \int_0^{\pi} (\pi - \theta) \log (\sin \theta) d\theta ;$$

$$\therefore \int_0^{\pi} \theta \log (\sin \theta) d\theta = \frac{\pi}{2} \int_0^{\pi} \log (\sin \theta) d\theta = - \frac{\pi^2}{2} \log (2).$$

119. **Theorem of Frullani.**—To prove that

$$\int_0^{\infty} \frac{\phi(ax) - \phi(bx)}{x} dx = \phi(0) \log \left(\frac{b}{a} \right).$$

Let $u = \int_0^h \dfrac{\phi(z) - \phi(\mathrm{o})}{z}\, dz$; substitute ax for z, and we get

$$u = \int_0^{\frac{h}{a}} \frac{\phi(ax) - \phi(\mathrm{o})}{x}\, dx.$$

If we substitute b for a, we get

$$u = \int_0^{\frac{h}{b}} \frac{\phi(bx) - \phi(\mathrm{o})}{x}\, dx;$$

$$\therefore \int_0^{\frac{h}{a}} \frac{\phi(ax)\,dx}{x} - \int_0^{\frac{h}{b}} \frac{\phi(bx)\,dx}{x} = \phi(\mathrm{o}) \int_{\frac{h}{b}}^{\frac{h}{a}} \frac{dx}{x} = \phi(\mathrm{o}) \log \frac{b}{a}. \quad (42)$$

$$\text{Hence } \int_0^{\frac{h}{a}} \frac{\phi(ax) - \phi(bx)}{x}\, dx - \int_{\frac{h}{a}}^{\frac{h}{b}} \frac{\phi(bx)\,dx}{x} = \phi(\mathrm{o}) \log\left(\frac{b}{a}\right). \quad (43)$$

If we suppose $h = \infty$, we get

$$\int_0^{\infty} \frac{\phi(ax) - \phi(bx)}{x}\, dx = \phi(\mathrm{o}) \log\left(\frac{b}{a}\right), \qquad (44)$$

provided $\displaystyle \int_{\frac{h}{b}}^{\frac{h}{a}} \frac{\phi(bx)}{x}\, dx = \mathrm{o}$ when $h = \infty$.

For example, let $\phi(x) = \cos x$, and, since the integral

$$\int_{\frac{h}{a}}^{\frac{h}{b}} \frac{\cos bx}{x}\, dx$$

evidently vanishes when $h = \infty$, we have

$$\int_0^{\infty} \frac{\cos ax - \cos bx}{x}\, dx = \log \frac{b}{a}.$$

Frullani's theorem plainly fails when $\phi(ax)$ tends to a definite limit when x becomes infinitely great. The formulæ can be exhibited, however, in this case in a simple shape, as was shown by Mr. E. B. Elliott.*

For, in (42) let $h = ab$, and it becomes

$$\int_0^b \frac{\phi(ax)dx}{x} - \int_0^a \frac{\phi(bx)dx}{x} = \phi(0) \log\left(\frac{b}{a}\right). \tag{45}$$

Again, if $\phi(\infty)$ denote the definite value to which $\phi(ax)$ tends when x increases indefinitely, then when h becomes infinite we may substitute $\phi(\infty)$ instead of $\phi(bx)$ in the integral

$$\int_{\frac{h}{a}}^{\frac{h}{b}} \frac{\phi(bx)}{x} \, dx \, ;$$

in which case it becomes

$$\phi(\infty) \int_{\frac{h}{a}}^{\frac{h}{b}} \frac{dx}{x} = \phi(\infty) \log\left(\frac{a}{b}\right).$$

On making this substitution in (43), we get

$$\int_0^\infty \frac{\phi(ax) - \phi(bx)}{x} \, dx = \left\{\phi(\infty) - \phi(0)\right\} \log\left(\frac{a}{b}\right). \tag{46}$$

For example, let $\phi(ax) = \tan^{-1}(ax)$ then we have $\phi(0) = 0$, and $\phi(\infty) = \dfrac{\pi}{2}$.

Accordingly we have

$$\int_0^\infty \frac{\tan^{-1} ax - \tan^{-1} bx}{x} \, dx = \frac{\pi}{2} \int_{\frac{h}{a}}^{\frac{h}{b}} \frac{dx}{x} = \frac{\pi}{2} \log\left(\frac{a}{b}\right).$$

---

* *Educational Times*, 1875. The student will find some remarkable extensions of the formulæ, given above, to Multiple Definite Integrals, by Mr. Elliott, in the *Proceedings* of the London Mathematical Society, 1876, 1877. Also by Mr. Lendesdorf, in the same Journal, 1878.

119 a. Remainder in Lagrange's Series.—We next proceed to show that the remainder in Lagrange's series (Diff. Calc., Art. 125) admits of being represented by a definite integral. This result, I believe, was first given by M. Popoff (*Comptes Rendus*, 1861, pp. 795-8).

The following proof, which at the same time affords a demonstration of the series, of a simple character, is due to M. Zolotareff :—

Let $z = x + y\,\phi(z)$; and consider the definite integral

$$s_n = \int_x^z \{y\,\phi(u) + x - u\}^n\, F'(u)\,du.$$

Differentiating this with respect to x, we get, by (33), Art. 114,

$$\frac{ds_n}{dx} = n\,s_{n-1} - y^n\{\phi(x)\}^n\, F'(x). \tag{47}$$

If in this we make $n = 1$, we get

$$s_0 = y\,\phi(x)\,F'(x) + \frac{ds_1}{dx} ;$$

but

$$s_0 = F(z) - F(x) ;$$

$$\therefore\; F(z) = F(x) + y\,\phi(x)\,F'(x) + \frac{ds_1}{dx}. \tag{48}$$

In like manner, making $n = 2$, we have

$$2s_1 = y^2\{\phi(x)\}^2\, F'(x) + \frac{ds_2}{dx} ;$$

$$\therefore\; \frac{ds_1}{dx} = \frac{y^2}{1\,.\,2}\frac{d}{dx}\left[\{\phi(x)\}^2\, F'(x)\right] + \frac{1}{1\,.\,2}\frac{d^2 s_2}{dx^2}.$$

Substituting in (48) it becomes

$$F(z) = F(x) + \frac{y}{1}\phi(x)\,F'(x) + \frac{y^2}{1\,.\,2}\frac{d}{dx}\left[\{\phi(x)\}^2\, F'(x)\right] + \frac{1}{1\,.\,2}\frac{d^2 s_2}{dx^2}.$$

Again,

$$s_2 = \frac{y^3}{3}\{\phi(x)\}^2\, F'(x) + \frac{ds_3}{dx} ;$$

$$\therefore \frac{1}{1 \cdot 2} \frac{d^2 s_2}{dx^2} = \frac{y^3}{1 \cdot 2 \cdot 3} \frac{d^2}{dx^2} \left[\{\phi(x)\}^3 F'(x) \right] + \frac{1}{1 \cdot 2 \cdot 3} \frac{d^3 s_3}{dx^3}.$$

$$\cdot \qquad \cdot \qquad \cdot \qquad \cdot \qquad \cdot \qquad \cdot$$

$$n s_{n-1} = y^n \{\phi(x)\}^n F'(x) + \frac{ds_n}{dx},$$

$$\frac{1}{1 \cdot 2 \ldots n-1} \frac{d^{n-1} s_{n-1}}{dx^{n-1}} = \frac{1}{1 \cdot 2 \ldots n} \frac{d^{n-1}}{dx^{n-1}} \left[\{\phi(x)\}^n F'(x) \right]$$
$$+ \frac{1}{1 \cdot 2 \ldots n} \frac{d^n s_n}{dx^n}.$$

Hence we get finally

$$F(z) = F(x) + \frac{y}{1} \phi(x) F'(x) + \frac{y^2}{1 \cdot 2} \frac{d}{dx} \left[\{(x)\}^2 F'(x) \right] + \&c.$$
$$+ \frac{1}{1 \cdot 2 \ldots n} \left(\frac{d}{dx} \right)^n \int_x^z [y \phi(u) + x - u]^n F'(u) \, du. \qquad (49)$$

Consequently the remainder in Lagrange's series is always represented by a definite integral.

We next proceed to consider a general class of Definite Integrals first introduced into analysis by Euler.

120. Gamma Functions.—It may be observed that there is no branch of analysis which has occupied the attention of mathematicians more than that which treats of Definite Integrals, both single and multiple; nor in which the results arrived at are of greater elegance and interest. It would be manifestly impossible in the limits of an elementary treatise to give more than a sketch of the results arrived at. At the same time the Gamma or Eulerian Integrals hold so fundamental a place, that no treatise, however elementary, would be complete without giving at least an outline of their properties. With such an outline we propose to conclude this Chapter.

The definitions of the Eulerian Integrals, both First and Second, have been given already in Art. 95.

The First Eulerian Integral, viz.,

$$\int_0^1 x^{m-1} (1 - x)^{n-1} \, dx,$$

is evidently a function of its two parameters, m and n; it is usually represented by the notation $B(m, n)$.

Thus, we have by definition

$$\int_0^1 x^{m-1} (1 - x)^{n-1} dx = B(m, n).$$

$$\int_0^\infty e^{-x} x^{p-1} dx = \Gamma(p). \tag{50}$$

The constants m, n, are supposed *positive* in all cases.

It is evident that the result in equation (14), Art. 95, still holds when p is of fractional form.

Hence, we have in all cases

$$\Gamma(p + 1) = p\Gamma(p). \tag{51}$$

This may be regarded as the fundamental property of Gamma Functions, and by aid of it the calculations of all such functions can be reduced to those for which the parameter p is comprised between any two consecutive integers. For this purpose the values of $\Gamma(p)$, or rather of log $\Gamma(p)$, have been tabulated by Legendre* to 12 decimal places, for all values of p (between 1 and 2) to 3 decimal places. The student will find Tables to 6 decimal places at the end of this chapter. By aid of such Tables we can readily calculate the approximate values of all definite integrals which are reducible to Gamma Functions.

It may be remarked that we have

$$\Gamma(1) = 1, \quad \Gamma(0) = \infty, \quad \Gamma(-p) = \infty,$$

p being any integer. For negative values of p which are not integer the function has a finite value.

Again, if we substitute zx instead of x, where z is a constant with respect to x, we obviously have

$$\int_0^\infty e^{-xz} x^{m-1} dx = \frac{\Gamma(m)}{z^m}. \tag{52}$$

---

* See *Traité des Fonctions Elliptiques*, Tome 2, Int. Euler, chap. 16.

With respect to the First Eulerian Integral, we have already seen (Art. 92) that

$$\int_0^1 x^{m-1}(1-x)^{n-1}\,dx = \int_0^1 x^{n-1}(1-x)^{m-1}\,dx\,;$$

$$\therefore\ B(m, n) = B(n, m).$$

Hence, the interchange of the constants m and n does not alter the value of the integral.

Again, if we substitute $\dfrac{y}{1+y}$ for x, we get

$$\int_0^1 x^{m-1}(1-x)^{n-1}\,dx = \int_0^\infty \frac{y^{m-1}\,dy}{(1+y)^{m+n}}.$$

Hence

$$\int_0^\infty \frac{y^{m-1}\,dy}{(1+y)^{m+n}} = B(m, n). \tag{53}$$

We now proceed to express $B(m, n)$ in terms of Gamma Functions.

121. **To prove that**

$$B(m, n) = \frac{\Gamma(m)\,\Gamma(n)}{\Gamma(m+n)}.$$

From equation (52) we have

$$\Gamma(m) = \int_0^\infty e^{-zx}\, z^m\, x^{m-1}\,dx.$$

Hence

$$\Gamma(m)\, e^{-z}\, z^{n-1} = \int_0^\infty e^{-z(1+x)}\, z^{m+n-1}\, x^{m-1}\,dx\,;$$

$$\therefore\ \Gamma(m)\int_0^\infty e^{-z}\, z^{n-1}\,dz = \int_0^\infty \left[\int_0^\infty e^{-z(1+x)}\, z^{m+n-1}\,dz\right] x^{m-1}\,dx.$$

[11]

But, if $z(1 + x) = y$, we get

$$\int_0^\infty e^{-z(1+x)} z^{m+n-1}\, dz = \frac{1}{(1+x)^{m+n}} \int_0^\infty e^{-y} y^{m+n-1}\, dy = \frac{\Gamma(m+n)}{(1+x)^{m+n}};$$

$$\therefore\ \Gamma(m)\,\Gamma(n) = \Gamma(m+n) \int_0^\infty \frac{x^{m-1}\, dx}{(1+x)^{m+n}}.$$

Accordingly, by (53), we have

$$B(m,\, n) = \frac{\Gamma(m)\,\Gamma(n)}{\Gamma(m+n)}. \tag{54}$$

Again, if $m = 1 - n$, we get, by (24),

$$\Gamma(n)\,\Gamma(1-n) = \int_0^\infty \frac{x^{n-1}\, dx}{1+x} = \frac{\pi}{\sin n\pi}. \tag{55}$$

If in this $n = \dfrac{1}{2}$, we get

$$\Gamma\!\left(\frac{1}{2}\right) = \sqrt{\pi}.$$

This agrees with (36), for if we make $x^2 = z$, we get

$$\int_0^\infty e^{-x^2}\, dx = \frac{1}{2} \int_0^\infty e^{-z} z^{-\frac{1}{2}}\, dz = \frac{\Gamma\!\left(\dfrac{1}{2}\right)}{2}. \tag{56}$$

Again, if we suppose in the double integral

$$\iint x^{m-1} y^{n-1}\, dx\, dy$$

x and y extended to all *positive* values, subject to the condition that $x + y$ is not greater than unity; then, integrating with respect to y, between the limits 0 and $1 - x$, the integral becomes

$$\frac{1}{n} \int_0^1 x^{m-1}(1-x)^n\, dx = \frac{1}{n} \frac{\Gamma(m)\,\Gamma(n+1)}{\Gamma(m+n+1)},\ \text{by (54)};$$

$$\therefore\ \iint x^{m-1} y^{n-1}\, dx\, dy = \frac{\Gamma(m)\,\Gamma(n)}{\Gamma(m+n+1)}; \tag{57}$$

in which x and y are always positive, and subject to the condition $x + y < 1$.

122. By aid of the relation in (54) a number of definite integrals are reducible to Gamma Functions.

For instance, we have

$$\int_0^\infty \frac{y^{m-1}\,dy}{(1+y)^{m+n}} = \int_0^1 \frac{y^{m-1}\,dy}{(1+y)^{m+n}} + \int_1^\infty \frac{y^{m-1}\,dy}{(1+y)^{m+n}}.$$

Now, substituting $\dfrac{1}{x}$ for y in the last integral, we get

$$\int_1^\infty \frac{y^{m-1}\,dy}{(1+y)^{m+n}} = \int_0^1 \frac{x^{n-1}\,dx}{(1+x)^{m+n}}.$$

Hence

$$\int_0^1 \frac{x^{m-1} + x^{n-1}}{(1+x)^{m+n}}\,dx = \frac{\Gamma(m)\,\Gamma(n)}{\Gamma(m+n)}. \tag{58}$$

Next, if we make $x = \dfrac{ay}{b}$, we get

$$\int_0^\infty \frac{x^{m-1}\,dx}{(1+x)^{m+n}} = a^m b^n \int_0^\infty \frac{y^{m-1}\,dy}{(ay+b)^{m+n}};$$

$$\therefore \int_0^\infty \frac{y^{m-1}\,dy}{(ay+b)^{m+n}} = \frac{\Gamma(m)\,\Gamma(n)}{a^m b^n\,\Gamma(m+n)}. \tag{59}$$

Again,* let $x = \sin^2\theta$, and we get

$$\int_0^1 x^{m-1}\,(1-x)^{n-1}\,dx = 2\int_0^{\frac{\pi}{2}} \sin^{2m-1}\theta\,\cos^{2n-1}\theta\,d\theta;$$

$$\therefore \int_0^{\frac{\pi}{2}} \sin^{2m-1}\theta\,\cos^{2n-1}\theta\,d\theta = \frac{\Gamma(m)\,\Gamma(n)}{2\,\Gamma(m+n)}. \tag{60}$$

This result may also be written as follows:

$$\int_0^{\frac{\pi}{2}} \sin^{p-1}\theta\,\cos^{q-1}\theta\,d\theta = \frac{\Gamma\left(\dfrac{p}{2}\right)\Gamma\left(\dfrac{q}{2}\right)}{2\,\Gamma\left(\dfrac{p+q}{2}\right)}. \tag{61}$$

---

* These results may be regarded as generalizations of the formulæ given in Arts. 93, 94, to which the student can readily see that they are reducible when the indices are integers.

If we make $q = 1$, we get

$$\int_0^{\frac{\pi}{2}} \sin^{p-1}\theta \, d\theta = \frac{\sqrt{\pi}}{2} \frac{\Gamma\left(\dfrac{p}{2}\right)}{\Gamma\left(\dfrac{p+1}{2}\right)}. \tag{62}$$

Again, if $p = q$ in (61) it becomes

$$\frac{\left\{\Gamma\left(\dfrac{p}{2}\right)\right\}^2}{2\,\Gamma(p)} = \int_0^{\frac{\pi}{2}} \sin^{p-1}\theta \cos^{p-1}\theta \, d\theta = \frac{1}{2^{p-1}} \int_0^{\frac{\pi}{2}} \sin^{p-1} 2\theta \, d\theta.$$

Let $2\theta = z$, and we have

$$\int_0^{\frac{\pi}{2}} \sin^{p-1} 2\theta \, d\theta = \frac{1}{2} \int_0^{\pi} \sin^{p-1} z \, dz = \int_0^{\frac{\pi}{2}} \sin^{p-1} z \, dz$$

$$= \frac{\sqrt{\pi}}{2} \frac{\Gamma\left(\dfrac{p}{2}\right)}{\Gamma\left(\dfrac{p+1}{2}\right)}.$$

Hence $\qquad \Gamma\left(\dfrac{p}{2}\right) \Gamma\left(\dfrac{p+1}{2}\right) = \dfrac{\sqrt{\pi}}{2^{p-1}} \Gamma(p).$

If we substitute $2m$ for p, this becomes

$$\Gamma(m)\,\Gamma\left(m + \frac{1}{2}\right) = \frac{\sqrt{\pi}}{2^{2m-1}}\,\Gamma(2m). \tag{63}$$

Again, make $y = \tan^2\theta$ in (59), and we get

$$\int_0^{\frac{\pi}{2}} \frac{\sin^{2m-1}\theta \cos^{2n-1}\theta \, d\theta}{(a\sin^2\theta + b\cos^2\theta)^{m+n}} = \frac{\Gamma(m)\,\Gamma(n)}{2a^m\,b^n\,\Gamma(m+n)}. \tag{64}$$

123. **To find the Value* of**

$$\Gamma\left(\frac{1}{n}\right) \Gamma\left(\frac{2}{n}\right) \Gamma\left(\frac{3}{n}\right) \dots \Gamma\left(\frac{n-1}{n}\right),$$

n being any integer.

---

* This important theorem is due to Euler, by whom, as already noticed, the Gamma Functions were first investigated.

Multiply the expression by itself, reversing the order of the factors, and we get its square under the form

$$\Gamma\left(\frac{1}{n}\right)\Gamma\left(1-\frac{1}{n}\right)\Gamma\left(\frac{2}{n}\right)\Gamma\left(1-\frac{2}{n}\right)\dots\Gamma\left(\frac{n-1}{n}\right)\Gamma\left(1-\frac{n-1}{n}\right),$$

that is, by (55),

$$\frac{\pi^{n-1}}{\sin\dfrac{\pi}{n}\,\sin\dfrac{2\pi}{n}\,\sin\dfrac{3\pi}{n}\dots\sin\dfrac{(n-1)\pi}{n}}.$$

To calculate this expression, we have by the theory of equations

$$\frac{1-x^{2n}}{1-x^2}$$

$$=\left(1-2x\cos\frac{\pi}{n}+x^2\right)\left(1-2x\cos\frac{2\pi}{n}+x^2\right)\dots\left(1-2x\cos\frac{(n-1)\pi}{n}+x^2\right).$$

Making successively in this, $x = 1$, and $x = -1$, and replacing the first member by its true value n, we get

$$n = \left(2\,\sin\frac{\pi}{2n}\right)^2\left(2\,\sin\frac{2\pi}{2n}\right)^2\dots\left(2\,\sin\frac{(n-1)\pi}{2n}\right)^2,$$

$$n = \left(2\,\cos\frac{\pi}{2n}\right)^2\left(2\,\cos\frac{2\pi}{2n}\right)^2\dots\left(2\,\cos\frac{(n-1)\pi}{2n}\right)^2,$$

whence, multiplying and extracting the square root,

$$n = 2^{n-1}\sin\frac{\pi}{n}\,\sin\frac{2\pi}{n}\dots\sin\frac{(n-1)\pi}{n}.$$

Hence, it follows that

$$\Gamma\left(\frac{1}{n}\right)\Gamma\left(\frac{2}{n}\right)\dots\Gamma\left(\frac{n-1}{n}\right)=\frac{(2\pi)^{\frac{n-1}{2}}}{n^{\frac{1}{2}}}. \tag{65}$$

124. To find the values of

$$\int_0^\infty e^{-ax} \cos bx\, x^{m-1}\, dx, \text{ and} \int_0^\infty e^{-ax} \sin bx\, x^{m-1}\, dx.$$

If in (52) $a - b\sqrt{-1}$ be substituted* for z the equation becomes

$$\int_0^\infty e^{-ax} e^{bx\sqrt{-1}} x^{m-1}\, dx = \frac{\Gamma(m)}{(a - b\sqrt{-1})^m} = \frac{\Gamma(m)\,(a + b\sqrt{-1})^m}{(a^2 + b^2)^m}.$$

Let $a = (a^2 + b^2)^{\frac{1}{2}} \cos\theta$, then $b = (a^2 + b^2)^{\frac{1}{2}} \sin\theta$, and the preceding result becomes

$$\int_0^\infty e^{-ax} (\cos bx + \sqrt{-1}\, \sin bx)\, x^{m-1}\, dx$$

$$= \frac{\Gamma(m)}{(a^2 + b^2)^{\frac{m}{2}}} (\cos\theta + \sqrt{-1}\, \sin\theta)^m$$

$$= \frac{\Gamma(m)}{(a^2 + b^2)^{\frac{m}{2}}} (\cos m\theta + \sqrt{-1}\, \sin m\theta).$$

Hence, equating real and imaginary parts, we have

$$\left.\begin{array}{l} \displaystyle\int_0^\infty e^{-ax} \cos bx\, x^{m-1}\, dx = \dfrac{\Gamma(m)}{(a^2 + b^2)^{\frac{m}{2}}} \cos m\theta \\[2em] \displaystyle\int_0^\infty e^{-ax} \sin bx\, x^{m-1}\, dx = \dfrac{\Gamma(m)}{(a^2 + b^2)^{\frac{m}{2}}} \sin m\theta \end{array}\right\}, \qquad (66)$$

in which $\theta = \tan^{-1}\left(\dfrac{b}{a}\right)$.

If we make $a = 0$, θ becomes $\dfrac{\pi}{2}$, and these formulæ become

---

$$\left.\begin{aligned}
\int_0^\infty \cos bx\, x^{m-1}\, dx &= \frac{\Gamma(m)}{b^m} \cos \frac{m\pi}{2}, \\[2ex]
\int_0^\infty \sin bx\, x^{m-1}\, dx &= \frac{\Gamma(m)}{b^m} \sin \frac{m\pi}{2}
\end{aligned}\right\} . \qquad (67)$$

It may be observed that these latter integrals can be arrived at in another manner, as follows :—

From (52) we have

$$\Gamma(n)\, \frac{\cos bz}{z^n} = \int_0^\infty e^{-zx} x^{n-1} \cos bz\, dx;$$

$$\therefore\ \Gamma(n) \int_0^\infty \frac{\cos bz\, dz}{z^n} = \int_0^\infty \int_0^\infty e^{-zx} \cos bz\, x^{n-1}\, dx\, dz.$$

But, by (32), we have

$$\int_0^\infty e^{-xz} \cos bz\, dz = \frac{x}{b^2 + x^2};$$

$$\therefore\ \int_0^\infty \frac{\cos bz\, dz}{z^n} = \frac{1}{\Gamma(n)} \int_0^\infty \frac{x^n\, dx}{b^2 + x^2}.$$

$$= \frac{b^{n-1}}{\Gamma(n)} \frac{\pi}{2 \cos \dfrac{n\pi}{2}}, \text{ by } (27),$$

in which n must be positive and < 1.

In like manner we find

$$\int_0^\infty \frac{\sin bz\, dz}{z^n} = \frac{b^{n-1}}{\Gamma(n)} \frac{\pi}{2 \sin \dfrac{n\pi}{2}}.$$

The results in (67) follow from these by aid of the relation contained in equation (55).

EXAMPLES.

1. $\displaystyle\int_0^1 x^m (1 - x^n)^p\, dx.$ *Ans.* $\displaystyle \frac{\Gamma(p + 1)\, \Gamma\left(\dfrac{m + 1}{n}\right)}{n\Gamma\left(p + 1 + \dfrac{m + 1}{n}\right)}.$

2. $\displaystyle\int_0^1 \frac{x^{m-1}(1 - x)^{n-1}\, dx}{(a + x)^{m+n}}.$,, $\displaystyle \frac{\Gamma(m)\, \Gamma(n)}{a^n (1 + a)^m\, \Gamma(m + n)}.$

3. Prove that

$$\int_0^1 \frac{x^2\, dx}{(1 - x^4)^{\frac{1}{2}}} \times \int_0^1 \frac{dx}{(1 + x^4)^{\frac{1}{2}}} = \frac{\pi}{2\sqrt{2}}.$$

4. $\displaystyle\int_0^\infty \cos\left(b z^{\frac{1}{n}}\right) dz.$,, $\displaystyle \frac{\Gamma(n + 1)\cos\left(n\,\dfrac{\pi}{2}\right)}{b^n}.$

5. $\displaystyle\int_0^1 \frac{dx}{\sqrt{1 - x^n}}.$,, $\displaystyle \frac{\sqrt{\pi}}{n}\,\frac{\Gamma\left(\dfrac{1}{n}\right)}{\Gamma\left(\dfrac{1}{2} + \dfrac{1}{n}\right)}.$

6. $\displaystyle\int_0^\infty \frac{\sin bx}{x}\, dx.$,, $\displaystyle \frac{\pi}{2}.$

123. **Numerical Calculation of Gamma Functions.**—The following Table gives the values of $\log \Gamma(p)$, to six decimal places, for all values of p between 1 and 2 (taken to three decimal places).

It may be observed that we have $\Gamma(1) = \Gamma(2) = 1$, and that for all values of p between 1 and 2, $\Gamma(p)$ is positive and less than unity; and hence the values of $\log \Gamma(p)$ are negative for all such values. Consequently, as in ordinary trigonometrical logarithmic Tables, the Tabular logarithm is obtained by adding 10 to the natural logarithm. The method of calculating these Tables is too complicated for insertion in an elementary Treatise.

Log $\Gamma(p)$.

p	0	1	2	3	4	5	6	7	8	9
1.00		9750	9500	9251.	9003	8755	8509	8263	8017	7773
1.01	9.997529	7285	7043	6801	6560	6320	6080	5841	5602	5365
1.02	5128	4892	4656	4421	4187	3953	3721	3489	3257	3026
1.03	2796	2567	2338	2110	1883	1656	1430	1205	$\overline{0}$981	0775
1.04	0533	0311	0089	$\overline{9}$868	$\overline{9}$647	9427	$\overline{9}$208	8989	$\overline{8}$772	8554
1.05	9.988338	8122	7907	7692	7478	7265	7052	6841	6629	6419
1.06	6209	6000	5791	5583	5378	5169	4963	4758	4553	4349
1.07	4145	3943	3741	3539	3338	3138	2939	2740	2541	2344
1.08	2147	1951	1755	1560	1365	1172	0978	0786	0594	0403
1.09	0212	0022	$\overline{9}$833	9644	9456	$\overline{9}$269	9082	$\overline{8}$900	$\overline{8}$710	$\overline{8}$525
1.10	9.978341	8157	7974	7791	7610	7428	7248	7068	6888	6709
1.11	6531	6354	6177	6000	5825	5650	5475	5301	5128	4955
1.12	4783	4612	4441	4271	4101	3932	3764	3596	3429	3262
1.13	3096	2931	2766	2602	2438	2275	2113	1951	1790	1629
1.14	1469	1309	1150	0992	0835	0677	0521	0365	0210	0055
1.15	9.969901	9747	9594	9442	9290	9139	8988	8838	8688	8539
1.16	8390	8243	8096	7949	7803	7658	7513	7369	7225	7082
1.17	6939	6797	6655	6514	6374	6234	6095	5957	5818	5681.
1.18	5544	5408	5272	5137	5002	4868	4734	4601	4469	4337
1.19	4205	4075	3944	3815	3686	3557	3429	3302	3175	3048
1.20	2922	2797	2672	2548	2425	2302	2179	2057	1936	1815
1.21	1695	1575	1456	1337	1219	1101	0984	0867	0751	0636
1.22	0521	0407	0293	0180	0067	$\overline{9}$955	$\overline{9}$843	$\overline{9}$732	$\overline{9}$621	$\overline{9}$511
1.23	9.959401	9292	9184	9076	8968	8861	8755	8649	8544	8439
1.24	8335	8231	8128	8025	7923	7821	7720	7620	7520	7420
1.25	7321	7223	7125	7027	6930	6834	6738	6642	6547	6453
1.26	6359	6267	6173	6081	5989	5898	5807	5716	5627	5537
1.27	5449	5360	5273	5185	5099	5013	4927	4842	4757	4673
1.28	4589	4506	4423	4341	4259	4178	4097	4017	3938	3858
1.29	3780	3702	3624	3547	3470	3394	3318	3243	3168	3094
1.30	3020	2947	2874	2802	2730	2659	2588	2518	2448	2379
1.31	2310	2242	2174	2106	2040	1973	1907	1842	1777	1712
1.32	1648	1585	1522	1459	1397	1336	1275	1214	1154	1094
1.33	1035	0977	0918	0861	0803	0747	0690	0634	0579	0524
1.34	0470	0416	0362	0309	0257	0205	0153	0102	0051	0001
1.35	9.949951	9902	9853	9805	9757	9710	9663	9617	9571	9525
1.36	9480	9435	9391	9348	9304	9262	9219	9178	9136	9095
1.37	9054	9015	8975	8936	8898	8859	8822	8785	8748	8711
1.38	8676	8640	8605	8571	8537	8503	8470	8437	8405	8373
1.39	8342	8311	8280	8250	8221	8192	8163	8135	8107	8080
1.40	8053	8026	8000	7975	7950	7925	7901	7877	7854	7831
1.41	7808	7786	7765	7744	7723	7703	7683	7664	7645	7626
1.42	7608	7590	7573	7556	7540	7524	7509	7494	7479	7465
1.43	7451	7438	7425	7413	7401	7389	7378	7368	7357	7348
1.44	7338	7329	7321	7312	7305	7298	7291	7284	7278	7273
1.45	7262	7263	7259	7255	7251	7248	7246	7244	7242	7241
1.46	7240	7239	7239	7240	7240	7242	7243	7245	7248	7251
1.47	7254	7258	7262	7266	7271	7277	7282	7289	7295	7302
1.48	7310	7317	7326	7334	7343	7353	7363	7373	7384	7395
1.49	7407	7419	7431	7444	7457	7471	7485	7499	7514	7529

Log $\Gamma(p)$.

p	0	1	2	3	4	5	6	7	8	9
1.50	9.947545	7561	7577	7594	7612	7629	7647	7666	7685	7704
1.51	7724	7744	7764	7785	7806	7828	7850	7873	7896	7919
1.52	7943	7967	7991	8016	8041	8067	8093	8120	8146	8174
1.53	8201	8229	8258	8287	8316	8346	8376	8406	8437	8468
1.54	8500	8532	8564	8597	8630	8664	8698	8732	8767	8802
1.55	8837	8873	8910	8946	8983	9021	9059	9097	9135	9174
1.56	9214	9254	9294	9334	9375	9417	9458	9500	9543	9586
1.57	9629	9672	9716	8761	9806	9851	9896	9942	9989	0035
1.58	9.950082	0130	0177	0225	0274	0323	0372	0422	0472	0522
1.59	0573	0624	0676	0728	0780	0833	0886	0939	0993	1047
1.60	1102	1157	1212	1268	1324	1380	1437	1494	1552	1610
1.61	1668	1727	1786	1845	1905	1965	2025	2086	2147	2209
1.62	2271	2333	2396	2459	2522	2586	2650	2715	2780	2845
1.63	2911	2977	3043	3110	3177	3244	3312	3380	3449	3517
1.64	3587	3656	3726	3797	3867	3938	4010	4081	4154	4226
1.65	4299	4372	4446	4519	4594	4668	4743	4819	4894	4970
1.66	5047	5124	5201	5278	5356	5434	5513	5592	5671	5740
1.67	5830	5911	5991	6072	6154	6235	6317	6400	6482	6566
1.68	6649	6733	6817	6901	6986	7072	7157	7243	7322	7416
1.69	7503	7590	7678	7766	7854	7943	8032	8122	8211	8301
1.70	8391	8482	8573	8664	8756	8848	8941	9034	9127	9220
1.71	9314	9409	9502	9598	9693	9788	9884	9980	0077	0174
1.72	9.960271	0369	0467	0565	0664	0763	0862	0961	1061	1162
1.73	1262	1363	1464	1566	1668	1770	1873	1976	2079	2183
1.74	2287	2391	2496	2601	2706	2812	2918	3024	3131	3238
1.75	3345	3453	3561	3669	3778	3887	3996	4105	4215	4326
1.76	4436	4547	4659	4770	4882	4994	5107	5220	5333	5447
1.77	5561	5675	5789	5904	6019	6135	6251	6367	6484	6600
1.78	6718	6835	6953	7071	7189	7308	7427	7547	7666	7787
1.79	7907	8023	8149	8270	8392	8514	8636	8759	8882	9005
1.80	9129	9253	9377	9501	9626	9751	9877	0008	0129	0255
1.81	9.970383	0509	0637	0765	0893	1021	1150	1279	1408	1538
1.82	1668	1798	1929	2060	2191	2322	2454	2586	2719	2852
1.83	2985	3118	3252	3386	3520	3655	3790	3925	4061	4197
1.84	4333	4470	4606	4744	4881	5019	5157	5295	5434	5573
1.85	5712	5852	5992	6132	6273	6414	6555	6697	6838	6980
1.86	7123	7266	7408	7552	7696	7840	7984	8128	8273	8419
1.87	8564	8710	8856	9002	9149	9296	9443	9591	9739	9887
1.88	9.980036	9184	0333	0483	0633	0783	0933	1084	1234	1386
1.89	1537	1689	1841	1994	2147	2299	2453	2607	2761	2915
1.90	3069	3224	3379	3535	3690	3846	4003	4159	4316	4474
1.91	4631	4789	4947	5105	5264	5423	5582	5742	5902	6062
1.92	6223	6383	6544	6706	6867	7029	7192	7354	7517	7680
1 93	7844	8007	8171	8336	8500	8665	8830	8996	9161	9327
1.94	9494	9660	9827	9995	0162	0330	0498	0666	0835	1004
1.95	9.991173	1343	1512	1683	1853	2024	2195	2366	2537	2709
1.96	2881	3054	3227	3399	3573	3746	3920	4094	4269	4443
1.97	4618	4794	4969	5145	5321	5498	5674	5851	6029	6206
1.98	6384	6562	6740	6919	7098	7277	7457	7637	7817	7997
1.99	8178	8359	8540	8722	8903	9085	9268	9450	9633	9816

EXAMPLES.

1. $\displaystyle\int_0^a \frac{dx}{\sqrt{a-x}}.$ *Ans.* $2\sqrt{a}.$

2. If $f(x) = f(a+x)$ for all values of x, prove that

$$\int_0^{na} f(x)\,dx = n \int_0^a f(x)\,dx,$$

where n is an integer.

3. $\displaystyle\int_0^a \frac{dx}{\sqrt{ax-x^2}}.$,, $\pi.$

4. $\displaystyle\int_1^2 \frac{dx}{x\sqrt{x^2-1}}.$,, $\dfrac{\pi}{3}.$

5. $\displaystyle\int_0^1 \sin^{-1} x\,dx.$,, $\dfrac{\pi}{2} - 1.$

6. $\displaystyle\int_0^1 \frac{dx}{(1+x)\sqrt{1+2x-x^2}}.$,, $\dfrac{\pi}{4\sqrt{2}}.$

7. $\displaystyle\int_{-\infty}^{\infty} \frac{dx}{a+2bx+cx^2},$ $ac-b^2$ being positive. ,, $\dfrac{\pi}{\sqrt{ac-b^2}}.$

8. Prove that

$$\int_0 \frac{dx}{a+2bx^2+cx^4} = \frac{\pi}{2\sqrt{ah}}, \text{ where } h = 2(\sqrt{ac}+b).$$

9. $\displaystyle\int_0^{\pi} \frac{dx}{1+\cos\theta\cos x}.$ *Ans.* $\dfrac{\pi}{\sin\theta}.$

10. $\displaystyle\int_0^{\frac{\pi}{2}} \frac{dx}{1+\cos\theta\cos x}.$, $\dfrac{\theta}{\sin\theta}.$

11. $\displaystyle\int_0^{\frac{\pi}{2}} \frac{dx}{a^2\sin^2 x + b^2\cos^2 x}.$, $\dfrac{\pi}{2ab}.$

12. $\displaystyle\int_0^{\frac{\pi}{2}} \frac{dx}{(a^2\sin^2 x + b^2\cos^2 x)^2}.$,, $\dfrac{\pi(a^2+b^2)}{4a^3 b^3}.$

13. $\displaystyle\int_0^a \sqrt{a^2 - x^2}\, \cos^{-1}\frac{x}{a}\, dx.$ *Ans.* $\dfrac{\pi^2 a^2}{16} + \dfrac{a^2}{4}.$

14. $\displaystyle\int_{-1}^{+1} \frac{dx}{(a - bx)\sqrt{1 - x^2}},\ a > b.$,, $\dfrac{\pi}{\sqrt{a^2 - b^2}}.$

15. $\displaystyle\int_a^\beta \frac{dx}{\sqrt{(x - a)(\beta - x)}}.$,, $\pi.$

16. $\displaystyle\int_{a-\sqrt{a^2-b^2}}^{a+\sqrt{a^2-b^2}} \frac{(y^2 + b^2)\, y\, dy}{\sqrt{4a^2 y^2 - (y^2 + b^2)^2}}.$,, $\pi a^2.$

17.   Show that $\displaystyle\int_0^\infty \frac{\sin ax \cos bx}{x}\, dx = \frac{\pi}{2}$, or 0, according as $a >$ or $< b$; and that when $a = b$ the value of the integral is $\dfrac{\pi}{4}$.

18. $\displaystyle\int_{-1}^{+1} \frac{dx}{\sqrt{(1 - 2ax + a^2)(1 - 2bx + b^2)}},\ ab < 1.$ *Ans.* $\dfrac{1}{\sqrt{ab}}\log\left(\dfrac{1 + \sqrt{ab}}{1 - \sqrt{ab}}\right).$

19. $\displaystyle\int_0^{\frac{\pi}{4}} \tan^5 x\, dx.$,, $\dfrac{1}{2}\left(\log 2 - \dfrac{1}{2}\right).$

20. $\displaystyle\int_0^{\frac{3\pi}{4}} \frac{\sin x\, dx}{1 + \cos^2 x}.$,, $\dfrac{\pi}{4} + \tan^{-1}\dfrac{1}{\sqrt{2}}.$

21. If every infinitesimal element of the side c of any triangle be divided by its distance from the opposite angle C, and the sum taken, show that its value is

$$\log\left(\cot\frac{A}{2}\, \cot\frac{B}{2}\right).$$

22. Being given the base of a triangle; if the sum of every element of the base multiplied by the square of the distance from the vertex be constant, show that the locus of the vertex is a circle.

23. $\displaystyle\int_0^{\frac{\pi}{2}} \frac{\cos^2\theta \sin\theta\, d\theta}{1 + e^2 \cos^2\theta}.$ *Ans.* $\dfrac{1}{e^2} - \dfrac{\tan^{-1}e}{e^3}.$

24. $\displaystyle\int_0^{\frac{\pi}{2}} \frac{\cos^2\theta \sin\theta\, d\theta}{\sqrt{1 + e^2 \cos^2\theta}}.$,, $\dfrac{\sqrt{1 + e^2}}{2e^2} - \dfrac{\log(e + \sqrt{1 + e^2})}{2e^3}.$

25. Deduce the expansions for $\sin x$ and $\cos x$ from Bernoulli's series.

26. Show that the integral

$$\int_0^1 x^n (\log x)^m \, dx$$

can be immediately evaluated by the method of Art. 111, when m is an integer.

27. $\quad \displaystyle\int_0^\infty \frac{\tan^{-1}(ax)\,dx}{x(1+x^2)}$ $\qquad\qquad$ *Ans.* $\dfrac{\pi}{2}\log(1+a)$.

28. Find the value of

$$\int_0^\pi \log(1 - 2a\cos x + a^2)\,dx,$$

distinguishing between the cases where a is $>$ or < 1.

$\qquad\qquad$ *Ans.* $a < 1$, its value is 0.
$\qquad\qquad\quad$,, $\quad a > 1$, its value is $2\pi\log a$.

29. If $f(x)$ can be expanded in a series of the form

$$a_0 + a_1 \cos x + a_2 \cos 2x + \ldots + a_n \cos nx + \ldots,$$

show t a any coefficient after a_0 can be exhibited in the form of a definite integrah t

$$\textit{Ans. } \quad a_n = \frac{2}{\pi}\int_0^\pi f(x)\cos nx\,dx.$$

30. Find the analogous theorem when $f(x)$ can be expanded in a series of sines of multiples of x; and apply the method to prove the relation

$$x = 2\left(\sin x - \frac{\sin 2x}{2} + \frac{\sin 3x}{3} - \text{&c.}\right),$$

when x lies between $\pm\,\pi$.

31. Prove the relation

$$\int_0^{\frac{\pi}{2}} \frac{d\theta}{\sqrt{\sin\theta}} \times \int_0^{\frac{\pi}{2}} \sqrt{\sin\theta}\,d\theta = \pi.$$

32. Express the definite integral

$$\int_0^{\frac{\pi}{2}} \frac{d\theta}{\sqrt{1 - \kappa^2 \sin^2\theta}}$$

in the form of a series, κ being < 1.

$$\textit{Ans. } \frac{\pi}{2}\left(1 + \left(\frac{1}{2}\right)^2\kappa^4 + \left(\frac{1\cdot 3}{2\cdot 4}\right)^2\kappa^4 + \left(\frac{1\cdot 3\cdot 5}{2\cdot 4\cdot 6}\right)^2\kappa^6 + \text{&c.}\right).$$

33. $\displaystyle\int_0^{\frac{\pi}{2}} \frac{\log\left(1 + \cos a \cos x\right) dx}{\cos x}.$ $Ans.\ \dfrac{1}{2}\left(\dfrac{\pi^2}{4} - a^2\right).$

34. $\displaystyle\int_0^{\infty} x e^{-ax} \cos bx\, dx,$ where $a > 0.$,, $\dfrac{a^2 - b^2}{(a^2 + b^2)^2}.$

35. $\displaystyle\int_0^{\infty} \frac{\tan^{-1} ax \tan^{-1}\beta x}{x^2}\, dx.$,, $\dfrac{\pi}{2} \log\left\{\dfrac{(a+\beta)^{a+\beta}}{a^a \beta^\beta}\right\}.$

36. $\displaystyle\int_0^{\frac{\pi}{2}} \log\left(a^2 \cos^2\theta + \beta^2 \sin^2\theta\right) d\theta.$,, $\pi \log \dfrac{a + \beta}{2}.$

37. $\displaystyle\int_0^{\frac{\pi}{2}} \log\left(\frac{a + b\sin\theta}{a - b\sin\theta}\right) \frac{d\theta}{\sin\theta},\ a > b.$,, $\pi \sin^{-1}\left(\dfrac{b}{a}\right).$

38. $\displaystyle\int_0^{1} \frac{dx}{(1 - x^6)^{\frac{1}{6}}}.$,, $\dfrac{\pi}{3}.$

39. $\displaystyle\int_0^{1} \frac{dx}{(1 - x^n)^{\frac{1}{n}}}.$,, $\dfrac{\pi}{n \sin \dfrac{\pi}{n}}.$

40. $\displaystyle\int_0^{\pi} \frac{\cos rx\, dx}{1 - 2a \cos x + a^2}.$,, $\dfrac{\pi a^r}{1 - a^2}.$

41. Find the sum of the series

$$\frac{n}{n^2 + 1^2} + \frac{n}{n^2 + 2^2} + \frac{n}{n^2 + 3^2} + \ldots + \frac{n}{2n^2}.$$

when n is increased indefinitely.

This is evidently represented by the definite integral

$$\int_0^{1} \frac{dx}{1 + x^2},\ \text{or} = \frac{\pi}{4}.$$

42. Find the limit of the sum

$$\frac{1}{\sqrt{n^2 - 1^2}} + \frac{1}{\sqrt{n^2 - 2^2}} + \frac{1}{\sqrt{n^2 - 3^2}} + \ldots + \frac{1}{\sqrt{n^2 - (n-1)^2}},$$

when $n = \infty.$ $Ans.\ \dfrac{\pi}{2}.$

43. Prove that

$$\int_0^{\frac{\pi}{2}} \cos^m x \cos nx \, dx = \frac{m(m-1)}{m^2 - n^2} \int_0^{\frac{\pi}{2}} \cos^{m-2} x \cos nx \, dx \; ;$$

and hence, deduce the values of the integrals

$$\int_0^{\frac{\pi}{2}} \cos^{2m} x \cos(2n+1) x \, dx, \text{ and } \int_0^{\frac{\pi}{2}} \cos^{2m+1} x \cos 2nx \, dx,$$

when m and n are integers.

44. $\int_0^{\pi} \log(1 - 2a \cos \theta + a^2) \cos n\theta \, d\theta$, when $a^2 < 1$.   *Ans.* $-\dfrac{\pi a^n}{n}$.

45. $\int_{-\infty}^{\infty} \cos \dfrac{\pi x^2}{2} dx.$

46. $\int_0^1 \dfrac{\log(1+x)}{1+x^2} \, dx.$,, $\dfrac{\pi}{8} \log 2.$

47. Prove the following equation :

$$\int_0^{\pi} \frac{d\theta}{(1 - 2a \cos \theta + a^2)^n} = \frac{1}{(1 - a^2)^{n-1}} \int_0^{\pi} (1 - 2a \cos \theta + a^2)^{n-1} d\theta.$$

48. Prove the more general equation

$$\int_0^{\pi} \frac{\sin^m \theta \, d\theta}{(1 - 2a \cos \theta + a^2)^n} = \frac{1}{(1 - a^2)^{2n-m-1}} \int_0^{\pi} \frac{\sin^m \theta \, d\theta}{(1 - 2a \cos \theta + a^2)^{1+m-n}},$$

in which $m + 1$ is positive.

CHAPTER VII.

AREAS OF PLANE CURVES.

126. **Areas of Curves.**—The simplest method of regarding the area of a curve is to suppose it referred to rectangular axes of co-ordinates; then, the area included between the curve, the axis of x, and the two ordinates corresponding to the values x_0 and x_1 of x, is represented by the definite integral

$$\int_{x_0}^{x_1} y\, dx.$$

For, let the area in question be represented by the space $ABVT$, and suppose BV divided into n equal intervals, and the corresponding ordinates drawn, as in the accompanying figure.

Then the area of the portion $PMNQ$ is less than the rectangle $pMNQ$, and greater than $PMNq$.

Hence the entire area $ABVT$ is less than the sum of the rectangles represented by $pMNQ$, and greater than the sum of the rectangles $PMNq$; but the difference between these latter sums is the sum

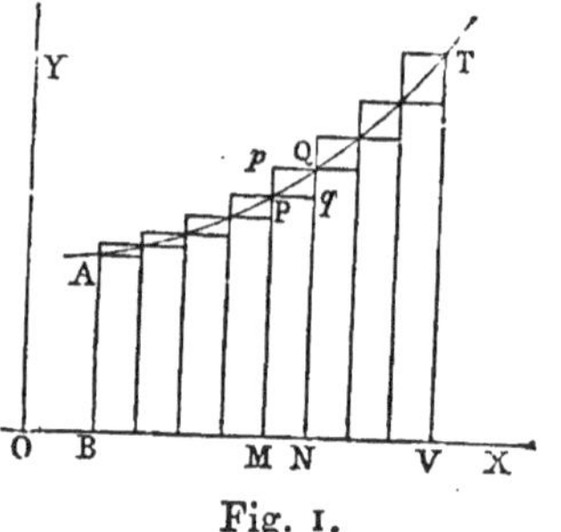

Fig. 1.

of the rectangles $Pp\,Qq$, or (since the rectangles have equal bases) the rectangle under MN and the difference between TV and AB. Now, by supposing the number n increased indefinitely, MN can be made indefinitely small, and hence the rectangle $MN\,(TV - AB)$ also becomes infinitely small. Consequently the difference between the area $ABVT$ and the sum of the rectangles $PMNq$ becomes evanescent at the same time.

If now the co-ordinates of P be denoted by x and y, and MN by Δx, it follows that the area $ABVT$ is the limiting value* of $\Sigma(y\,\Delta x)$ when the increment Δx becomes infinitely small ;

or area $ABVT = \displaystyle\int_{x_0}^{x_1} y\,dx$; where $x_1 = OV$, $x_0 = OB$.

It should be observed that this result requires that y continue finite, and of the same sign, between the limits of integration.

If y change its sign between the limits, i.e. if the curve cut the axis of x, the preceding definite integral represents the difference of the areas at opposite sides of the axis of x.

In such cases it is preferable to consider each area separately, by dividing the integral into two parts, separated by the value of x for which y vanishes.

The preceding mode of proof obviously applies also to the case where the co-ordinate axes are oblique; in which case the area is represented by

$$\sin\omega \int_{x_0}^{x_1} y\,dx,$$

where ω represents the angle between the axes.

In applying these formulæ the value of y is found in terms of x by means of the equation of the curve : thus, if $y = f(x)$ be this equation, the area is represented by

$$\int f(x)\,dx,$$

taken between suitable limits.

Conversely, the value of any definite integral, such as

$$\int_a^b f(x)\,dx,$$

may be represented geometrically by the area of a definite portion of the curve represented by the equation

$$y = f(x).$$

---

* This demonstration is substantially that given by Newton (see *Principia*, Lib. I., Sect. I., Lemma 2) ; and is the geometrical representation of the result established in Art. 90.

The modification in the proof when the elements of BV are considered unequal, but each infinitely small, is easily seen. It may be remarked that the result here given is but a particular case of the general principle laid down in Arts. 38, 39, *Diff. Calc.*

[12]

On account of this property the process of integration was called, by Newton and the early writers on the Calculus, the *method of quadratures.*

Again, it is plain that the area between the curve, the axis of y, and two ordinates to that axis, is represented by

$$\int x\,dy,$$

taken between the proper limits: the co-ordinate axes being supposed rectangular.

We proceed to illustrate this method of determining areas by a few applications, commencing with the simplest examples.

127. **The Circle.**—Taking the equation of a circle in the form

$x^2 + y^2 = a^2$, we get $y = \sqrt{a^2 - x^2}$,

and the area is represented by

$$\int \sqrt{a^2 - x^2}\,dx,$$

taken between proper limits.

For instance, to find the area of the portion represented by $APDE$ in the accompanying figure. Let $x = a \cos \theta$, then the area in question plainly is represented by

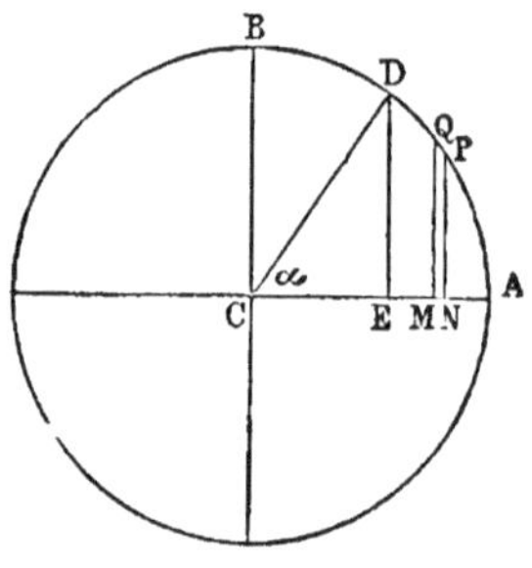

Fig. 2.

$$a^2 \int_0^a \sin^2\theta\,d\theta = \frac{a^2}{2}(a - \sin a \cos a); \text{ where } a = \angle DCA.$$

This result is also evident from geometry; for the area $DPAE$ is the difference between $DPAC$ and DCE, or is

$$\frac{a^2 a}{2} - \frac{a^2 \sin a \cos a}{2}.$$

The area of the quadrant ACB is got by making $a = \dfrac{\pi}{2}$; and accordingly is $\dfrac{\pi a^2}{4}$: hence the entire area of the circle is πa^2.

128. The Ellipse.—From the equation of the ellipse

$$\frac{x^2}{a^2} + \frac{y^2}{b^2} = 1, \text{ we get } y = \frac{b}{a}\sqrt{a^2 - x^2},$$

and the element of area is

$$\frac{b}{a}\sqrt{a^2 - x^2}\,dx;$$

but this is $\dfrac{b}{a}$ times the area of the corresponding element of the circle whose radius is a: consequently the area of any portion of the ellipse is $\dfrac{b}{a}$ times that of the corresponding part of the circle. This is also evident from geometry.

The area of the entire ellipse is πab.

Again, if the equation of an ellipse be given in the form $Ax^2 + By^2 = C$, its area is evidently $\dfrac{\pi C}{\sqrt{AB}}$.

As an application of oblique axes, let it be proposed *to find the area of the segment of an ellipse cut off by any chord DD'.*

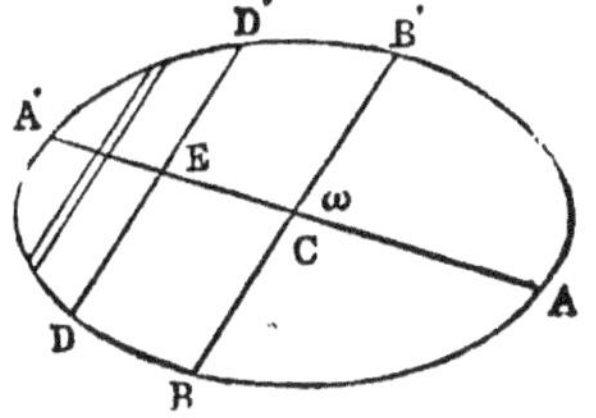

Fig. 3.

Draw the diameter AA', conjugate to the chord, and BB' parallel to it. Then, C being the centre, let

$$CA' = a', \ CB' = b', \ ACB' = \omega,$$

and the equation of the ellipse is $\dfrac{x^2}{a'^2} + \dfrac{y^2}{b'^2} = 1$; hence the area $DA'D'$ is represented by

$$2\frac{b'}{a'}\sin\omega\int_{CE}^{CA'}\sqrt{a'^2 - x^2}\,dx = a'b'\sin\omega\,(a - \sin a\cos a),$$

where

$$\cos a = \frac{CE}{CA'}.$$

Again, $a'\,b'\sin\omega = ab$, by an elementary property of the ellipse, a and b being the semiaxes.

Hence the area of the segment in question is

$$ab\,(a - \sin a\cos a).$$
$$[12\ a]$$

This result can also be deduced immediately from the circle by the method of orthogonal projection.

It may be observed that if we denote the area of an elliptic sector, measured from the axis major to a point whose co-ordinates are x, y, by S, we may write

$$\frac{x}{a} = \cos\frac{2S}{ab} = \cos a, \qquad \frac{y}{b} = \sin\frac{2S}{ab} = \sin a.$$

129. **The Parabola.**—Taking the equation of the parabola in the form

$$y^2 = px, \text{ we get } y = \sqrt{px}.$$

Hence the area of the portion APN is

$$p^{\frac{1}{2}} \int x^{\frac{1}{2}} dx, \text{ or } \frac{2}{3} p^{\frac{1}{2}} x^{\frac{3}{2}}, \text{ i.e. } \frac{2}{3} xy.$$

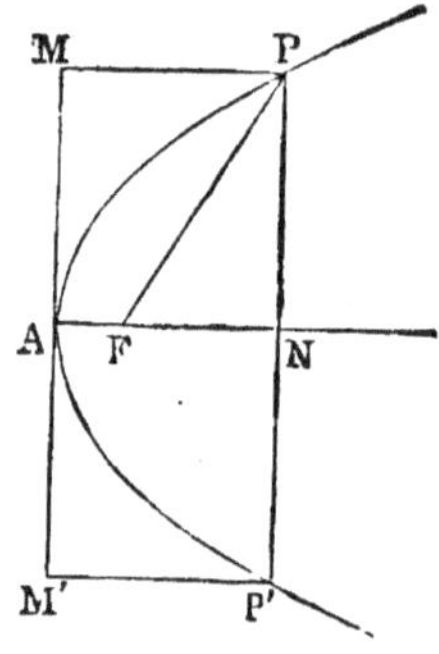

Fig 4.

Consequently, the area of the segment PAP', cut off by a chord perpendicular to the axis, is $\frac{2}{3}$ of the rectangle $PMM'P'$.

It is easily seen that a similar relation holds for the segment cut off by any chord.

More generally, let the equation of the curve be $y = ax^n$, where n is positive.

Here $\qquad \int y\,dx = a \int x^n\,dx = \dfrac{ax^{n+1}}{n+1} + \text{const.}$

If the area be counted from the origin, the constant vanishes, and the expression for the area becomes

$$\frac{ax^{n+1}}{n+1}, \quad \text{or } \frac{xy}{n+1}.$$

Hence, the area is in a constant ratio to the rectangle under the co-ordinates. A corresponding result holds for oblique axes. The discussion, when n is negative, is left to the student.

EXAMPLE.

Express the area of a segment of a parabola cut off by any focal chord in terms of l, the length of the chord, and p, the parameter of the parabola.

Ans. $\dfrac{l^{\frac{3}{2}} p^{\frac{1}{2}}}{6}$.

130. **The Hyperbola.**—The simplest form of the equation of a hyperbola is where the asymptotes are taken for co-ordinate axes; in this case its equation is of the form $xy = c^2$.

Hence, denoting the angle between the asymptotes by ω, the area between the curve and an asymptote is denoted by

$$c^2 \sin \omega \int \frac{dx}{x}, \text{ or } c^2 \sin \omega \log \left(\frac{x_1}{x_0}\right),$$

where x_1 and x_0 are the abscissæ of the limiting points.

If the curve be referred to its axes, its equation is

$$\frac{x^2}{a^2} - \frac{y^2}{b^2} = 1 \; ;$$

and the element of area $y\,dx$ becomes

$$\frac{b}{a} \sqrt{x^2 - a^2}\,dx.$$

Hence the area is represented by

$$\frac{b}{a} \int \sqrt{x^2 - a^2}\,dx,$$

taken between proper limits.

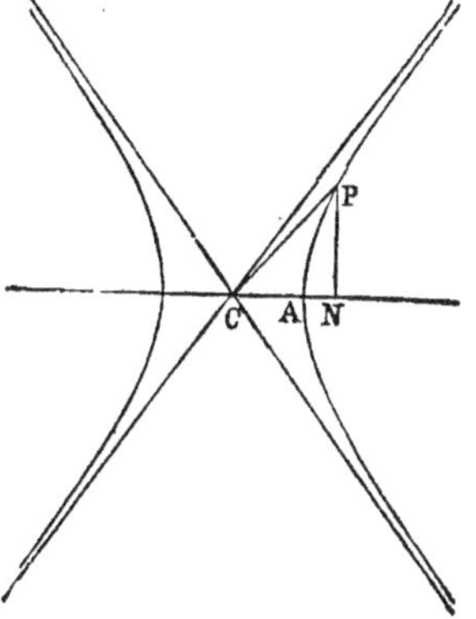

Fig. 5.

Again, $\int \sqrt{x^2 - a^2}\,dx = \int \frac{x^2\,dx}{\sqrt{x^2 - a^2}} - a^2 \int \frac{dx}{\sqrt{x^2 - a^2}}.$

Also, integrating by parts, we have

$$\int \sqrt{x^2 - a^2}\,dx = x \sqrt{x^2 - a^2} - \int \frac{x^2\,dx}{\sqrt{x^2 - a^2}}.$$

Adding, and dividing by 2, we get

$$\int \sqrt{x^2 - a^2}\,dx = \frac{x\sqrt{x^2 - a^2}}{2} - \frac{a^2}{2} \int \frac{dx}{\sqrt{x^2 - a^2}}$$

$$= \frac{x\sqrt{x^2 - a^2}}{2} - \frac{a^2}{2} \log (x + \sqrt{x^2 - a^2}).$$

Accordingly, if we suppose the area counted from the summit A, we have

$$APN = \frac{b}{2a}\,x\sqrt{x^2 - a^2} - \frac{ab}{2}\,\log\left(\frac{x + \sqrt{x^2 - a^2}}{a}\right)$$

$$= \frac{xy}{2} - \frac{ab}{2}\,\log\left(\frac{x}{a} + \frac{y}{b}\right).$$

Again, since the triangle $CPN = \frac{1}{2}xy$, it follows that

$$\text{sector } ACP = \frac{ab}{2}\,\log\left(\frac{x}{a} + \frac{y}{b}\right).$$

For a geometrical method of finding the area of a hyperbolic sector, see Salmon's *Conics*, Art. 395.

130 (*a*). **Hyperbolic Sine and Cosine.**—If S represent the sector ACP, the final equation of the preceding Article becomes

$$\frac{ab}{2}\,\log\left(\frac{x}{a} + \frac{y}{b}\right) = S, \tag{1}$$

which may also be written

$$\frac{x}{a} + \frac{y}{b} = e^v,$$

introducing a single letter v to denote the quantity

$$\log\left(\frac{x}{a} + \frac{y}{b}\right) = \frac{2S}{ab} = v.$$

Hence, by the equation of the hyperbola, we get

$$\frac{x}{a} - \frac{y}{b} = e^{-v}.$$

Thus, in analogy with the last result of Art. 128, calling the following functions the hyperbolic cosine and hyperbolic sine of v, and for brevity writing them $\cosh v$, and $\sinh v$,

$$e^v + e^{-v} = 2\cosh v, \quad e^v - e^{-v} = 2\sinh v, \tag{2}$$

the co-ordinates of any point on the curve are

$$\frac{x}{a} = \cosh v = \cosh\frac{2S}{ab}, \quad \frac{y}{b} = \sinh v = \sinh\frac{2S}{ab}.$$

We might have treated the matter differently by introducing the angle ϕ defined by the equation $x = a \sec \phi$, and therefore $y = b \tan \phi$ (for the geometric meaning of this transformation, see Salmon's *Conics*, Art. 232); whence (1) may be written*

$$\frac{2S}{ab} = v = \log \tan \left(\frac{\pi}{4} + \frac{\phi}{2} \right):$$

and we see that the hyperbolic cosine of a real quantity is the secant, and the hyperbolic sine the tangent of the same real angle. Also, since

$$\sin \phi = \frac{\sinh v}{\cosh v}, \quad \cos \phi = \frac{1}{\cosh v}, \quad \cot \phi = \frac{1}{\sinh v}, \quad \operatorname{cosec} \phi = \frac{\cosh v}{\sinh v},$$

we can obviously extend the names of the other trigonometrical functions likewise. Again, putting in (2) for v, $u\sqrt{-1}$, or iu, they become, by Art. 8,

$$\cos u = \cosh iu, \quad i \sin u = \sinh iu.$$

131. The Catenary.—If an inelastic string of uniform density be allowed to hang freely from two fixed points, the curve which it assumes is called the Catenary.

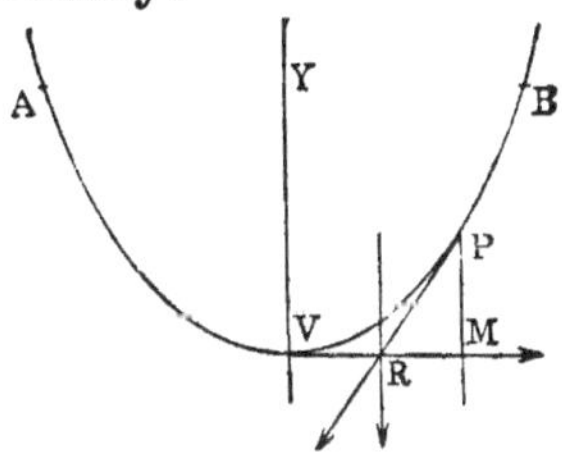

Its equation can be easily arrived at from elementary mechanics, as follows :—

Let V be the lowest point on the curve; then any portion VP of the string must be in equilibrium under the action of the tensions at its extremities, and its own weight, W.

Fig. 6.

Let A be the tension at V; T that at P, which acts along PR, the tangent at P; $\angle PRM = \phi$. Then, by the property of the triangle of force, we have

$$W : A = PM : RM;$$

$$\therefore W = A \tan \phi.$$

---

* When ϕ is related to v by this equation, ϕ is what Professor Cayley (*Elliptic Functions*, p. 56) calls the gudermannian of v, after Professor Gudermann, and writes the inverse equation $\phi = gd\,v$.

Again, if s be the length of VP, and a that of the portion of the string whose weight is A, we have, since the string is uniform,

$$W = A\,\frac{s}{a};$$

$$\therefore\ s = a \tan \phi.$$

This is the intrinsic equation of the catenary. (Diff. Calc., Art. 242 (a).)

Its equation in Cartesian co-ordinates can be easily arrived at.

For, on the vertical through V take $VO = a$, and draw OX in the horizontal direction, and assume OX and OY as axes of co-ordinates. Let

$$PN = y, \quad ON = x,$$

then

$$\frac{dy}{dx} = \tan \phi,$$

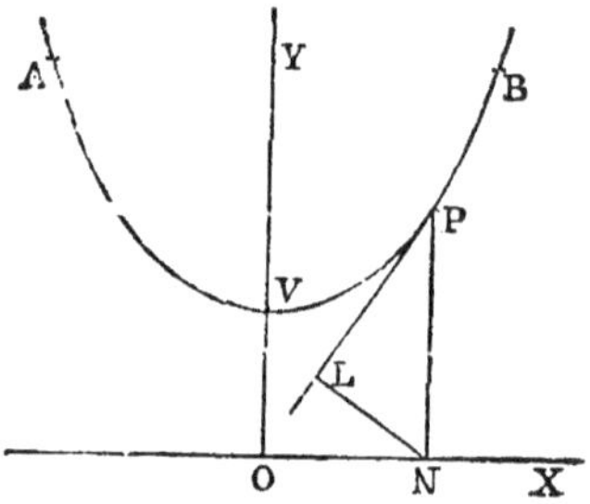

Fig. 7.

$$\frac{dy}{ds} = \sin \phi, \qquad \frac{dx}{ds} = \cos \phi\ ;$$

$$\therefore\ \frac{dy}{d\phi} = \frac{dy}{ds}\frac{ds}{d\phi} = a\,\frac{\sin \phi}{\cos^2 \phi}, \quad \frac{dx}{d\phi} = \frac{a}{\cos \phi}.$$

Hence $\qquad y = a \sec \phi, \ x = a \log (\sec \phi + \tan \phi).$ $\qquad$ (3)

No constant is added to either integral, since $y = a$, and $x = 0$, when $\phi = 0$.

From the latter equation we get

$$\sec \phi + \tan \phi = e^{\frac{x}{a}}\ ;$$

also $\qquad\qquad \sec \phi - \tan \phi = \dfrac{1}{\sec \phi + \tan \phi} = e^{-\frac{x}{a}}.$

Hence, we have

$$2 \sec \phi = e^{\frac{x}{a}} + e^{-\frac{x}{a}}, \quad 2 \tan \phi = e^{\frac{x}{a}} - e^{-\frac{x}{a}}.$$

Consequently,

$$y = \frac{a}{2}\left(e^{\frac{x}{a}} + e^{-\frac{x}{a}}\right). \qquad (4)$$

Also

$$s = \frac{a}{2}\left(e^{\frac{x}{a}} - e^{-\frac{x}{a}}\right). \qquad (5)$$

In the notation of last Article these equations may be written

$$\frac{y}{a} = \cosh\frac{x}{a} \quad \text{and} \quad \frac{s}{a} = \sinh\frac{x}{a}.$$

Again, if NL be drawn perpendicular to the tangent at P, we have

$$NL = PN\cos\phi ; \ \therefore\ NL = a. \qquad (6)$$

Also

$$PL = NL\tan\phi ; \ \therefore\ PL = s = PV. \qquad (7)$$

The area of any portion $VPNO$ is

$$\frac{a}{2}\int_0^x\left(e^{\frac{x}{a}} + e^{-\frac{x}{a}}\right)dx = \frac{a^2}{2}\left(e^{\frac{x}{a}} - e^{-\frac{x}{a}}\right) = a\,(y^2 - a^2)^{\frac{1}{2}}. \qquad (8)$$

Accordingly, the area $VPNO$ is double that of the triangle PNL.

EXAMPLES.

1. To find the area of the oval of the parabola of the third degree with a double point

$$cy^2 = (x - a)(x - b)^2.$$

The area in question is represented by

$$\frac{2}{\sqrt{c}}\int_a^b (b - x)\sqrt{x - a}\,dx.$$

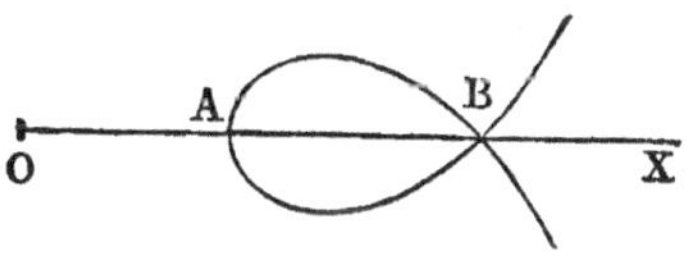

Fig. 8.

Let $x - a = z^2$, and we easily find the area* to be $\dfrac{8\,(b - a)^{\frac{5}{2}}}{3\cdot5\,c^{\frac{1}{2}}}$.

2. Find the whole area of the curve $a^2y^2 = x^3(2a - x)$.   *Ans.* πa^2.

3. Find the whole area between the cissoid $x^3 = y^2(a - x)$ and its asymptote.

---

* The student will find little difficulty in proving that this area is $\dfrac{2\sqrt{2}}{5}$ times the rectangle which circumscribes the oval, having its sides parallel to the co-ordinate axes.

Since $x - a = 0$ is the equation of the asymptote the area in question is represented by

$$\int_0^a \frac{x^{\frac{3}{2}}\,dx}{(a-x)^{\frac{1}{4}}}.$$

Let $x = a\sin^2\theta$, and this becomes

$$2a^2 \int_0^{\frac{\pi}{2}} \sin^4\theta\,d\theta :$$

hence the area in question is $\dfrac{3}{8}\pi a^2$.

4. Find the area of the loop of the curve

$$a^3 y^2 = x^4(b + x).$$

This curve has been considered in Art. 262, Diff. Calc. Its form is exhibited in the annexed figure; and the area of the loop is plainly

$$\frac{2}{a^{\frac{3}{2}}} \int_{-b}^0 x^2 \sqrt{b + x}\,dx.$$

Let $b + x = z^2$, and it is easily seen that the area in question is represented by

$$\frac{8 \cdot b^{\frac{7}{2}}}{3 \cdot 5 \cdot 7 \cdot a^{\frac{3}{2}}}.$$

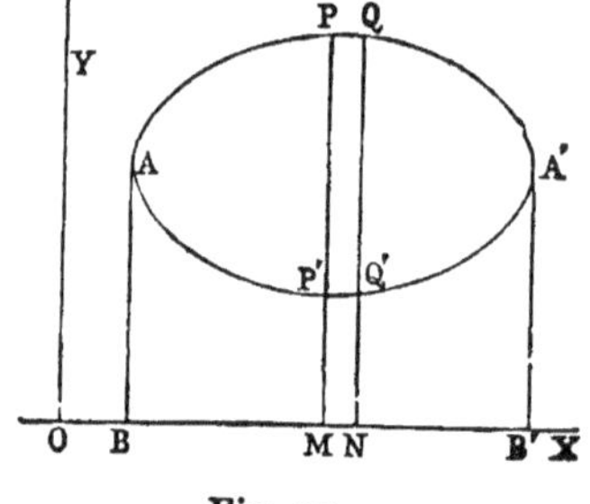

Fig. 9.

5. Find the area between the witch of Agnesi

$$xy^2 = 4a^2(2a - x)$$

and its asymptote.

Ans. $4\pi a^2$.

132. In finding the whole area of a closed curve, such as that represented in the figure, we suppose lines, PM, QN, &c., drawn parallel to the axis of y; then, assuming each of these lines to meet the curve in but two points, and making $PM = y_2$, $P'M = y_1$, the elementary area $PQQ'P'$ is represented by $(y_2 - y_1)\,dx$, and the entire* area by

$$\int_{OB}^{OB'} (y_2 - y_1)\,dx ;$$

Fig. 10.

in which OB, OB' are the limiting values of x.

---

* This form still holds when the axis of x intersects the curve, for the ordinates below that axis have a negative sign, and $(y_2 - y_1)\,dx$ will still represent the element of the area between two parallel ordinates.

For example, let it be proposed to find the whole area of an ellipse given by the general equation

$$ax^2 + 2hxy + by^2 + 2gx + 2fy + c = 0.$$

Here, solving for y, we easily find

$$y_2 - y_1 = \frac{2}{b} \sqrt{(h^2 - ab) x^2 + 2 (hf - bg) x + f^2 - bc}.$$

Also, the limiting values of x are the roots of the quadratic expression under the radical sign.

Accordingly, denoting these roots by a and β, and observing that $h^2 - ab$ is negative for an ellipse, the entire area is represented by

$$\frac{2 \sqrt{ab - h^2}}{b} \int_a^\beta \sqrt{(x - a)(\beta - x)}\, dx.$$

To find this, assume $x - a = (\beta - a) \sin^2 \theta$;
then $\beta - x = (\beta - a) \cos^2 \theta$,
and we get

$$\int_a^\beta \sqrt{(x - a)(\beta - x)}\, dx = 2 (\beta - a)^2 \int_0^{\frac{\pi}{2}} \sin^2 \theta \cos^2 \theta\, d\theta$$

$$= \frac{\pi}{8} (\beta - a)^2.$$

Again, $(\beta - a)^2 = 4 \cdot \dfrac{(hf - bg)^2 + (f^2 - bc)(ab - h^2)}{(ab - h^2)^2}$

$$= \frac{4b(af^2 + bg^2 + ch^2 - 2fgh - abc)}{(ab - h^2)^2}.$$

Hence the area of the ellipse is represented by

$$\frac{\pi(af^2 + bg^2 + ch^2 - 2fgh - abc)}{(ab - h^2)^{\frac{3}{2}}}.$$

This result can be verified without difficulty, by determining the value of the rectangle under the semiaxes of an ellipse, in terms of the coefficients of its general equation.

It is worthy of observation that if we suppose a closed curve to be described by the motion of a point round its entire perimeter, the whole *inclosed area is represented by* $\int y\, dx$, *taken for every point around the entire curve.*

Thus, in the preceding figure, if we proceed from A to A' along the upper portion of the curve, the corresponding part of the integral $\int y\,dx$ represents the area $APA'B'B$. Again, in returning from A' to A along the lower part of the curve, the increment dx is negative, and the corresponding part of $\int y\,dx$ is also negative (assuming that the curve does not intersect the axis of x), and represents the area $A'P'ABB'$, taken with a negative sign. Consequently, the whole area of the closed curve is represented by the integral $\int y\,dx$, taken for all points on the curve.

The student will find no difficulty in showing that this proof is general, whatever be the form of the curve, and whatever the number of points in which it is met by the parallel ordinates.

To avoid ambiguity, the preceding result may be stated as follows :—*The area of any closed curve is represented by*

$$\int y\,\frac{dx}{ds}\,ds$$

taken through the entire perimeter of the curve, the element of the curve being regarded as positive throughout.

The preceding is on the hypothesis that the curve has no double point. If the curve cut itself, so as to form two loops, it is easily seen that $\int y\,\dfrac{dx}{ds}\,ds$, when taken round the entire perimeter, represents the difference between the areas of the two loops. The corresponding result in the case of three or more loops can be readily determined.

133. In many cases, instead of determining y in terms of x, we can express them both in terms of a single variable, and thus determine the area by expressing its element in terms of that variable.

For instance, in the ellipse, if we make $x = a \sin \phi$, we get $y = b \cos \phi$, and $y\,dx$ becomes $ab \cos^2 \phi\, d\phi$, the integral of which gives the same result as before.

In like manner, to find the area of the curve

$$\left(\frac{x}{a}\right)^{\frac{2}{3}} + \left(\frac{y}{b}\right)^{\frac{2}{3}} = 1.$$

Let $x = a \sin^3 \phi$, then $y = b \cos^3 \phi$, and $y\,dx$ becomes

$$3ab \sin^2 \phi \cos^4 \phi\, d\phi :$$

hence the entire area of the curve is represented by

$$12ab \int_0^{\frac{\pi}{2}} \sin^2\phi \, \cos^4\phi \, d\phi \;=\; \frac{3}{8}\,\pi ab.$$

EXAMPLES.

1. Find the whole area of the evolute of the ellipse

$$\frac{x^2}{a^2} + \frac{y^2}{b^2} = 1.$$

Ans. $\dfrac{3\pi(a^2 - b^2)^2}{8ab}.$

2. Find the whole area of the curve

$$\left(\frac{x}{a}\right)^{\frac{2}{2m+1}} + \left(\frac{y}{b}\right)^{\frac{2}{2n+1}} = 1.$$

Ans. $\dfrac{1 \cdot 3 \cdot 5 \, \ldots \, (2m + 1) \cdot 1 \cdot 3 \cdot 5 \, \ldots \, (2n + 1)}{2 \cdot 4 \cdot 6 \quad \ldots \ldots \ldots \quad 2\,(m + n + 1)}\,\pi ab.$

134. **The Cycloid.**—In the cycloid, we have (Diff. Calc., Art. 272),

$$x = a\,(\theta - \sin\theta), \quad y = a\,(1 - \cos\theta);$$

$$\therefore \int y\,dx = a^2 \int (1 - \cos\theta)^2\,d\theta = 4a^2 \int \sin^4\frac{\theta}{2}\,d\theta.$$

Taking θ between 0 and π, we get $3\pi a^2$ for the entire area between the cycloid and its base.

The area of the cycloid admits also of an elementary geometrical deduction, as follows :—

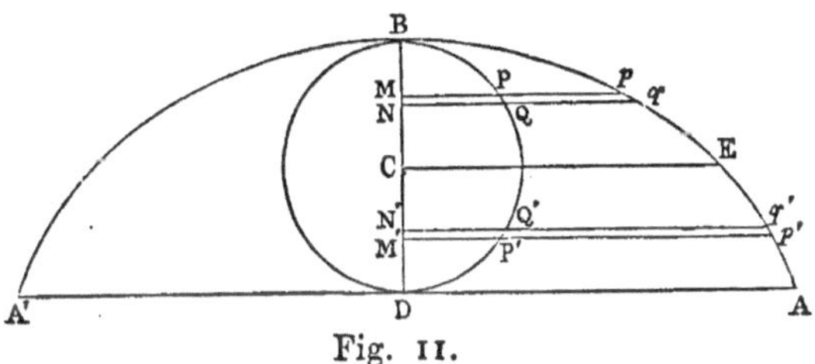

Fig. 11.

It is obviously sufficient to find the area between the semicircle BPD and the semi-cycloid BpA. To determine this, let points P and P' be taken on the semicircle such that arc BP = arc DP' : draw MPp and $M'P'p'$ perpendicular to BD. Take MN and $M'N'$ of equal length, and draw Nq and $N'q'$, also perpendicular to BD : then, by the fundamental property of the cycloid, the line Pp = arc BP, and $P'p'$ = arc BP' : $\therefore Pp + P'p'$ = semicircle = πa.

Now, if the interval MN be regarded as indefinitely small, the sum of the elementary areas $PpqQ$ and $P'p'q'Q'$ is equal to the rectangle under MN and the sum of Pp and $P'p'$, or to $\pi a \times MN$.

Again, if the entire figure be supposed divided in like manner, it is obvious that the whole area between the semi-circle and the cycloid is equal to πa multiplied by the sum of the elements MN, taken from B to the centre C, i.e. equal to πa^2.

Consequently the whole area of the cycloid is $3\pi a^2$, as before.

The area of a prolate or curtate cycloid can be obtained in like manner.

135. **Areas in Polar Co-ordinates.**—Suppose the curve APB to be referred to polar co-ordinates, O being the pole, and let OP, OQ, OR represent consecutive radii vectores, and PL, QM, arcs of circles described with O as centre. Then the area $OPQ = OPL + PLQ$; but PLQ becomes evanescent in comparison with OPL when P and Q are infinitely near points; consequently, in the limit the elementary area $OPQ =$ area $OPL = \dfrac{r^2 d\theta}{2}$;

r and θ being the polar co-ordinates of P.

Hence the sectorial area AOB is represented by

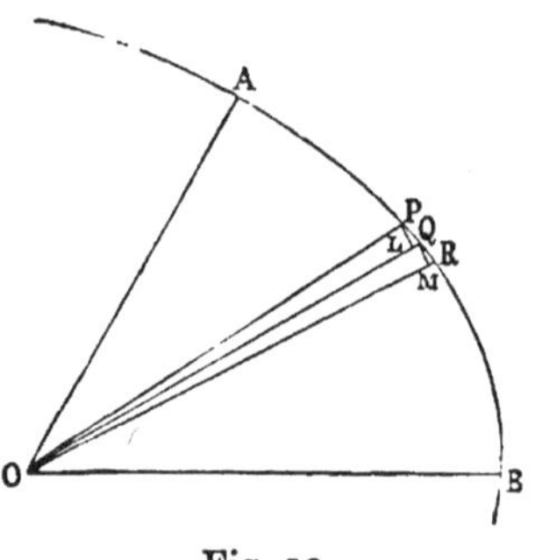

Fig. 12.

$$\frac{1}{2}\int_{\beta}^{a} r^2 \, d\theta,$$

where a and β are the values of θ corresponding to the limiting points A and B.

136. **Area of Pedals of Ellipse and Hyperbola.**—For example, let it be proposed to find the area of the locus of the foot of the perpendicular from the centre on a tangent to an ellipse.

Writing the equation of the ellipse in the form $\dfrac{x^2}{a^2} + \dfrac{y^2}{b^2} = 1$, the equation of the locus in question is obviously

$$r^2 = a^2 \cos^2 \theta + b^2 \sin^2 \theta.$$

Hence its area is

$$\frac{a^2}{2}\int \cos^2\theta\,d\theta + \frac{b^2}{2}\int \sin^2\theta\,d\theta = \frac{a^2+b^2}{4}\theta + \frac{a^2-b^2}{4}\sin\theta\cos\theta.$$

The entire area of the locus is

$$\frac{\pi}{2}(a^2+b^2).$$

The equation of the corresponding locus for the hyperbola is

$$r^2 = a^2\cos^2\theta - b^2\sin^2\theta.$$

In finding its area, since r must be real, we must have $a^2\cos^2\theta - b^2\sin^2\theta$ positive : accordingly, the limits for θ are o and $\tan^{-1}\dfrac{a}{b}$.

Integrating between these limits, and multiplying by 4, we get for the entire area

$$ab + (a^2 - b^2)\tan^{-1}\frac{a}{b}.$$

In this case, if we had at once integrated between $\theta = $ o and $\theta = 2\pi$, we should have found for the area $(a^2 - b^2)\dfrac{\pi}{2}$. This anomaly would arise from our having integrated through an interval for which r^2 is negative, and for which, therefore, the corresponding part of the curve is imaginary.

The expression for the area of the pedal of an ellipse with respect to any origin will be given in a subsequent Article.

EXAMPLES.

1. Show that the entire area of the Lemniscate

$$r^2 = a^2\cos 2\theta$$

is a^2.

2. In the hyperbolic spiral

$$r\theta = a,$$

prove that the area bounded by any two radii vectores is proportional to the difference between their lengths.

3. Find the area of a loop of the curve

$$r^2 = a^2\cos n\theta. \qquad\qquad\qquad Ans.\ \frac{a^2}{n}.$$

4. Find the area of the loop of the Folium of Descartes, whose equation is

$$x^3 + y^3 = 3axy.$$

Transforming to polar co-ordinates, we have

$$r = \frac{3a\,\cos\theta\,\sin\theta}{\sin^3\theta + \cos^3\theta}.$$

Again, the limiting values of θ are 0 and $\dfrac{\pi}{2}$;

$$\therefore \text{Area} = \frac{9a^2}{2} \int_0^{\frac{\pi}{2}} \frac{\sin^2\theta\,\cos^2\theta\,d\theta}{(\sin^3\theta + \cos^3\theta)^2}.$$

Let $\tan\theta = u$, and this expression becomes

$$\frac{9a^2}{2} \int_0^{\infty} \frac{u^2\,du}{(1 + u^3)^2} = \frac{3a^2}{2}.$$

5. To find the area of the Limaçon

$$r = a\cos\theta + b.$$

Here we must distinguish between two cases.

(1). Let $b > a$. In this case the curve consists of one loop, and its area is

$$\frac{1}{2} \int_0^{2\pi} (a\cos\theta + b)^2 d\theta = \left(b^2 + \frac{a^2}{2}\right)\pi.$$

When $b = a$, the curve becomes a Cardioid, and the area $\dfrac{3\pi a^2}{2}$.

(2). Let $b < a$. The curve in this case has two loops, as in the figure (see Diff. Calc., Art. 269), the outer loop corresponding to

$$r = a\cos\theta + b,$$

the inner to

$$r = a\cos\theta - b.$$

To find the area of the inner loop, we take θ between the limits 0 and a, where $a = \cos^{-1}\left(\dfrac{b}{a}\right)$; and the entire area is

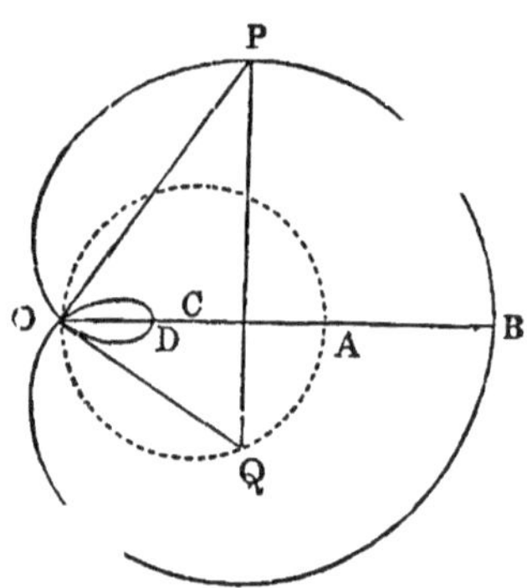

Fig. 13.

$$\int_0^{a} (a\cos\theta - b)^2 d\theta$$

$$= \int_0^{a} (a^2\cos^2\theta - 2ab\cos\theta + b^2)\,d\theta$$

$$= \left(\frac{a^2}{2} + b^2\right)a + \frac{a^2}{2}\sin a\cos a - 2ab\sin a$$

$$= \left(\frac{a^2}{2} + b^2\right)\cos^{-1}\frac{b}{a} - \frac{3}{2}b\sqrt{a^2 - b^2}.$$

It is easily seen that the sum of the areas of the two loops is obtained by integrating between the limits o and 2π, and accordingly is

$$\pi\left(\frac{a^2}{2} + b^2\right),$$

as in the former case.

137. Area of a Closed Curve by Polar Co-ordinates.—In finding the whole area of a closed curve by polar co-ordinates we distinguish between two cases.   When the origin O is outside, we suppose tangents OT, OT', drawn from O, and vectors OP, OQ, &c., drawn to cut the curve; then, if these lines intersect it in but two points each, the element of area $PpqQ$ is the difference between the areas POQ and pOq; or, in the limit, is $\frac{1}{2}(r_1^2 - r_2^2)\,d\theta$, where $OP = r_1$, $Op = r_2$.

Hence, the expression

$$\tfrac{1}{2}\textstyle\int(r_1^2 - r_2^2)\,d\theta,$$

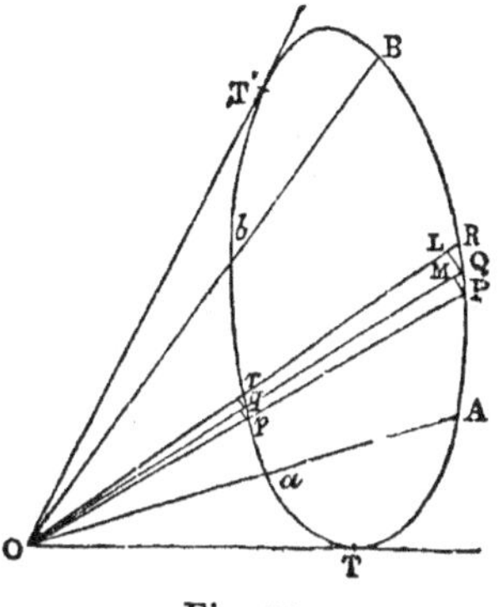

Fig. 14.

taken between the limits corresponding to the tangents OT and OT', represents the entire included area.

If the origin lie inside the curve, its whole area is in general represented by $\frac{1}{2}\int(r_1^2 + r_2^2)\,d\theta$, taken between the limits $\theta = o$, and $\theta = \pi$.

We shall illustrate these results by applying them to the circle

$$r^2 - 2rc\cos\theta + c^2 = a^2.$$

If the origin be outside, we have $c > a$, and $r_1 + r_2 = 2c\cos\theta$, and $r_1 r_2 = c^2 - a^2$; $\therefore$ $r_1 - r_2 = 2\sqrt{a^2 - c^2\sin^2\theta}$.

Hence $(r_1^2 - r_2^2)\,d\theta = 4c\cos\theta\sqrt{a^2 - c^2\sin^2\theta}\,d\theta$; and the limiting values of θ are $\pm\sin^{-1}\dfrac{a}{c}$.

Hence the whole area is

$$2c\int_{-\sin^{-1}\frac{a}{c}}^{\sin^{-1}\frac{a}{c}}\cos\theta\sqrt{a^2 - c^2\sin^2\theta}\,d\theta.$$

$\lceil 13 \rceil$

Let $c \sin \theta = a \sin \phi$, and this integral transforms into

$$2a^2 \int_{-\frac{\pi}{2}}^{\frac{\pi}{2}} \cos^2 \phi \, d\phi = \pi a^2.$$

Again, if the origin be inside, we have $c < a$, and

$$\frac{1}{2}\left(r_1{}^2 + r_2{}^2\right) = a^2 + c^2 \cos 2\theta\,;$$

$$\therefore \int_0^{\pi}\left(r_1{}^2 + r_2{}^2\right) d\theta = \int_0^{\pi}\left(a^2 + c^2 \cos 2\theta\right) d\theta = \pi a^2.$$

The method given above may be applied to find the area included between two branches of the same spiral curve. As an example, let us consider the spiral of Archimedes.

138. **The Spiral of Archimedes.**—The equation of this curve is $r = a\theta$, and its form, for *positive* values* of θ, is represented in the accompanying figure, in which O is the pole and OA the line from which θ is measured. Let any line drawn through O meet the different branches of the spiral in points $P, Q, R,$ &c.: then, if $OP = r$, and $\angle POA = \theta$, we have, from the equation of the curve,

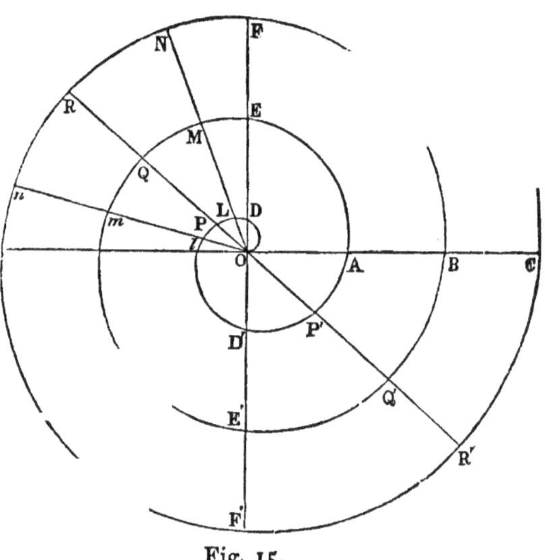

Fig. 15.

$$OP = a\theta, \quad OQ = a(\theta + 2\pi), \quad OR = a(\theta + 4\pi), \text{ &c.}$$

---

* It should be noted that when negative values of θ are taken, we get for the remaining half of the spiral a curve symmetrically situated with respect to the prime vector OA.

Hence $PQ = QR = \&\text{c}., = 2a\pi = c$ (suppose); i. e. the intercepts between any two consecutive branches of the spiral are of constant length.

Again, let $OQ = r_1$, $OR = r_2 = r_1 + c$, and the area between the two corresponding branches is

$$\frac{1}{2}\int (r_2{}^2 - r_1{}^2)\, d\theta = c \int r_1 d\theta + \frac{c^2}{2}\int d\theta.$$

Now, suppose MN and mn represent the limiting lines, and let β and a be the corresponding values of θ; then the area $nNMm$ will be equal to

$$c \int_a^\beta a\theta\, d\theta + \frac{c^2}{2}\int_a^\beta d\theta = \frac{c}{2}(\beta - a)(aa + a\beta + c)$$

$$= \frac{c}{2}(\beta - a)(OM + On). \tag{9}$$

If $\beta - a = \pi$, this gives for the area of the portion between two consecutive branches $QE'Q'$ and $RF'R'$, intercepted by any right line RR' drawn through the pole, $\frac{\pi}{2}RQ \cdot QR'$, i.e. half the area of the ellipse whose semi-axes are RQ and $R'Q$.

139. **Another Expression for Area.**—The formula in Article 137 still holds, obviously, when AB and ab represent portions of different curves.

It is also easily seen, as in Art. 132, that if a point be supposed to move round any closed boundary, the included area is in all cases represented by $\frac{1}{2}\int r^2 d\theta$, taken round the entire boundary, whatever be its form; the elementary angle $d\theta$ being taken with its proper sign throughout.

Again, if we transform to rectangular axes by the relations $x = r \cos \theta$, $y = r \sin \theta$, we get

$$\tan \theta = \frac{y}{x}; \quad \therefore \quad \frac{d\theta}{\cos^2\theta} = \frac{x\,dy - y\,dx}{x^2}.$$

Hence
$$r^2 d\theta = x\,dy - y\,dx;$$

[13 a]

and the area swept out by the radius vector is represented by the integral

$$\frac{1}{2}\int (x\,dy - y\,dx),$$

taken between suitable limits; a result which can also be easily arrived at geometrically.

140. **Area of Elliptic Sector. Lambert's Theorem.**—It is of importance in Astronomy to be able to express the area AFP swept out by the focal radius vector of an ellipse. This can be arrived at by integration from the polar equation of the curve; it is, however, more easily obtained geometrically.

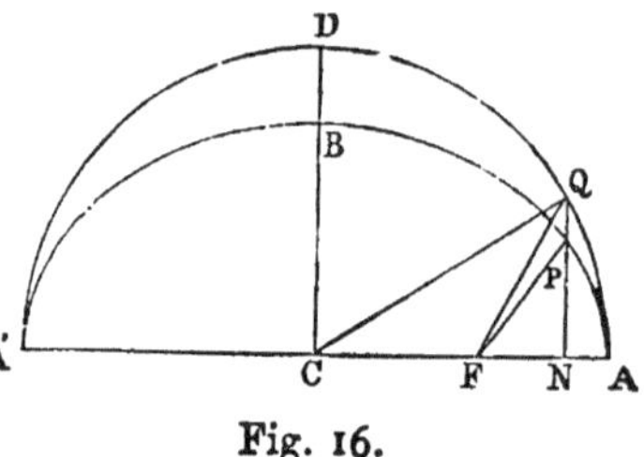

Fig. 16.

For, if the ordinate PN be produced to meet the auxiliary circle in Q, we have

$$\text{area } AFP = \frac{b}{a} \times \text{area } AFQ = \frac{b}{a}(ACQ - CFQ)$$

$$= \frac{ab}{2}(u - e \sin u), \qquad (10)$$

where $u = \angle ACQ$.

By aid of this result, the area of any elliptic sector can be expressed in terms of the focal distances of its extremities, and of the chord joining them.

For (Fig. 17), let QFP represent the sector, and let $FP = \rho$, $FQ = \rho'$, $PQ = \delta$; then, denoting by u and u' the eccentric angles corresponding to P and Q, the area of the sector QFP, by (10), is represented by

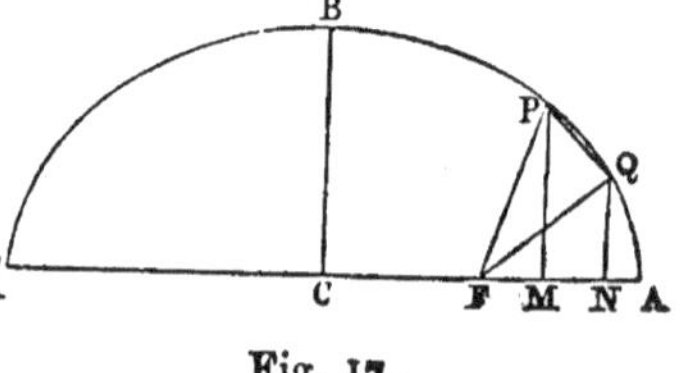

Fig. 17.

$$\frac{ab}{2}\left\{u - u' - e(\sin u - \sin u')\right\}.$$

We proceed to show that this result can be written in the form

$$\frac{ab}{2}\{\phi - \phi' - (\sin\phi - \sin\phi')\}. \tag{11}$$

where ϕ and ϕ' are given by the equations

$$\sin\frac{\phi}{2} = \frac{1}{2}\sqrt{\frac{\rho + \rho' + \delta}{a}}, \qquad \sin\frac{\phi'}{2} = \frac{1}{2}\sqrt{\frac{\rho + \rho' - \delta}{a}}.$$

For, assume that ϕ and ϕ' are determined by the equations

$$u - u' = \phi - \phi', \quad e(\sin u - \sin u') = \sin\phi - \sin\phi'. \tag{a}$$

The latter gives

$$e \sin\frac{u - u'}{2} \cos\frac{u + u'}{2} = \sin\frac{\phi - \phi'}{2} \cos\frac{\phi + \phi'}{2},$$

or by the former, $\quad e \cos\dfrac{u + u'}{2} = \cos\dfrac{\phi + \phi'}{2}.$

Again, since the co-ordinates of P and Q are $a\cos u$, $b\sin u$, and $a\cos u'$, $b\sin u'$, respectively, we have

$$\delta^2 = a^2(\cos u - \cos u')^2 + b^2(\sin u - \sin u')^2$$

$$= 4\sin^2\frac{u - u'}{2}\left(a^2\sin^2\frac{u + u'}{2} + b^2\cos^2\frac{u + u'}{2}\right)$$

$$= 4a^2\sin^2\frac{u - u'}{2}\left(1 - e^2\cos^2\frac{u + u'}{2}\right)$$

$$= 4a^2\sin^2\frac{\phi - \phi'}{2}\sin^2\frac{\phi + \phi'}{2};$$

$$\therefore\ \delta = 2a\sin\frac{\phi - \phi'}{2}\sin\frac{\phi + \phi'}{2} = a(\cos\phi' - \cos\phi). \tag{b}$$

Again, from the ellipse, we have

$$\rho = a(1 - e\cos u), \qquad \rho' = a(1 - e\cos u'),$$

$$\therefore\ \rho + \rho' = 2a - ae(\cos u + \cos u') = 2a - 2ae\cos\frac{u + u'}{2}\cos\frac{u - u'}{2}$$

$$= 2a - 2a\cos\frac{\phi + \phi'}{2}\cos\frac{\phi - \phi'}{2} = 2a - a(\cos\phi + \cos\phi'). \tag{c}$$

Hence, adding and subtracting (*b*) and (*c*), we get

$$\frac{\rho + \rho' + \delta}{a} = 2\left(1 - \cos\phi\right) = 4\sin^2\frac{\phi}{2},$$

$$\frac{\rho + \rho' - \delta}{a} = 2\left(1 - \cos\phi'\right) = 4\sin^2\frac{\phi'}{2},$$

which proves the theorem in question.

Consequently, the *area* of any focal sector of an ellipse can be expressed in terms of the focal distances of its extremities, of the chord which joins them, and of the axes of the curve.*

141. We next proceed to an elementary principle which is sometimes useful in determining areas, viz. :—

The area of any portion of the curve represented by the equation

$$F\left(\frac{x}{a},\ \frac{y}{b}\right) = c$$

is ab times the area of the corresponding portion of the curve

$$F\left(x,\ y\right) = c.$$

This result is obvious, for the former equation is transformed into the latter, by the assumption $\frac{x}{a} = x',\ \frac{y}{b} = y'$; and hence $y\,dx$ becomes $ab\,y'dx'$;

$$\therefore \int y\,dx = ab \int y'\,dx',$$

the integrals being taken through corresponding limits—a result which is also easily shown by projection.

Thus, for example, the area of the ellipse $\frac{x^2}{a^2} + \frac{y^2}{b^2} = 1$

---

* This remarkable result is an extension, by Lambert (in his treatise entitled : *Insigniores orbitæ cometarum proprietates*, published in 1761), of the corresponding formula for a parabola given by Euler in *Miscell. Berolin*, 1743. It furnishes an expression for the time of describing any arc of a planet's orbit, in terms of its chord, the distances of its extremities from the sun, and the major axis of the orbit ; neglecting the disturbing action of the other bodies of the solar system.

reduces to that of the circle; and the area of the hyperbola

$$\frac{x^2}{a^2} - \frac{y^2}{b^2} = 1$$

to that of the equilateral hyperbola $x^2 - y^2 = 1$.

Again, let it be proposed to find the area of the curve

$$\left(\frac{x^2}{a^2} + \frac{y^2}{b^2}\right)^2 = \frac{x^2}{l^2} + \frac{y^2}{m^2}.$$

The transformed equation is

$$(x^2 + y^2)^2 = \frac{a^2 x^2}{l^2} + \frac{b^2 y^2}{m^2};$$

or, in polar co-ordinates,

$$r^2 = \frac{a^2 \cos^2\theta}{l^2} + \frac{b^2 \sin^2\theta}{m^2}.$$

But the whole area of this (Art. 136) is $\dfrac{\pi}{2}\left(\dfrac{a^2}{l^2} + \dfrac{b^2}{m^2}\right)$.

Consequently the whole area of the proposed curve is

$$\frac{\pi}{2} ab \left(\frac{a^2}{l^2} + \frac{b^2}{m^2}\right).$$

It may be remarked that the equations

$$F\left(\frac{x}{a}, \ \frac{y}{a}\right) = c, \qquad F(x, y) = c,$$

represent similar curves, and their corresponding linear dimensions are as $a : 1$. Consequently the areas of similar curves are as the squares of their dimensions; as is also obvious from geometry.

142. **Area of a Pedal Curve.**—If from any point perpendiculars be drawn to the tangents to any curve, the

locus of their feet is a new curve, called the pedal of the original (Diff. Calc., Art. 187).

If p and ω be the polar co-ordinates of N, the foot of the perpendicular from the origin O, then the polar element of area of the locus described by N is plainly $\dfrac{p^2 d\omega}{2}$, and the sectorial area of any portion is accordingly represented by

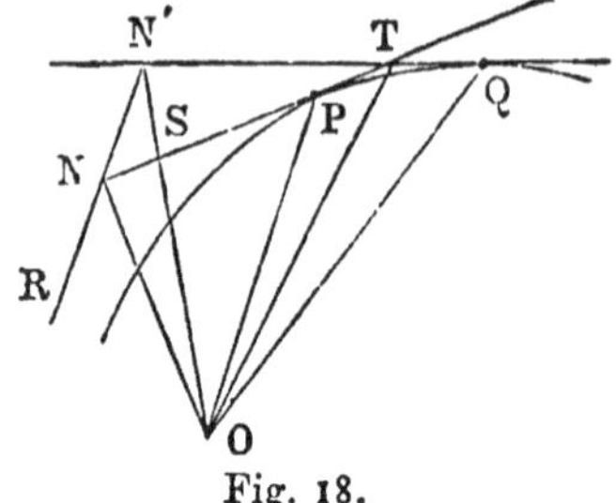
Fig. 18.

$$\frac{1}{2}\int p^2 d\omega,$$

taken between proper limits.

There is another expression for the area of a closed pedal curve which is sometimes useful.

Let S_1 denote the whole area of the pedal, and S that of the original curve; then the area included between the two curves is ultimately equal to the sum of the elements represented by NTN' in the figure.

Hence $\qquad S_1 = S + \Sigma NTN' = S + \dfrac{1}{2}\displaystyle\int PN^2 d\omega.$ $\qquad$ (12)

Again, by the preceding,

$$S_1 = \frac{1}{2}\int ON^2 d\omega.$$

Accordingly, by addition,

$$2S_1 = S + \frac{1}{2}\int OP^2 d\omega. \qquad (13)$$

It is easily seen that equation (12) admits of being stated in the following form:—

The whole area of the pedal of any closed curve is equal to the sum of the areas of the curve and of the pedal of its evolute: both pedals having the same origin.

For, PN is equal in length to the perpendicular from O on the normal at P: and hence $\dfrac{1}{2}PN^2 d\omega$ represents the element of area of the locus described by the foot of this perpendicular, i.e. of the pedal of the evolute of the original curve.

For example, it follows from Art. 136 that *the area of the pedal of the evolute of an ellipse is $\frac{\pi}{2}(a - b)^2$, the centre being origin.*

143. **Area of Pedal of Ellipse for any Origin.—**
Suppose O to be the pedal origin, and OM, OM' perpendiculars on two parallel tangents to the ellipse; draw CN the perpendicular from the centre C; let $OM = p_1$, OM' $= p_2$, $CN = p$, $OC = c$, $\angle OCA$ $= a$, $\angle ACN = \omega$; then

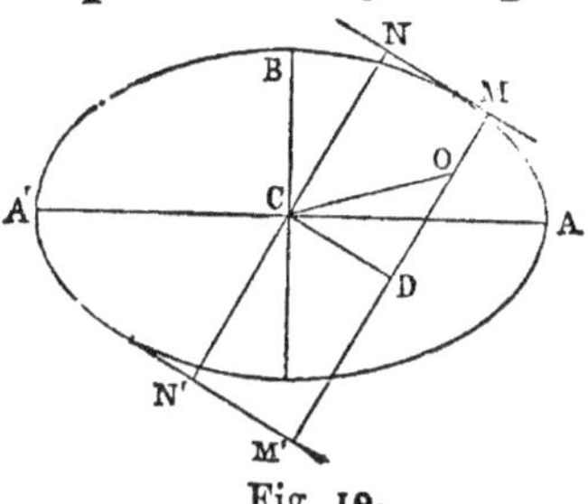

Fig. 19.

$$p_1 = MD - OD = p - c \cos (\omega - a),$$

$$p_2 = p + c \cos (\omega - a).$$

Again, the whole area of the pedal is

$$\frac{1}{2} \int_0^\pi (p_1^2 + p_2^2)\, d\omega = \int_0^\pi \{p^2 + c^2 \cos^2 (\omega - a)\}\, d\omega$$

$$= \int_0^\pi p^2 d\omega + c^2 \int_0^\pi \cos^2 (\omega - a)\, d\omega = \frac{\pi}{2}(a^2 + b^2 + c^2). \quad (14)$$

That is, the area of the pedal with respect to O as origin exceeds the area of its pedal with respect to C by half the area of the circle whose radius is OC.

If the origin O lie outside the ellipse, the pedal consists of two loops intersecting at O and lying one inside the other; and in that case the expression in (14) represents the sum of the areas of the two loops, as can be easily seen.

The result established above is a particular case of a general theorem of Steiner, which we next proceed to consider.

144. **Steiner's Theorem on Areas of Pedal Curves.**
Suppose A to be the whole area of the pedal of any closed curve with respect to any internal origin O, and A' the area

of its pedal with respect to another origin O'; then, if p and p' be the lengths of the perpendiculars from O and O' on a tangent to the curve, we have

$$A = \frac{1}{2}\int_0^{2\pi} p^2 d\omega, \quad A' = \frac{1}{2}\int_0^{2\pi} p'^2 d\omega.$$

Also, adopting the notation of the last article,

$$p' = p - c\cos(\omega - a) = p - x\cos\omega - y\sin\omega\,;$$

where x, y represent the co-ordinates of O' with respect to rectangular axes drawn through O. Hence we get

$$A' - A = \frac{1}{2}\int_0^{2\pi} (x\cos\omega + y\sin\omega)^2 d\omega$$

$$- x\int_0^{2\pi} p\cos\omega\, d\omega - y\int_0^{2\pi} p\sin\omega\, d\omega.$$

But $\displaystyle\int_0^{2\pi}\cos^2\omega\, d\omega = \pi, \quad \int_0^{2\pi}\sin^2\omega\, d\omega = \pi, \quad \int_0^{2\pi}\sin\omega\cos\omega\, d\omega = 0.$

Also, for a given curve, $\displaystyle\int_0^{2\pi} p\cos\omega\, d\omega$ and $\displaystyle\int_0^{2\pi} p\sin\omega\, d\omega$ are constants when O is given. Denoting their values by g and h, we have

$$A' - A = \frac{\pi}{2}(x^2 + y^2) - gx - hy. \tag{15}$$

This equation shows that if O be fixed, *the locus of the origin O', for which the area of the pedal of a closed curve is constant, is a circle.*[*] The centre of this circle is the same, whatever be the given area, and all the circles got by varying the pedal area are concentric.

---

* It can be seen, without difficulty, from the demonstration given above, that when the curve is not closed, the locus of the origin for pedals of equal area is a conic: a theorem due to Prof. Raabe, of Zurich. See *Crelle's Journal,* vol. l., p. 193.

The student will find a discussion of these theorems by Prof. Hirst in the *Transactions of the Royal Society,* 1863, in which he has investigated the corresponding relations connecting the volumes of the pedals of surfaces.

If the origin O be supposed taken at the centre of this circle, the constants g and h will disappear; and, in this case, the pedal area is a minimum, and *the difference between the areas of the pedals is equal to half the area of the circle whose radius is the distance between the pedal origins.*

For example, if we take the origin at the centre, the pedal of a circle, whose radius is a, is the circle itself. For any other origin the pedal is a limaçon; hence the whole area of a limaçon is $\pi\left(a^2 + \dfrac{b^2}{2}\right)$, as found in Art. 136, Ex. 5.

145. Areas of Roulettes on Rectilinear Bases. The connexion between the areas of roulettes and of pedals is contained in a very elegant theorem,* also due to Steiner, which may be stated as follows:—

When a closed curve rolls on a right line, the area between the right line and the roulette generated in a complete revolution by any point invariably connected with the rolling curve is double the area of the pedal of the rolling curve, this pedal being taken with respect to the generating point as origin.

To prove this, suppose O to be the describing point in any

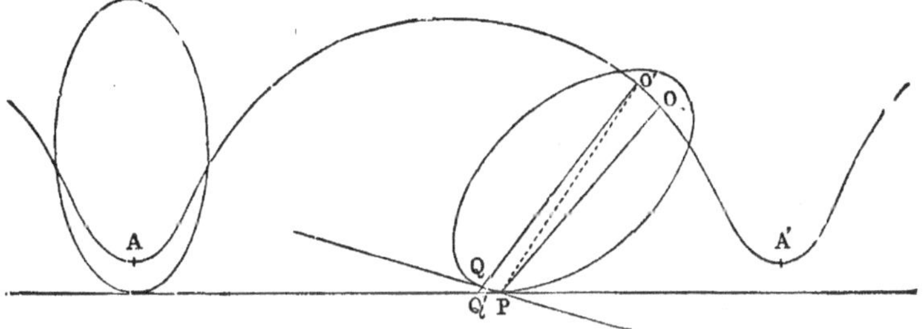

Fig 20.

position of the rolling curve, and P the corresponding point of contact. Let O' represent an infinitely near position of the describing point, Q' the corresponding point of contact, and Q

---

a point on the curve such that $PQ = PQ'$; then Q is the point which coincides with Q' in the new position of the rolling curve; and, denoting the angle between the tangents at P and Q (the angle of contingence) by $d\omega$, we have $OPO' = d\omega$, since we may regard the curve as turning round P at the instant (Diff. Calc., Art. 275).

Moreover, QQ' ultimately is infinitely small in comparison with QP, and consequently the elementary area $OPQ'O'$ is ultimately the sum of the areas POO' and $QO'P$, neglecting an area which is infinitely small in comparison with either of these areas.

Again, if $OP = r$, we have $POO' = \dfrac{r^2 d\omega}{2}$, and area $QO'P$ $= QOP$ in the limit.

Also the sum of the elements QOP in an entire revolution is equal to the area (S) of the rolling curve. Consequently the entire area of the roulette described by O is

$$S + \tfrac{1}{2} \int r^2 d\omega.$$

But we have already seen (13) that this is double the area of the pedal of the curve with respect to the point O; which establishes our proposition.

Again, from Art. 144, it follows that there is one point in any closed curve for which the entire area of the corresponding roulette is a minimum. Also, *the area of the roulette described by any other point exceeds that of the minimum roulette by the area of the circle whose radius is the distance between the points.*

For instance, if a circle roll on a right line, its centre describes a parallel line, and the area between these lines after a complete revolution is equal to the rectangle under the radius of the circle and its circumference; i.e. is $2\pi a^2$; denoting the radius by a.

Consequently, for a point on the circumference, the area generated is $2\pi a^2 + \pi a^2$, or $3\pi a^2$; which agrees with the area found already for the cycloid.

In like manner, by Steiner's theorem, the area of the ordinary cycloid is the same as that of the cardioid: and the area of a prolate or curtate cycloid the same as that of a limaçon.

Again, if an ellipse roll on a right line, the area of the path described by any point can be immediately obtained.

For example, the pedal of an ellipse with respect to a focus is the circle described on its axis major. Hence, *if an ellipse roll upon a right line, the area of the roulette described by its focus in a complete revolution is double the area of the auxiliary circle.* Also, the area of the roulette described by the centre of the ellipse is equal to the sum of the circles described on the axes of the ellipse as diameters, and is less than the area of the roulette described by any other point.

146. **General Case of Area of Roulette.**—If the curve, instead of rolling on a right line, roll on another curve, it is easily seen that the method of proof given in the last article still holds; provided we take, instead of $d\omega$, the sum of the angles of contingence of the two curves at the point P.

Hence the element of area OPO' is in this case

$$\frac{1}{2} OP^2 d\omega \left(1 + \frac{d\omega'}{d\omega} \right), \text{ or } \frac{1}{2} OP^2 d\omega \left(1 + \frac{\rho}{\rho'} \right),$$

where ρ and ρ' are the radii of curvature at P of the rolling and fixed curves, respectively.

Hence it follows that the area between the roulette, the fixed curve, and the two extreme normals, after a complete revolution, is represented by

$$S + \frac{1}{2} \int r^2 d\omega \left(1 + \frac{\rho}{\rho'} \right).$$

If a closed curve roll on a curve identical with itself, having corresponding points always in contact, the formula for the area generated becomes

$$S + \int r^2 d\omega.$$

In this case the area generated is four times that of the corresponding pedal; a result which appears at once geometrically by drawing a figure.

EXAMPLES.

1. If A be the area of a loop of the curve $r^m = a^m \cos m\theta$, and A_1 the area of its pedal with respect to the polar origin, prove that

$$A_1 = \left(1 + \frac{m}{2}\right) A.$$

It is easily seen, as in Diff. Calc., Art. 190, that the angle between the radius vector and the perpendicular on the tangent is $m\theta$; and $\therefore \omega = (m + 1)\theta$

Hence, by Art. 142,

$$2A_1 = A + \frac{m + 1}{2} \int r^2 d\theta = (m + 2) A.$$

2. If a circle of radius b roll on a circle of radius a, and if A denote the area, after a complete revolution, between the fixed circle, the roulette described by any point, and the extreme normals; and if A' be the area of the pedal of the circle with respect to the generating point, prove that

$$Aa + Bb = 2(a + b) A'.$$

where B is the area of the rolling circle.

3. Apply this result to find the area included between the fixed circle and the arc of an epicycloid extending from one cusp to the next.

147. **Holditch's Theorem.***—If a line CC' of a given length move with its extremities on two fixed closed curves, to find, in terms of the areas of the two fixed curves, an expression for the whole area of the curve generated, in a complete revolution, by any given point P situated on the moving line.

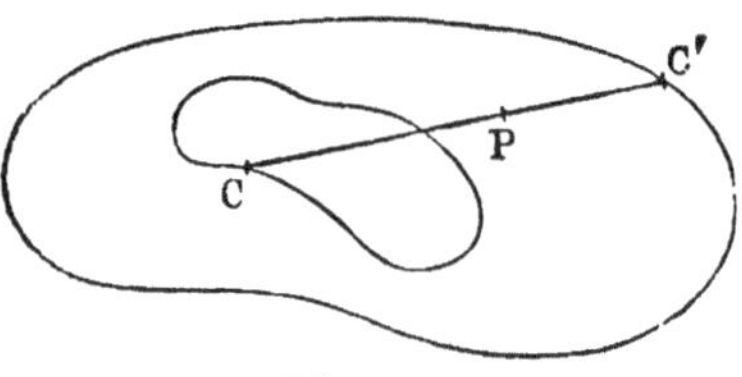

Fig. 21.

Let $CP = c$, $PC' = c'$, and suppose (x_1, y_1), (x, y), and (x_2, y_2) to be the co-ordinates of the points C, P, and C', respectively, with reference to any rectangular axes.

---

* This simple and elegant theorem appeared, in a modified form, as the Prize Question, by Mr. Holditch, under the name of "Petrarch," in the Lady's and Gentleman's Diary for the year 1858. The first proof given above is due to Mr. Woolhouse, and contains his extension of Mr. Holditch's theorem.

Then, if θ be the angle made by CC' with the axis of y, we have evidently

$$x_1 = x - c \sin \theta, \quad y_1 = y - c \cos \theta,$$

$$x_2 = x + c' \sin \theta, \quad y_2 = y + c' \cos \theta.$$

Hence we have

$$y_1 dx_1 = y\,dx - c \cos \theta\,(dx + y\,d\theta) + c^2 \cos^2 \theta\,d\theta\,;$$

$$y_2 dx_2 = y\,dx + c' \cos \theta\,(dx + y\,d\theta) + c'^2 \cos^2 \theta\,d\theta.$$

Multiplying the former equation by c', and the latter by c, and adding, we get

$$c' y_1 dx_1 + c y_2 dx_2 = (c + c')\,y\,dx + (c + c')\,cc'\,\cos^2 \theta\,d\theta\,;$$

$$\therefore\ c' \int y_1 dx_1 + c \int y_2 dx_2 = (c + c') \int y\,dx + (c + c')\,cc' \int \cos^2 \theta\,d\theta.$$

If we suppose the rod to make a complete revolution, so as to return to its original position, and if we denote by (C), (C'), (P), the areas of the curves described by the points C, C', and P, respectively, we shall have (since in this case the angle θ revolves through 2π)

$$c'\,(C) + c\,(C') = (c + c')(P) + \pi\,(c + c')\,cc',$$

or
$$\frac{c'\,(C) + c\,(C')}{c + c'} = (P) + \pi cc'. \tag{16}$$

This determines the area (P) in terms of the areas (C), (C') and of the segments c, c'.

When the extremities C, C' move on the same identical curve we have $(C) = (C')$, and hence $(C) - (P) = \pi cc'$.

Consequently, if *a chord of given length move inside any closed curve, having a tracing point P at the distances c and c' from its ends, the area comprised between the two curves is equal to* $\pi cc'$.

More generally, if the extremities C, C' move on curves of equal area, we have, as before,

$$(C) - (P) = \pi cc'. \tag{17}$$

Should the extremities, instead of revolving, oscillate back to their former positions, then $(C) = 0$, $(C') = 0$, and

$\therefore (P) = -\pi cc'$. The negative sign implies that the area is described in a direction contrary to that in which the rod revolves.

Again, if the rod returns to its original position after n revolutions, the limits for θ become o and $2n\pi$, and equation (16) becomes

$$\frac{c'(C) + c(C')}{c + c'} = (P) + n\pi cc'. \tag{18}$$

If $(C) = (C')$, this gives

$$(C) - (P) = n\pi cc'. \tag{19}$$

If the line oscillate back to its former position, without making a revolution, we have $n = 0$, and (19) becomes

$$(C) = (P).$$

Hence, in this case, if two points describe curves of equal area, then any point on the line joining these points describes a curve of the same area.

The theorem in (16) can also be proved simply in another manner, as follows:—

Let O denote the point of intersection of the moving line CC' with its infinitely near position; that is to say, the point of contact with its envelope; and let $OP = r$. Adopting the same notation as before, let (O) represent the area of the envelope, and it is easily seen that

$$(C) - (O) = \tfrac{1}{2}\int_0^{2\pi}(OC)^2\,d\theta = \tfrac{1}{2}\int_0^{2\pi}(c - r)^2\,d\theta,$$

$$(C') - (O) = \tfrac{1}{2}\int_0^{2\pi}(OC')^2\,d\theta = \tfrac{1}{2}\int_0^{2\pi}(c' + r)^2\,d\theta,$$

$$(P) - (O) = \tfrac{1}{2}\int(OP)^2\,d\theta = \tfrac{1}{2}\int r^2\,d\theta\,;$$

hence

$$c'(C) + c(C') - (c + c')(P) = \tfrac{1}{2}\int_0^{2\pi}\{c'(c - r)^2 + c(c' + r)^2 - (c + c')r^2\}\,d\theta$$

$$= cc'(c + c')\pi,$$

as before.

A remarkable extension of Holditch's theorem was given by Mr. E. B. Elliott, in the *Messenger of Mathematics,* February, 1878.

Mr. Elliott supposed the length of the moving line $C'C$ to vary, but that it is in all positions divided in the constant ratio $m : n$ in a point P.

Then, if C travel round the perimeter of any closed area (C), and C' move simultaneously round another area (C'), the two motions being quite independent and subject to no restrictions whatever, except that both are continuous, having no abrupt passage from one position to another finitely differing from it, then P will travel simultaneously round the perimeter of another closed area (P).

Adopting the same notation as before, we have

$$(m + n)\, x = m x_1 + n x_2, \quad (m + n)\, y = m y_1 + n y_2 ;$$

$$\therefore\ (m + n)^2 y\, dx = (m y_1 + n y_2)(m\, dx_1 + n\, dx_2)$$

$$= m^2 y_1 dx_1 + n^2 y_2 dx_2 + mn\, (y_2 dx_1 + y_1 dx_2)$$

$$= (m + n)(m y_1\, dx_1 + n y_2\, dx_2) - mn\, (y_2 - y_1)\, d\, (x_2 - x_1).$$

Integrating for a complete circuit, and dividing by $(m + n)$, we have

$$(m + n)\,(P) = m\,(C) + n\,(C') - \frac{mn}{m + n} \int (y_2 - y_1)\, d\,(x_2 - x_1). \quad (20)$$

This result is stated as follows by Mr. Elliott:—

Through any fixed point in the plane of a closed area S let radii vectores be drawn to all points in its perimeter, and let chords AB, parallel and equal to the radii vectores, be placed with one extremity A in each case in the perimeter of a closed area (A), and the other B on that of another (B); then, if the points A, B, travel respectively all round the perimeters, and do not in either case return to their first positions from the same sides as that towards which they left them; and, if

(C) represent the area described by a point always dividing BA in the constant ratio $m : n$, then the areas (A), (B), (C), (S) are connected by the following relation :

$$(C) = \frac{m\,(A) + n\,(B)}{m + n} - \frac{mn}{(m + n)^2}\,(S). \qquad (21)$$

This follows immediately from (20) by altering the notation.

Areas described in opposite directions of rotation must be taken with opposite signs.

For particular modifications in this result, as also for its extension to surfaces, the student is referred to Mr. Elliott's paper ; as also to Mr. Leudesdorf's papers in the same Journal.

147 (a). **Kempe's Theorem.**—We next proceed to the consideration of a singularly elegant theorem[*] discovered by Mr. Kempe, and which may be stated as follows :—

If one plane sliding upon another start from any position, move in any manner, and return to its original position after making one or more complete revolutions; then every point in the moving area describes a closed curve, and *the locus, in the moving plane, of points which describe equal areas is a circle; and by varying the area we get a system of concentric circles* for loci.

This result can be readily deduced from Holditch's theorem, for if we suppose A, B, C, to be three points which generate equal areas; it can easily be seen that any fourth point, D, which generates the same area, lies on the circle circumscribing ABC.

Let AB and CD intersect in P, then, let (P) represent the area described by the point P, as before; and n the number of revolutions made before AB returns to its original position : then we have, by (19), denoting by

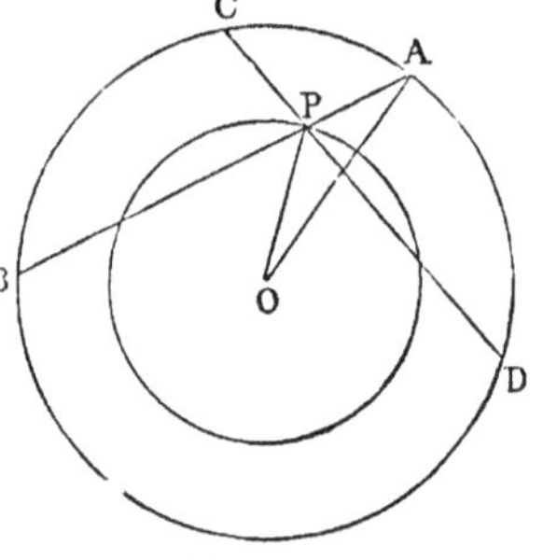

Fig. 22.

---

[*] *Messenger of Mathematics*, July, 1878.

(C) the common area described by each of the points $A, B, C, D,$

$$(C) - (P) = n\pi\, AP \cdot PB,$$

and, by same theorem,

$$(C) - (P) = n\pi\, CP \cdot PD;$$

hence

$$AP \cdot PB = CP \cdot PD;$$

consequently $A, B, C, D,$ lie on the circumference of the same circle.

Again, let O be the centre of this circle, and join OP and OA, then the preceding equation gives

$$(C) - (P) = n\pi\,(OA^2 - OP^2).$$

Hence all points which describe an area equal to that of (P) lie on a circle, having O for centre, and OP for radius, which establishes the second part of the theorem.

For the effect of two or more loops in the area described by a moving point see Art. 132.

148. **Areas by Approximation.**—In many cases it is necessary to approximate to the value of the area included within a closed contour. The usual method is by drawing a convenient number of parallel ordinates at equal intervals; then, when a rough approximation is sufficient, we may regard the area of the curve as that of the polygon got by joining the points of intersection of the parallel ordinates with the curve. Hence, if h be the common distance between the ordinates, and if

$$y_0,\ y_1,\ y_2,\ \&c.,\ y_n,$$

represent the system of parallel ordinates, the area of the polygon, since it consists of a number of trapeziums of equal breadth, is plainly represented by

$$h\left\{\frac{y_0 + y_n}{2} + y_1 + y_2 + \&c. + y_{n-1}\right\}.$$

$$[14\,a]$$

Hence the rule: *add together the halves of the extreme ordinates, and the whole of the intermediate ordinates, and multiply the result by the common interval.*

When a nearer approximation is required, the method next in simplicity supposes the curve to consist of a number of parabolic arcs; each parabola having its axis parallel to the equidistant ordinates, and being determined by three of those ordinates.

To find the area of the parabola passing through the points whose ordinates are y_0, y_1, y_2; let $y = a + \beta x + \gamma x^2$ be the equation of the parabola, and, for simplicity, assume the origin at the foot of the intermediate ordinate y_1, then we have

$$y_0 = a - \beta h + \gamma h^2, \quad y_1 = a, \quad y_2 = a + \beta h + \gamma h^2.$$

Again, the area between the first and third ordinate is

$$\int_{-h}^{h} (a + \beta x + \gamma x^2)\, dx = 2h\left(a + \gamma\, \frac{h^2}{3}\right).$$

But $y_0 + y_2 = 2y_1 + 2\gamma h^2$: hence the area in question is

$$\frac{h}{3} \left\{ y_0 + 4y_1 + y_2 \right\}.$$

Now, if we suppose the number of intervals n to be even, and add the different parabolic areas, we get, as an approximation to the area, the expression

$$\frac{h}{3} \left\{ y_0 + y_n + 4\left(y_1 + y_3 + \&c. + y_{n-1}\right) + 2\left(y_2 + y_4 + \&c. + y_{n-2}\right) \right\}.$$

Hence the rule: *add together the first and last ordinates, twice every second intermediate ordinate, and four times each remaining ordinate; and multiply by one-third of the common interval.*

We get a closer approximation by supposing the number of equal intervals a multiple of 3, and regarding the curve as a series of parabolæ of the third degree, each being determined by four equidistant ordinates. To find the area corresponding to one of these parabolic curves, let y_0, y_1, y_2, y_3 be four equidistant ordinates, and for convenience assume the origin midway between y_1 and y_2; then if the equation of the parabolic curve be

$$y = a + \beta x + \gamma x^2 + \delta x^3,$$

and the common interval on the axis of x be denoted by $2h$, we have

$$y_0 = a - 3\beta h + 9\gamma h^2 - 27\delta h^3,$$
$$y_1 = a - \beta h + \gamma h^2 - \delta h^3,$$
$$y_2 = a + \beta h + \gamma h^2 + \delta h^3,$$
$$y_3 = a + 3\beta h + 9\gamma h^2 + 27\delta h^3.$$

Hence $y_0 + y_3 = 2(a + 9\gamma h^2), \quad y_1 + y_2 = 2(a + \gamma h^2).$

Again, the parabolic area between y_0 and y_3 is

$$\int_{-3h}^{3h} (a + \beta x + \gamma x^2 + \delta x^3)\,dx = 3h(2a + 6\gamma h^2).$$

Substituting in this the values of a and γ obtained from the two preceding equations, the expression for the area becomes

$$\frac{3h}{4}\{y_0 + y_3 + 3(y_1 + y_2)\}.$$

If the corresponding expressions be added together, we easily arrive at the following rule:*—Add together the first and last ordinates, *twice* every third intermediate ordinate, and *thrice* each remaining ordinate; and multiply by $\frac{3}{8}$ths of the common interval.

It is readily seen that these rules also apply to the approximation to any closed area, by drawing a system of lines, parallel and equidistant, and adopting the intercepts made by the curve instead of the ordinates, in each rule.

Since every definite integral may be represented by a

---

* This and the preceding are commonly called " Simpson's rules " for calculating areas; they were however previously noticed by Newton (see *Opuscula. Method. Diff.*, Prop. 6, scholium) as a particular application of the method of interpolation. By taking seven equidistant ordinates, Mr. Weddle (*Camb. and Dub. Math. Jour.*, 1854), obtained the following simple and important rule for finding the area:—*To five times the sum of the even ordinates add the middle ordinate and all the odd ordinates, multiply the sum by three-tenths of the common interval, and the product will be the required area, approximately.* The proof, which is too long for insertion here, will be found in Mr. Weddle's memoir: and also, with applications, in Boole's *Calculus of Finite Differences.* The student is referred to Bertrand's *Calc. Int.*, l. i, ch. xii., for more general and accurate methods of approximation by Cotes and Gauss.

curvilinear area, the methods given above are applicable to the approximate determination of any such integral.

In practice the accuracy of these methods is increased by increasing the number of intervals.

149. Planimeters.—Several mechanical contrivances have been introduced for the purpose of practically estimating the area inclosed within any curved boundary. Such instruments are called Planimeters. The simplest and most elegant is that of Professor Amsler of Schaffhausen. It consists of two arms jointed together so as to move in perfect freedom in one plane. A point at the extremity of one arm is made a fixed centre round which the instrument turns; and a wheel is fixed to, and turns on the other arm as an axis, and records by its revolution the area of the figure traced out by a point on this arm. From its construction it is plain that the revolving wheel registers only the motion which is perpendicular to the moving arm on which it revolves.

In the practical application of the instrument it is necessary that the two arms, CA and AB, should return to their original position after the tracing point B has been moved round the entire boundary of the required area.

We shall commence by showing that the length registered by the wheel while B has moved round the entire closed area is independent of the wheel's position on the moving arm; *i.e.* is the same as if the wheel be supposed placed at the joint.

To prove this, suppose P to represent the point on the arm at which the centre of the revolving wheel is situated. Let $A'B'$ represent a new position of AB very near to AB, and P' the corresponding position of the point P. Draw PN perpendicular to $A'B'$; then PN represents the length registered by the wheel while the arm moves from AB to the infinitely near position $A'B'$.

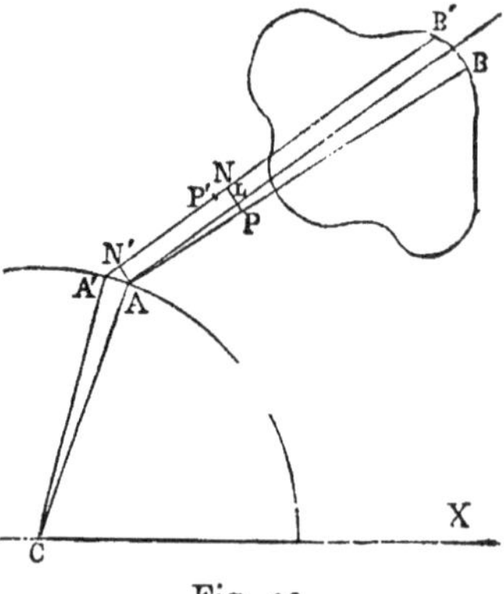

Fig. 23.

Next, draw AN' perpendicular, and AL parallel, to $A'B'$.

Let $PN = ds'$, $AN' = ds$, $AP = c$, $PAL = d\phi$; then $PN = PL + AN'$, or $ds' = ds + c\,d\phi$.

Now, if we suppose AB after a complete circuit of the curve to return to its original position, we have obviously $\Sigma(d\phi) = 0$; and therefore $\Sigma(ds') = \Sigma(ds)$, i.e. the whole length registered by the revolving wheel at P is the same as if it were placed at A.

Next, let x and y be the co-ordinates of B with respect to rectangular axes drawn through C, and let $AC = a$, $AB = b$, $\angle ACX = \theta$; and suppose ϕ the angle which BA produced makes with the axis of x; then we shall have

$$x = a\cos\theta + b\cos\phi, \quad y = a\sin\theta + b\sin\phi.$$

Hence $\quad x\,dy - y\,dx = a^2 d\theta + b^2 d\phi + ab\cos(\theta - \phi)\,d(\theta + \phi).$

Also $\quad ds = AN' = AA'\sin AA'N = a\,d\theta\cos(\theta - \phi).$

But $\qquad\qquad \theta + \phi = 2\theta - (\theta - \phi);$

$$\therefore\ ab\cos(\theta - \phi)\,d(\theta + \phi)$$
$$= 2ab\cos(\theta - \phi)d\theta - ab\cos(\theta - \phi)\,d(\theta - \phi)$$
$$= 2b\,ds - ab\cos(\theta - \phi)\,d(\theta - \phi).$$

Consequently

$$x\,dy - y\,dx = a^2 d\theta + b^2 d\phi + 2b\,ds - ab\cos(\theta - \phi)\,d(\theta - \phi).$$

But, by Art. 139, the area traced out by B in a complete revolution is represented by $\frac{1}{2}\int(x\,dy - y\,dx)$ taken around the entire curve.

Also, since AC and AB return to their original positions, the integrals of the terms $a^2 d\theta$, $b^2 d\phi$ and $ab\cos(\theta - \phi)\,d(\theta - \phi)$ disappear; and hence the area in question is equal to bS, where S denotes the entire length registered by the revolving wheel.

On account of the importance of the principle of this instrument, the following proof, for which I am indebted to Prof. Ball, based on elementary geometrical principles, is also added.

Let C, A, B represent, as before, the positions of the fixed centre, the joint, and the tracing point, respectively; and suppose R to represent the position of the roller, or revolving wheel; then draw CP and RS perpendicular to AB.

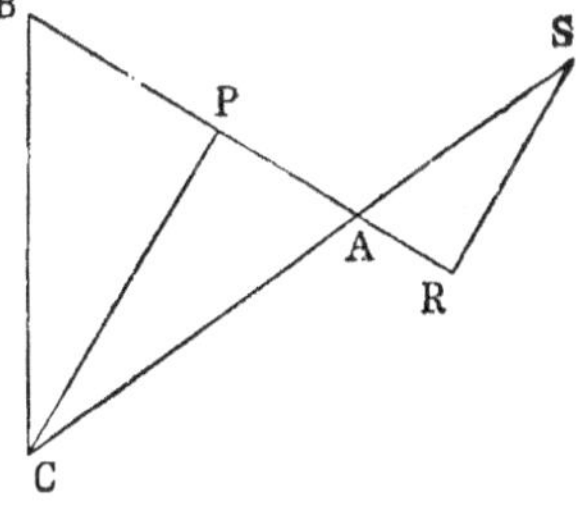

Fig. 24.

Let $\quad AC = a,\ AB = b,\ AR = l,\ BC = r.$

Now, if the instrument be rotated about C through an angle θ without altering the angle CAB, it is easily seen that the circumference of the roller is rotated through an arc represented by

$$PR \cdot \theta = \left(l + \frac{a^2 + b^2 - r^2}{2b}\right)\theta.$$

Again, if the instrument be rotated about S through a small angle the roller does not revolve. Hence a curve can be drawn through B, such that, if the tracing point B be moved along it, the roller will not revolve.

Now, let $\lambda\mu,\ \lambda'\mu'$ be the two adjacent circles described with C as centre, and suppose $\alpha\alpha'$ and $\beta\beta'$ two adjacent *non-rolling* curves, such as just stated: and suppose the tracing point B to move round the indefinitely small area $\alpha\alpha'\beta\beta$: then the arc through which the roller has turned is represented by

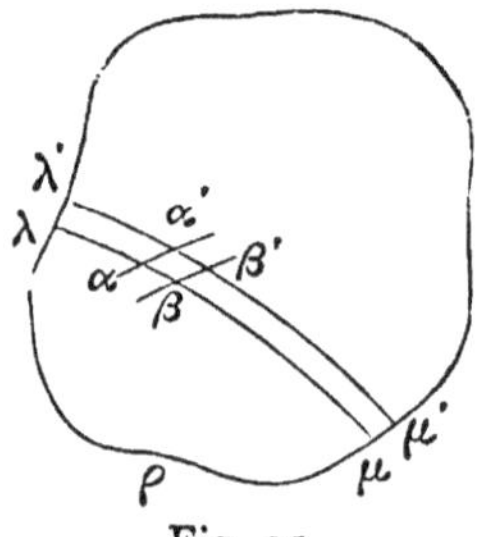

Fig. 25.

$$\left(l + \frac{a^2 + b^2 - r^2}{2b}\right)\delta\theta - \left(l + \frac{a^2 + b^2 - (r + \delta r)^2}{2b}\right)\delta\theta$$

$$= \frac{r\,\delta r\,\delta\theta}{b} = \text{area of } \frac{\alpha\alpha'\beta'\beta}{b},$$

since $\alpha\beta = r\,\delta\theta$; and $\delta r = \alpha\alpha' \sin\beta$.

Now suppose the instrument works correctly for the area $\lambda\lambda'\alpha'\alpha$, then it will work correctly for the area $\lambda\lambda'\beta'\beta$; for, start from α to λ, λ', α', then the area $\alpha\lambda\lambda'\alpha'$ must be registered, since the roller does not turn in moving from α' to α; proceed then from α' to β', β, α, then, by what has been just proved, the area $\alpha'\beta'\beta\alpha$ will be added. Hence the instrument will work correctly for the strip $\lambda\lambda'\mu'\mu$.

Again, suppose the instrument works correctly for the area $\lambda\mu\rho$, then it will work correctly for $\lambda'\mu'\rho$; for suppose we start from λ to ρ, μ, and back to λ : then start from λ to

μ, μ', λ' and λ; the two journeys from λ to μ and μ to λ will neutralize each other, and it follows that if the instrument works correctly for the area $\lambda\mu\rho$, it will work correctly for the area $\lambda'\mu'\rho$: hence, if the instrument works correctly for any portion of the area, however small, it works correctly for the entire area.

The student will find a description of Amsler's Planimeter, with another mode of demonstration, in a communication by Mr. F. J. Bramwell, C.E., to the British Association.—See Report, 1872, pp. 401–412.

EXAMPLES.

1. Find the whole area between the curve

$$x^2 y^2 + a^2 b^2 = a^2 y^2$$

and its asymptotes. *Ans.* $2\pi ab.$

2. Find the whole area of the curve

$$a^2 y^4 = x^4 (a^2 - x^2).$$
,, $\dfrac{8a^3}{5}.$

3. Find the whole area of the curve

$$\left(\frac{x}{a}\right)^2 + \left(\frac{y}{b}\right)^{\frac{2}{3}} = 1.$$
,, $\dfrac{3}{4}\pi ab.$

4. Find the whole area included between the folium of Descartes

$$x^3 + y^3 - 3axy = 0$$

and its asymptote. *Ans.* $\dfrac{3a^2}{2}.$

5. In the logarithmic curve $y = a^x$, prove that the area between the axis of x and any two ordinates is proportional to the difference between the ordinates.

6. Find the area of a loop of the curve

$$r = a \cos n\theta.$$
Ans. $\dfrac{\pi a^2}{n}.$

7. Find the area of a loop of the curve

$$r = a \cos n\theta + b \sin n\theta.$$
,, $(a^2 + b^2)\dfrac{\pi}{n}.$

The equation of the curve may be written in the form

$$r = \sqrt{a^2 + b^2}\,\cos(n\theta + a),$$

where $\tan a = -\dfrac{b}{a}$; and consequently its area can be found from the preceding example.

8. Find the area of a loop of the curve

$$r^2 = a^2 \cos n\theta + b^2 \sin n\theta.$$
Ans. $\dfrac{\sqrt{a^4 + b^4}}{n}.$

9. Find the area of the tractrix.

The characteristic property of the tractrix is that the intercept on a tangent to the curve between its point of contact and a fixed right line is constant.

Denoting the constant by a, and taking the origin O at the point for which the tangent OA is perpendicular to the axis, we have, P being any point on the curve

$$PT = a, \quad PN = y,$$

$$\frac{dy}{dx} = -\tan PTN = -\frac{y}{\sqrt{a^2 - y^2}};$$

$$\therefore \; y\,dx = -\sqrt{a^2 - y^2}\,dy.$$

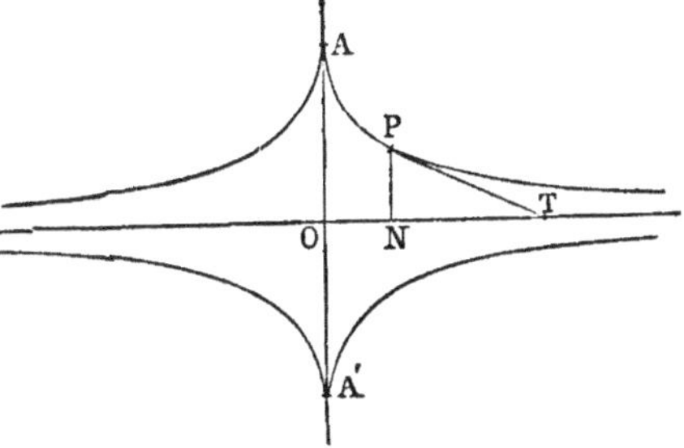
Fig. 26.

Hence the element of the area of the tractrix is equal to that of a circle of radius a.

It follows immediately that the whole area between the four infinite branches of the tractrix is equal to πa^2. This example furnishes an instance of our being able to determine the area of a curve from a geometrical property of the curve, without a previous determination of its equation.

If the equation of the tractrix be required, it can be derived from its differential equation

$$dx = -\frac{\sqrt{a^2 - y^2}\,dy}{y},$$

from which we get

$$x + \sqrt{a^2 - y^2} = a \log \frac{a + \sqrt{a^2 - y^2}}{y}.$$

That the equation of the tractrix depends on logarithms was noticed by Newton. See his Second Epistle to Oldenburg (Oct. 1676). This was, I believe, the first example of the determination of the equation of a curve by integration; or, what at the time was called the *inverse method of tangents*.

10. If each focal radius vector of an ellipse be produced a constant length c, show that the area between the curve so formed and the ellipse is $\pi c(2b + c)$, b being the semi-axis minor of the ellipse.

11. Find the area of a loop of the curve $r^n = a^n \cos n\theta$.

$$Ans. \quad \frac{a^2}{2}\sqrt{\pi}\,\frac{\Gamma\left(\frac{1}{2} + \frac{1}{n}\right)}{\Gamma\left(\frac{1}{n}\right)}.$$

12. If a right line carrying three tracing points A, B, C, move in any manner in a plane, returning to its original position after making a complete revolution; and if (A), (B), (C) represent the entire areas of the closed curves described by the points A, B, C, respectively, prove that

$$BC \times (A) + CA \times (B) + AB \times (C) + \pi . AB . BC . CA = 0,$$

in which the lines AB, BC, &c., are taken with their proper signs; i.e., $AB = -BA$, &c.

13. A, B, C, D, are four points rigidly connected together, and moving in any way in a plane ; if they describe closed curves, of areas (A), (B), (C), (D), respectively; and if x, y, z, be the areolar co-ordinates of D referred to the triangle ABC, prove that

$$(D) = x\,(A) + y\,(B) + z\,(C) - \pi t^2,$$

where t is the length of the tangent from D to the circle circumscribed to the triangle ABC. Mr. Leudesdorf, *Messenger of Mathematics*, 1878.

This follows immediately: for let P be the point of intersection of the lines AB and CD, then, by (18), we get a relation between (A), (B), and (P); and also between (C), (D), and (P). If P be eliminated between these equations we get the required result.

14. Show that a corresponding equation connects the areas of the pedals of any given closed curve with respect to four points A, B, C, D, taken respectively as pedal origin. *Mr. Leudesdorf.*

15. If a curve be referred to its radius vector r and the perpendicular p on the tangent, prove that its area is represented by

$$\frac{1}{2} \int \frac{pr\,dr}{\sqrt{r^2 - p^2}}.$$

16. A chord of constant length (c) moves about within a parabola, and tangents are drawn at its extremities; find the total area between the parabola and the locus of intersection of the tangents.

$$\text{Ans. } \frac{\pi c^2}{2}.$$

17. From the centre of an ellipse a tangent is drawn to a semicircle described on an ordinate to the axis major; prove that the polar equation of the locus of the point of contact is

$$r^2 = \frac{a^2 b^2}{b^2 + (a^2 + b^2)\tan^2\theta};$$

and that the whole area of the locus is

$$\frac{\pi}{2} \frac{a^2 b}{\sqrt{a^2 + b^2} + b}.$$

18. Apply the three methods of approximation of Art. 148 to the calculation to 6 decimal places of the definite integral $\int_0^1 \frac{dx}{1 + x}$, adopting $\frac{1}{12}$ as the common interval in each case.   *Ans.* (1), .693669.   (2), .693266.   (3), .693224.

The real value of the integral being log 2, or .693147, to the same number of decimal places.

19. Prove that the sectorial area bounded by two focal vectors r and r' of a parabola is represented by

$$\frac{a^{\frac{1}{2}}}{3} \left\{ \left(\frac{r + r' + c}{2}\right)^{\frac{3}{2}} - \left(\frac{r + r' - c}{2}\right)^{\frac{3}{2}} \right\},$$

where c is the chord of the arc, and a the semiparameter of the parabola.

20. Show that the whole area of the inverse of the ellipse $\dfrac{x^2}{a^2} + \dfrac{y^2}{b^2} = 1$ is represented by

$$\frac{\pi k^4}{\left(1 - \dfrac{\alpha^2}{a^2} - \dfrac{\beta^2}{b^2}\right)^2} \left\{ \frac{1}{a^2} + \frac{1}{b^2} + \left(\frac{1}{a^2} - \frac{1}{b^2}\right)\left(\frac{\alpha^2}{a^2} - \frac{\beta^2}{b^2}\right) \right\},$$

where α, β, are the co-ordinates of the origin of inversion, and k is the radius of the circle of inversion.

21. A given arc of a plane curve turns through a given angle round a fixed point in its plane; what is the area described?

22. Given the base of a triangle, prove that the polar equation of the locus of its vertex, when the vertical angle is double one of its base angles is

$$r = \frac{a\,(2\,\cos 2\theta + 1)}{2\,\cos \theta}.$$

Hence show that the entire area of the loop of the curve is $\dfrac{3a^2\sqrt{3}}{4}$.

23. O is a point within a closed oval curve, P any point on the curve, QPQ' a straight line drawn in a given direction such that $QP = PQ' = PO$; prove that as P moves round the curve, Q, Q', trace out two closed loops the sum of whose areas is twice the area of the original curve. *Camb. Trip. Exam.*, 1874.

24. Prove that the area of the pedal of the cardioid $r = a\,(1 - \cos\theta)$ taken with respect to an internal point at the distance c from the pole is

$$\frac{3\pi}{8}\,(5a^2 - 2ac + 2c^2). \qquad\qquad (\textit{Ibid.}, 1876.)$$

25. The co-ordinates of a point are expressed as follows:

$$x = \frac{3\theta}{\theta^3 + 1}, \quad y = \frac{3\theta^2}{\theta^3 + 1};$$

find the equation of the curve described by the point, and the area of the portion of the plane inclosed thereby.

CHAPTER VIII.

LENGTHS OF CURVES.

150. Length of Curves referred to Rectangular Axes.
The usual mode of considering the length of a curve is by
treating it as the limit of a polygon when each of its sides is
infinitely small.   If the curve be referred to rectangular axes
of co-ordinates, the length of the chord joining the points
(x, y) and $(x + dx, y + dy)$ is $\sqrt{dx^2 + dy^2}$, and, consequently, if
s represent the length of the curve measured from a fixed
point on it, we shall have $ds = \sqrt{dx^2 + dy^2}$, or, integrating,

$$s = \int \sqrt{1 + \left(\frac{dy}{dx}\right)^2}\, dx, \tag{1}$$

taken between suitable limits.

The value of $\dfrac{dy}{dx}$ in terms of x is to be got from the equation of the curve, and thus the finding of s is reducible to a
question of integration.

The determination of the length of an arc of a curve is
called its *rectification*.

It is evident that if y be taken for the independent variable
we shall have

$$s = \int \sqrt{1 + \left(\frac{dx}{dy}\right)^2}\, dy.$$

Again, when x and y are given functions of a single variable ϕ, we have

$$s = \int \left\{\left(\frac{dx}{d\phi}\right)^2 + \left(\frac{dy}{d\phi}\right)^2\right\}\, d\phi.$$

In each case the form of the equation of the curve determines which of these formulæ should be employed.

The curves whose lengths can be obtained in finite terms (compare Art. 2) are very limited in number. We proceed to consider some of the simplest cases.

151. **The Parabola.**—Writing the equation of the parabola in the form $y^2 = 2mx$, we get $\dfrac{dx}{dy} = \dfrac{y}{m}$.

Hence
$$s = \frac{1}{m} \int \sqrt{y^2 + m^2}\, dy.$$

The value of this integral can be obtained from that of the area of a hyperbola (Art. 130), by substituting y for x, and m^2 for $-a^2$.

Thus we have

$$s = \frac{y\sqrt{y^2 + m^2}}{2m} + \frac{m}{2} \log\left(\frac{y + \sqrt{y^2 + m^2}}{m}\right), \qquad (2)$$

the arc being measured from the vertex of the curve.

152. **The Catenary.**—The equation of the catenary (Art. 131), is

$$y = \frac{a}{2}\left(e^{\frac{x}{a}} + e^{-\frac{x}{a}}\right).$$

Hence

$$\frac{dy}{dx} = \frac{1}{2}\left(e^{\frac{x}{a}} - e^{-\frac{x}{a}}\right),$$

$$\frac{ds}{dx} = \left(1 + \frac{dy^2}{dx^2}\right)^{\frac{1}{2}} = \frac{1}{2}\left(e^{\frac{x}{a}} + e^{-\frac{x}{a}}\right),$$

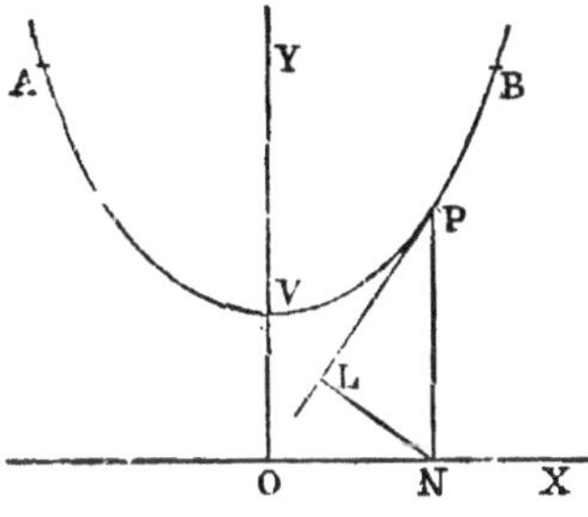

Fig. 27.

$$\therefore s = \frac{1}{2}\int e^{\frac{x}{a}}\,dx + \frac{1}{2}\int e^{-\frac{x}{a}}\,dx = \frac{a}{2}\left(e^{\frac{x}{a}} - e^{-\frac{x}{a}}\right) + \text{const.}$$

If s be measured from the vertex V, we have

$$s = \frac{a}{2}\left(e^{\frac{x}{a}} - e^{-\frac{x}{a}}\right);$$

the same result as already arrived at in Art. 131.

Again, since $PL = PV$, and NL is constant, it follows that the catenary is the evolute of the tractrix (see Ex. 9, p. 219).

153. **Semi-cubical Parabola.**—The equation of this curve is of the form $ay^2 = x^3$.

hence
$$y = \frac{x^{\frac{3}{2}}}{a^{\frac{1}{2}}}; \quad \therefore \frac{dy}{dx} = \frac{3}{2}\left(\frac{x}{a}\right)^{\frac{1}{2}}, \quad \frac{ds}{dx} = \left(1 + \frac{9x}{4a}\right)^{\frac{1}{2}};$$

$$\therefore s = \int\left(1 + \frac{9x}{4a}\right)^{\frac{1}{2}} dx = \frac{8a}{27}\left(1 + \frac{9x}{4a}\right)^{\frac{3}{2}} + \text{const.}$$

If the arc be measured from the vertex, we get

$$s = \frac{8a}{27}\left\{\left(1 + \frac{9x}{4a}\right)^{\frac{3}{2}} - 1\right\}.$$

The semi-cubical parabola is the first curve whose length was determined. This result was discovered by William Neil, in 1660.

154. **Rectification of Evolutes.**—It may be noted that the rectification of the semi-cubical parabola is an immediate consequence of its being the evolute of the ordinary parabola (see Diff. Calc., Art. 239). In like manner the length of any curve can be found if it be the evolute of a known curve, from the property that any portion of the arc of the evolute is the difference between the two corresponding radii of curvature of the curve of which it is the evolute.

For, example, we get by this means the lengths of the cycloid, the epicycloid and the hypocycloid.

Again, since the equation of the evolute of an ellipse is

$$(ax)^{\frac{2}{3}} + (by)^{\frac{2}{3}} = (a^2 - b^2)^{\frac{2}{3}},$$

the length of any arc of this curve can be at once found.

This can also be readily got otherwise; for, writing the equation in the form

$$\left(\frac{x}{a}\right)^{\frac{2}{3}} + \left(\frac{y}{\beta}\right)^{\frac{2}{3}} = 1,$$

and making $x = a \sin^3 \phi$, we get $y = \beta \cos^3 \phi$, and

$$ds = (dx^2 + dy^2)^{\frac{1}{2}} = 3 \sin\phi \cos\phi (a^2 \sin^2\phi + \beta^2 \cos^2\phi)^{\frac{1}{2}} d\phi$$

$$= \frac{3(a^2 \sin^2\phi + \beta^2 \cos^2\phi)^{\frac{1}{2}}}{2(a^2 - \beta^2)} d(a^2 \sin^2\phi + \beta^2 \cos^2\phi).$$

Hence

$$s = \frac{(a^2 \sin^2 \phi + \beta^2 \cos^2 \phi)^{\frac{3}{2}}}{a^2 - \beta^2} + \text{const.}$$

If the arc be measured from the point $x = 0$, $y = \beta$, we get the constant

$$= \frac{-\beta^3}{a^2 - \beta^2}, \text{ and } s = \frac{(a^2 \sin^2 \phi + \beta^2 \cos^2 \phi)^{\frac{3}{2}} - \beta^3}{a^2 - \beta^2}.$$

If $a = \beta$, the expression for ds becomes $3a \sin \phi \cos \phi \, d\phi$; hence we get $s = \dfrac{3}{2} a \sin^2 \phi$, the arc being measured from the same point as above.

EXAMPLES.

1. Find the length of the logarithmic curve $y = ca^x$.

Here $\qquad \log y = x \log a + \log c$; $\quad \therefore \dfrac{dx}{dy} = \dfrac{b}{y}$, where $b = \dfrac{1}{\log a}$.

Hence

$$s = \int \frac{(b^2 + y^2)^{\frac{1}{2}} dy}{y} = \int \frac{y \, dy}{(b^2 + y^2)^{\frac{1}{2}}} + \int \frac{b^2 \, dy}{y (b^2 + y^2)^{\frac{1}{2}}}$$

$$= (b^2 + y^2)^{\frac{1}{2}} + b \, \log \frac{(b^2 + y^2)^{\frac{1}{2}} - b}{y}.$$

2. Find the length of the tractrix.

Here, by definition (see fig. 26), we have $PT = a$;

$$\therefore \sin PTN = \frac{y}{a}, \quad \text{hence } \frac{ds}{dy} = -\frac{a}{y};$$

$$\therefore s = -a \int \frac{dy}{y} = -a \log y + \text{const.}$$

If the arc be measured from the vertex A, we get

$$\text{arc } AP = a \log \left(\frac{a}{y}\right).$$

3. Find in what cases the curves represented by $a^m y^n = x^{m+n}$ are rectifiable. Here we have

$$s = \int \left\{ 1 + \left(\frac{m+n}{n}\right)^2 \left(\frac{x}{a}\right)^{\frac{2m}{n}} \right\}^{\frac{1}{2}} dx.$$

[15]

Substituting b for $\dfrac{(m+n)^2}{n^2 a^{\frac{2m}{n}}}$, and making $1 + bx^{\frac{2m}{n}} = z^2$, this becomes

$$s = \frac{n}{mb} \int \left(\frac{z^2 - 1}{b} \right)^{\frac{n}{2m} - 1} z^2 \, dz.$$

This expression is immediately integrable when $\dfrac{n}{2m}$ is a positive integer.

Hence, if $\dfrac{n}{2m} = r$, we see that curves of the form $ay^{2r} = x^{2r+1}$ are rectifiable.

Again, if $\dfrac{n}{2m}$ be a negative integer, the expression under the integral sign becomes rational, and can accordingly be integrated. This leads to the form $y^{2r} = ax^{2r-1}$. Accordingly, all curves comprised in the equation $ay^m = x^{m \pm 1}$ are rectifiable, m being any integer. (Compare Art. 62).

155. **The Ellipse.**—The simplest expression for the arc of an ellipse is obtained by taking $x = a \sin \phi$, whence

$$y = b \cos \phi, \text{ and } ds = (a^2 \cos^2 \phi + b^2 \sin^2 \phi)^{\frac{1}{2}} \, d\phi;$$

$$\therefore \; s = \int (a^2 \cos^2 \phi + b^2 \sin^2 \phi)^{\frac{1}{2}} d\phi.$$

It is often more convenient to write this in the form

$$s = a \int (1 - e^2 \sin^2 \phi)^{\frac{1}{2}} d\phi, \tag{3}$$

e being the eccentricity of the ellipse.

It may be observed that ϕ is the complement of the *eccentric* angle belonging to the point (x, y).

The length of an elliptic quadrant is represented by the definite integral

$$a \int_0^{\frac{\pi}{2}} (1 - e^2 \sin^2 \phi)^{\frac{1}{2}} \, d\phi.$$

We postpone the further consideration of elliptic arcs to a subsequent part of the Chapter.

156. **Rectification in Polar Co-ordinates.**—If the curve be referred to polar co-ordinates we plainly have (Diff. Calc., Art. 180) $ds^2 = dr^2 + r^2 d\theta^2$; hence we get

$$s = \int \left(r^2 + \frac{dr^2}{d\theta^2} \right)^{\frac{1}{2}} d\theta, \quad \text{or } s = \int \left(1 + \frac{r^2 d\theta^2}{dr^2} \right)^{\frac{1}{2}} dr. \tag{4}$$

For example, the length of the spiral of Archimedes, $r = a\theta$, is given by the equation

$$s = \frac{1}{a} \int (r^2 + a^2)^{\frac{1}{2}}\, dr.$$

Comparing this with the formula (2) for the parabola, it follows that the length of any arc of the spiral, measured from its pole, is equal to that of a parabola measured from its vertex.

EXAMPLES.

1. Cardioid, $\qquad\qquad r = a(1 + \cos\theta).$

Here $\dfrac{dr}{d\theta} = -a\sin\theta$, and hence

$$s = a \int \{(1 + \cos\theta)^2 + \sin^2\theta\}^{\frac{1}{2}} d\theta = 2a \int \cos\frac{\theta}{2}\, d\theta = 4a \sin\frac{\theta}{2} + \text{constant}.$$

The constant becomes zero if we measure s from the point for which $\theta = 0$.

2. Logarithmic spiral, $\qquad\qquad r = a^\theta.$

Here, if $b = \dfrac{1}{\log a}$, we get

$$\frac{r\, d\theta}{dr} = b; \quad \therefore\ s = \int_{r_0}^{r_1} (1 + b^2)^{\frac{1}{2}} dr = (1 + b^2)^{\frac{1}{2}} (r_1 - r_0).$$

Accordingly, the length of any arc is proportional to the difference between the vectors of its extremities; a result which also follows immediately from the property that the curve cuts its radius vector at a constant angle.

3. $\qquad\qquad\qquad\qquad r^m = a^m \cos m\theta.$

Taking the logarithmic differentials, we get $\dfrac{dr}{r\, d\theta} = -\tan m\theta$;

$$\therefore\ \frac{ds}{r\, d\theta} = \sec m\theta.$$

Hence $\qquad\qquad s = a \int (\cos m\theta)^{\frac{1}{m} - 1} d\theta.$

Or, writing ϕ for $m\theta$,

$$s = \frac{a}{m} \int (\cos\phi)^{\frac{1}{m} - 1} d\phi.$$

This is readily integrated when $\dfrac{1}{m}$ is an integer (see Art. 56).

[15 a]

Whatever be the value of m, we can express the complete length of a loop of the curve in Gamma Functions. For if we integrate between o and $\frac{\pi}{2}$, we obviously get the length of half the loop.

Hence the length of the loop (Art. 122) is

$$\frac{a\sqrt{\pi}}{m}\,\frac{\Gamma\left(\dfrac{1}{2m}\right)}{\Gamma\left(\dfrac{m+1}{2m}\right)}.$$

157. **Formula of Legendre on Rectification.**— Another formula* of considerable utility in rectification follows immediately from the result obtained in Art. 192, Diff. Calc. For, if this result be written in the form

$$\frac{d(s-t)}{d\omega} = p, \text{ we get } s - t = \int p\,d\omega. \tag{5}$$

Consequently, the total increment of $s - t$ between any two points on a curve is equal to $\int p\,d\omega$ taken between the same two points.

For example, in the parabola we have $p = \dfrac{a}{\cos\omega}$, and hence

$$s - t = a\int\frac{d\omega}{\cos\omega} = a\log\tan\left(\frac{\pi}{4} + \frac{\omega}{2}\right) + \text{const.}$$

If we measure the arc from the vertex of the curve, and observe that $t = \dfrac{dp}{d\omega}$, this gives

$$s = \frac{a\sin\omega}{\cos^2\omega} + a\log\tan\left(\frac{\pi}{4} + \frac{\omega}{2}\right).$$

The student can without difficulty identify this result with that given in Art. 151.

---

* This theorem is due to Legendre. See *Traité des Fonctions Elliptiques*, tome ii., p. 588.

It should be observed that when the curve is closed, its whole length is, in general, represented by

$$\int_0^{2\pi} p\,d\omega.$$

Equation (5) furnishes a simple method of expressing the intrinsic equation of a curve, when we are given its equation in terms of p and ω.

For, if $p = f(\omega)$ we have

$$s = \frac{dp}{d\omega} + \int p\,d\omega = f'(\omega) + \int f(\omega)\,d\omega, \qquad (6)$$

taken between suitable limits.

158. **Application to Ellipse. Fagnani's Theorem.** In the ellipse we have

$$p^2 = a^2 \cos^2\omega + b^2 \sin^2\omega.$$

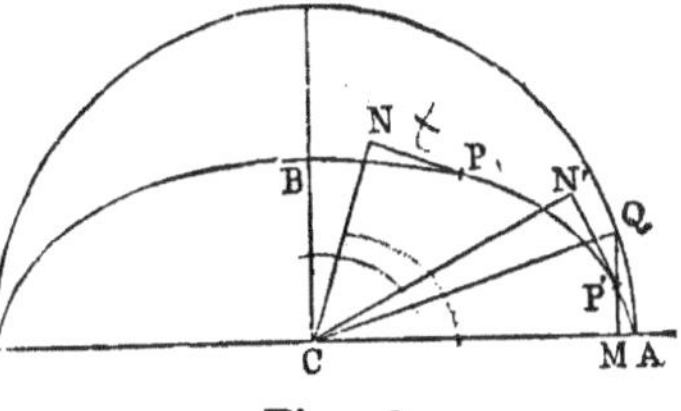

Fig. 28.

Hence, measuring the arc from the vertex A, and observing that in this case PN is to be taken with a negative sign, we have

$$\text{arc } AP + PN = \int_0^a (a^2 \cos^2\omega + b^2 \sin^2\omega)^{\frac{1}{2}}\,d\omega,$$

where $a = \angle ACN$.

But, in Art. 155, we have found that if ϕ be measured from the vertex B, the arc is represented by

$$\int (a^2 \cos^2\phi + b^2 \sin^2\phi)^{\frac{1}{2}}\,d\phi.$$

Consequently, if we make $\angle BCQ = a = \angle ACN$, and draw QM perpendicular to the axis major meeting the curve in P', we shall have

$$\text{arc } BP' = \text{arc } AP + PN,$$

or, taking away the common arc PP',

$$BP - AP' = PN. \qquad (7)$$

This remarkable result is known as Fagnani's Theorem*, and shows that we can in an indefinite number of ways find two arcs of an ellipse whose difference is expressible by a right line.

We add a few properties connecting the points P and P' in this construction.

EXAMPLES.

1. If (x, y) and (x', y') be the co-ordinates of P and P', respectively; prove the following :—

$$(1). \quad PN = \frac{e^2 xx'}{a}, \qquad (2). \quad PN = P'N', \qquad (3). \quad CN \cdot CN' = CA \cdot CB,$$

$$(4). \quad CP^2 + CN'^2 = CA^2 + CB^2 = CP'^2 + CN^2.$$

2. Divide an elliptic quadrant into two parts whose difference shall be equal to the difference of the semiaxes.

This takes place when P and P' coincide; in which case $CN = \sqrt{ab}$, and $PN = a - b$.

We shall designate the point so determined on the elliptic quadrant as Fagnani's point.

3. Show that if a tangent be drawn at Fagnani's point, the intercepts between its point of contact and its points of intersection with the axes are respectively equal in length to the semi-axes of the ellipse.

4. If the lines PN and $P'N'$ be produced to meet, show that they intersect on the confocal hyperbola which passes through the points of intersection of the tangents to the ellipse at its vertices. Show also that this hyperbola cuts the ellipse in Fagnani's point.

---

* Fagnani, *Giornale de' Letterati d'Italia*, 1716, reprinted in his *Produzioni Matematiche*, 1750. It may be noted that if we integrate the equation of Art. 116, *Diff. Calc.*, taking the angle C as obtuse, and adopting zero for the lowest limit in each integral, we obtain

$$\int_0^a \sqrt{1 - k^2 \sin^2 a}\, da + \int_0^b \sqrt{1 - k^2 \sin^2 b}\, db$$

$$= \int_0^c \sqrt{1 - k^2 \sin^2 c}\, dc + k^2 \sin a \sin b \sin c,$$

where k is defined by the equation $\sin C = k \sin c$, and a, b, c are connected by the relation

$$\cos c = \cos a \cos b - \sin a \sin b \sqrt{1 - k^2 \sin^2 c}.$$

This equation furnishes a relation between three elliptic arcs, from which Fagnani's theorem can be readily deduced, as well as many other theorems connected with such arcs. See Legendre, *Fonc. Ellip.*, tome i., ch. 9.

The equation of PN is

$$x \sin \theta + y \cos \theta = \sqrt{a^2 \sin^2 \theta + b^2 \cos^2 \theta},$$

and that of $P'N'$ is

$$\frac{x \cos \theta}{a} + \frac{y \sin \theta}{b} = 1.$$

If we eliminate θ, we get

$$\frac{x^2}{a} - \frac{y^2}{b} = a - b,$$

which represents the hyperbola in question.

159. **The Hyperbola.**—In the hyperbola we have

$$p^2 = a^2 \cos^2 \omega - b^2 \sin^2 \omega.$$

Hence, measuring the arc from the vertex A of the curve, we find, since ω is measured below the axis,

$$PN - AP = \int_0^a (a^2 \cos^2 \omega - b^2 \sin^2 \omega)^{\frac{1}{2}} d\omega, \qquad (8)$$

where $a = \angle ACN$.

As we proceed along the hyperbola the perpendicular p diminishes, and vanishes when the tangent becomes the asymptote.

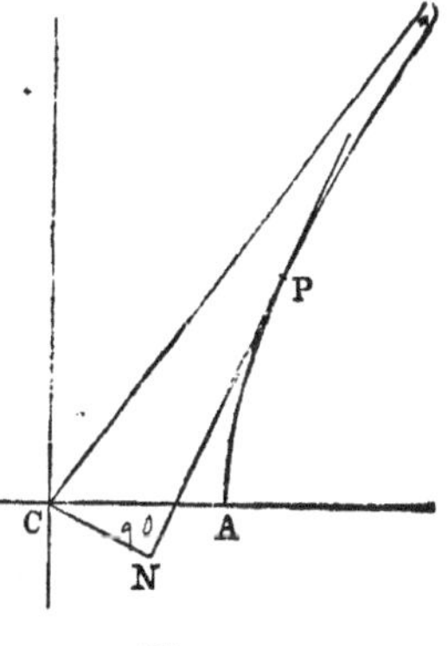

Fig. 29.

Moreover, as the limit of ω in this case becomes $\tan^{-1}\dfrac{a}{b}$, it follows that the difference between the asymptote and the infinite hyperbolic arc, measured from the vertex, is represented by the definite integral

$$\int_0^{\tan^{-1}\frac{a}{b}} (a^2 \cos^2 \omega - b^2 \sin^2 \omega)^{\frac{1}{2}} d\omega.$$

EXAMPLES.

1. If $a > b$, prove that

$$\int (a + b \cos \phi)^{\frac{1}{2}} d\phi$$

is represented by an elliptic arc, and that the semiaxes of the ellipse are the greatest and least values of $(a + b \cos \phi)^{\frac{1}{2}}$.

2. If $a < b$, prove that

$$\int (a + b \cos \phi)^{\frac{1}{2}} d\phi$$

is represented by the difference between a right line and a hyperbolic arc.

160. **Landen's Theorem on a Hyperbolic Arc.**—
We next proceed to establish an important theorem, due to
Landen;[*] namely, that *any arc of a hyperbola can be expressed
in terms of the arcs of two ellipses.*

This can be easily seen as follows:—In any triangle,
adopting the usual notation, we have

$$c = a \cos B + b \cos A.$$

Now, representing by C the external angle at the vertex
C, we have $C = A + B$, and hence

$$cdC = (a \cos B + b \cos A)\, dA + (a \cos B + b \cos A)\, dB.$$

Consequently, supposing the sides a and b constant, and
the remaining parts variable, we have

$$\int cdC = \int a \cos B\, dA + \int b \cos A\, dB + 2a \sin B + \text{const.},$$

or

$$\int \sqrt{a^2 + b^2 + 2ab \cos C}\, dC = \int \sqrt{a^2 - b^2 \sin^2 A}\, dA + \int \sqrt{b^2 - a^2 \sin^2 B}\, dB$$

$$+ 2a \sin B + \text{const.} \qquad (9)$$

Now, if we suppose $a > b$, $\int \sqrt{a^2 - b^2 \sin^2 A}\, dA$ represents
(Art. 155) the arc of an ellipse, of axis major $2a$ and eccen-
tricity $\dfrac{b}{a}$.　Also $\int \sqrt{b^2 - a^2 \sin^2 B}\, dB$ represents (Art. 159) the
difference between a right line and the arc of a hyperbola,
whose axis major is b and eccentricity $\dfrac{a}{b}$.

Again, $\sqrt{a^2 + b^2 + 2ab \cos C} = \sqrt{(a - b)^2 \sin^2 \dfrac{C}{2} + (a + b)^2 \cos^2 \dfrac{C}{2}}$,

---

* Landen, *Philosophical Transactions*, 1775; also, *Mathematical Memoirs*,
1780.

and consequently the integral

$$\int \sqrt{a^2 + b^2 + 2ab \cos C}\, dC$$

represents an arc of the ellipse whose semiaxes are $a + b$ and $a - b$.

Hence, Landen's theorem follows immediately.

It should be noted that the limiting values of A, B and C are connected by the relations

$$a \sin B = b \sin A, \text{ and } C = A + B.$$

Again, if we suppose the angle A to increase from o to π, the external angle C will increase at the same time from o to π, while B will commence by increasing from o to a, and afterwards diminish from a to o $\left(\text{where } a = \sin^{-1}\dfrac{b}{a}\right)$. Moreover, in the latter stage $b \cos A$ is negative, and dB also negative, consequently the term $b \cos A\, dB$ is positive throughout the entire integration ; and the total value of

$\int \sqrt{b^2 - a^2 \sin^2 B}\, dB$ is represented by $2 \displaystyle\int_0^a \sqrt{b^2 - a^2 \sin^2 B}\, dB.$

Hence, substituting ϕ for $\dfrac{C}{2}$, and integrating between the limits indicated, we get, after dividing by 2,

$$\int_0^{\frac{\pi}{2}} \{(a + b)^2 \sin^2\phi + (a - b)^2 \cos^2\phi\}^{\frac{1}{2}}\, d\phi$$

$$= \int_0^{\frac{\pi}{2}} (a^2 - b^2 \sin^2 A)^{\frac{1}{2}}\, dA + \int_0^a (b^2 - a^2 \sin^2 B)^{\frac{1}{2}}\, dB. \tag{10}$$

Accordingly, *the difference between the length of the asymptote and of the infinite arc of a hyperbola is equal to the difference between two elliptic quadrants.* This result is also due to Landen.

We next proceed to two important theorems, which may be regarded as extensions of Fagnani's theorem.

161. Theorem* of Dr. Graves.—If from any point P on the exterior of two confocal ellipses, tangents PT and PT' be drawn to the interior, then the difference $(PT + PT' - TT')$ between the sum of the tangents and the arc between their points of contact is constant.

For, draw the tangents QS and QS' from a point Q, regarded as infinitely near to P, and drop the perpendiculars PN and QN'; then, since the conics are confocal, we have

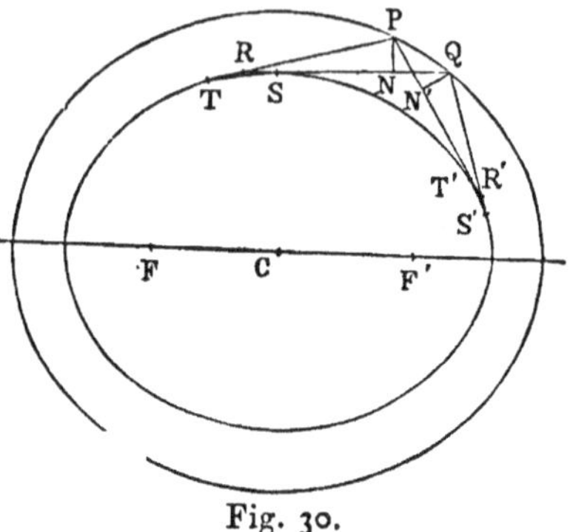

Fig. 30.

$$\angle PQN = \angle QPN'; \therefore PN' = QN.$$

Also, $PT = TR + RN = TR + RS + SN = TS + SN$

$$= TS + SQ - QN.$$

In like manner

$$PT' = PN' + S'Q - T'S';$$

$$\therefore PT + PT' = QS + QS' + TS - T'S',$$

or $\qquad PT + PT' - TT' = QS + QS' - SS'.$

Hence, $PT + PT' - TT'$ does not change in passing to the consecutive point Q; which proves that $PT + PT' - TT'$ has a constant value.

---

* This elegant theorem was arrived at by Dr. Graves, now Bishop of Limerick, for the more general case of spherical conics, from the reciprocal theorem, viz. :— If two spherical conics have the same cyclic arcs, then any arc touching the inner will cut from the outer a segment of constant area. (See Graves' translation of Chasles on *Cones and Spherical Conics*, p. 77, Dublin, 1841.)

It should be remarked that the theorems of this and of the following article were investigated independently by M. Chasles. The student will find in the *Comptes Rendus*, 1843, 1844, a number of beautiful applications by that great geometrician of these theorems, as well to properties of confocal conics, as also to the addition of elliptic functions of the first species.

This value can be readily expressed by taking the point at B', one of the extremities of the minor axis of the exterior ellipse. Let D be the point of contact of the tangent drawn from B', and drop DM, and DN perpendicular to CA and CB, respectively.

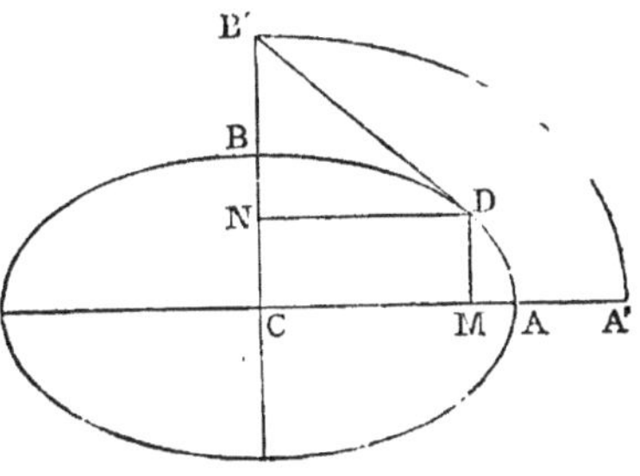

Fig. 31.

Let $CA = a$, $CB = b$, $CA' = a'$, $CB' = b'$, e the eccentricity of interior ellipse. Then, by Art. 155, the length of arc

$$BD = a \int_0^a (1 - e^2 \sin^2\phi)^{\frac{1}{2}} d\phi,$$

where

$$\cos a = \frac{DM}{CB} = \frac{CN}{CB} = \frac{CB}{CB'} = \frac{b}{b'}.$$

Again,

$$B'D^2 = B'N^2 + DN^2 = (b' - b\cos a)^2 + a^2 \sin^2 a$$

$$= \left(b' - \frac{b^2}{b'}\right)^2 + a^2\left(1 - \frac{b^2}{b'^2}\right);$$

hence

$$B'D = \frac{a'}{b'}\sqrt{b'^2 - b^2} = a' \sin a.$$

Consequently we have

$$B'D - BD = a' \sin a - a \int_0^a (1 - e^2 \sin^2\phi)^{\frac{1}{2}} d\phi,$$

Hence, in general,

$$PT + PT' - TT' = 2a' \sin a - 2a \int_0^a (1 - e^2 \sin^2 \phi)^{\frac{1}{2}} d\phi, \qquad (11)$$

where

$$a = \cos^{-1}\left(\frac{b}{b'}\right).$$

The analogous theorem, due to Professor Mac Cullagh, may be stated as follows :—

162. **Theorem.**—If tangents PT, PT' be drawn to an ellipse from any point on a confocal hyperbola, then the difference of the tangents is equal to the difference of the arcs TK and KT'.

The proof is left to the student, and is nearly identical with that given for the previous theorem.

This result still holds when the tangents are drawn from a point on an ellipse to a confocal hyperbola, provided that the tangents both touch the same branch of the hyperbola; as can be seen without difficulty.

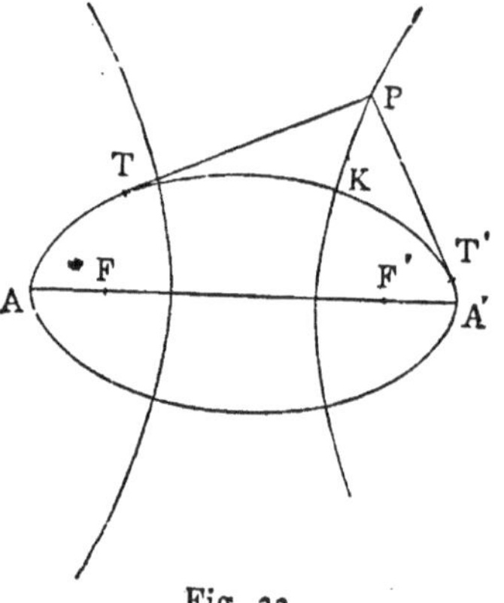

Fig. 32.

As an application* we shall prove another theorem of Landen; viz., that the *difference between the length of the asymptote and of the infinite branch of a hyperbola can be expressed in terms of an arc of the hyperbola.*

For, let the tangent at A meet the asymptote in D, and suppose a confocal ellipse drawn through D. Then, regarding DT as a tangent to the hyperbola, it follows, by the theorem just established, that the difference between DT and KT is equal to the difference between DA and AK.

Consequently the difference between the asymptote CT and the hyperbolic branch AT is equal to $DA + DC - 2KA$. Consequently the required difference is expressible in terms of given lines and of the hyperbolic arc AK.

Fig. 33.

---

* I am indebted to Dr. Ingram for this application of Professor M'Cullagh's theorem.

We next proceed to consider two important curves whose rectification depends on that of the ellipse.

163. **The Limaçon.**—From the equation of the limaçon,

$$r = a \cos \theta + b, \text{ we get } \frac{dr}{d\theta} = - a \sin \theta,$$

and hence

$$ds = (a^2 + b^2 + 2ab \cos \theta)^{\frac{1}{2}} d\theta;$$

$$\therefore s = \int \left\{ (a + b)^2 \cos^2 \frac{\theta}{2} + (a - b)^2 \sin^2 \frac{\theta}{2} \right\}^{\frac{1}{2}} d\theta.$$

Accordingly, the rectification of the limaçon depends on that of the ellipse whose semiaxes are $a + b$ and $a - b$.

164. **The Epitrochoid and Hypotrochoid.**—The epitrochoid is represented by the equations (see Diff. Calc., Art. 284)

$$x = (a + b) \cos \theta - c \cos \frac{a + b}{b} \theta,$$

$$y = (a + b) \sin \theta - c \sin \frac{a + b}{b} \theta.$$

Hence

$$\frac{dx}{d\theta} = - (a + b) \left\{ \sin \theta - \frac{c}{b} \sin \frac{a + b}{b} \theta \right\},$$

$$\frac{dy}{d\theta} = (a + b) \left\{ \cos \theta - \frac{c}{b} \cos \frac{a + b}{b} \theta \right\}.$$

Squaring and adding we get

$$\left(\frac{ds}{d\theta} \right)^2 = \left(\frac{a + b}{b} \right)^2 \left\{ b^2 + c^2 - 2bc \cos \frac{a\theta}{b} \right\};$$

$$\therefore s = \frac{a + b}{b} \int \left\{ b^2 + c^2 - 2bc \cos \frac{a\theta}{b} \right\}^{\frac{1}{2}} d\theta.$$

Hence, substituting $\frac{2b\phi}{a}$ for θ, we get

$$s = \frac{2 (a + b)}{a} \int \{ (b + c)^2 \sin^2 \phi + (b - c)^2 \cos^2 \phi \}^{\frac{1}{2}} d\phi.$$

Consequently the length of an arc of the epitrochoid is equal to that of an ellipse.

The corresponding form for the hypotrochoid is obtained by changing the sign of b.

165. **Steiner's Theorem on Rectification of Roulettes.**—If any curve roll on a right line, the length of the arc of the roulette described by any point is equal to that of the corresponding arc of the pedal, taken with respect to the generating point as origin.

For (see fig. 20, Art. 145), the element OO' of the roulette is equal to $OPd\omega$.

Again, to find the element of the pedal. Since the angles at N and N' are right, the quadrilateral $NN'TO$ is inscribable in a circle, and consequently $NN' = OT \sin NON'$. But, in the limit, NN' becomes the element of the pedal, and OT becomes OP: hence the element of pedal is $OPd\omega$; consequently the element of the pedal is equal to the corresponding element of the roulette; $\therefore$ &c.

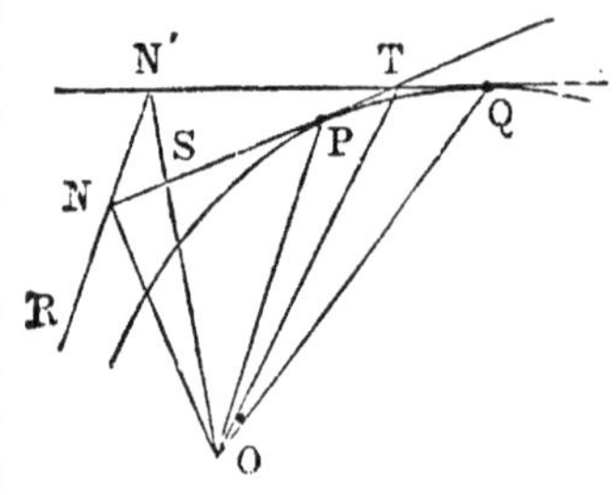

Fig. 34.

We proceed to point out a few elementary examples of this principle. In the first place it follows that the length of an arc of the cycloid is the same as that of the cardioid; and the length of the trochoid as that of the limaçon. Again, if an ellipse roll on a right line, the length of the roulette described by either focus is equal to the corresponding arc of the auxiliary circle.

Moreover, it is easily seen, as in Art. 146, that, if one curve roll on another, the elements ds and ds', of the roulette, and of the corresponding pedal are connected by the relation

$$ds = ds'\left(1 + \frac{\rho}{\rho'}\right).$$

In the case of one circle rolling on another, this relation shows that the arcs of epicycloids and of epitrochoids are proportional to the arcs of cardioids and of limaçons, which agrees with the results established already.

166. Oval of Descartes.—We next proceed to the rectification of the Ovals of Descartes, some properties of which curves we have given in chapter xx., Diff. Calc.

The curve is defined as the locus of a point whose distances, r and r', from two fixed points are connected by the equation

$$mr + lr' = d,$$

where l, m, d are constants.

For convenience we shall write the equation in the form

$$mr + lr' = nc, \quad (12)$$

where c is the distance between the fixed points.

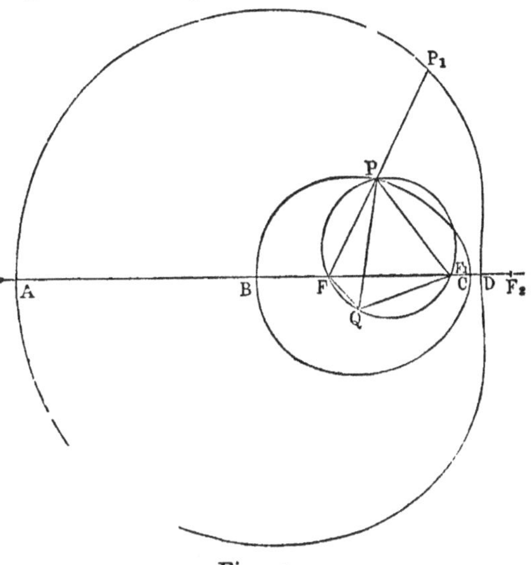

Fig. 35.

The polar equation of the curve is easily got. For, let F and F_1 be the fixed points, and $\angle F_1 FP = \theta$, then we have

$$r'^2 = r^2 + c^2 - 2rc \cos \theta \; ;$$

also from (12),

$$l^2 r'^2 = (nc - mr)^2,$$

hence the polar equation of the locus is readily seen to be

$$r^2 - 2rc \frac{mn - l^2 \cos \theta}{m^2 - l^2} + c^2 \frac{n^2 - l^2}{m^2 - l^2} = 0. \quad (13)$$

For simplicity we shall write this in the form

$$r^2 - 2r\Omega + C = 0. \quad (14)$$

Solving this equation for r, we get

$$r = \Omega \pm \sqrt{\Omega^2 - C}, \text{ or } FP_1 = \Omega + \sqrt{\Omega^2 - C}, \; FP = \Omega - \sqrt{\Omega^2 - C}.$$

It can be seen without difficulty that, so long as l, m, n are real and unequal, the curve consists of two ovals, one lying inside the other, as in the figure.

Again we get from (14), by differentiation

$$(r - \Omega)\, dr = r\Omega'\, d\theta, \quad \text{where } \Omega' = \frac{d\Omega}{d\theta};$$

$$\therefore \frac{dr}{r\, d\theta} = \frac{\Omega'}{r - \Omega} = \frac{\Omega'}{\sqrt{\Omega^2 - C}}; \text{ hence } \frac{ds}{r\, d\theta} = \frac{\sqrt{\Omega^2 + \Omega'^2 - C}}{\sqrt{\Omega^2 - C}}.$$

$$\text{Or} \qquad ds = \frac{\Omega\sqrt{\Omega^2 + \Omega'^2 - C}}{\sqrt{\Omega^2 - C}}\, d\theta \pm \sqrt{\Omega^2 + \Omega'^2 - C}\, d\theta, \quad (15)$$

the upper sign corresponding to the outer oval, and the lower to the inner.

Hence the difference between the two corresponding elementary arcs is equal to

$$2\sqrt{\Omega^2 + \Omega'^2 - C}\, d\theta, \quad \text{or,} \quad 2\sqrt{a^2 + 2ab\, \cos\theta + b^2 - C}\, d\theta,$$

(writing Ω in the form $a + b\,\cos\theta$); this plainly represents the element of an ellipse. Consequently, the difference between two corresponding arcs of the ovals can be represented by the arc of an ellipse. This remarkable theorem is due to Mr. W. Roberts (Liouville, 1847, p. 195). Some years after its publication it was shown by Professor Genocchi (Tortolini, 1864, p. 97), that the arc* of a Cartesian is expressible in terms of three elliptic arcs.

In order to establish this result we commence by proving one or two elementary properties of the curve.

Suppose a circle described through F, F_1, and P; and let PQ be the normal at P to the oval, meeting the circle in Q, and join FQ and F_1Q; then let $\angle\, FPQ = \omega$, and $F_1PQ = \omega'$; and since $m\dfrac{dr}{ds} + l\dfrac{dr'}{ds} = 0$, we have $l\,\sin\omega' = m\,\sin\omega$;

$$\therefore FQ : F_1Q = l : m.$$

---

* For the proof of this theorem given in the text I am indebted to Mr. Panton.

Also, since $mr + lr' = nc$; and (by Ptolemy's theorem)

$$FP . F_1Q + F_1P . FQ = FF_1 . PQ,$$

we have

$$\frac{FQ}{l} = \frac{F_1Q}{m} = \frac{PQ}{n}.$$

Hence, denoting the common value of these fractions by u, we have

$$FQ = lu, \quad F_1Q = mu, \quad PQ = nu.$$

Again

$$\tan \omega = \frac{dr}{r\,d\theta} = \frac{\Omega'}{\sqrt{\Omega^2 - C}}; \quad \therefore \cos \omega = \frac{\sqrt{\Omega^2 - C}}{\sqrt{\Omega^2 + \Omega'^2 - C}}.$$

Hence the first term in the expression for ds in (15) is equal to

$$\frac{\Omega\,d\theta}{\cos \omega} = \frac{c}{m^2 - l^2} \frac{mn - l^2 \cos \theta}{\cos \omega}\,d\theta.$$

Again, let $\quad \angle FPF_1 = \psi, \quad \angle PF_1C = \phi,$

and we have the two following relations between the angles θ, ϕ, ψ:

$$\phi = \theta + \psi, \quad l \sin \theta + m \sin \phi = n \sin \psi. \qquad (16)$$

Hence

$$d\phi - d\theta = d\psi, \quad l \cos \theta\,d\theta + m \cos \phi\,d\phi = n \cos \psi\,d\psi;$$

$$\therefore (mn - l^2 \cos \theta)d\theta = m (n + l \cos \phi)d\phi - n (m + l \cos \psi)d\psi,$$

or

$$\frac{mn - l^2 \cos \theta}{\cos \omega}\,d\theta = m \frac{n + l \cos \phi}{\cos \omega}\,d\phi - n \frac{m + l \cos \psi}{\cos \omega}\,d\psi. \quad (17)$$

Again, from the triangle FPQ, we have

$$r \cos \omega = PQ + FQ \cos \phi = (n + l \cos \phi)u;$$

$$\therefore \frac{n + l \cos \phi}{\cos \omega} = \frac{r}{u} = \sqrt{l^2 + n^2 + 2ln \cos \phi}.$$

[16]

In the same manner it can be shown that

$$\frac{m + l \cos \psi}{\cos \omega} = \frac{c}{u} = \sqrt{l^2 + m^2 + 2lm \cos \psi}.$$

Hence we have

$$\int \frac{\Omega \, d\theta}{\cos \omega} = \frac{mc}{m^2 - l^2} \int \sqrt{l^2 + n^2 + 2ln \cos \phi} \, d\phi$$

$$- \frac{nc}{m^2 - l^2} \int \sqrt{l^2 + m^2 + 2lm \cos \psi} \, d\psi. \qquad (18)$$

Each of these latter integrals is represented by the arc of an ellipse, and, accordingly, the arc of a Cartesian Oval is expressible in the required manner.

It should be noted that the limiting values of θ, ϕ, and ψ are connected by the relations given in (16).

Again, it can be shown without difficulty that *the axes of the ellipses are the lines (AB, CD), (AC, BD), and (AD, BC), respectively*: a result also given by Signor Genocchi. First, with respect to the ellipse whose element is $\sqrt{\Omega^2 + \Omega'^2 - C} \, d\theta$, it is plain that its axes are the greatest and least values of $2\sqrt{\Omega^2 + \Omega'^2 - C}$, or of $2\sqrt{a^2 + b^2 + 2ab \cos \theta - C}$; but these are $2\sqrt{(a + b)^2 - C}$ and $2\sqrt{(a - b)^2 - C}$, which are plainly the same as the greatest and least values of PP_1; and, consequently, are AB and CD.

Again, from the equation $mr + lr' = nc$, we get

$$m\,FB + l(FB + c) = nc; \qquad \therefore FB = \frac{(n - l)\,c}{l + m}.$$

In like manner,

$$FC = \frac{(n + l)\,c}{l + m}.$$

Again, since we get the points on the outer oval by changing the sign of l, we have

$$FA = \frac{(n + l)\,c}{m - l}, \qquad FD = \frac{(n - l)\,c}{m - l};$$

and, consequently,

$$AD = \frac{2nc}{m-l}, \quad BC = \frac{2nc}{l+m},$$

$$AC = \frac{2mc\,(n+l)}{m^2-l^2}, \quad BD = \frac{2mc\,(n-l)}{m^2-l^2};$$

but these are readily seen to be the values for the axes of the ellipses in (18).

It should be noted that if we substitute in (15) the values for a and b, the expression for the element ds becomes of the following symmetrical form :

$$ds = \frac{mc}{m^2-l^2}\sqrt{l^2+n^2+2ln\cos\phi}\,d\phi - \frac{nc}{m^2-l^2}\sqrt{l^2+m^2+2lm\cos\psi}\,d\psi$$

$$\pm \frac{lc}{m^2-l^2}\sqrt{m^2+n^2-2mn\cos\theta}\,d\theta. \tag{19}$$

We shall conclude the Chapter with a brief account of the rectification of curves of double curvature.

167. **Rectification of Curves of Double Curvature.** If the points in a curve be not situated in the same plane, the curve is said to be one of double curvature. The expression for its length is obtained in an analogous manner to that adopted for plane curves; for, if we refer the curve to a system of rectangular axes in space, and denote the co-ordinates of two consecutive points by (x, y, z), $(x+dx, y+dy, z+dz)$, we get for the element of length, ds, the value

$$ds = \sqrt{dx^2 + dy^2 + dz^2}.$$

The curve is commonly supposed to be determined by the intersection of two cylindrical surfaces, whose equations are of the form

$$f(x, y) = 0, \qquad \phi(x, z) = 0.$$

From these equations, if $\dfrac{dy}{dx}$ and $\dfrac{dz}{dx}$ be determined, the formula of rectification is

$$s = \int\left\{1 + \left(\frac{dy}{dx}\right)^2 + \left(\frac{dz}{dx}\right)^2\right\}^{\frac{1}{2}}dx. \tag{20}$$

[16 a]

When z is taken as the independent variable, this formula becomes

$$s = \int \left\{ 1 + \left(\frac{dx}{dz}\right)^2 + \left(\frac{dy}{dz}\right)^2 \right\}^{\frac{1}{2}} dz \; ;$$

the limits being in each case determined by the conditions of the question.

The simplest example is that of the helix, or the curve formed by the thread of a screw. From its mode of generation it is easily seen that the helix is represented by two equations of the form

$$x = a \cos\left(\frac{z}{b}\right), \quad y = a \sin\left(\frac{z}{b}\right).$$

Hence

$$\frac{dx}{dz} = - \frac{a}{b} \sin\left(\frac{z}{b}\right), \quad \frac{dy}{dz} = \frac{a}{b} \cos\left(\frac{z}{b}\right) ;$$

$$\therefore \; ds = \left(1 + \frac{a^2}{b^2}\right)^{\frac{1}{2}} dz, \quad \text{or } s = \left(1 + \frac{a^2}{b^2}\right)^{\frac{1}{2}} z \; ;$$

the arc being measured from the point in which the helix meets the plane of xy.

This result can also be readily established geometrically.

EXAMPLES.

1. Find the length of the curve whose equations are

$$y = \frac{x^2}{2a}, \quad z = \frac{x^3}{6a^2}.$$

Here $\quad s = \int \left(1 + \frac{x^2}{a^2} + \frac{x^4}{4a^4}\right)^{\frac{1}{2}} dx = \int \left(1 + \frac{x^2}{2a^2}\right) dx = x + \frac{x^3}{6a^2} = x + z \; ;$

the arc being measured from the origin.

This is a case of a system of curves which are readily rectified; for, in general, whenever

$$\left(\frac{dy}{dx}\right)^2 = 2 \frac{dz}{dx},$$

we have

$$\left(1 + \frac{dy^2}{dx^2} + \frac{dz^2}{dx^2}\right)^{\frac{1}{2}} = \left(1 + \frac{dz}{dx}\right),$$

and therefore $\quad ds = dx + dz, \quad \text{or} \quad s = x + z + \text{const.}$

Thus, if $y = f(x)$ be one of the equations of a curve, we get $\dfrac{dy}{dx} = f'(x)$, and hence, if a second equation be determined from the equation

$$\frac{dz}{dx} = \frac{1}{2}\left\{f'(x)\right\}^2,$$

the length of the curve is represented by $x + z + \text{const.}$; the value of the constant being determined by the conditions of the problem.

For instance, if $y = a \sin x$, we get $f'(x) = a \cos x$, and

$$\frac{dz}{dx} = \frac{a^2}{2} \cos^2 x; \quad \therefore \ z = \frac{a^2}{4}(x + \cos x \sin x).$$

Hence the length of the curve of intersection of the cylindrical surfaces

$$y = a \sin x, \qquad z = \frac{a^2}{4}(x + \cos x \sin x)$$

is $z + x$; the length being measured from the origin.

2. $y = 2\sqrt{ax} - x, \quad z = x - \dfrac{2}{3}\sqrt{\dfrac{x^3}{a}}.$ *Ans.* $s = x + y - z.$

3. $\dfrac{x^2}{a^2} - \dfrac{y^2}{b^2} = 1, \quad x = \dfrac{a}{2}(e^{\frac{z}{a}} + e^{-\frac{z}{a}})$, the length being measured from the point

of intersection of the curve with the plane of xy.

$$\textit{Ans. } s = \frac{(a^2 + b^2)^{\frac{1}{2}}}{a}(x^2 - a^2)^{\frac{1}{2}}.$$

1. Find the length of any arc of the catenary

$$y = \frac{a}{2}\left(e^{\frac{x}{a}} + e^{-\frac{x}{a}}\right),$$

and show that the area between the curve, the axis of x, and the ordinates at two points on the curve, is equal to a times the length of the arc terminated by those points.

2. In any curve prove that $s = \int \dfrac{r\,dr}{\sqrt{r^2 - p^2}}$, and hence find the length of a parabolic arc.

3. Show that the integral $\int \dfrac{x\,dx}{\sqrt{bx^2 - x^4 - c^2}}$ may be represented by an arc of a circle, and find the limiting values of x for its possibility.

4. Show that the length of an elliptic arc is represented by $\int \sqrt{\dfrac{a^2 - e^2 x^2}{a^2 - x^2}}\, dx$, where a is the semiaxis major, and e the eccentricity.

5. Express the length of an elliptic quadrant in a series of ascending powers of its eccentricity.

$$Ans.\ \frac{\pi a}{2}\left\{1 - \left(\frac{1}{2}\right)^2\frac{e^2}{1} - \left(\frac{1 \cdot 3}{2 \cdot 4}\right)^2\frac{e^4}{3} - \left(\frac{1 \cdot 3 \cdot 5}{2 \cdot 4 \cdot 6}\right)^2\frac{e^6}{5} - \&\text{c.}\right\}.$$

6. Prove that the integral of

$$\frac{x^2\,dx}{\sqrt{(x^2 - \beta^2)(a^2 - x^2)}}$$

can be represented by an arc of the ellipse whose semiaxes are a and β.

7. Show that the rectification of the sinusoid $y = b \sin x$ is the same as that of an ellipse.

8. Prove that the whole length of the *first negative pedal* of an ellipse, taken with respect to a focus, is equal to the circumference of the circle described on the axis minor as diameter.

9. Show that the length of an arc of the curve $r = a \sin n\theta$ is equal to that of an arc of the ellipse whose semiaxes are a and na.

10. If, from the equation of a curve referred to rectangular co-ordinates, we form an equation in polar co-ordinates, by taking $r = y$ and $r\,d\theta = dx$, then the lengths of the corresponding arcs of the two curves are equal, and the area $\int y\,dx$ of the former curve is equal to the corresponding sectorial area of the latter.

11. Prove that the difference between the lengths of the two loops of the limaçon $r = a \cos \theta + b$ is equal to $8b$: a being greater than b.

12. Being given three points A, B, C on the circumference of an ellipse, show that we can always find, at either side of C, a fourth point D such that the difference between AB and CD shall be equal to a right line.

13. If a circle be described touching two tangents to an ellipse and also touching the ellipse, prove that the point of contact with the ellipse divides the elliptic arc between the points of contact of the tangents into two parts, whose difference is equal to the difference of the lengths of the tangents (Chasles, *Comptes Rendus*, 1843).

14. Prove that the entire length of any closed curve is represented by $\int \frac{p\,ds}{\rho}$ taken round the entire curve ; ρ being the radius of curvature at any point, and p the length of the perpendicular from any fixed point on the tangent.

15. If $e^y = \dfrac{e^x + 1}{e^x - 1}$ be the equation of a curve, prove that $\dfrac{ds}{dx} = \dfrac{e^{2x} + 1}{e^{2x} - 1}$, and hence rectify the curve.

16. Calculate approximately, by the tables of Art. 125, the whole length of a loop of the curve $r^{\frac{2}{3}} = a^{\frac{2}{3}} \cos \frac{4}{5}\theta$.

Here, by Ex. 3, Art. 156, the required length is

$$\frac{5}{4} a \sqrt{\pi} \; \frac{\Gamma\left(\dfrac{5}{8}\right)}{\Gamma\left(\dfrac{9}{8}\right)}, \text{ or } 2a \sqrt{\pi} \; \frac{\Gamma\left(\dfrac{13}{8}\right)}{\Gamma\left(\dfrac{9}{8}\right)} .$$

Hence, taking logarithms, and observing that $\dfrac{13}{8} = 1.625$, and $\dfrac{9}{8} = 1.125$, we get as the required approximation $a \times 3.29488$. The figure of this curve is exhibited in Art. 268, Diff. Calc.

17. In a Cartesian Oval whose two internal foci coincide, prove that the difference of the two arcs, intercepted by any two transversals from the external focus, is equal to a straight line which may be found. [The above curve is the inverse of an ellipse from a focus.]—Professor Crofton, *Educ. Times,* June, 1874.

From (13) Art. 166, it follows, making $n = m$, that the equation of the limaçon, in this case, is

$$r^2 + 2rc \, \frac{l^2 \cos\theta - m^2}{l^2 - m^2} + c^2 = 0,$$

which is of the form

$$r^2 + 2r(\alpha \cos\theta - \beta) + (\alpha - \beta)^2 = 0.$$

Hence, by (15), the difference between two corresponding elementary arcs is

$$4\sqrt{\alpha\beta} \cos \frac{\theta}{2} \, d\theta.$$

Consequently, if θ_1 and θ_2 be the values of θ for the two transversals in question, we get the difference of the corresponding arcs

$$= 8\sqrt{\alpha\beta}\left(\sin\frac{\theta_2}{2} - \sin\frac{\theta_1}{2}\right).$$

Also, it can be readily seen that the distance between the vertices of the limaçon is $4\sqrt{\alpha\beta}$; $\therefore$ &c.

18. Show that the length of an arc of the ellipse $\dfrac{x^2}{a^2} + \dfrac{y^2}{b^2} = 1$ is represented by the integral

$$a^2 b^2 \int \frac{d\theta}{(a^2 \cos^2\theta + b^2 \sin^2\theta)^{\frac{3}{2}}}$$

This result is easily seen, for we have $ds = \rho\, d\theta$, and $\rho = \dfrac{a^2 b^2}{p^3}$; $\therefore$ &c.

19. Show, in like manner, that the length of a hyperbolic arc is represented by

$$a^2 b^2 \int \frac{d\theta}{(a^2 \cos^2\theta - b^2 \sin^2\theta)^{\frac{3}{2}}}$$

20. Hence prove that the integral

$$\int \frac{dx}{(a - bx^2)^{\frac{3}{2}} (a' - b'x^2)^{\frac{1}{2}}}$$

is represented by an elliptic arc when $ab' > ba'$, and by a hyperbolic arc when $ab' < ba'$.

21. Prove that the differential of the arc of the curve found by cutting in the ratio $n : 1$ the normals to the cycloid

$$y = a + b \cos u, \quad x = au + b \sin u,$$

is

$$\sqrt{(a + nb)^2 + 4nab \sin^2 \frac{u}{2}}\, du.$$

22. Each element of the periphery of an ellipse is divided by the diameter parallel to it: find the sum of all the elementary quotients extended to the entire ellipse.

$$\textit{Ans. } \pi.$$

23. In the figure of Art. 158, if $\alpha = \angle ACN'$, and $\beta = \angle BCN$, prove that

$$\frac{\tan \alpha}{a} = \frac{\tan \beta}{b}.$$

24. Find the length, measured from the origin, of the curve

$$x^2 = a^2 \left(1 - e^{\frac{y}{a}}\right).$$

$$\textit{Ans. } s = a \log \left(\frac{a + x}{a - x}\right) - x.$$

25. Find the length, measured from $\phi = 0$, of the curve which is represented by the equations

$$x = (2a - b) \sin \phi - (a - b) \sin^3 \phi,$$
$$y = (2b - a) \cos \phi - (b - a) \cos^3 \phi.$$

$$\textit{Ans. } s = \tfrac{1}{2}(a + b)\phi + \tfrac{3}{2}(a - b) \sin \phi \cos \phi.$$

26. Prove that the sides of a polygon of maximum perimeter inscribed in a conic are tangents to a confocal conic.—Chasles, *Comptes Rendus*, 1845.

27. To two arcs of an equilateral hyperbola, whose difference is rectifiable, correspond equal arcs of the lemniscate which is the pedal of the hyperbola. *Ibid.*

28. The tangents at the extremities of two arcs of a conic, whose difference is rectifiable, form a quadrilateral, whose sides are tangents to the same circle.—*Ibid.*

29. In an equilateral hyperbola prove that

$$r\,ds = \tfrac{1}{2}a^2\,d(\tan 2\theta),$$

and hence show that $\int r\,ds$ taken between any two points on the curve is equal to the rectangle under the chord joining the points and the line connecting the middle point of the chord with the centre of the hyperbola.   **Mr. W. S. M'Cay.**

30. If

$$x = a\,\frac{z + z^3}{1 + z^4}, \qquad y = a\,\frac{z - z^3}{1 + z^4}$$

be any point on a curve, show that the arc is the integral of

$$a\sqrt{2}\,\frac{dz}{\sqrt{1 + z^4}}. \qquad\qquad \text{(M. Serret}$$

What curve do the equations represent ?

31. Through any point in a plane two conics of a confocal system can be drawn.   If the distance between the foci be $2c$, and the transverse semi-axes of these conics be μ, ν, prove the following expression for any arc of a curve

$$ds^2 = (\mu^2 - \nu^2)\left\{\frac{d\mu^2}{\mu^2 - c^2} + \frac{d\nu^2}{c^2 - \nu^2}\right\}.$$

32. Prove that the following relation is satisfied by the μ and ν of any point on a tangent to the ellipse for which μ has the value μ_1 :

$$\frac{d\mu}{\sqrt{(\mu^2 - c^2)(\mu^2 - \mu_1^2)}} \pm \frac{d\nu}{\sqrt{(c^2 - \nu^2)(\mu_1^2 - \nu^2)}} = 0.$$

33. The arc of the envelope of the right line $x \sin a - y \cos a = f(a)$ is the integral of $(f(a) + f''(a))\,da.$ (Hermite, *Cours d'Analyse.*)

34. The arc of the curve in which $y^2 + a^2 x^2 - 2ax = 0$ and $z^2 - b^2 x^2 + 2bx = 0$ intersect, if $a^2 = 1 + b^2$, is

$$\int \frac{\sqrt{2(a - b)}\,dx}{\sqrt{x(2 - ax)(2 - bx)}}. \qquad\qquad (Ibid).$$

35. Show that the arc of the curve $\dfrac{x^m}{a^m} + \dfrac{y^m}{b^m} = 1$ depends on an integral of the form

$$\int dz\,\sqrt{a^2(1 + z)^k + b^2(1 - z)^k}, \quad\text{where } k = \frac{2}{m} - 2.$$

36. Show that rectification may, in general, be reduced to quadratures as follows :—

Produce each ordinate of the curve to be rectified until the whole length is in a constant ratio to the corresponding normal divided by the old ordinate, then the locus of the extremity of the ordinate so produced is a curve whose area is in a constant ratio to the length of the given curve.

By this theorem Van Huraet rectified the semi-cubical parabola nearly simultaneously with Wm. Neil.

CHAPTER IX.

VOLUMES AND SURFACES OF SOLIDS.

168. Solids.—The Prism and Cylinder.—The most simple solid is the cube, which is accordingly the measure of all solids, as the square is that of all areas. Hence the finding the volume of a solid is called its *cubature*. Before proceeding to the application of the Integral Calculus to finding the volumes and surfaces of solids we propose to show how, in certain cases, such volumes and surfaces can be found from geometrical considerations. In the first place, the volume of a rectangular parallelepiped is measured by the continued product of the three adjacent edges; and that of any parallelepiped by the area of a face multiplied by its distance from the opposite face.

Again, the volume of a right prism is measured by the product of its altitude into the area of its base. For example, the volume of the right prism represented in the figure is measured by the area of the polygon $ABCDE$, multiplied by the altitude AA'. Again, since each lateral face, $AB\,B'A'$ for example, is a rectangle, it follows that the sum of the areas of all the faces (exclusive of the two bases), i.e. the area of the surface of the prism, is equal to the rectangle under the altitude and the perimeter of the polygon which forms its base.

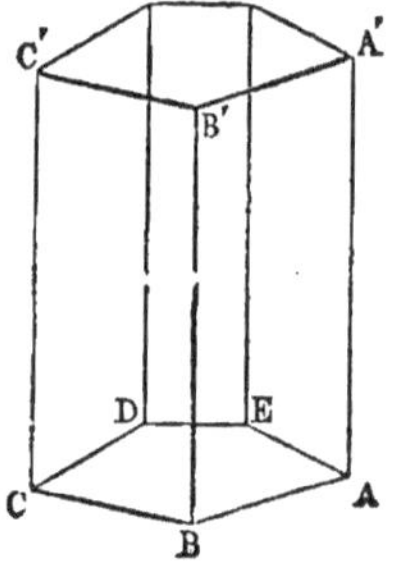

Fig. 36.

This and the preceding result still hold in the limit, when the base, instead of a polygon, is a closed curve of any form, in which case the surface generated is called a *cylinder*. Hence, if V denote the volume of the portion of a cylinder bounded by two planes drawn perpendicular to its edges, h its height, and A the area of its base, we get $V = Ah$.

Again, if Σ denote the superficial area of a cylinder, bounded as before, and S the length of the curve which forms its base, we have $\Sigma = Sh$.

169. **The Pyramid and Cone.**—If the angular points of a polygon be joined to any external point, the solid so formed is called a *pyramid*. Any section of a pyramid by a plane parallel to its base is a polygon similar to that which forms the base, and the ratio of their homologous sides is the same as that of the distances of the planes from the vertex of the pyramid. Hence it follows that pyramids standing on the same base, and whose vertices lie in a plane parallel to the base, are equal in volume. For, the sections made by any plane parallel to the base are equal in every respect ; and, consequently, if we suppose the pyramids divided into an indefinite number of slices by planes parallel to the base, the volumes of the corresponding slices will be the same for all the pyramids; and hence the entire volumes are equal.

Also, if two pyramids have equal altitudes, but stand on different polygonal bases, the volumes of the pyramids will be to each other in the same proportion as the areas of the polygonal bases. For, this proportion holds between the areas of the sections made by any plane parallel to the base ; and consequently between the slices made by two infinitely near planes.

Again, the pyramid whose base is one of the faces of a cube, and whose vertex is at the centre of the cube, is the one-sixth part of the cube; for the entire cube can be divided into six equal pyramids, one for each face. Hence, denoting the side of a cube by a, the volume of the pyramid in question is represented by $\dfrac{a^3}{6}$; i. e. by the product of the area of its base into one-third of its height.

Now, if we vary the base, without altering the height, from what has been established above it follows that the volume of any pyramid is the area of its base multiplied by one-third of its height.*

---

* This demonstration is taken from Clairaut's *Élémens de Géométrie*. The student is supposed familiar with the more ancient proof, from the property that a triangular prism can be divided into three pyramids of equal volume.

If the base of the pyramid be any closed curve, the solid so formed is called a cone; and we infer that the *volume of a cone is equal to one-third of the product of the area of its base into its height.*

If the base of a pyramid be a regular polygon, and the vertex be equidistant from the angular points of the polygon, the pyramid is called a *right pyramid.*

In this case each *face* of the pyramid is an isosceles triangle, whose area is the rectangle under the side of the polygon and half the perpendicular of the triangle. Hence the surface of the pyramid is equal to the rectangle under the semi-perimeter of the regular polygon and the perpendicular common to each face of the pyramid.

Again, if we suppose the number of sides of the regular polygon to become infinite, the pyramid becomes a right cone; and we infer that the entire surface of a right cone is equal to the rectangle under the semi-circumference of its circular base and the length of an edge of the cone.

Hence, if a be the semi-angle of the cone, l the length of an edge, and r the radius of its base, we have $r = l \sin a$, and the surface of the cone is represented by $\pi l^2 \sin a$.

If a right cone be divided by two planes ABC, DEF, perpendicular to its axis, as in figure, the part intercepted by the planes is called a *truncated* cone.

The surface of a truncated cone is easily expressed; for if $OA = l$, $OD = l'$, the required surface is $\pi \sin a \, (l^2 - l'^2)$, or $\pi (l - l')(l + l') \sin a$.

Now, if the circular section LMN be drawn bisecting the distance between ABC and DEF, the circumference of the circle LMN is $\pi (l + l') \sin a$. Hence the surface of the truncated cone is equal to the rectangle under the edge AD and the circumference of LMN its mean section.

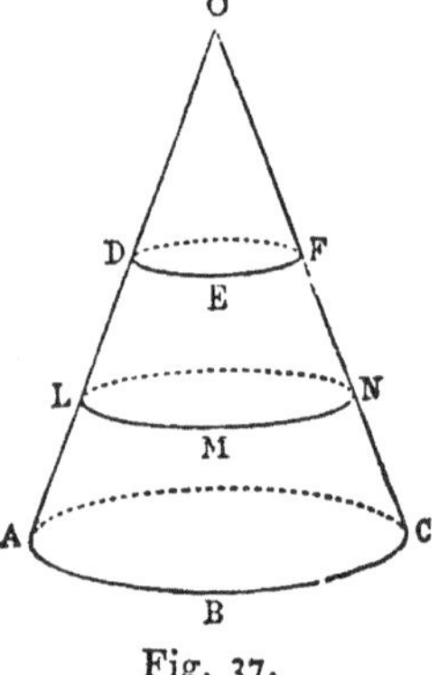

Fig. 37.

170. **Surface and Volume of a Sphere.**—To find the superficial area of a sphere; suppose a regular polygon inscribed in a semicircle, and let the figure revolve around the diameter AB; then each side of the polygon, PQ for example, will describe a truncated cone.

Now, from the centre C draw CD perpendicular to PQ, and construct, as in figure; then, by the preceding Article, the surface generated by PQ is equal to $2\pi\,PQ\,.\,DI.$

Again, by similar triangles, we have $DC : DI = PQ : MN$; $\therefore\ PQ\,.\,DI = DC\,.\,MN.$

Accordingly, since the perpendicular CD is of same length for each side of the polygon, the surface generated by the entire polygon in a complete revo-

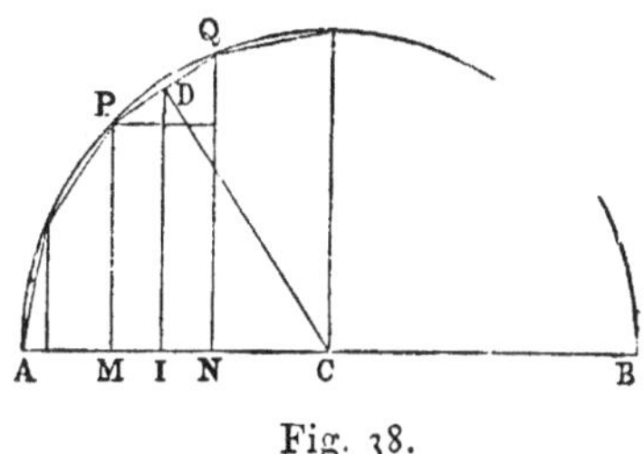

Fig. 38.

lution is equal to $2\pi\,CD\,.\,AB = 4\pi\,R^2\cos\dfrac{\pi}{n}$; where n represents the number of sides of the polygon, and R the radius of the circle.

If we suppose n to become infinite, the solid generated by the polygon becomes a sphere; and we get $4\pi\,R^2$ for the entire surface of the sphere. Hence, the surface of a sphere is equal to four times the area of one of its great circles.

Again, it is easy to find the surface generated by any number of sides of the polygon. Thus, for example, that generated by all the sides lying between the points A and Q is plainly equal to $2\pi\,CD\,.\,AN.$

Hence, in the limit, the surface generated in a complete revolution by the arc AQ is equal to $2\pi\,.\,AC\,.\,AN.$ Such a portion of a sphere is called a *spherical cap*.

Again, suppose the points A and Q connected; then, since $AQ^2 = AB\,.\,AN$, it follows that the area of the spherical cap generated by the arc AQ is equal to the area of the circle whose radius is the chord AQ.

The volume of a sphere is readily found from its surface; for we may regard the volume as consisting of an infinitely great number of pyramids, having their common vertex at the centre, and whose bases form the entire surface. But the volume of each pyramid is represented by the product of one-third of its height (i. e. the radius) by its base. Hence the entire volume of the sphere is one-third of its radius multiplied by its surface, i. e. $\dfrac{4\pi}{3}R^3.$

EXAMPLES.

1. If a sphere and its circumscribing cylinder be cut by planes perpendicular to the axis of the cylinder, prove that the intercepted portions of the surfaces are equal in area.

2. Prove that the volume of a sphere is to that of its circumscribing cylinder in the proportion of 2 to 3 : and that their surfaces also are in the same proportion. These results were discovered by Archimedes.

171. **Surfaces of Revolution.**—In the preceding we have regarded a sphere as generated by the revolution of a circle around a diameter. In general, if any plane be supposed to revolve around a fixed line situated in it, every point in the plane will describe a circle, and any curve lying in the plane will generate a surface.

Such a surface is called a *surface of revolution;* and the fixed line, round which the revolution takes place, is called the *axis* of revolution.

It is obvious that the section of a surface of revolution made by any plane drawn perpendicular to its axis is a circle.

If we suppose any solid of revolution to be cut by a series of planes perpendicular to its axis, the volume of the solid intercepted between any two such sections may be regarded as the limit of the sum of an indefinite number of thin cylindrical plates.

Now, if we suppose the generating curve to be referred to rectangular axes, the axis of revolution being that of x, the area of the circle generated by a point (x, y) is plainly equal to πy^2, and the cylindrical plate standing on it, whose thickness is dx, is represented by $\pi y^2 dx$.

Hence, the element of volume of the surface of revolution is $\pi y^2 dx$, and the entire volume comprised between two sections, corresponding to the abscissæ a and β, is obviously represented by the definite integral

$$\pi \int_{a}^{\beta} y^2 dx,$$

in which the value of y in terms of x is to be got from the equation of the generating curve.

In like manner, the volume of the surface generated by the revolution of a curve around the axis of y is represented by $\pi \int x^2 dy$, taken between suitable limits.

Again, we may regard the surface generated by any element ds of the curve as being ultimately a portion of the surface of a truncated cone, as in Art. 170; and hence the surface generated by ds in a complete revolution round the axis of x is represented by $2\pi y ds$; and accordingly the entire surface generated is represented by

$$2\pi \int y ds,$$

taken between proper limits.

We proceed to apply these formulæ to a few elementary examples.

172. **The Sphere.**—Let $x^2 + y^2 = a^2$ be the equation of the generating circle; then, substituting $a^2 - x^2$ for y^2, we get for the volume

$$V = \pi \int (a^2 - x^2)\, dx = \pi \left(a^2 x - \frac{x^3}{3} \right) + \text{const.}$$

If we take o and a as limits, we get $\dfrac{2\pi a^3}{3}$ for the volume of the hemisphere; $\therefore$ the entire volume of the sphere is $\dfrac{4\pi a^3}{3}$, as in Art. 170.

To find the volume of a spherical cap, let h be the length of the portion of the diameter cut off by the bounding plane, and we get for the corresponding volume

$$\pi \int_{a-h}^{a} (a^2 - x^2)\, dx = \pi h^2 \left(a - \frac{h}{3} \right).$$

Again, to find the superficial area, we have

$$ds = \left(1 + \frac{dy^2}{dx^2} \right)^{\frac{1}{2}} dx = \left(1 + \frac{x^2}{y^2} \right) dx = \frac{a}{y}\, dx; \quad \therefore\ y\, ds = a\, dx.$$

Hence, the surface of the zone contained between two parallel planes corresponding to the abscissæ x_1 and x_0 is

$$2\pi \int_{x_0}^{x_1} a\, dx = 2\pi a (x_1 - x_0);$$

that is the product of the circumference of a great circle by the breadth of the zone. This agrees with Art. 170.

173. **Right Cone.**—If a denote, as before, the angle which the right line which generates a cone makes with its axis of revolution, we get $y = x \tan a$, taking the vertex of the cone as origin, and the axis of revolution as that of x; accordingly, the element of volume is $\pi \tan^2 a \, x^2 \, dx$.

Hence, if h denote the height of the cone, we get its volume equal to

$$\pi \tan^2 a \int_0^h x^2 \, dx = \frac{\pi h^3}{3} \tan^2 a \,;$$

i.e. $\dfrac{h}{3} \times$ area of its base, as in Art. 169.

Again, to find its surface, we have $ds = \sec a \, dx$;

$$\therefore \; 2\pi \int y \, ds = 2\pi \tan a \sec a \int_0^h x \, dx = \pi h^2 \tan a \sec a \,;$$

which agrees with the result already obtained.

EXAMPLES.

1. The base of a cylinder is a circle whose area is equal to the surface of a sphere of radius 5 ft.; being given that the volume of the cylinder is equal to the sum of the volumes of two spheres of radii 9 ft. and 16 ft., find the height of the cylinder.   *Ans.* $64\frac{1}{3}$ ft.

2. A solid sector is cut out of a sphere of 10 ft. radius, by a cone the angle of which is 120°; find the radius of the sphere whose solid contents are equal to those of the sector.   *Ans.* $5\sqrt[3]{2}$.

3. Two cones have a common base, the radius of which is 12 ft.; the altitude of one is 9 ft.; and that of the other is 5 ft.; find the radius of a sphere whose entire surface is equal to the sum of the areas of the cones.

Ans. $2\sqrt{21}$ ft.

174. **Paraboloid of Revolution.**—Writing the equation of a parabola in the form $y^2 = 2mx$, we get for the volume of the solid generated by its revolution round the axis of x

$$2\pi m \int x \, dx = \pi m x^2 + \text{const.} = \frac{\pi}{2} y^2 x + \text{const.}$$

Hence, the volume of the surface generated by the revolution of the part of a parabola between its vertex and the point (x_1, y_1) is represented by $\dfrac{\pi}{2} y_1^2 x_1$, i.e. is equal to half the volume of the circumscribing cylinder.

Again, to find the surface of the paraboloid, we have

$$y\,ds = y\left(1 + \frac{y^2}{m^2}\right)^{\frac{1}{2}} dy = \frac{1}{m}\,(y^2 + m^2)^{\frac{1}{2}}\,y\,dy.$$

Hence, the surface of the paraboloid, between the same limits as above, is represented by

$$\frac{2\pi}{m}\int_0^{y_1} (y^2 + m^2)^{\frac{1}{2}}\,y\,dy = \frac{2\pi}{3m}\left\{(y_1^2 + m^2)^{\frac{3}{2}} - m^3\right\}.$$

175. **Spheroids of Revolution.**—If we suppose an ellipse to revolve round its axis major, the surface generated by the revolving curve is called a *prolate spheroid.* If it revolve round the axis minor the surface is called an *oblate spheroid.*

The volume of a spheroid is easily obtained; for, taking $\dfrac{x^2}{a^2} + \dfrac{y^2}{b^2} = 1$ as the equation of the curve, we get, on substituting $b^2\left(1 - \dfrac{x^2}{a^2}\right)$ for y^2,

$$V = \pi\,\frac{b^2}{a^2}\int (a^2 - x^2)\,dx = \frac{\pi b^2}{a^2}\,x\left(a^2 - \frac{x^2}{3}\right) + \text{const.}$$

Hence the entire volume is $\dfrac{4\pi}{3}ab^2$. In like manner, the volume of an oblate spheroid is obviously $\dfrac{4\pi}{3}ba^2$.

176. **Surface of Spheroid.**—In the case of a prolate spheroid we have

$$ds = \left(1 + \frac{b^4 x^2}{a^4 y^2}\right)^{\frac{1}{2}} dx\,;$$

$$\therefore\, y\,ds = \left(y^2 + \frac{b^4}{a^4}x^2\right)^{\frac{1}{2}} dx = \left(b^2 - \frac{b^2}{a^2}e^2 x^2\right)^{\frac{1}{2}} dx = \frac{be}{a}\left(\frac{a^2}{e^2} - x^2\right)^{\frac{1}{2}} dx.$$

[17]

Hence, if $CN = x_1$, $CM = x_0$, we get for S, the zone generated in a complete revolution by the arc PQ,

$$S = 2\pi \, \frac{be}{a} \int_{x_0}^{x_1} \left(\frac{a^2}{e^2} - x^2 \right)^{\frac{1}{2}} dx.$$

Now, if we take $CD = \dfrac{a}{e}$,

and construct an ellipse whose semiaxes are CD and CB, it is easily seen

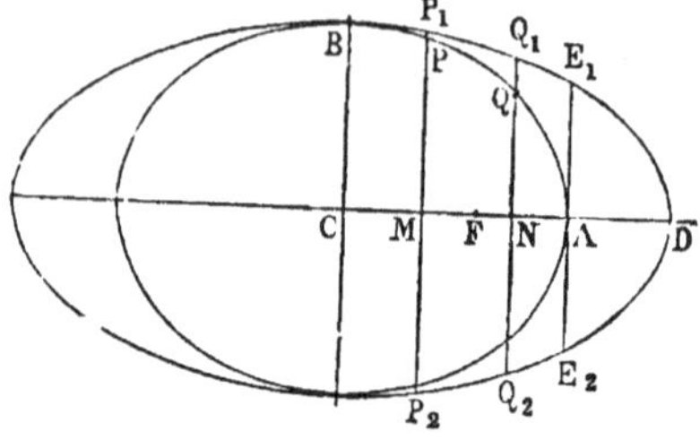

Fig. 39.

(Art. 129) that the elementary area between two consecutive ordinates of this ellipse is $\dfrac{be}{a}\left(\dfrac{a^2}{e^2} - x^2 \right)^{\frac{1}{2}} dx$.   Hence it follows that the area of the zone generated by the arc PQ is π times the area of the portion $P_1Q_1Q_2P_2$ of this ellipse.

Again, if AE_1 be the tangent at the vertex of the original ellipse, we see that the entire surface of the spheroid is 4π × the area $BCAE_1$; but this is seen, without difficulty, to be

$$2\pi b^2 + 2\pi \, \frac{ab}{e} \sin^{-1} e. \tag{1}$$

In like manner, we get for the surface S generated by the revolution of an ellipse round its minor axis

$$S = 2\pi \int x \, ds = 2\pi \int \left(a^2 + \frac{a^4 e^2}{b^4} y^2 \right)^{\frac{1}{2}} dy$$

$$= 2\pi \, \frac{a^2 e}{b^2} \int \left(y^2 + \frac{b^4}{a^2 e^2} \right)^{\frac{1}{2}} dy.$$

If this be integrated, as in Art. 151, we get, after some obvious reductions,

$$S = \pi \frac{ay}{b^2} (a^2 e^2 y^2 + b^4)^{\frac{1}{2}} + \pi \frac{b^2}{e} \log \frac{aey + (a^2 e^2 y^2 + b^4)^{\frac{1}{2}}}{b^2}.$$

If this be taken between the limits 0 and b, and doubled, we get for the entire surface of the ellipsoid

$$2\pi a^2 + \pi \frac{b^2}{e} \log \left(\frac{1 + e}{1 - e} \right). \tag{2}$$

It is readily seen, as in the former case, that the surface of any zone of this ellipsoid is π times the area of a corresponding portion of the hyperbola

$$\frac{x^2}{a^2} - \frac{a^2 e^2 y^2}{b^4} = 1$$

bounded by lines drawn parallel to the axis of x.

The area of the surface generated by the revolution of a hyperbola round either axis admits of a similar investigation.

EXAMPLES.

1. Find the volume of the surface generated by the revolution of a cycloid round its base.

Here, referring the cycloid to DA and DB as co-ordinate axes, we have (see Diff. Calc., Art. 272)

$$x = a(\phi + \sin \phi), \quad y = a(1 + \cos \phi),$$

where $\angle PCL = \phi$.

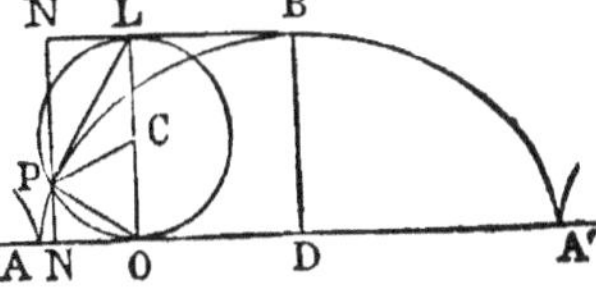

Fig. 40.

Hence

$$dV = \pi y^2 dx = \pi a^3 (1 + \cos \phi)^3 d\phi;$$

$\therefore$ for the entire volume V, we get

$$V = 2\pi a^3 \int_0^\pi (1 + \cos \phi)^3 d\phi = 16\pi a^3 \int_0^\pi \cos^6 \frac{\phi}{2} d\phi$$

$$= 32\pi a^3 \int_0^{\frac{\pi}{2}} \cos^6 \theta \, d\theta, \quad \text{making } \frac{\phi}{2} = \theta.$$

Hence

$$V = 5\pi^2 a^3.$$

2. Find the whole surface generated in the same case.

Here

$$S = 2\pi \int y \, ds = 4\pi a^2 \int (1 + \cos \phi) \cos \frac{\phi}{2} d\phi;$$

hence the entire surface is

$$32\pi a^2 \int_0^\pi \cos^3 \frac{\phi}{2} d\phi = \frac{64\pi a^2}{3}.$$

$$[17\,a]$$

3. Find the volume and the surface of the solid generated by the revolution of the tractrix round its axis.

(1). Here we have

$$y^3 dx = - (a^2 - y^2)^{\frac{1}{2}} y \, dy \, ;$$

hence the volume generated by the portion AP is

$$\pi \int_y^a (a^2 - y^2)^{\frac{1}{2}} y \, dy = \frac{\pi}{3} (a^2 - y^2)^{\frac{3}{2}}.$$

The volume generated by the entire tractrix is $\dfrac{2\pi}{3} a^3$; i.e. half the volume of the sphere whose radius is OA.

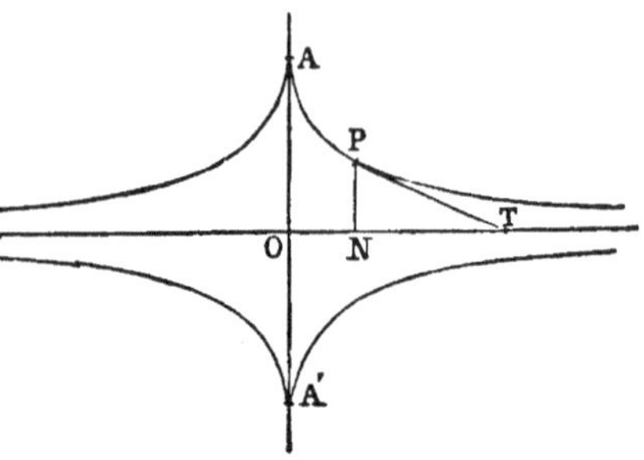

Fig. 41.

(2). The surface generated by AP is

$$2\pi \int y \, ds = 2\pi a \int_y^a dy \quad \text{(see Ex. 2, Art. 154)}$$

$$= 2\pi a (a - y).$$

Hence the entire surface generated is $2\pi a^2$; i.e. half the surface of the sphere of radius OA.

4. Find the volume, and also the surface, generated by the revolution of the catenary around the axis of x.

(1). Here the volume of the solid generated by VP is represented by

$$\pi \int_0^x y^2 dx = \frac{\pi a^2}{4} \int_0^x \left(e^{\frac{2x}{a}} + e^{-\frac{2x}{a}} + 2 \right) dx$$

$$= \frac{\pi a^2}{4} \left\{ \frac{a}{2} \left(e^{\frac{2x}{a}} - e^{-\frac{2x}{a}} \right) + 2x \right\}$$

$$= \frac{\pi a}{2} (ys + ax),$$

where $s = PV$.

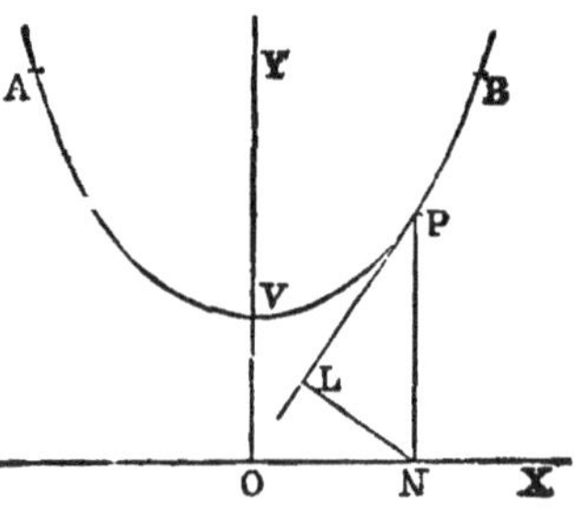

Fig. 42.

(2). Again, since

$$ds = \tfrac{1}{2} \left(e^{\frac{x}{a}} + e^{-\frac{x}{a}} \right) dx = \frac{y \, dx}{a},$$

we have

$$2\pi \int y \, ds = \frac{2\pi}{a} \int y^2 dx.$$

Consequently the surface generated by PV in a complete revolution is $\dfrac{2}{a}$ × the volume generated; i.e. $= \pi(ys + ax)$.

5. In the same curve to find the surface generated by its revolution round the axis OV.

Here

$$S = 2\pi \int x\,ds = \pi \int x e^{\frac{x}{a}}\,dx + \pi \int x e^{-\frac{x}{a}}\,dx.$$

Again

$$\int_0^x x e^{\frac{x}{a}}\,dx = ax e^{\frac{x}{a}} - a \int_0^x e^{\frac{x}{a}}\,dx = a\left(x e^{\frac{x}{a}} - a e^{\frac{x}{a}} + a\right).$$

Also the value of

$$\int_0^x x e^{-\frac{x}{a}}\,dx$$

is obtained by changing the sign of a in the last result.

Hence

$$\int_0^x x e^{-\frac{x}{a}}\,dx = a^2 - ax e^{-\frac{x}{a}} - a^2 e^{-\frac{x}{a}};$$

$$\therefore S = \pi \left\{ 2a^2 + ax \left(e^{\frac{x}{a}} - e^{-\frac{x}{a}} \right) - a^2 \left(e^{\frac{x}{a}} + e^{-\frac{x}{a}} \right) \right\}$$

$$= 2\pi(a^2 + xs - ay).$$

177. Annular Solids.—If a closed curve, which is symmetrical with respect to a right line, be made to revolve round a parallel line, then the superficial area generated in a complete revolution is equal to the product of the length of the moving curve into the circumference of the circle whose radius is the distance between the parallel lines.

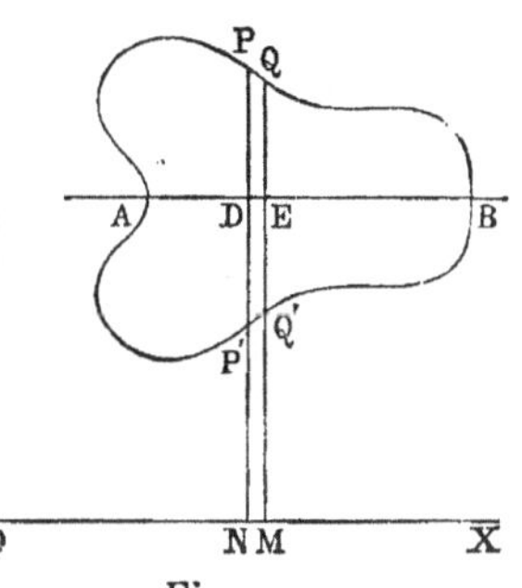

Fig. 43.

This is easily proved: for let $APBP'$ be any curve, symmetrical with respect to AB, and suppose OX to be the axis of revolution; and draw PN, QM two indefinitely near lines perpendicular to the axis. It is evident that $PQ = P'Q'$. Again, let $PN = y$, $P'N = y'$, $PQ = P'Q' = ds$, $DN = b$; then the sum of the elementary zones described by PQ and $P'Q'$ in a complete revolution is represented by

$$2\pi(y + y')\,ds = 4\pi b\,ds.$$

Consequently the surface generated by the entire curve is $2\pi bS$, where S denotes the whole length of the curve.

A similar theorem holds for the volume of the solid generated : viz., the volume generated is equal to the product of the area of the revolving curve into the circumference of the same circle as before.

For the volume of this solid is plainly represented by

$$\pi \int (y^2 - y'^2)\, dx,$$

or by

$$\pi \int (y - y')(y + y')\, dx = 2\pi b \int (y - y')\, dx.$$

But the area of the curve is represented by

$$\int (y - y')\, dx :$$

consequently, denoting this area by A, and the volume by V, we have

$$V = 2\pi b \times A.$$

In these results the axis of revolution is supposed not to intersect the curve; if it does, the expression $2\pi b \times A$ represents the difference between the volumes of the surfaces generated by the portions of the curve lying at opposite sides of the axis of revolution; as is readily seen. A similar alteration must be made in the former theorem in this case.

If a circle revolve round any external axis situated in its plane, the surface generated is called a spherical ring. From the preceding it follows that the entire surface of such a ring is $4\pi^2 ab$; where a is the radius of the circle, and b the distance of its centre from the axis of revolution.

In like manner the volume of the ring is $2\pi^2 a^2 b$.

It would be easy to add other applications of these theorems.

178. **Guldin's* Theorems.**—The results established in the preceding Article are but particular cases of two general

---

* Guldin, *Centrobaryica, seu de centro gravitatis trium specierum quantitatis continuæ*, 1635. Guldin arrived at his principle by induction from a small number of elementary cases, but his attempt at a general demonstration was an eminent failure. See Montucla *Hist. des Math.*, tom. ii. p. 34. Montucla has shown, tom. ii. p. 92, that Guldin's theorems can be established from geometrical considerations, without recourse to the Calculus.

propositions, usually called Guldin's Theorems, but originally enunciated by Pappus (see Walton's *Mechanical Problems,* p. 42, third Edition). They may be stated as follows:—

(1). If a plane curve revolve round any external axis, situated in its plane, *the area of the surface generated is equal to the product of the perimeter of the revolving curve by the length of the path described, during the revolution, by the centre of gravity of that perimeter.*

(2). Under the same circumstances, *the volume of the solid generated is equal to the product of the area of the generating curve into the path described by the centre of gravity of the revolving area.*

To prove the former, let s denote the whole length of the curve, x, y, the co-ordinates of one of its points, $\bar{x}$, $\bar{y}$, those of the centre of gravity of the curve; then, from the definition of these latter, we have

$$\bar{y} = \frac{\int y\,ds}{s};$$

$$\therefore \ 2\pi\bar{y}s = 2\pi \int y\,ds,$$

i.e. the surface generated by revolution round the axis of x is equal to the product of S, the length of the generating curve, into $2\pi\bar{y}$, the path described by the centre of gravity.

To prove the second proposition; let A denote the area of the generating curve, and dA the element of area corresponding to any point x, y. Also let $\bar{x}$, $\bar{y}$ be the co-ordinates of the centre of gravity of the area, then

$$\bar{y} = \frac{\Sigma\,y\,dA}{A} = \frac{\iint y\,dx\,dy}{A} \ \text{(substituting } dx\,dy \text{ for } dA\text{)};$$

$$\therefore \ 2\pi\bar{y}A = 2\pi \iint y\,dx\,dy = \pi \int y^2\,dx\,;$$

where the integral is supposed taken for every point round the perimeter of the curve: but, from Art. 171, the integral at the right-hand side represents the volume of the solid generated; hence the proposition in question follows.

For example, the volume of the ring generated by the revolution of an ellipse around any exterior line situated in its plane is at once $2\pi^2 abc$, where a and b are the semiaxes of the ellipse, and c is the distance of its centre from the axis of revolution.

It may be noted that these results still hold if we suppose the curve, instead of making a complete revolution, to turn round the axis through any angle. For, let θ be the circular measure of the angle of rotation, and in the former case we have

$$\theta \bar{y} s = \theta \int y\, ds.$$

But $\theta \bar{y}$ is the length of the path described by the centre of gravity, and $\theta \int y\, ds$ is the area of the surface generated by the curve; $\therefore$ &c.

In like manner the second proposition can be shown to hold.

Again, Guldin's theorems are still true if we suppose the rotation to take place around a number of different axes in succession; in which case the centre of gravity, instead of describing a single circle, would describe a number of arcs of circles consecutively; and the whole area of the surface generated will still be measured by the product of the length of the generating curve into the path of its centre of gravity; for this result holds for the part of the surface corresponding to each axis of revolution separately, and therefore holds for the sum.

Again, in the limit, when we suppose each separate rotation indefinitely small, we deduce the following theorem. If any plane curve move so that the path of its centre of gravity is at each instant perpendicular to the moving plane, then the surface generated by the curve is equal to the length of the curve into the path described by its centre of gravity.

The corresponding theorem holds for the volume of the surface generated.

These extensions of Guldin's theorems were given by Leibnitz (*Act. Erud.* Lips., 1695).

179. **Expression for Volume of any Solid.**—The method given in Art. 171 of investigating the volume bounded by a surface of revolution can be readily extended to a solid bounded in any manner. For, if we suppose the volume divided into slices by a system of parallel planes, the entire volume may, as before, be regarded as the limit of the sum

of a number of infinitely thin cylindrical plates. Thus, if we suppose a system of rectangular co-ordinate axes taken, and the cutting planes drawn parallel to that of xy; then, if A_z represent the area of the section made by a plane drawn at the distance z from the origin, the entire volume is denoted by

$$\int A_z\, dz,$$

taken between proper limits.

The area A_z is to be determined in each case as a function of z from the conditions of the bounding surface.

For example, to find the volume of the portion of a cone cut off by any plane; we take the origin at the vertex, and the axis of z perpendicular to the cutting plane; then, if B denote the area of the base, and h the height of the cone, it is easily seen that we have

$$A_z : B = z^2 : h^2, \ \text{or} \ A_z = \frac{Bz^2}{h^2};$$

$$\therefore \ V = \frac{B}{h^2}\int_0^h z^2\, dz = \frac{1}{3} B \times h; \ \text{as in Art. } 169.$$

If the cutting planes be parallel to that of yz, the volume is denoted by $\int A_x\, dx$; where A_x denotes the area of the section at the distance x from the origin.

180. **Volume of Elliptic Paraboloid.**—Let it be proposed to find the volume of the portion of the elliptic paraboloid

$$\frac{x^2}{p} + \frac{y^2}{q} = 2z,$$

cut off by a plane drawn perpendicular to the axis of the surface. Here, considering z as constant, the area of the ellipse

$$\frac{x^2}{p} + \frac{y^2}{q} = 2z, \ \text{by Art. } 128, \ \text{is} \ 2\pi z\sqrt{pq}.$$

Hence, denoting by c the distance of the bounding plane from the vertex of the surface, we have

$$V = 2\pi\sqrt{pq}\int_0^c z\, dz = \pi c^2\sqrt{pq}.$$

This result admits of being exhibited in another form ; for if B be the area of the elliptic section made by the bounding plane, we have

$$B = 2\pi c \sqrt{pq}.$$

Hence $V = \frac{1}{2}$ circumscribing cylinder, as in paraboloid of revolution.

181. **The Ellipsoid.**—Next, to find the volume of the ellipsoid

$$\frac{x^2}{a^2} + \frac{y^2}{b^2} + \frac{z^2}{c^2} = 1.$$

The section of the surface at the distance z from the origin is the ellipse

$$\frac{x^2}{a^2} + \frac{y^2}{b^2} = 1 - \frac{z^2}{c^2}:$$

the area of this ellipse is

$$\pi\left(1 - \frac{z^2}{c^2}\right)ab, \text{ i.e. } A_z = \pi\left(1 - \frac{z^2}{c^2}\right)ab.$$

Hence, denoting the entire volume by V, we have

$$V = 2\pi ab \int_0^c \left(1 - \frac{z^2}{c^2}\right)dz = \frac{4}{3}\pi abc.$$

182. **Case of Oblique Axes.**—It is sometimes more convenient to refer the surface to a system of oblique axes. In this case, if, as before, we take the cutting planes parallel to that of xy, and if ω be the angle the axis of z makes with the plane of xy, the expression for the volume becomes

$$\sin \omega \int A_z dz,$$

taken between proper limits, where A_z represents the area of the section, as in the former case.

For example, let us seek the volume of the portion of an ellipsoid cut off by any plane.

Suppose $DED'E'$ to represent the section made by the plane, and $ABA'B'$ the parallel central section. Take OA, OB, the axes of this section as axes of x and y respectively; and the conjugate diameter OC as axis of z.

Then the equation of the surface is

$$\frac{x^2}{a'^2} + \frac{y^2}{b'^2} + \frac{z^2}{c'^2} = 1;$$

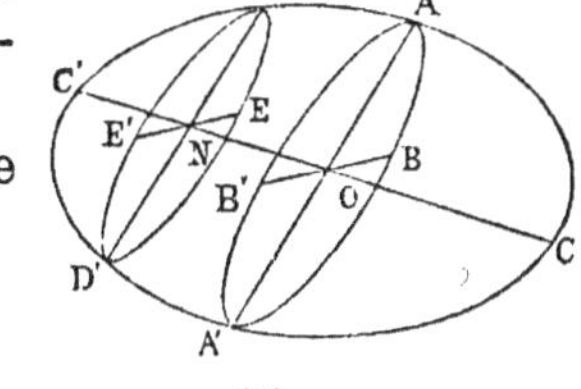

Fig. 44.

where $OA = a'$, $OB = b'$, $OC = c'$.

It will now be convenient to transfer the origin to the point C', without altering the directions of the axes, when the equation of the surface becomes

$$\frac{x^2}{a'^2} + \frac{y^2}{b'^2} = \frac{2z}{c'} - \frac{z^2}{c'^2}.$$

The area A_z of the section, by Art. 128, is

$$\pi a' b' \left(\frac{2z}{c'} - \frac{z^2}{c'^2} \right); \tag{3}$$

hence, denoting $C'N$ by h, the volume cut off by the plane DED' is represented by

$$\pi a' b' \sin \omega \int_0^h \left(\frac{2z}{c'} - \frac{z^2}{c'^2} \right) dz,$$

or

$$\pi a' b' \sin \omega \left(\frac{h^2}{c'} - \frac{h^3}{3c'^2} \right).$$

But, by a well-known theorem,* we have

$$a'b'c' \sin \omega = abc,$$

where a, b, c, are the principal semiaxes of the surface.

Hence the expression for the volume V in question becomes

$$V = \pi abc \left(\frac{h^2}{c'^2} - \frac{h^3}{3c'^3} \right); \tag{4}$$

---

* Salmon's *Geometry of Three Dimensions*, Art. 96.

or, denoting $\dfrac{C'N}{C'O}$ by k,

$$V = \pi abck^2\left(1 - \frac{k}{3}\right). \tag{5}$$

This result shows that the volume cut off is constant for all sections for which k has the same value. Again, since $\dfrac{ON}{OC'} = 1 - k$, the locus of N is a similar ellipsoid; and we infer that *if a plane cut a constant volume from an ellipsoid, the locus of the centre of the section is a similar and similarly situated ellipsoid.*

183. **Elliptic Paraboloid.**—The corresponding results for the elliptic paraboloid can be deduced from the preceding by adopting the usual method of such derivation: viz., by taking

$$a^2 = pc, \quad b^2 = qc,$$

and afterwards making c infinite; observing that in this case the ratio $\dfrac{c}{c'}$ becomes unity.

Making these substitutions in (4), it becomes

$$V = \pi\sqrt{pq}\,h^2\left(1 - \frac{h}{3c'}\right), \text{ or } \pi h^2\sqrt{pq}, \text{ since } c' = \infty.$$

Hence, if a constant length be measured on any diameter of an elliptic paraboloid and a conjugate plane drawn, then the volume* of the segment cut from the paraboloid by the plane is constant.

Again, the area of an elliptic section by (3) is

$$\pi a'b'\left(\frac{2h}{c'} - \frac{h^2}{c'^2}\right), \text{ or } \frac{\pi abc}{c'\sin\omega}\left(\frac{2h}{c'} - \frac{h^2}{c'^2}\right).$$

---

* For a more direct investigation the student is referred to a memoir "On some Properties of the Paraboloid," *Quarterly Journal of Mathematics*, June, 1874, by Professor Allman.

On making the same substitutions, this becomes for the paraboloid

$$\frac{2\pi\sqrt{pq}}{\sin\omega}\,h.$$

Now, if we suppose a cylinder to stand on this section, the volume of the portion cut off by the parallel tangent plane to the paraboloid is obtained by multiplying the area of the section by $h\sin\omega$; and, consequently, is

$$2\pi\sqrt{pq}\,h^2,$$

i. e. is double the corresponding volume of the paraboloid.

This is an extension of the theorem of Art. 180.

EXAMPLES.

1. Prove that the volume of the segment cut from a paraboloid by any plane is $\frac{3}{4}$ths of that of the circumscribing cone standing on the section made by the plane as base.

2. A cylinder intersects the plane of xy in an ellipse of semiaxes $OA = a$, $OB = b$, and the plane of xz in an ellipse of semiaxes $OA = a$, $OC = c$; the edges of the cylinder being parallel to BC; find the volume of the portion of the cylinder bounded by the three co-ordinate planes.   *Ans.* $\frac{1}{3}abc$.

3. The axes of two equal right cylinders intersect at right angles; find the volume common to both.   *Ans.* $\frac{16}{3}a^3$, where a is the radius of either cylinder. This surface is called a *Groin*.

184. **Volume by Double Integration.**—In the application of the preceding method of finding volumes the area represented by A_x, instead of being immediately known, requires in general a previous integration; so that the determination of the volume of a surface involves two successive integrations, and consequently V is expressed by a *double* integral.

Thus, as the area A_x lies in a plane parallel to that of yz, its value, as in Art. 126, may generally be represented by $\int z\,dy$, taken between proper limits. Hence V may be represented by

$$\int\left[\int z\,dy\right]dx\,;$$

or, adopting the usual notation, by

$$\int\int z\,dy\,dx,$$

taken between limits determined by the data of the question.

The value of z is supposed given by a relation $z = f(x, y)$, by means of the equation of the bounding surface; hence

$$\int z\, dy = \int f(x, y)\, dy.$$

In the determination of this integral we regard x as constant (since all the points in the area have the same value of x), and integrate with respect to y between its proper limits.

Thus, if y_1 and y_0 denote the limiting values of y, the definite integral

$$\int_{y_0}^{y_1} f(x, y)\, dy$$

becomes a function of x: this function, when integrated with respect to x between the proper limits, determines the volume in question.

If x_1 and x_0 denote the limits of x, V may be represented by the double integral

$$\int_{x_0}^{x_1} \int_{y_0}^{y_1} f(x, y)\, dy\, dx.$$

We shall exemplify this by a figure, in which we suppose the volume bounded by the plane of xy, by a cylinder perpendicular to that plane, and also by any surface.* Let $RPR'Q$ represent the section of the cylinder by the plane of xy; and suppose $PMNQ$ to be the section of the volume by a plane parallel to yz at the distance x from the origin. Let $PL = y_1$, $QL = y_0$, then the area $PMNQ$ is represented by the integral

$$\int_{y_0}^{y_1} z\, dy.$$

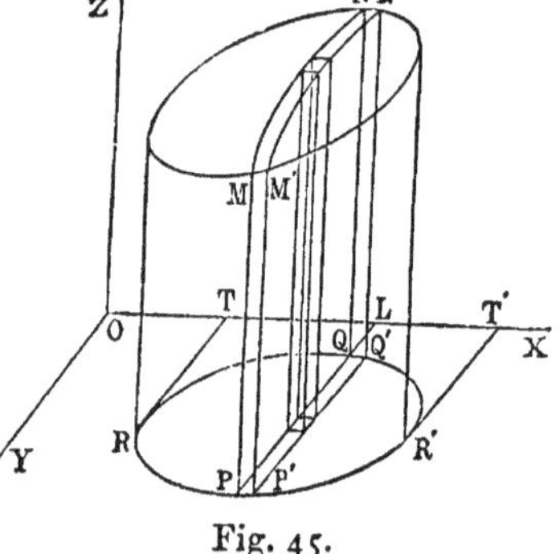

Fig. 45.

The values* of y_1 and y_0 in terms of x are obtained from the equation of the curve $RPR'Q$.

Again, suppose $P'M'N'Q'$ to represent the parallel section at the infinitesimal distance dx from $PMNQ$, then the elementary volume between $PMNQ$ and $P'M'N'Q'$ is represented by

$$dx \int_{y_0}^{y_1} z\, dy.$$

Now, if RT and $R'T'$ be tangents to the bounding curve, drawn perpendicular to the axis of x, and if $OT' = x_1$, $OT = x_0$, the entire volume is represented by

$$\int_{x_0}^{x_1} \int_{y_0}^{y_1} z\, dy\, dx.$$

It should be observed that $z\, dy\, dx$ represents the volume of the parallelepiped whose height is z, and whose base is the infinitesimal rectangle having dx and dy as sides; and consequently the volume may be regarded as the sum of all such parallelepipeds corresponding to every point within the area $RPR'Q$.

It is also plain that we shall arrive at the same result whether we integrate first with respect to x, and afterwards with respect to y, or *vice-versâ*; i. e. whether we conceive the volume divided into slices parallel to the plane of xz, or to that of yz.

We shall illustrate the preceding by an example.†

Suppose $RPR'Q$ to be the circle

$$(x - a)^2 + (y - b)^2 = R^2,$$

and the bounding surface the hyperbolic paraboloid

$$xy = cz;$$

---

* In our investigation we have assumed that the parallels intersect the curve in but two points each; the general case is omitted, as the solution in such cases can be rarely obtained, and also as the investigation is unsuited for an elementary treatise.

† This and the next example are taken from Cauchy's *Applications Géométriques du Calcul Infinitésimal*, p. 109.

then we have

$$y_0 = b - \sqrt{R^2 - (x-a)^2}, \quad y_1 = b + \sqrt{R^2 - (x-a)^2},$$

and

$$\int_{y_0}^{y_1} z\,dy = \frac{1}{c}\int_{y_0}^{y_1} xy\,dy = \frac{x}{2c}(y_1^2 - y_0^2) = \frac{2bx}{c}\sqrt{R^2 - (x-a)^2}.$$

Again, $\qquad x_1 = a + R, \quad x_0 = a - R;$

$$\therefore\; V = \frac{2b}{c}\int_{a-R}^{a+R} \sqrt{R^2 - (x-a)^2}\,x\,dx.$$

Now let $x - a = R \sin\theta$, and we get

$$V = \frac{2bR^2}{c}\int_{-\frac{\pi}{2}}^{\frac{\pi}{2}} \cos^2\theta\,(a + R\sin\theta)\,d\theta.$$

But $\qquad \displaystyle\int_{-\frac{\pi}{2}}^{\frac{\pi}{2}} \cos^2\theta\,d\theta = \frac{\pi}{2}, \qquad \int_{-\frac{\pi}{2}}^{\frac{\pi}{2}} \cos^2\theta \sin\theta\,d\theta = 0,$

$$\therefore\; V = \pi\,\frac{ab R^2}{c}.$$

Again, if for the cylindrical surface which has for its base the circle we substitute a system of four planes $x = x_0$, $x = X$, $y = y_0$, $y = Y$, we get

$$V = \int_{x_0}^{X}\int_{y_0}^{Y} \frac{xy}{c}\,dy\,dx$$

$$= \frac{1}{4c}(X^2 - x_0^2)(Y^2 - y_0^2)$$

$$= (X - x_0)(Y - y_0)\,\frac{x_0 y_0 + x_0 Y + X y_0 + XY}{4c}$$

$$= (X - x_0)(Y - y_0)\,\frac{z_1 + z_2 + z_3 + z_4}{4},$$

ich z_1, z_2, z_3, z_4, are the ordinates of the four corner
 of the portion of the surface in question.

ain, from the well-known properties of the surface, in
o construct the hyperbolic paraboloid it is sufficient
e the gauche quadrilateral whose summits are the
ities of the ordinates z_1, z_2, z_3, z_4; then a right line
g on a pair of opposite sides of this quadrilateral, and
sed in a plane parallel to the other pair, will generate
raboloid in question.

nce we arrive at the following proposition :—

wing traced a gauche quadrilateral on the four lateral
f a right prism standing on a rectangular base, if a
line move on two opposite sides of this quadrilateral
 parallel to the planes of the faces which contain the
wo sides, then the volume cut from the prism by the
 so generated is equal to the product of the area of
tangular base of the prism by one-fourth of the sum
 edges of the prism between the vertices of the
gle and those of the quadrilateral.

5. **Double Integration.**—From the preceding Article
adily seen that the double integral

$$\iint f(x,\ y)\, dy\, dx$$

represented geometrically by a volume ; and the deter-
on of the double integral, when the limits are given, is
ae as the finding the volume of a solid with correspond-
its.

r instance, the example in the preceding page is equi-
to finding the value of the double integral

$$\iint xy\, dx\, dy$$

for all values of x and y subject to the condition

$$(x - a)^2 + (y - b)^2 - R^2 < 0;$$

milarly in other cases.

hen the limits of x and y are constants, as in

$$\int_a^{a'} \int_b^{b'} f(x,\ y)\, dy\, dx,$$

[18]

the double integral represents the volume cut by the surface

$$z = f(x, y)$$

from the parallelepiped whose base is the rectangle formed by the lines

$$x = a, \quad x = a', \quad y = b, \quad y = b'.$$

It is plain that in this case the order of integration is indifferent, as already seen in Art. 115.

186. It is sometimes more convenient to refer the curve $RPR'Q$ to polar co-ordinates, in which case we conceive the area divided into infinitesimal rectangles of the type $r\, dr\, d\theta$.

The corresponding parallelepiped is represented by $zr\, dr\, d\theta$, and the expression for V becomes

$$V = \iint zr\, dr\, d\theta,$$

taken between proper limits.

For instance, if the bounding surface be a sphere, whose centre is the origin, we have

$$z = \sqrt{a^2 - r^2},$$

and the equation becomes

$$V = \iint \sqrt{a^2 - r^2}\, r\, dr\, d\theta\,;$$

but

$$\int \sqrt{a^2 - r^2}\, r\, dr = -\tfrac{1}{3}(a^2 - r^2)^{\frac{3}{2}}.$$

Hence, if V denote the volume included between the sphere and the *exterior* surface of the cylinder, we shall have

$$V = \tfrac{1}{3}\int (a^2 - r^2)^{\frac{3}{2}} d\theta,$$

where we suppose each *radius* of the sphere to cut the cylinder in but one point.

For example, let the base of the cylinder be the pedal of an ellipse whose major axis coincides with a diameter of the sphere; then

$$r^2 = a^2 \cos^2\theta + b^2 \sin^2\theta,$$

and

$$V = \tfrac{1}{3}(a^2 - b^2)^{\frac{3}{2}} \int \sin^3\theta\, d\theta.$$

this be integrated between the limits o and $\frac{\pi}{2}$ we get

ι of the entire volume; hence the entire volume

$$V = \frac{16}{9}(a^2 - b^2)^{\frac{3}{2}}.$$

EXAMPLES.

sphere is cut by a right cylinder, the radius of whose base is half that
here, and one of whose edges passes through the centre of the sphere;
volume common to both surfaces.

$$Ans. \quad \frac{2\pi a^3}{3} - \frac{8a^3}{9}, \ a \text{ being the radius of the sphere.}$$

the base of the cylinder be the complete curve represented by the
$r = a \cos n\theta$, where n is any integer, find the volume of the solid be-
e surface of the sphere and the external surface of the cylinder.

ι. It is readily seen, as in Art. 141, that *the volume in-
within the surface represented by the equation*

$$F\left(\frac{x}{a}, \ \frac{y}{b}, \ \frac{z}{c}\right) = \text{o}$$

‹ *the volume of the surface*

$$F(x, y, z) = \text{o}.$$

r, let $\frac{x}{a} = x'$, $\frac{y}{b} = y'$, $\frac{z}{c} = z'$, and we shall have

$$z\,dx\,dy = abc\,z'\,dx'\,dy',$$

$$\therefore \ \int\int z\,dx\,dy = abc\int\int z'\,dx'\,dy';$$

proves the theorem.

nce, for example, the determination of the volume of
psoid is reduced to that of a sphere.

ain, if the point (x, y, z) move along a plane, the cor-
ding point (x', y', z') will describe another plane. From
operty the expression for the volume of an ellipsoidal
rt. 182) can be immediately deduced from that of a
al cap (Art. 170).

[18 a]

In like manner the volume included between a *cone enveloping an ellipsoid and the surface of the ellipsoid is reducible to the corresponding volume for a sphere.*

188. **Quadrature on the Sphere.**—We next propose to give a brief discussion of quadrature on a sphere, and commence with the results on the subject usually given in treatises on Spherical Trigonometry. In the first place, since the area of a lune is to that of the entire sphere as the angle of the lune to four right angles, the area of a lune of angle A is represented by $2R^2A$; where R is the radius of the sphere, and A is expressed in circular measure.

Again, the area of a spherical triangle ABC is expressed by $R^2(A + B + C - \pi)$; for, the sum of the three lunes exceeds the hemisphere by twice the area of the triangle, as is easily seen from a figure.

Hence, it readily follows that the area Σ of a spherical polygon of n sides is represented by

$$\Sigma = R^2\{A + B + C + \&\text{c.} - (n - 2)\pi\};$$

A, B, C, &c., being the angles of the polygon.

This result admits of being expressed in terms of the sides of the polar polygon; for, representing these sides by a', b', c', &c., we have

$$A = \pi - a', \quad B = \pi - b', \&\text{c.},$$

and consequently

$$\Sigma = R^2\{2\pi - (a' + b' + c' + \&\text{c.})\}.$$

Or, denoting the perimeter of the polar figure by S,

$$\Sigma + RS = 2\pi R^2. \tag{6}$$

This proof is perfectly general, and holds in the limit, when the polygon becomes any curve; and, accordingly, the area bounded by any closed spherical curve is connected with the perimeter of its polar curve by the relation (6).

Again, the spherical area bounded by a lesser circle (Art. 170) admits of a simple expression. If ρ denote the circular radius of the circle, or the arc from its pole to its circumference, the area in question is represented by

$$2\pi R^2(1 - \cos \rho);$$

e fig. Art. 170) we have

$$AN = AC - CN = R(1 - \cos\rho).$$

is result also follows immediately as a simple case of
on (6).

ain, the area bounded by the lesser circle and by two
awn to its pole is plainly represented by

$$R^2 a (1 - \cos\rho),$$

a is the circular measure of the angle between the arcs.
e can now find an expression for the area bounded by
osed curve on a sphere; for
sition of any point P on the
e can be expressed by means
arc OP drawn to a fixed
and of the angle POX
n this arc and a fixed arc
h O. These are called the
o-ordinates of the point, and
nalogous to ordinary polar
inates on a plane.

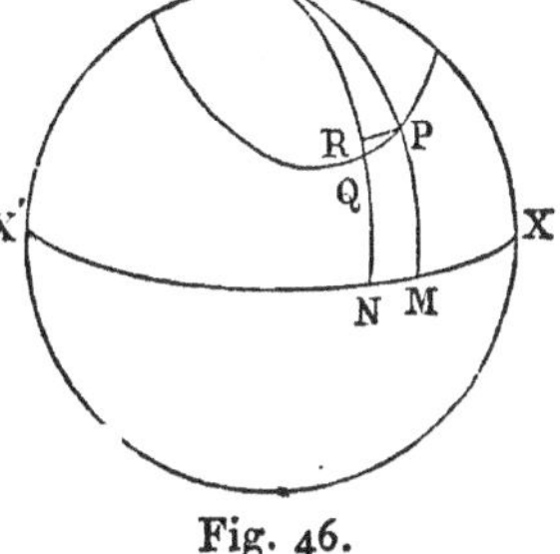

Fig. 46.

w, let $OP = \rho$, and $POX = \omega$;
ny curve on the sphere may be supposed to be expressed
elation between ρ and ω.

ain, suppose OQ to represent an infinitely near vector,
raw PR perpendicular to OP; then, neglecting in
nit the area PQR, the elementary area OPQ by the
ing is represented by

$$R^2 (1 - \cos\rho)\, d\omega.$$

ence the area bounded by two vectors from O is
sed by the integral $R^2 \int (1 - \cos\rho)\, d\omega$, taken between
le limits.

the curve be closed, the entire superficial area becomes

$$R^2 \int_0^{2\pi} (1 - \cos\rho)\, d\omega.$$

e value of $\cos\rho$ in terms of ω is to be determined in
ase by means of the equation of the bounding curve.

The integral $R^2 \displaystyle\int_0^{2\pi} \cos\rho\, d\omega$ obviously represents the area included between the closed curve and the great circle which has O for its pole.

The length of the curve can also be represented by a definite integral; for, regarding PRQ as ultimately a right-angled triangle, we have in the limit,

$$PQ^2 = PR^2 + RQ^2 : \text{ also } PR = \sin\rho\, d\omega.$$

Hence
$$ds^2 = dr^2 + \sin^2\rho\, d\omega^2,$$

or
$$ds = d\omega \sqrt{\sin^2\rho + \left(\frac{d\rho}{d\omega}\right)^2};$$

$$\therefore\ s = \int d\omega \sqrt{\sin^2\rho + \left(\frac{d\rho}{d\omega}\right)^2}.$$

Again, it is manifest from (6) that the determination of the length of any spherical curve is reducible to finding the area of its polar curve, and *vice versâ*.

EXAMPLES.

1. Find the area of the portion of the surface of a sphere which is intercepted by a right cylinder, one of whose edges passes through the centre of the sphere, and the radius of whose base is half that of the sphere.

Here, the equation of the base may be written in the form $r = R \sin\omega$, R being the radius of the sphere, and ω being measured from the tangent to the circular base.

Again, from the sphere we have $r = R \sin\rho$; $\therefore\ \rho = \omega$ is the equation of the curve of intersection of the sphere and the cylinder; hence the area in question is

$$2R^2 \int_0^{\frac{\pi}{2}} (1 - \cos\omega)\, d\omega = 2R^2 \left(\frac{\pi}{2} - 1\right).$$

This being doubled gives the whole intercepted area $= 2\pi R^2 - 4R^2$.

This is the celebrated Florentine enigma, proposed by Vincent Viviani as a challenge to the Mathematicians of his time, in the following form :—" Inter venerabilia olim Græciæ monumenta extat adhuc, perpetuo quidem duraturum, Templum augustissimum ichnographia circulari Almæ Geometriæ dicatum, quod Testudine intus perfecte hemisphærica operitur : sed in hac fenestrarum quatuor æquales areæ (circum ac supra basin hemisphæræ ipsius dispositarum) tali configuratione, amplitudine, tantaque industria, ac ingenii acumine sunt exstructæ, detractis, superstes curva Testudinis superficies, pretioso opere musivo Tetragonismi vere geometrici sit capax."—*Acta Eruditorum*, Leipsic, 1692. [ontucla, *Histoire des Mathématiques*, tome ii., p. 94.]

general, if $r = f(\omega)$ be the equation of the base of a cylinder, it is easily iat the equation of the curve of its intersection with the sphere may be i in the form $R \sin \rho = f(\omega)$.

r example, let the diameter of the right cylinder be less than half that sphere; then writing the equation of the base in the form $r = a \sin \omega$, a is the diameter of the section, we get $R \sin \rho = a \sin \omega$, or $\sin \rho = \kappa \sin \omega$ κ is < 1), as the equation of the curve of intersection of the sphere and linder.

nce the intercepted area is denoted by

$$2R^2 \int_0^{\frac{\pi}{2}} (1 - \sqrt{1 - \kappa^2 \sin^2 \omega})\, d\omega = \pi R^2 - 2R^2 \int_0^{\frac{\pi}{2}} \sqrt{1 - \kappa^2 \sin^2 \omega}\, d\omega.$$

nce the area in question depends on the rectification of an ellipse.

Find the area of the portion of the surface of the cylinder intercepted by here, in the preceding.

re the area in question is easily seen to be represented by $2 \int z\, ds$, where otes the element of the curve which forms the base, corresponding to the

w (1), when the diameter of the base is equal to the radius of the sphere, ve

$$z = R \cos \omega, \text{ and } ds = R\, d\omega;$$

a in question $= 2R^2 \int_0^{\frac{\pi}{2}} \cos \omega\, d\omega = 4R^2$; i.e. the square of the diameter of here.

When the diameter is less than the radius of the sphere,

$$\int z\, ds = 2a \int \sqrt{R^2 - a^2 \sin^2 \omega}\, d\omega = 2aR \int \sqrt{1 - \kappa^2 \sin^2 \omega}\, d\omega; \therefore \text{ &c.}$$

89. **Quadrature of Surfaces.**—In seeking the area portion of any surface we regard it as the limit of a ber of infinitely small elements, each of which is con ed as a portion of a plane which is ultimately a tangent ɔ to the surface. Now let dS denote such an element of superficial area, and $d\sigma$ its projection on a fixed plane h makes the angle θ with the plane of the element; then, elementary geometry, we shall have

$$d\sigma = \cos \theta\, dS, \text{ or } dS = \sec \theta\, d\sigma.$$

Ience
$$S = \int \sec \theta\, d\sigma,$$

i between suitable limits.

The applications of this formula usually involve *double integration*, and are generally very complicated ; there is, however, one mode by which the determination of the area of a portion of a surface can be reduced to a single integration, and by whose aid its value can in some cases be found ; viz., by supposing the surface divided into zones by a system* of curves along each of which the angle θ between the tangent plane and a fixed plane is constant ; then, if dS denote the superficial area of the zone between the two infinitely near curves corresponding to the angles θ and $\theta + d\theta$; and, if dA be the projection of this area on the fixed plane, we shall have $dS = \sec\theta\, dA$.

If we suppose the surface referred to a rectangular system of axes, the fixed plane being that of xy ; and adopting the usual notation, if we take λ, μ, ν as the direction angles of the normal at any point on the surface, we get for dS, the area of the zone between the curves corresponding to ν and $\nu + d\nu$, the equation

$$dS = \sec\nu\, dA,$$

where A denotes the area of the projection on the plane of xy of the closed curve defined by the equation $\nu = $ constant.

Now whenever we can express the area A in terms of ν and constants, then the area of a portion of the surface, bounded by two curves of the system in question, is reducible to a single integration.

The most important applications of this method are furnished by surfaces of the second degree, to which we proceed to apply it, commencing with the paraboloid.

190. **Quadrature of the Paraboloid.**—Writing the equation of the surface in the form

$$\frac{x^2}{p} + \frac{y^2}{q} = 2z,$$

---

* This method has been employed in a more or less modified form by M. Catalan, *Liouville*, tome iv., p. 323, by Mr. Jellett, *Camb. and Dub. Math. Journal*, vol. i., as also by other writers. The curves employed are called *parallel curves* by M. Lebesgne, *Liouville*, tome xi., p. 332, and *Curven isokliner Normalen*, by Dr. Schlömilch.

,tion of the tangent plane at the point (x, y, z) is

$$\frac{xX}{p} + \frac{yY}{q} = z + Z,$$

X, Y, Z are the co-ordinates of any point on the plane.
paring this with the equation

$$X \cos \lambda + Y \cos \mu + Z \cos \nu = P,$$

$$\cos \lambda = -\frac{x}{p} \cos \nu, \quad \cos \mu = -\frac{y}{q} \cos \nu :$$

ting in the identical equation

$$\cos^2 \lambda + \cos^2 \mu + \cos^2 \nu = 1,$$

$$\frac{x^2}{p^2} + \frac{y^2}{q^2} = \tan^2 \nu. \tag{7}$$

sequently the curve along which the tangent plane
the angle ν with the tangent plane at the vertex is
d on that plane into the ellipse

$$\frac{x^2}{p^2} + \frac{y^2}{q^2} = \tan^2 \nu.$$

area A of this ellipse is $\pi pq \tan^2 \nu$; accordingly, we

$$dA = \pi pq \, d(\tan^2 \nu) ;$$

$\therefore \; dS = \pi pq \sec \nu \, d(\tan^2 \nu) = \pi pq \sec \nu \, d(\sec^2 \nu) ;$

ıe area of the paraboloidal cap bounded by the curve

$$\pi pq \int^a \sec \nu \, d(\sec^2 \nu) = \tfrac{2}{3} \pi pq (\sec^3 a - 1).$$

the area of the belt* between the curves

$$\nu = a \text{ and } \nu = a' \text{ is } \tfrac{2}{3} \pi pq (\sec^3 a' - \sec^3 a). \tag{8}$$

---

form for the quadrature of a paraboloid is, I believe, due to Mr. Jellett:
and Dub. Math. Journal, vol. i. p. 65. The proof given above is in
asure taken from Mr. Allman's paper in the *Quarterly Journal*, already

191. **Quadrature of the Ellipsoid.**—Proceeding in like manner to the ellipsoid

$$\frac{x^2}{a^2} + \frac{y^2}{b^2} + \frac{z^2}{c^2} = 1,$$

the equation of the tangent plane at the point (x, y, z) is

$$\frac{Xx}{a^2} + \frac{Yy}{b^2} + \frac{Zz}{c^2} = 1.$$

Hence, comparing with the equation

$$X \cos \lambda + Y \cos \mu + Z \cos \nu = P,$$

we get

$$\cos \lambda = \frac{c^2}{a^2} \frac{x}{z} \cos \nu, \qquad \cos \mu = \frac{c^2}{b^2} \frac{y}{z} \cos \nu.$$

Hence, we have

$$\cos^2 \nu \frac{c^4}{z^2} \left(\frac{x^2}{a^4} + \frac{y^2}{b^4} \right) = \cos^2 \lambda + \cos^2 \mu = \sin^2 \nu \, ;$$

or, substituting $1 - \dfrac{x^2}{a^2} - \dfrac{y^2}{b^2}$ for $\dfrac{z^2}{c^2}$,

$$\frac{x^2}{a^4} \left(a^2 \sin^2 \nu + c^2 \cos^2 \nu \right) + \frac{y^2}{b^4} \left(b^2 \sin^2 \nu + c^2 \cos^2 \nu \right) = \sin^2 \nu.$$

This shows that the projection on the plane of xy of a curve along which $\nu =$ constant is an ellipse.

Again the area A of this ellipse is

$$\frac{\pi a^2 b^2 \sin^2 \nu}{(a^2 \sin^2 \nu + c^2 \cos^2 \nu)^{\frac{1}{2}} (b^2 \sin^2 \nu + c^2 \cos^2 \nu)^{\frac{1}{2}}},$$

and accordingly, the area dA of the elementary annulus between two consecutive ellipses is

$$\pi a^2 b^2 \frac{d}{d\nu} \left\{ \frac{\sin^2 \nu}{(a^2 \sin^2 \nu + c^2 \cos^2 \nu)^{\frac{1}{2}} (b^2 \sin^2 \nu + c^2 \cos^2 \nu)^{\frac{1}{2}}} \right\} d\nu.$$

The corresponding elementary ellipsoidal zone dS is represented by

$$\frac{\pi a^2 b^2}{\cos \nu} \frac{d}{d\nu} \left\{ \frac{\sin^2 \nu}{(a^2 \sin^2 \nu + c^2 \cos^2 \nu)^{\frac{1}{2}} (b^2 \sin^2 \nu + c^2 \cos^2 \nu)^{\frac{1}{2}}} \right\} d\nu.$$

ow, if S denote the superficial area* between two
corresponding to $\nu = a$ and $\nu = a'$, after one or two
ions, it is easily seen that

$$S = \pi a^2 b^2 c^2 (I + I'),\qquad (9)$$

$$I = \int_a^{a'} \frac{\sin \nu\, d\nu}{(b^2 \sin^2 \nu + c^2 \cos^2 \nu)^{\frac{3}{2}} (a^2 \sin^2 \nu + c^2 \cos^2 \nu)^{\frac{1}{2}}},$$

$$I' = \int_a^{a'} \frac{\sin \nu\, d\nu}{(a^2 \sin^2 \nu + c^2 \cos^2 \nu)^{\frac{3}{2}} (b^2 \sin^2 \nu + c^2 \cos^2 \nu)^{\frac{1}{2}}}.$$

is easily shown that the former of these integrals is
sented by an arc of an ellipse, and the latter by an arc
yperbola; it being assumed that $a > b > c$.
or, assuming $a^2 - c^2 = a^2 e^2$, and $b^2 - c^2 = b^2 e'^2$, and
ig $\cos \nu = x$, we get

$$I = \frac{1}{ab^3} \int_{\cos a}^{\cos a} \frac{dx}{(1 - e'^2 x^2)^{\frac{3}{2}} (1 - e^2 x^2)^{\frac{1}{2}}},$$

$$I' = \frac{1}{a^3 b} \int_{\cos a'}^{\cos a} \frac{dx}{(1 - e^2 x^2)^{\frac{3}{2}} (1 - e'^2 x^2)^{\frac{1}{2}}}.$$

gain, let $ex = \sin \theta$ in the former integral, and $e'x = \sin \theta$
latter, and we get

$$I = \frac{e^2}{ab^3} \int \frac{d\theta}{(e^2 - e'^2 \sin^2 \theta)^{\frac{3}{2}}},$$

$$I' = \frac{e'^2}{a^3 b} \int \frac{d\theta}{(e'^2 - e^2 \sin^2 \theta)^{\frac{3}{2}}}.$$

ow, since $e > e'$, the former integral represents an
an ellipse, and the latter an arc of a hyperbola.   (See
9, p. 249).

This form for the quadrature of an ellipsoid is given by Mr. Jellett in
moir already referred to. He has also shown that the ellipse and the
ola in question are the focal conics of the reciprocal ellipsoid; a result
can be easily arrived at from the forms of I and I' given above.
application to the hyperboloid, and further development of these results,
ident is referred to Mr. Jellett's memoir.

192. **Integration over a Closed Surface.**—We shall conclude this Chapter with the consideration of some general formulæ in double integration relative to any closed surface. We commence by adopting the same notation as in Art. 189, where λ, μ, ν are taken as the angles which the exterior normal at the element dS makes with the positive directions of the axes of x, y, z, respectively.

Again, let each element of the surface be projected on the plane of xy, and suppose* for simplicity that each z ordinate meets the surface in but two points: then, if the indefinitely small cylinder standing on any element dA in the plane of xy intersects the surface in the two elementary portions dS_1 and dS_2 (where dS_1 is the upper, and dS_2 the lower element), and if ν_1 and ν_2 be the corresponding values of ν, it is plain that ν_1 is an acute, and ν_2 an obtuse angle, and we have

$$dA = \cos \nu_1 dS_1 = - \cos \nu_2 dS_2.$$

Hence, if we take into account all the elements of the surface, attending to the sign of $\cos \nu$, we shall have

$$\int\int \cos \nu \, dS = 0.$$

In like manner we get

$$\int\int \cos \lambda \, dS = 0, \text{ and } \int\int \cos \mu \, dS = 0 ;$$

the integrals extending in each case over the whole of the closed curve

These formulæ are comprised in the equation

$$\int\int (a \cos \lambda + \beta \cos \mu + \gamma \cos \nu) \, dS = 0. \qquad (10)$$

Again, if z_1 and z_2 be the values of z corresponding to the element dA, then, denoting by dV the element of volume standing on dA and intercepted by the surface, we plainly have

$$dV = (z_1 - z_2) \, dA = z_1 dS_1 \cos \nu_1 + z_2 dS_2 \cos \nu_2,$$

---

* It it easily seen that this and the following demonstrations are perfectly general, inasmuch as each ordinate must meet a closed surface in an even number of points, which may be considered in pairs.

ie sum of all such elements, that is, the whole volume,
lently represented by

$$\iint z \cos \nu \, dS.$$

', denoting the whole volume by V, we have

$$V = \iint x \cos \lambda \, dS = \iint y \cos \mu \, dS = \iint z \cos \nu \, dS \, ;$$

itegrals, as before, being extended over the entire
e.
rain, it is easily seen that we have

$$x \cos \nu \, dS = 0, \quad \iint y \cos \nu \, dS = 0, \quad \iint x \cos \mu \, dS = 0,$$

$$y \cos \lambda \, dS = 0, \quad \iint z \cos \lambda \, dS = 0, \quad \iint z \cos \mu \, dS = 0.$$

s in the first case, it readily appears that the elements
ual and opposite in pairs in each of these integrals.
iese results are comprised in the equation

$$\iota x + \beta y + \gamma z)(a' \cos \lambda + \beta' \cos \mu + \gamma' \cos \nu) \, dS$$
$$= (aa' + \beta\beta' + \gamma\gamma') \, V. \quad (11)$$

r a like reason, we have

$$\iota \cos \nu \, dS = 0, \quad \iint zx \cos \mu \, dS = 0, \quad \iint yz \cos \lambda \, dS = 0.$$

$$\iint x^2 \cos \nu \, dS = 0, \quad \iint x^2 \cos \mu \, dS = 0, \&c.$$

ixt, let us consider the integral

$$\iint xz \cos \nu \, dS.$$

is integral is equivalent to $\iint x \, dV$; consequently, if
, be the co-ordinates of the centre of gravity of the
id volume V, we get $\iint xz \cos \nu \, dS = \iint x \, dV = \bar{x} V$; in
anner $\iint xz \cos \lambda \, dS = \bar{z} V$.
rain, the integral

$$\iint z^2 \cos \nu \, dS$$

s of elements of the form $(z_1^2 - z_2^2) \, dA$; but

$$(z_1^2 - z_2^2) \, dA = (z_1 + z_2)(z_1 - z_2) \, dA$$
$$= (z_1 + z_2) \, dV.$$

But the z ordinate of the centre of gravity of dV is plainly $\dfrac{z_1 + z_2}{2}$, and consequently

$$\iint z^2 \cos \nu \, dS = 2 \iint \frac{z_1 + z_2}{2} dV = 2\bar{z} V.$$

In like manner it can be shown that

$$\iint x^2 \cos \lambda \, dS = 2\bar{x} V, \quad \iint y^2 \cos \mu \, dS = 2\bar{y} V.$$

Accordingly we have

$$V\bar{x} = \tfrac{1}{2}\iint x^2 \cos \lambda \, dS = \iint xy \cos \mu \, dS = \iint xz \cos \nu \, dS,$$

$$V\bar{y} = \iint yx \cos \lambda \, dS = \tfrac{1}{2}\iint y^2 \cos \mu \, dS = \iint yz \cos \nu \, dS,$$

$$V\bar{z} = \iint zx \cos \lambda \, dS = \iint zy \cos \mu \, dS = \tfrac{1}{2}\iint z^2 \cos \nu \, dS.$$

193. Expression for Volume of a Closed Surface. —Next, if we suppose a cone described with its vertex at the origin O, and standing on the elementary base dS, its volume is represented (Art. 169) by $\tfrac{1}{3}pdS$, where p is the length of the perpendicular drawn from O to the tangent plane at the point.

Also, if r be the distance of O from the point, and γ the angle which r makes with the *internal* normal, we have $p = r \cos \gamma$.

Hence the elementary volume is equal to $\tfrac{1}{3} r \cos \gamma \, dS$, and it is easily seen that if we integrate over the entire surface, the enclosed volume is represented by

$$\tfrac{1}{3}\iint r \cos \gamma \, dS.$$

194. Again, if we suppose a sphere of unit radius described with O as centre, and if $d\omega$ represent the superficial portion of this sphere intercepted by the elementary cone standing on dS, then it is easily seen that $\cos \gamma \, dS = r^2 d\omega$;

$$\therefore \ d\omega = \frac{\cos \gamma \, dS}{r^2}.$$

Now if O be inside the closed surface, and the integral be extended over the entire surface, it is plain that $\iint d\omega = 4\pi$, being the surface of the sphere of radius unity;

$$\therefore \ \iint \frac{\cos \gamma \, dS}{r^2} = 4\pi.$$

ain, if O be outside the surface, the cone will cut the
e in an even number of elements, for which the values
γ will be alternately positive and negative, and, the
ponding elements of the integral being equal but with
te signs, their sum is equal to zero, and we shall have

$$\iint \frac{\cos \gamma \, dS}{r^2} = 0.$$

O be situated on the surface, it follows in like manner

$$\iint \frac{\cos \gamma}{r^2} \, dS = 2\pi.$$

ence, we conclude that

$$\iint \frac{\cos \gamma}{r^2} \, dS = 4\pi, \; 2\pi, \text{ or } 0, \tag{12}$$

ling as the origin is inside, on, or outside the surface.
he multiple integrals introduced into this and the two
ling Articles are principally due to Gauss.
he student will find some important applications of
method in Bertrand's *Calc. Int.*, §§ 437, 455, 456,
&c.

EXAMPLES.

1. A sphere of 15 feet radius is cut by two parallel planes at distances of 3 and 7 feet from its centre; find the superficial area of the portion of the surface included between the planes approximately.   *Ans.* 376.9908 sq. feet.

2. Being given the slant height of a right cone, find the cosine of half its vertical angle when its volume is a maximum.

$$\text{\textit{Ans.}}\quad \frac{1}{\sqrt{3}}.$$

3. Prove that the volume of a truncated cone of height h is represented by

$$\frac{\pi h}{3}\,(R^2 + Rr + r^2),$$

where R and r are the radii of its two bases.

4. A cone is circumscribed to a sphere of radius R, the vertex of the cone being at the distance D from the centre; find the ratio of the superficial area of the cone to that of the sphere.

$$\text{\textit{Ans.}}\quad \frac{D^2 - R^2}{4DR}.$$

5. Two spheres, A and B, have for radii 9 feet and 40 feet; the superficial area of a third sphere C is equal to the sum of the areas of A and B; calculate the excess, in cubic feet, of the volume of C over the sum of the volumes of A and B.   *Ans.* 17558.

6. If any arc of a plane curve revolve successively round two parallel axes, show that the difference of the surfaces generated is equal to the product of the length of the arc into the circumference of the circle described by any point on either axis turning round the other.

If the axes of revolution lie at opposite sides of the curve, the sum of the surfaces must be taken instead of the difference.

7. Find, in terms of the sides, the volume of the solid generated by the complete revolution of a triangle round its side c.

$$\text{\textit{Ans.}}\quad \frac{4\pi}{3}\,\frac{s\,(s-a)\,(s-b)\,(s-c)}{c}.$$

8. Apply Guldin's theorem to determine the distance, from the centre, of the centre of gravity, (1) of a semicircular area; (2) of a semicircular arc.

$$\text{\textit{Ans.}}\quad (1)\ \frac{4a}{3\pi}, \quad (2)\ \frac{2a}{\pi}.$$

9. If a triangle revolve round any external axis, lying in its plane, find an expression for the area of the surface generated in a complete revolution.

10. Prove that the volume cut from the surface

$$z^n = Ax^2 + By^2$$

by any plane parallel to that of xy, is $\dfrac{1}{n+1}$th part of the cylinder standing on the plane section, and terminated by the plane of xy.

ι cone is circumscribed to a sphere of 23 feet radius, the vertex of the
ιg 265 feet distant from the centre of the sphere ; find the ratio of the
ιl area of the cone to that of the sphere.

'he axis of a right circular cylinder passes through the centre of a
find the volume of the solid included between the concave surface of the
ιd the convex surface of the cylinder.

$\frac{\pi c}{6}{}^3$, where c is the length of the portion of any edge of the cylinder

ed by the sphere.

question is the same as that of finding the volume of the solid generated
egment of a circle cut off by any chord, in a revolution round the
parallel to the chord.

'ind the volume of the solid generated by the revolution of an arc of a
ιnd its chord.   *Ans.* $2\pi a \left\{ \dfrac{(2a^2 + c^2)\sin a}{3} - ca \right\}$,

$=$ radius, $c =$ distance of chord from centre, and $\cos a = \dfrac{c}{a}$.

is we suppose the arc less than a semicircle : the modification when it
ɾ is easily seen.

f the ellipsoid of revolution,

$$x^2 + z^2 + \frac{a^2 y^2}{b^2} = a^2,$$

ιyperboloid

$$x^2 + z^2 - \frac{a^2 - b^2}{b^2} y^2 = a^2,$$

ɤ two planes perpendicular to the axis of revolution, prove that the
ercepted on the two surfaces are of equal area.

'ind the entire volume bounded by the positive sides of the three co-
ρlanes, and

$$\left(\frac{x}{a}\right)^{\frac{1}{2}} + \left(\frac{y}{b}\right)^{\frac{1}{2}} + \left(\frac{z}{c}\right)^{\frac{1}{2}} = 1, \qquad\qquad Ans. \ \frac{abc}{90}.$$

'ind the volume of the surface generated by the revolution of an arc of
a round its chord ; the chord being perpendicular to the axis of the

$\dfrac{8}{15}\pi b^2 c$, where c is the length of the chord, and b the intercept made
:he diameter of the parabola passing through the middle point of the

. sphere of radius r is cut by a plane at distance d from the centre ; find
ence of the volumes of the two cones having as a common base the
which the plane cuts the sphere, and whose vertices are the opposite
:he diameter perpendicular to the cutting plane.
           Ans. $\frac{2}{3}\pi d\,(r^2 - d^2)$.

18. Find the area of a spherical triangle; and prove that if a curve traced on a sphere have for its equation $\sin \lambda = f(l)$, λ denoting latitude, and l longitude, the area between the curve and the equator $= \int f(l)\,dl$.

19. Show that the volume contained between the surface of a hyperboloid of one sheet, its asymptotic cone, and two planes parallel to that of the real axes, is proportional to the distance between those planes.

20. Find the entire volume of the surface

$$\left(\frac{x}{a}\right)^{\frac{2}{3}} + \left(\frac{y}{b}\right)^{\frac{2}{3}} + \left(\frac{z}{c}\right)^{\frac{2}{3}} = 1. \qquad\qquad Ans. \ \frac{4\pi abc}{5 \cdot 7}.$$

21. The vertex of a cone of the second degree is in the surface of a sphere, and its internal axis is the diameter passing through its vertex ; find the volume of the portion of the sphere intercepted within the cone.

22. Prove that the volume of the portion of a cylinder intercepted between any two planes is equal to the product of the area of a perpendicular section into the distance between the centres of gravity of the areas of the bounding sections.

23. If A be the area of the section of any surface made by the plane of xy, prove, as in Art. 192, that

$$A = \iint \cos \nu \, dS,$$

the integral being extended through the portion of the surface which lies above the plane of xy.

24. If a right cone stand on an ellipse, prove that its volume is represented by

$$\frac{\pi}{3} \ (OA . OA')^{\frac{3}{2}} \sin^2 \alpha \cos \alpha;$$

where O is the vertex of the cone, A and A' the extremities of the major axis of the ellipse, and α is the semi-angle of the cone.

25. In the same case prove that the superficial area of the cone is

$$\frac{\pi}{3} (OA + OA') \ (OA . OA')^{\frac{1}{2}} \sin \alpha.$$

CHAPTER X.

INTEGRALS OF INERTIA.

Integrals of Inertia.—The following integrals are [so?]h frequent occurrence in mechanical investigations, [that it?] is proposed to give a brief discussion of them in this [chapt]er.

[If] each element of the mass of any solid body be supposed multiplied by the square of its distance from any fixed line, and the sum extended throughout every element [of the] body, the quantity thus obtained is called the *moment [of iner]tia of the body with respect to the fixed line or axis.*

[H]ence, denoting the element of mass by dm, its distance [from t]he axis by p, and the moment of inertia by I, we have

$$I = \Sigma p^2 dm. \tag{1}$$

[In] like manner, if each element of mass of a body be [multi]plied by the square of its distance from a plane, the [sum o]f such products is called the *moment of inertia of the [body r]elative to the plane.*

[If] the system be referred to rectangular axes of co-[ordina]tes, then the expression for the moment of inertia [relativ]e to the axis of z is obviously represented by

$$\Sigma (x^2 + y^2) dm.$$

[Si]milarly, the moments of inertia relative to the axes of [x and] y are represented by $\Sigma (y^2 + z^2) dm$ and $\Sigma (x^2 + z^2) dm$, [respec]tively.

[A]gain, the quantities $\Sigma x^2 dm$, $\Sigma y^2 dm$, $\Sigma z^2 dm$, are the [mome]nts of inertia of the body with respect to the planes [yz,] xz, and xy, respectively. Also the quantities $\Sigma xy dm$, [$\Sigma xz dm$,] $\Sigma yz dm$, are called the *products of inertia* relative to [the sa]me system of co-ordinate axes.

[In] like manner the *moment of inertia of the body with [refere]nce to a point* is $\Sigma r^2 dm$, where r denotes the distance of [the el]ement dm from the point. Thus the moment of inertia [relati]ve to the origin is $\Sigma (x^2 + y^2 + z^2) dm$.

[19 a]

196. **Moments of Inertia relative to Parallel Axes, or Planes.**—The following result is of fundamental importance :—*The moment of inertia of a body with respect to any axis exceeds its moment of inertia with respect to a parallel axis drawn through its centre of gravity, by the product of the mass of the body into the square of the distance between the parallel axes.*

For, let I be the moment of inertia relative to the axis through the centre of gravity, I' that for the parallel axis, M the mass of the body, and a the distance between the axes.

Then, taking the centre of gravity as origin, the fixed axis through it as the axis of z, and the plane through the parallel axes for that of zx, we shall have

$$I = \Sigma (x^2 + y^2)\, dm, \quad I' = \Sigma\{(x + a)^2 + y^2\}\, dm.$$

Hence
$$I' - I = 2a\, \Sigma x\, dm + a^2 \Sigma\, dm = a^2 M,$$

since $\Sigma x\, dm = 0$ as the centre of gravity is at the origin ;

$$\therefore\ I' = I + a^2 M. \tag{2}$$

Consequently, the moment of inertia of a body relative to any axis can be found when that for the parallel axis through its centre of gravity is known.

Also, the moments of inertia of a body are the same for all parallel axes situated at the same distance from its centre of gravity.

Again, it may be observed that of all parallel axes that which passes through the centre of gravity of a body has the least moment of inertia.

It is also apparent that the same theorem holds if the moments of inertia be taken with respect to parallel planes, instead of parallel axes.

A similar property also connects the moment of inertia relative to any point with that relative to the centre of gravity of the body.

In finding the moment of inertia of a body relative to any axis, we usually suppose the body divided into a system of indefinitely thin plates, or *laminæ*, by a system of planes perpendicular to the axis; then, when the moment of inertia is determined for a lamina, we seek by integration to find that of the entire body.

7. **Radius of Gyration.**—If k denote the distance
an axis at which the entire mass of a body should be
ıtrated that its moment of inertia relative to the axis
·emain unaltered, we shall have

$$Mk^2 = I = \Sigma p^2 dm. \tag{3}$$

ıe length k is called the radius of gyration of the body
:espect to the fixed axis.

. homogeneous bodies, which shall be here treated of
pally, since the mass of any part varies directly as its
.e, the preceding equation may be written in the form

$$k^2 V = \Sigma p^2 dV,$$

dV denotes the element of volume, and V the entire
ıe of the body.

ence, in homogeneous bodies, the value of k is indepen-
)f the density of the body, and depends only on its form.
'e shall in our investigations represent the moment of
ı in the form

$$I = Mk^2 ;$$

ıt is plain that in its determination *for homogeneous*
we may take the element of volume for the element of mass,
ıe total volume of the body instead of its mass.

lso, in finding the moment of inertia of a lamina, since its
ı of gyration is independent of the thickness of the lamina,
ıy take the element of area instead of the element of
and the total area of the lamina instead of its mass.

ı8. If A and B be the moments of inertia of an infi-
thin plate, or lamina, with respect to two rectangular
)X, OY, lying in its plane, and if C be the moment of
ı relative to OZ drawn perpendicular to the plane, we

$$C = A + B. \tag{4}$$

)r, we have in this case $A = \Sigma y^2 dm$, $B = \Sigma x^2 dm$, and
ı$(x^2 + y^2) dm$.

gain, for every two rectangular axes in the plane of the
a, at any point, we have

$$\Sigma x^2 dm + \Sigma y^2 dm = \text{const.}$$

ence, if one be a maximum, the other is a minimum, and
:rsâ.

'e shall, in all investigations concerning laminæ, take C
e moment of inertia relative to a line perpendicular to
.mina.

199. Uniform Rod, Rectangular Lamina.—We commence with the simple case of a rod, the axis being perpendicular to its length, and passing through either extremity.

Let x be the distance of any element dm of the rod from the extremity; then, since the rod is uniform, dm is proportional to dx, and we may assume $dm = \mu\,dx$: hence, the moment of inertia I is represented by $\mu\,\Sigma x^2 dx$, or by

$$\mu \int_0^l x^2 dx,$$

where l is the length of the rod.

Hence
$$I = \frac{\mu\,l^3}{3} = M\frac{l^2}{3}.$$

If the axis be drawn through the middle point of the rod, perpendicular to its length, the moment of inertia is plainly the same for each half of the rod, and we shall have in this case

$$I = M\frac{l^2}{12}.$$

Next, let us take a rectangular lamina, and suppose the axis drawn through its centre, parallel to one of its sides.

Here, it is evident that the lamina may be regarded as made up of an infinite number of parallel rods of equal length, perpendicular to the axis, each having the same radius of gyration, and consequently the radius of gyration of the lamina is the same as that of one of the rods.

Accordingly, we have, denoting the lengths of the sides of the rectangle by $2a$ and $2b$, and the moments of inertia round axes through the centre parallel to the sides, by A and B, respectively,

$$A = \frac{1}{3}Mb^2, \quad B = \frac{1}{3}Ma^2. \tag{5}$$

Hence also, by (4), the moment of inertia round an axis through the centre of gravity and perpendicular to the plane of the lamina, is

$$\frac{1}{3}M(a^2 + b^2). \tag{6}$$

By applying the principle of Art. 196 we can now find its moments of inertia with respect to any right line either lying in, or perpendicular to, the plane of the lamina.

0. **Rectangular Parallelepiped.**—Since a parallel-
d may be conceived as consisting of an infinite number
minæ, each of which has the same radius of gyration
ve to an axis drawn perpendicular to their planes, it
vs that the radius of gyration of the parallelepiped is
ame as that of one of the laminæ.

[ence, if the length of the sides of the parallelepiped be
b, and 2c, respectively; and, if A, B, C be respectively
1oments of inertia relative to three axes drawn through
entre of gravity, parallel to the edges of the parallel-
d, we have, by the last,

$$\frac{1}{3} M(b^2 + c^2), \quad B = \frac{1}{3} M(c^2 + a^2), \quad C = \frac{1}{3} M(a^2 + b^2). \qquad (7)$$

01. **Circular Plate, Cylinder.**—If the axis be
n through its centre, perpendicular to the plane of a
lar ring of infinitely small breadth, since each point of
ing may be regarded as at the same distance r from the
its moment of inertia is $r^2 dm$, where dm represents its

Ience, considering each ring as an element of a circular
, and observing that $dm = \mu\, 2\pi r\, dr$, we get for C, the
ent of inertia of the circular plate of radius a,

$$C = 2\pi\mu \int_0^a r^3 dr = \frac{\pi\mu a^4}{2} = M\frac{a^2}{2}.$$

'onsequently, the moment of inertia of a ring whose
: and inner radii are a and b, respectively, with respect to
ame axis, is

$$2\pi\mu \int_b^a r^3 dr = \pi\mu \frac{a^4 - b^4}{2} = M\frac{a^2 + b^2}{2}.$$

1gain, by (4), the moment of inertia of a circular plate
t any diameter is $M\frac{a^2}{4}$, since the moments of inertia are
ously the same respecting all diameters.

n like manner, the moment of inertia of a ring relative
1y diameter is

$$M\frac{a^2 + b^2}{4}.$$

Also, the moment of inertia of a right cylinder about its axis of figure is

$$M \frac{a^2}{2},$$

a being the radius of the section of the cylinder.

Again, the moment of inertia relative to any edge of the cylinder is $\frac{3}{2} Ma^2$.

202. **Right Cone.**—To find the moment of inertia of a right cone relative to its axis, we conceive it divided into an infinite number of circular plates, whose centres lie along the axis; and, denoting by x the distance of the centre of any section from the vertex of the cone, and by a the semi-angle of the cone, we have

$$I = \frac{\pi \mu \tan^4 a}{2} \int_0^h x^4\, dx = \frac{\pi \mu b^4 h}{10},$$

where h is the height of the cone, and b the radius of its base.

Hence, since by Art. 169 the volume of the cone is $\frac{\pi}{3} b^2 h$, we have

$$I = \frac{3}{10} Mb^2. \tag{8}$$

203. **Elliptic Plate.**—Next let us suppose the lamina an ellipse, of semi-axes a and b; and let A and B be the moments of inertia relative to these axes, respectively.

Describe a circle with the axis minor for diameter, and suppose the lamina divided into rods by sections perpendicular to this axis. Let B' be the moment of inertia for the circle round its diameter.

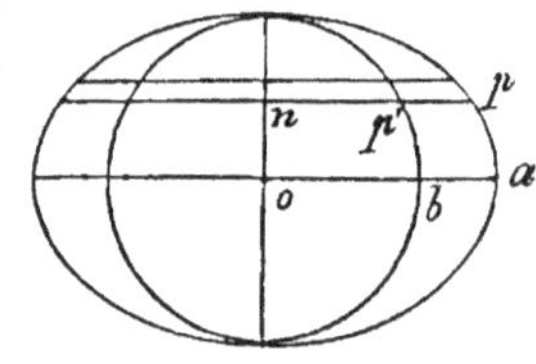

Fig. 47.

Then, denoting by dB and dB' the moments of inertia of corresponding rods, we have

$$dB : dB' = (np)^3 : (np')^3 = (oa)^3 : (ob)^3 = a^3 : b^3;$$

$$\therefore B : B' = a^3 : b^3.$$

t B', by Art. 201, is $\dfrac{M' b^2}{4}$;

$$\therefore\ B = \frac{M'}{4}\frac{a^3}{b} = \frac{M}{4} a^2.$$

rly,

$$A = \frac{M}{4} b^2.$$

nce the moment C round a line through the centre of ipse, perpendicular to its plane, is

$$\frac{M}{4}(a^2 + b^2). \tag{9}$$

is plain, as before, that the expression for the moment tia of an elliptical cylinder relative to its axis is of the orm.

. **Sphere.**—If we suppose a sphere divided into an number of concentric spherical shells, the moment of of each shell is plainly the same for all diameters; cordingly, representing the mass of any element of a y dm, and by x, y, z any point on it, we have

$$\Sigma x^2 dm = \Sigma y^2 dm = \Sigma z^2 dm.$$

$$\Sigma (x^2 + y^2 + z^2) dm = \Sigma r^2 dm\,;$$

$$\therefore\ \Sigma (x^2 + y^2) dm = \frac{2}{3}\Sigma r^2 dm.$$

nce, (a) the moment of inertia of a shell whose radius th respect to any diameter is $\dfrac{2}{3} mr^2$, where m repre-

he mass of the shell.

ain, (b) for a solid sphere of radius R, since the volume ndefinitely thin shell of radius r is $4\pi r^2 dr$, we get

$$\Sigma r^2 dv = 4\pi \int_0^R r^4 dr = \frac{4}{5}\pi R^5 = \frac{3}{5} V R^2.$$

this is substituted, the moment of inertia of a solid eneous sphere relative to any diameter is found to be

$$\frac{2}{5} M R^2. \tag{10}$$

205. **Ellipsoid.**—Let the equation of an ellipsoid be

$$\frac{x^2}{a^2} + \frac{y^2}{b^2} + \frac{z^2}{c^2} = 1 \, ;$$

and suppose A, B, C to be the moments of inertia relative to the axes a, b, c, respectively; then

$$C = \mu \Sigma \left(x^2 + y^2\right) dV = \mu \iiint \left(x^2 + y^2\right) dx\, dy\, dz.$$

Now, let
$$\frac{x}{a} = x', \quad \frac{y}{b} = y', \quad \frac{z}{c} = z',$$

and we get

$$C = \mu\, abc \iiint \left(a^2 x'^2 + b^2 y'^2\right) dx'\, dy'\, dz',$$

where the integrals are extended to all points within the sphere

$$x'^2 + y'^2 + z'^2 = 1.$$

But, by the last example we have

$$\iiint x'^2\, dx'\, dy'\, dz' = \iiint y'^2\, dx'\, dy'\, dz' = \frac{4}{15}\,\pi \, ;$$

$$\therefore \ C = \frac{4}{15}\,\pi \mu\, abc \left(a^2 + b^2\right) = \frac{M}{5}\left(a^2 + b^2\right). \qquad (11)$$

In like manner,

$$A = \frac{M}{5}\left(b^2 + c^2\right), \quad B = \frac{M}{5}\left(c^2 + a^2\right).$$

It should be remarked that the moments of inertia of the ellipsoid with respect to its three *principal planes* are

$$\frac{M}{5}a^2, \quad \frac{M}{5}b^2, \quad \frac{M}{5}c^2, \text{ respectively.}$$

:06. **Moments of Inertia of a Lamina.**—Suppose
any plane lamina is referred to two rectangular axes
m through any origin O, and that a is the angle which
right line through O, lying in the plane, makes with the
of x; then, if I be the moment of inertia of the lamina
ive to this line, we have

$$I = \Sigma p^2 \, dm = \Sigma \left(y \cos a - x \sin a\right)^2 dm$$

$$= \cos^2 a \, \Sigma y^2 \, dm + \sin^2 a \, \Sigma x^2 \, dm - 2 \sin a \cos a \, \Sigma xy \, dm$$

$$= a \cos^2 a + b \sin^2 a - 2h \sin a \cos a; \qquad (12)$$

re a and b represent the moments of inertia relative to
axes of x and y, respectively; and h is the product of
tia relative to the same axes.

Again, supposing X and Y to be the co-ordinates of a point
n on the same line at a distance R from the origin, we

$$\cos a = \frac{X}{R}, \sin a = \frac{Y}{R}; \text{ and, consequently,}$$

$$IR^2 = aX^2 + bY^2 - 2hXY.$$

ordingly, if an ellipse be constructed whose equation is

$$aX^2 + bY^2 - 2hXY = \text{const.}, \qquad (13)$$

1ave

$$IR^2 = \text{const.};$$

, consequently, the moment of inertia relative to any line
vn through the origin varies inversely as the square of
corresponding radius vector of this ellipse.

The form and position of this ellipse are evidently inde-
dent of the particular axes assumed; but its equation is
e simple if the axes, major and minor, of the ellipse had
1 assumed as the axes of co-ordinates. Again, since in
 case the coefficient of XY disappears from the equa-
 of the curve, we see that there exists at every point in
 dy one pair of rectangular axes for which the quantity
: $\Sigma xy \, dm = 0$.

This pair of axes is called the *principal axes* at the
1t; and the corresponding moments of inertia are called the
icipal moments of inertia of the lamina relative to the point.

Again, if A and B represent the principal moments of inertia, equation (12) becomes

$$I = A \cos^2 a + B \sin^2 a. \qquad (14)$$

Hence, for a lamina, the moment of inertia relative to any axis through a point can be found when the principal moments relative to the point are determined.

The equation of the ellipse (13) becomes, when referred to the principal axes,

$$AX^2 + BY^2 = \text{const.}$$

207. **Momental Ellipse.**—Since the moments of inertia for all axes are determined when those relative to the centre of gravity are known, it is sufficient to consider the case where the origin is at the centre of gravity. With reference to this case, the ellipse

$$AX^2 + BY^2 = \text{const.} \qquad (15)$$

is called the *momental ellipse* of the lamina.

Again, if two different distributions of matter in the same plane have a common centre of gravity, and have the same principal axes and principal moments of inertia, at that point, they have the same moments of inertia relative to all axes.

This is an immediate consequence of (14). Hence it is easily seen that the moments of inertia for any lamina are the same as for the system of four equal masses, each $\dfrac{M}{4}$, placed on the two central principal axes, at the four distances $\pm a$ and $\pm b$, from the centre of gravity, where a and b are determined by the equations

$$A = \frac{1}{2} Mb^2, \quad B = \frac{1}{2} Ma^2.$$

Again, if two systems of the same total mass, in a plane, have a common centre of gravity, and have equal moments of inertia relative to any three axes, through their common centre of gravity, they have the same moments of inertia for all axes.

ıis follows immediately since an ellipse is determined
its centre and three points on its circumference are

gain, it may be observed that the boundary of an
cal lamina may be regarded as the momental ellipse of
mina.
or, if I be the moment of inertia relative to any
ter making the angle a with the axis major, we have

$$I = A \cos^2 a + B \sin^2 a.$$

oy Art. 203,

$$A = \frac{M}{4} b^2, \quad B = \frac{M}{4} a^2 \, ;$$

$$\therefore I = \frac{M}{4} \left(b^2 \cos^2 a + a^2 \sin^2 a \right)$$

$$= \frac{M}{4} a^2 b^2 \left(\frac{\cos^2 a}{a^2} + \frac{\sin^2 a}{b^2} \right)$$

$$= \frac{M}{4} \frac{a^2 b^2}{r^2}.$$

ə the moment of inertia varies inversely as the square
semi-diameter r ; and, consequently, the ellipse may be
led as its own momental ellipse.

ı8. **Products of Inertia of Lamina.**—Suppose the
a referred to its principal axes at a point O ; and let p
be the distances of any element dm from two axes,
make the angles a and β with the axis of x ; then we

$$m = \Sigma \, (y \cos a - x \sin a)(y \cos \beta - x \sin \beta) \, dm$$

$$= \cos a \cos \beta \, \Sigma y^2 \, dm + \sin a \sin \beta \, \Sigma x^2 \, dm$$
$$- \sin (a + \beta) \, \Sigma xy \, dm$$

$$= A \cos a \cos \beta + B \sin a \sin \beta,$$

$$A = \Sigma y^2 \, dm, \quad B = \Sigma x^2 \, dm, \text{ and } \Sigma xy \, dm = \text{o}.$$

ə, if $\Sigma pq \, dm = \text{o}$, we have

$$A \cos a \cos \beta + B \sin a \sin \beta = \text{o},$$

and accordingly the axes are a pair of conjugate diameters of the momental ellipse

$$AX^2 + BY^2 = \text{const.}$$

Hence, if two laminæ in the same plane have for any point two pairs of axes for which $\Sigma pq\,dm = 0$ and $\Sigma p'q'\,dm' = 0$, they have the same principal axes at the point. This follows from the easily established property, that if two ellipses have two pairs of conjugate diameters in common, they must be similar and coaxal.

209. **Triangular Lamina and Prism.**—Suppose a triangular lamina, whose sides are a, b, c, to be divided into a system of rods parallel to a side a; and let A represent the moment of inertia relative to a line parallel to the side a, and drawn through the opposite vertex; also let p be the perpendicular of the triangle on the side a, and x the distance of an elementary rod from the vertex; then we have, since the mass dm of the

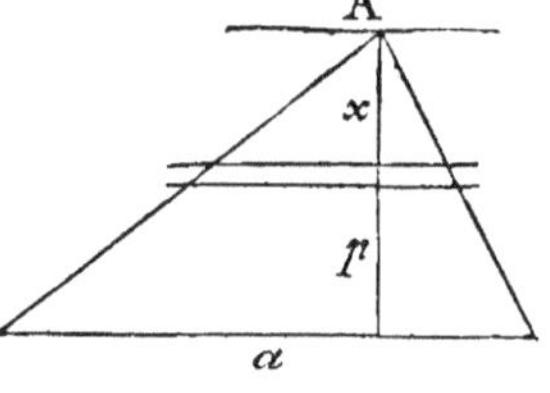

Fig. 48.

elementary rod may be represented by $\mu\dfrac{ax}{p}dx$,

$$A = \Sigma x^2\,dm = \mu\,\Sigma x^2 \frac{ax}{p}\,dx$$

$$= \mu\,\frac{a}{p}\int_0^p x^3\,dx = \mu\,\frac{ap^3}{4} = \frac{M}{2}p^2.$$

In like manner, let B and C be the moments of inertia relative to lines drawn through the other vertices parallel to b and c; and let q, r be the corresponding perpendiculars of the triangle, and we have

$$B = \frac{M}{2}q^2, \quad C = \frac{M}{2}r^2.$$

Again, if A_0, B_0, C_0, represent the moments of inertia

ive to three parallels to the sides, drawn through the
:e of gravity of the lamina, we have, by (2),

$$A_0 = \frac{1}{18} M p^2, \quad B_0 = \frac{1}{18} M q^2, \quad C_0 = \frac{1}{18} M r^2. \qquad (16)$$

Also, if A_1, B_1, C_1, be the moments of inertia relative
ιe sides a, b, c, respectively, it follows, in like manner,
. (2), that

$$A_1 = \frac{1}{6} M p^2, \quad B_1 = \frac{1}{6} M q^2, \quad C_1 = \frac{1}{6} M r^2. \qquad (17)$$

Again, it is readily seen that the values of A, A_0, A_1, &c.,
;he same as if the whole mass M were divided into three
ιl masses, placed respectively at the middle points of the
; of the lamina.

Consequently, by Art. 207, the moments of inertia of the
ιgular lamina relative to all axes are the same as for
e masses, each $\dfrac{M}{3}$, placed at the middle points of the
; of the triangle.

Hence, if I be the moment of inertia of a triangular
ιna with respect to the perpendicular to its plane drawn
ugh its centre of gravity, we have

$$I = \frac{1}{36} M (a^2 + b^2 + c^2). \qquad (18)$$

This expression also holds for the moment of inertia of a
t triangular prism with respect to *its axis*.*

In like manner the moments of inertia of the triangular
ιna relative to the three perpendiculars to its plane,
vn through its vertices, are

$$M\left(b^2 + c^2 - \frac{a^2}{3}\right), \quad \frac{1}{4} M\left(c^2 + a^2 - \frac{b^2}{3}\right), \quad \frac{1}{4} M\left(a^2 + b^2 - \frac{c^2}{3}\right);$$

the same expressions hold for a triangular prism relative
ιs edges.

By the axis of a prism is understood the right line drawn through its
e of gravity parallel to its edges.

210. Momental Ellipse of a Triangle.—It can be shown without difficulty that the ellipse which touches at the middle points of the sides may be taken for the momental ellipse of the triangle.

For, let x, y, z be the middle points of the sides, and it is easily seen that o is the centre of this ellipse; also, if I_1, I_2, I_3 be the moments of inertia of the

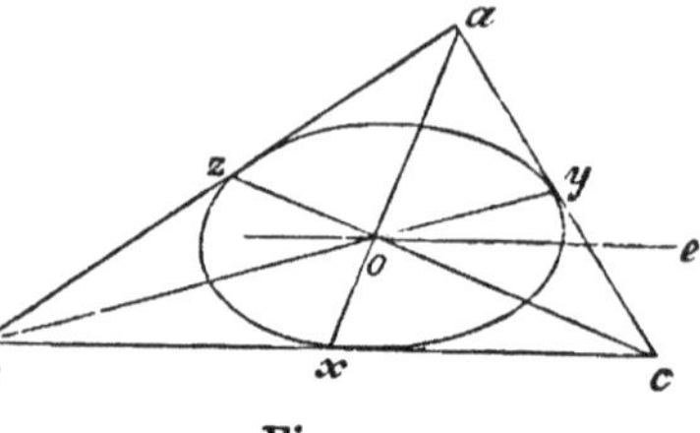

Fig. 49.

lamina relative to the lines ax, by, cz, respectively, it can be readily shown from (17), that we have

$$I_1 : I_2 : I_3 = \frac{1}{(ax)^2} : \frac{1}{(by)^2} : \frac{1}{(cz)^2}$$

$$= \frac{1}{(ox)^2} : \frac{1}{(oy)^2} : \frac{1}{(oz)^2}.$$

Accordingly, by Art. 207, the ellipse xyz may be taken for the momental ellipse of the lamina.

211. Tetrahedron.—If a solid tetrahedron be supposed divided into thin laminæ parallel to one of its faces, and if A, B, C, D represent its moments of inertia with regard to the four *planes* drawn respectively through its vertices parallel to its faces; then, denoting the areas of the corresponding faces by a, b, c, d, and the corresponding perpendiculars of the tetrahedron by p, q, r, s, respectively, it is easily seen, as in Art. 209, that we shall have

$$A = \Sigma x^2 dm = \mu \Sigma x^2 a\frac{x^2}{p^2}\, dx = \mu \frac{a}{p^2} \int_0^p x^4\, dx$$

$$= \mu \frac{ap^3}{5} = \frac{3}{5} M p^2.$$

In like manner we have

$$B = \frac{3}{5} M q^2, \quad C = \frac{3}{5} M r^2, \quad D = \frac{3}{5} M s^2.$$

gain, if A_0, B_0, C_0, D_0 be the corresponding moments of
a relative to the parallel planes drawn through the
) of gravity of the tetrahedron, we have, by (2),

$$\frac{3}{30} Mp^2, \quad B_0 = \frac{3}{80} Mq^2, \quad C_0 = \frac{3}{80} Mr^2, \quad D_0 = \frac{3}{80} Ms^2. \quad (19)$$

lso, if A_1, B_1, C_1, D_1 be the moments of inertia relative
, four faces of the tetrahedron, we have

$$\frac{1}{10} Mp^2, \quad B_1 = \frac{1}{10} Mq^2, \quad C_1 = \frac{1}{10} Mr^2, \quad D_1 = \frac{1}{10} Ms^2. \quad (20)$$

2. Solid Ring.*—If a plane closed curve, which is
etrical with respect to an axis AB, be made to revolve

a parallel axis, lying in
ıne, but not intersecting the
, to prove that the moment
rtia I of the generated solid,
with respect to the axis of
ction, is represented by

$$M(h^2 + 3k^2),$$

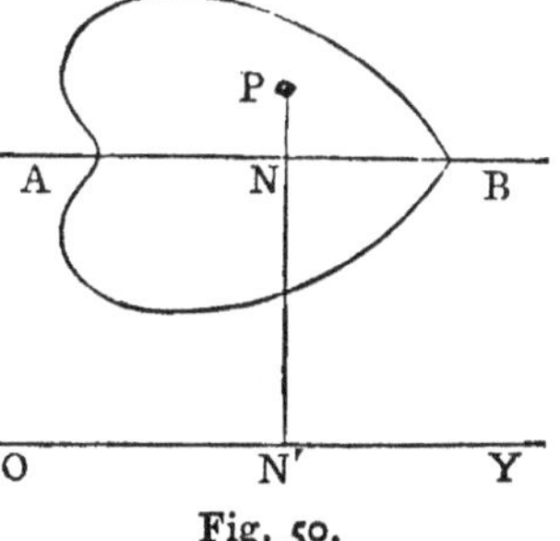

Fig. 50.

M is the mass of the solid,
distance between the parallel
and k the radius of gyration
generating area relative to its axis.

ır, if the axis of revolution be taken as the axis of x,
f y, Y be the distances of any point P within the
ıting area from AB, and from OX, respectively; and,
be the corresponding element of the area, then the
e of the elementary ring generated by dA is $2\pi Y dA$,
s mass $2\pi\mu Y dA$; hence the moment of inertia of this
ıtary ring, relative to the axis of X, is $2\pi\mu Y^3 dA$.
lingly, we have

$$I = 2\pi\mu \Sigma Y^3 dA = 2\pi\mu \Sigma (h + y)^3 dA$$

$$= 2\pi\mu \Sigma (h^3 + 3h^2 y + 3hy^2 + y^3) dA.$$

ıe theorems of this Article were given by Professor **Townsend in the**
ıy Journal of Mathematics, 1869.

Moreover, since the curve is symmetrical with respect to the axis AB, it is easily seen that we have

$$\Sigma y \, dA = 0, \quad \Sigma y^3 dA = 0.$$

Also, by definition, $\quad \Sigma y^2 dA = Ak^2.$

Hence $\qquad\qquad I = 2\pi \mu h A (h^2 + 3k^2).$

Again, by Art. 177, $\quad M = 2\pi \mu h A;$

$$\therefore I = M(h^2 + 3k^2). \tag{21}$$

This leads immediately to some important cases.

Thus, for example, the moment of inertia of a circular ring, of radius a, round its axis is

$$M\left(h^2 + \frac{3}{4}a^2\right).$$

Again, if a square of side a revolve round any line in its plane, situated at the distance h from its centre, we have

$$I = M(h^2 + a^2).$$

There is no difficulty in adding other examples.

213. **General Expression for Products of Inertia.** —We shall conclude this Chapter with a short discussion of the general case of the moments and products of inertia, for any body, or system.

Let us suppose the system referred to three rectangular planes, and let p, q, r represent the respective distances of any element dm from the three planes

$$x \cos a + y \cos \beta + z \cos \gamma = 0,$$
$$x \cos a' + y \cos \beta' + z \cos \gamma' = 0,$$
$$x \cos a'' + y \cos \beta'' + z \cos \gamma'' = 0.$$

Then

$$\Sigma pq \, dm = \Sigma (x\cos a + y\cos\beta + z\cos\gamma)(x\cos a' + y\cos\beta' + z\cos\gamma')\,dm$$
$$= \cos a \cos a' \Sigma x^2 dm + \cos\beta\cos\beta' \Sigma y^2 dm + \cos\gamma\cos\gamma' \Sigma z^2 dm$$
$$+ (\cos a \cos\beta' + \cos\beta\cos a')\Sigma xy\,dm$$
$$+ (\cos\gamma\cos a' + \cos a\cos\gamma')\Sigma zx\,dm$$
$$+ (\cos\beta\cos\gamma' + \cos\gamma\cos\beta')\Sigma yz\,dm;$$

and we get similar expressions for $\Sigma pr\,dm$ and $\Sigma qr\,dm$.

Now, suppose that we take

$$\Sigma x^2 dm = a, \quad \Sigma y^2 dm = b, \quad \Sigma z^2 dm = c,$$

$$\Sigma yz\, dm = f, \quad \Sigma xz\, dm = g, \quad \Sigma xy\, dm = h;$$

the preceding equation may be written

$$\Sigma pq\, dm = \cos a\, (a \cos a' + h \cos \beta' + g \cos \gamma')$$
$$+ \cos \beta\, (h \cos a' + b \cos \beta' + f \cos \gamma')$$
$$+ \cos \gamma\, (g \cos a' + f \cos \beta' + c \cos \gamma'); \qquad (22)$$

g with similar expressions for $\Sigma rp\, dm$ and $\Sigma qr\, dm$.

214. **Principal Axes.**—Next, let us suppose that the
les are so assumed as to satisfy the equations

$$\Sigma pq\, dm = 0, \quad \Sigma rp\, dm = 0, \quad \Sigma qr\, dm = 0;$$

ι it is easily seen* that these planes are a system of con-
ite diametral planes in the ellipsoid represented by the
ation

$$aX^2 + bY^2 + cZ^2 + 2fYZ + 2gZX + 2hXY = \text{const.} \quad (23)$$

ice it follows that at any point there exists *one system of
ıngular planes for which the corresponding products of
tia, for any body, vanish:* viz., *the principal planes of the
eding ellipsoid.*†
These three planes are called the *principal planes* of the
y relative to the point, and the right lines in which they
rsect are called the *principal axes* for the point.
Again, every two solids have for every point at least one
mon system of planes for which $\Sigma pq\, dm = 0$, $\Sigma rp\, dm = 0$,
·dm = 0, $\Sigma p'q'\, dm' = 0$, $\Sigma r'p'\, dm' = 0$, $\Sigma q'r'\, dm' = 0$;
·re the unaccented letters refer to the elements of one
1, and the accented to those of the other.
This is obvious from the property that every two con-
;ric ellipsoids have one common system of diametral planes.

. Salmon's *Geometry of Three Dimensions*, Art. 72.
The exceptional cases when the ellipsoid is of revolution, or is a sphere,
be considered subsequently.

[20 a]

Again, if two solids have for any point more than one system of planes for which the foregoing six products of inertia vanish, they must have the same principal planes at the point. This follows since the two ellipsoids in that case must be similar and coaxal.

215. **Principal Moments of Inertia.**—Let us now suppose the co-ordinate planes to be the principal planes of the body for the origin, then the moment of inertia relative to the plane

$$x \cos a + y \cos \beta + z \cos \gamma = 0$$

is

$$\Sigma p^2 dm = \Sigma (x \cos a + y \cos \beta + z \cos \gamma)^2 dm$$

$$= \cos^2 a \, \Sigma x^2 dm + \cos^2 \beta \, \Sigma y^2 dm + \cos^2 \gamma \, \Sigma z^2 dm, \quad (24)$$

since in this case we have

$$\Sigma xy \, dm = 0, \quad \Sigma zx \, dm = 0, \quad \Sigma yz \, dm = 0.$$

Again, let I be the moment of inertia of the body relative to the line through the origin whose direction angles are a, β, γ; then we have

$$I + \Sigma p^2 dm = \Sigma r^2 dm = \Sigma (x^2 + y^2 + z^2) \, dm;$$

$$\therefore \; I = \cos^2 a \, \Sigma (y^2 + z^2) \, dm + \cos^2 \beta \, \Sigma (z^2 + x^2) \, dm$$

$$+ \cos^2 \gamma \, \Sigma (x^2 + y^2) \, dm;$$

or
$$I = A \cos^2 a + B \cos^2 \beta + C \cos^2 \gamma, \quad (25)$$

where A, B, C are the moments of inertia of the body relative to its three principal axes.

A, B, C are called the *three principal moments of inertia* of the body relative to the origin.

If the centre of gravity be taken as the origin, the corresponding values of A, B, C are called the *principal moments of inertia of the body.*

We suppose, in general, that A is the greatest, and C the least of the three principal moments.

It follows from (25) that the moment of inertia of a body relative to any line passing through a given point is known, whenever the angles which the line makes with the principal axes are known, as also the moments of inertia relative to these axes.

16. **Ellipsoid of Gyration.**—Suppose, as before, the
referred to its three principal axes at any point, and let
c be the corresponding radii of gyration, i.e. let

$$A = Ma^2, \quad B = Mb^2, \quad C = Mc^2,$$

$I = Mk^2$; then equation (25) becomes

$$k^2 = a^2 \cos^2 \alpha + b^2 \cos^2 \beta + c^2 \cos^2 \gamma. \tag{26}$$

ow, if we suppose an ellipsoid described having the
ipal axes for the directions, and a, b, c for the lengths
corresponding semi-axes; then (26) shows that the
s of gyration of the body, relative to the perpendicular
the origin on any tangent plane to this ellipsoid, is
in length to this perpendicular. (Salmon's *Geometry*
ree Dimensions, Art. 89.)
he foregoing ellipsoid is called the *ellipsoid of gyration*
ve to the point. It should, however, be observed that
e ellipsoid of gyration of a body is meant the ellipsoid
e particular case where the origin is at the centre of
ty of the body.

17. **Momental Ellipsoid.**—If X, Y, Z be the co-
ates of a point R taken on the right line through the
O, whose direction angles are α, β, γ, we have

$$X = OR \cos \alpha, \quad Y = OR \cos \beta, \quad Z = OR \cos \gamma.$$

bstituting the values of $\cos \alpha$, $\cos \beta$, $\cos \gamma$, deduced
these equations, in (25), it becomes

$$I \cdot OR^2 = AX^2 + BY^2 + CZ^2.$$

ppose, now, that the point R lies on the ellipsoid

$$AX^2 + BY^2 + CZ^2 = \text{const.}, \tag{27}$$

e get $I \cdot OR^2 = \lambda$, denoting the constant by λ;

$$\therefore I = \frac{\lambda}{OR^2}. \tag{28}$$

ence the *moment of inertia relative to any axis, drawn*
h the origin, varies inversely as the square of the cor-
ding diameter of the ellipsoid (27).

From this property the ellipsoid is called the *momental ellipsoid* at the point.

When the origin is taken at the centre of gravity of the body, this ellipsoid is called the *central ellipsoid* of the body.

If two of the principal moments of inertia relative to any point be equal, the momental ellipsoid becomes one of revolution, and in this case all diameters perpendicular to its axis of revolution are principal axes relative to the point.

If the three principal moments at any point be equal, the ellipsoid becomes a sphere, and the moments of inertia for all axes drawn through the point are equal. Every such axis is a principal axis at the point.

For example, it is plain that the three principal moments for the centre of a cube are equal, and, consequently, its moments of inertia for all axes, through its centre, are equal.

218. **Equimomental Cone.**—Again, since

$$\cos^2 a + \cos^2 \beta + \cos^2 \gamma = 1,$$

equation (25) may be written in the form

$$(A - I)\cos^2 a + (B - I)\cos^2 \beta + (C - I)\cos^2 \gamma = 0\,;$$

hence the equation

$$(A - I)\,X^2 + (B - I)\,Y^2 + (C - I)\,Z^2 = 0 \qquad (29)$$

represents a cone such that the moment of inertia is the same for each of its edges. Such a cone is called an *equimomental cone* of the body.

Again, the three axes of any equimomental cone, for any solid, are the principal axes of the solid relative to the vertex of the cone.

When $I = B$, the cone breaks up into two planes; viz., the cyclic sections of the momental ellipsoid.

For a more complete discussion of the general theory of moments of inertia and principal axes, the student is referred to Routh's *Rigid Dynamics*, chapters I. and II.; as also to Professor Townsend's papers in the *Camb. and Dub. Math. Journal*, 1846, 1847.

EXAMPLES.

nd the expressions for the moments of inertia in the following, the bodies supposed homogeneous in all cases :—

A parallelogram, of sides a, b, and angle θ, with respect to its sides.

$$Ans. \quad \frac{M}{3} b^2 \sin^2 \theta, \quad \frac{M}{3} a^2 \sin^2 \theta.$$

A rod, of length a, with respect to an axis perpendicular to the rod and stance d from its middle point.

$$Ans. \quad M \left(\frac{a^2}{3} + d^2 \right).$$

An equilateral triangle, of side a, relative to a line in its plane at the e d from its centre of gravity.

$$Ans. \quad M \left(\frac{a^2}{24} + d^2 \right).$$

A right-angled triangle, of hypothenuse c, relative to a perpendicular to ne passing through the right angle.

$$Ans. \quad M \frac{c^2}{6}.$$

A hollow circular cylinder, relative to its axis.

$$Ans. \quad M \frac{r^2 + r'^2}{2}, \text{ where } r \text{ and } r' \text{ are the radii of the bounding circles.}$$

A truncated cone with reference to its axis.

$$Ans. \quad \frac{3M}{10} \frac{b^5 - b'^5}{b^3 - b'^3}, \text{ where } b \text{ and } b' \text{ are the radii of its bases.}$$

A right cone with respect to an axis drawn through its vertex perpen- to its axis.

$$Ans. \quad \frac{3M}{5} \left(h^2 + \frac{b^2}{4} \right), \text{ where } h \text{ denotes the altitude of the cone,}$$

he radius of its base.

An ellipsoid with respect to a diameter making angles a, β, γ with its

$$Ans. \quad \frac{M}{5} \left(a^2 \sin^2 a + b^2 \sin^2 \beta + c^2 \sin^2 \gamma \right).$$

Area bounded by two rectangles having a common centre, and whose re respectively parallel, with respect to an axis through their centre dicular to the plane.

$$Ans. \quad \frac{M}{12} \frac{(a^2 + b^2) ab - (a'^2 + b'^2) a' b'}{ab - a'b'}.$$

10. A square, of side a, relative to any line in its plane, passing through its centre.

$$Ans. \quad M\frac{a^2}{12}.$$

11. A regular polygon, or prism, with respect to its axis.

$$Ans. \quad \frac{M}{6}\left(R^2 + 2r^2\right),$$ where R and r are the radii of the circles circumscribed, and inscribed to the polygon.

12. Prove that a parallelogram and its maximum inscribed ellipse have the same principal axes at their common centre of figure.

13. Prove that the moments and products of inertia of any triangular lamina, of mass M, are the same as for three masses, each $\frac{M}{12}$, placed at the three vertices of the triangle, combined with a mass $\frac{3}{4}M$ placed at its centre of gravity.

14. Prove that the moments and products of inertia of any tetrahedron are the same as for four masses, each $\frac{M}{20}$, placed at the vertices of the tetrahedron, combined with a mass $\frac{4}{5}M$ placed at its centre of gravity.

15. If a system of equimomental axes, for any solid, all lie in a principal plane passing through its centre of gravity, prove that they envelop a conic, having that point for centre, and the principal axes in the plane for axes.

16. Prove also that the ellipses obtained by varying the magnitude of the moment of inertia form a confocal system.

17. Prove that the sum of the moments of inertia of a body relative to any three rectangular axes drawn through the same point is constant.

18. Prove that a principal axis belonging to the centre of gravity of a body is also a principal axis with respect to every point on its length.

19. Prove that the envelope of a plane for which the moment of inertia of a body is constant is an ellipsoid, confocal with the ellipsoid of gyration of the body.

20. If a system of equimomental planes pass through a point, prove that they envelop a cone of the second degree.

21. For different values of the constant moment the several enveloped cones are confocal?

22. The common axes of this system of cones are the three principal axes of the body for the point?

23. The three principal axes at any point are the normals to the three surfaces confocal to the ellipsoid of gyration, which pass through the point. (M. Binet, *Jour. de l'Ec. Poly.* 1813.)

CHAPTER XI.

MULTIPLE INTEGRALS.

. **Double Integration.**—In the preceding Chapters we
ə considered several cases of double and triple integra-
. in the determination of volumes and other problems
ɪected with surfaces. We now proceed to a short treat-
ɪt of the general problem of Multiple Integration, com-
ɪcing with double integrals.

The general form of a double integral may be written

$$\int_{x_0}^{X} \int_{y_0}^{Y} f(x,\ y)\,dx\,dy,$$

ɪhich we suppose the integration first taken with respect
, regarding x as constant. In this case, Y, y_0, the limits
, are, in general, functions of x; and the limits of x are
ɪtants.

Let us take for example the integral

$$U = \int_{0}^{a} \int_{x}^{\frac{a^2}{x}} x^{l-1} y^{m-1}\,dx\,dy,$$

ɪhich l is supposed greater than m.

Here
$$\int_{x}^{\frac{a^2}{x}} y^{m-1}\,dy = \frac{1}{m}\left(\frac{a^{2m}}{x^m} - x^m\right);$$

efore
$$U = \frac{1}{m}\int_{0}^{a} x^{l-1}\left(\frac{a^{2m}}{x^m} - x^m\right) dx = \frac{2a^{l+m}}{l^2 - m^2}.$$

ɪn many cases the variables are to be taken so as to in-
.e all values limited by a certain condition, which can be
ɪessed by an inequality: for instance, to find

$$U = \iint x^{l-1} y^{m-1}\,dx\,dy,$$

ɪnded to all *positive* values of x and y subject to the con-
ɪn $x + y < h.$

[21]

Here the limits for y are 0 and $h - x$; and the subsequent limits of x are 0 and h.

Hence
$$U = \int_0^h \int_0^{h-x} x^{l-1} y^{m-1} \, dx \, dy$$

$$= \frac{1}{m} \int_0^h x^{l-1} (h - x)^m \, dx.$$

Let $x = hu$, then

$$U = \frac{h^{l+m}}{m} \int_0^1 u^{l-1} (1 - u)^m \, du = \frac{h^{l+m} \, \Gamma(l) \, \Gamma(m)}{\Gamma(l + m + 1)}, \qquad (1)$$

by Art. 121.

220. **Change of Order of Integration.**—We have seen (Art. 115) that when the limits of x and y are constants in a double integral we may change the order of integration, the limits remaining unaltered. But when the limits of y are functions of x, if the order of integration be changed, it is necessary to find the new limits for x as functions of y. This is usually best obtained from geometrical considerations.

For example, in the integral

$$U = \int_0^a \int_x^{\frac{a^2}{x}} f(x, y) \, dx \, dy,$$

the limits for y are given by the right line $y = x$ and the hyperbola $xy = a^2$; and the integral extends to all points in the space included by the hyperbola AL, the right line OA, where A is the vertex of the hyperbola, and the axis of y. Draw AB perpendicular to the axis of y. Now when the order of integration is changed, we suppose the lines which divide the area into strips taken parallel to the axis of x instead of the axis of y. Thus the integral breaks up into two parts—one corresponding to

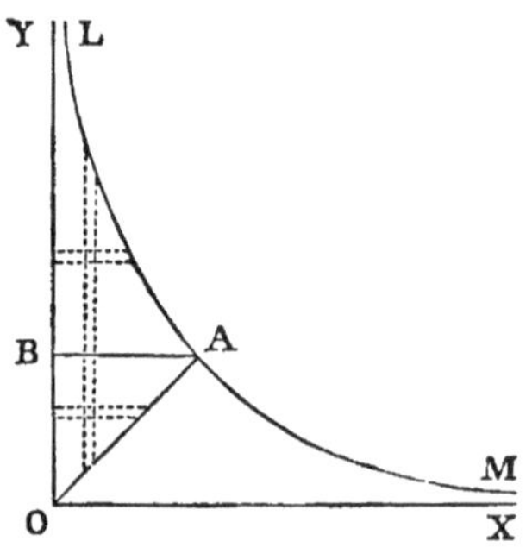

triangle OAB, the other to the remaining area : hence

$$U = \int_0^a \int_0^y f(x, y) \, dy \, dx + \int_a^\infty \int_0^{\frac{a^2}{y}} f(x, y) \, dy \, dx.$$

As another example, let us interchange the variables in integral

$$U = \int_0^a \int_{mx}^{lx} V \, dx \, dy.$$

Here, let OC and OD be the es represented by $y = lx$ and $= mx$; and let $OA = a$.
Then the integral is extended to points within the triangle OCD.
Accordingly, changing the order, get

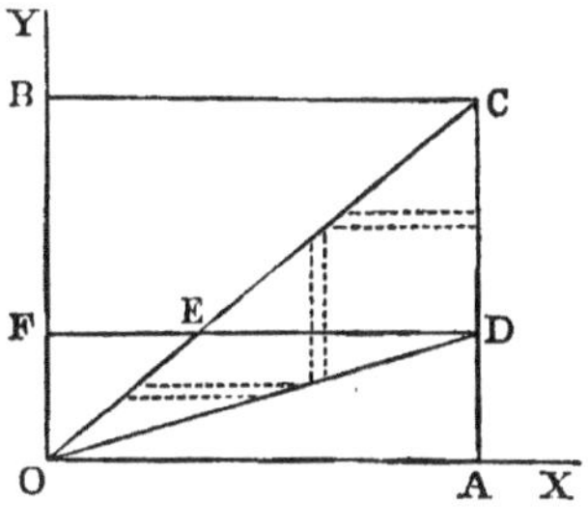

$$U = \int_{ma}^{la} \int_{\frac{y}{l}}^{a} V \, dy \, dx + \int_0^{ma} \int_{\frac{y}{l}}^{\frac{y}{m}} V \, dy \, dx.$$

EXAMPLES.

1. Find the value of the double integral

$$U = \int_0^a \int_0^x \frac{f'(y) \, dx \, dy}{\sqrt{(a-x)(x-y)}}.$$

Here, changing the order, the integral becomes

$$\int_0^a \int_y^a \frac{f'(y) \, dy \, dx}{\sqrt{(a-x)(x-y)}}.$$

But $\quad \int_y^a \dfrac{dx}{\sqrt{(a-x)(x-y)}} = \pi$; hence $U = \pi \{ f(a) - f(0) \}$.

2. Prove that

$$\int_0^{2a} \int_0^{\sqrt{2ax-x^2}} f(x, y) \, dx \, dy = \int_0^a \int_{a-\sqrt{a^2-y^2}}^{a+\sqrt{a^2-y^2}} f(x, y) \, dy \, dx.$$

$$[21\,a]$$

3. Hence find the value of

$$\int_0^{2a} \int_0^{\sqrt{2ax-x^2}} \frac{\phi'(u)\,(x^2 + y^2)\,x\,dx\,dy}{\sqrt{4a^2x^2 - (x^2 + y^2)^2}}.$$

$$Ans. \quad \pi a^2 \{\phi(a) - \phi(0,)\}.$$

4. Change the order of integration in the double integral

$$U = \int_0^{2a} \int_{\sqrt{2ax-x^2}}^{\sqrt{2ax}} V\,dx\,dy.$$

The limits of y are represented by the circle $x^2 + y^2 = 2ax$, and the parabola $y^2 = 2ax$; and we readily find that

$$U = \int_0^a \int_{\frac{y^2}{2a}}^{a-\sqrt{a^2-y^2}} V\,dy\,dx \; + \; \int_0^a \int_{a+\sqrt{a^2-y^2}}^{2a} V\,dy\,dx \; + \; \int_a^{2a} \int_{\frac{y^2}{2a}}^{a} V\,dy\,dx.$$

221. Dirichlet's Theorem.—The result given in equation (1) has been generalized by Dirichlet (Liouville's *Journal*, 1839), and extended to a large class of multiple integrals, as follows:

Commencing with three variables, let us consider the integral

$$U = \iiint x^{l-1}\, y^{m-1}\, z^{n-1}\, dx\, dy\, dz,$$

in which the variables are supposed always positive, and limited by the condition

$$x + y + z < 1.$$

In this case the limits of z are o and $1 - x - y$; those of y are o and $1 - x$; and those of x, o and 1.

Hence $\qquad U = \int_0^1 \int_0^{1-x} \int_0^{1-x-y} x^{-1}\, y^{m-1}\, z^{n-1}\, dx\, dy\, dz.$

It is easily seen, from (1), that

$$\int_0^{1-x} \int_0^{1-x-y} y^{m-1}\, z^{n-1}\, dy\, dz = (1 - x)^{m+n}\, \frac{\Gamma(m)\,\Gamma(n)}{\Gamma(m + n + 1)}.$$

refore

$$U = \frac{\Gamma(m)\,\Gamma(n)}{\Gamma(m+n+1)} \int_0^1 x^{l-1}\,(1-x)^{m+n}\,dx$$

$$= \frac{\Gamma(m)\,\Gamma(n)}{\Gamma(m+n+1)} \cdot \frac{\Gamma(l)\,\Gamma(m+n+1)}{\Gamma(l+m+n+1)} = \frac{\Gamma(l)\,\Gamma(m)\Gamma(n)}{\Gamma(l+m+n+1)}. \quad (2)$$

Again, in the same multiple integral, if x, y, z, being always positive, are subject to the condition

$$x + y + z < h,$$

get

$$U = h^{l+m+n}\frac{\Gamma(l)\,\Gamma(m)\,\Gamma(n)}{\Gamma(l+m+n+1)}. \quad (3)$$

This readily appears by substituting $x = hx'$, $y = hy'$, hz', in the multiple integral.

There is no difficulty in extending these results to any nber of variables. We proceed from (3) to the case of r variables; and so by induction to any number.

Thus, the value of the multiple integral

$$U = \iiint \ldots x^{l-1}\,y^{m-1}\,z^{n-1}\,\ldots dx\,dy\,dz\ldots,$$

ended to all positive values of x, y, z, &c., subject to the dition

$$x + y + z + \&c. < 1,$$

$$U = \frac{\Gamma(l)\,\Gamma(m)\,\Gamma(n)\,\ldots}{\Gamma(1+l+m+n+\ldots)}. \quad (4)$$

Again, in the integral

$$U = \iiint x^{l-1}\,y^{m-1}\,z^{n-1}\,dx\,dy\,dz,$$

pose the variables to be still always positive, but limited the condition

$$\left(\frac{x}{a}\right)^p + \left(\frac{y}{b}\right)^q + \left(\frac{z}{c}\right)^r < 1\,;$$

then making

$$\left(\frac{x}{a}\right)^p = u, \quad \left(\frac{y}{b}\right)^q = v, \quad \left(\frac{z}{c}\right)^r = w,$$

the integral transforms into

$$U = \frac{a^l b^m c^n}{pqr} \iiint u^{\frac{l}{p}-1}\, v^{\frac{m}{q}-1}\, w^{\frac{n}{r}-1}\, du\, dv\, dw,$$

where $\quad u + v + w < 1.$

Accordingly

$$U = \frac{a^l b^m c^n}{pqr} \frac{\Gamma\left(\frac{l}{p}\right) \Gamma\left(\frac{m}{q}\right) \Gamma\left(\frac{n}{r}\right)}{\Gamma\left(1 + \frac{l}{p} + \frac{m}{q} + \frac{n}{r}\right)}. \qquad (5)$$

Again, from (3), the value of the triple integral

$$\iiint x^{l-1}\, y^{m-1}\, z^{n-1}\, dx\, dy\, dz,$$

extended to all positive values, subject to the condition

$$x + y + z > u \text{ and } < u + du,$$

is

$$\frac{\Gamma(l)\,\Gamma(m)\,\Gamma(n)}{\Gamma(1 + l + m + n)}(l+m+n)\, u^{l+m+n-1}\, du, \text{ or } \frac{\Gamma(l)\Gamma(m)\Gamma(n)}{\Gamma(l+m+n)}\, u^{l+m+n-1} du.$$

Hence the multiple integral

$$\iiint F(x + y + z)\, x^{l-1}\, y^{m-1}\, z^{n-1}\, dx\, dy\, dz,$$

taken between the same limits, has for its value

$$\frac{\Gamma(l)\,\Gamma(m)\,\Gamma(n)}{\Gamma(l + m + n)}\, F(u)\, u^{l+m+n-1}\, du.$$

Accordingly, the value of the multiple integral

$$\iiint F(x + y + z)\, x^{l-1}\, y^{m-1}\, z^{n-1}\, dx\, dy\, dz,$$

ended to all positive values of the variables, subject to the condition

$$x + y + z < h,$$

$$\frac{\Gamma(l)\,\Gamma(m)\,\Gamma(n)}{\Gamma(l + m + n)} \int_0^h F(u)\, u^{l+m+n-1}\, du. \tag{6}$$

In like manner it is seen that if the multiple integral

$$U = \iiint F\left\{\left(\frac{x}{a}\right)^p + \left(\frac{y}{b}\right)^q + \left(\frac{z}{c}\right)^r\right\}\, x^{l-1}\, y^{m-1}\, z^{n-1}\, dx\, dy\, dz$$

extended to all positive values, subject to the condition

$$\left(\frac{x}{a}\right)^p + \left(\frac{y}{b}\right)^q + \left(\frac{z}{c}\right)^r < h,$$

have

$$U = \frac{a^l b^m c^n}{pqr} \frac{\Gamma\left(\dfrac{l}{p}\right) \Gamma\left(\dfrac{m}{q}\right) \Gamma\left(\dfrac{n}{r}\right)}{\Gamma\left(\dfrac{l}{p} + \dfrac{m}{q} + \dfrac{n}{r}\right)} \int_0^h F(u)\, u^{\frac{l}{p} + \frac{m}{q} + \frac{n}{r} - 1}\, du. \tag{7}$$

These results can be readily extended to any number of riables.

EXAMPLES.

1. Find the value of

$$\iint x^{l-1}\, y^{-l}\, e^{x+y}\, dx\, dy,$$

ended to all positive values, subject to $x + y < h$.

$$Ans. \quad \frac{\pi}{\sin l\pi}\, (e^h - 1).$$

2. More generally, prove that

$$\iint F'(x+y)\, x^{l-1}\, y^{-l}\, dx\, dy = \frac{\pi}{\sin l\pi}\{F(h) - F(o)\},$$

where
$$x + y < h.$$

3. Find the value of

$$\iiint .. dx_1\, dx_2 \ldots dx_n,$$

extended to all positive values of the variables, subject to the condition

$$x_1{}^2 + x_2{}^2 + \ldots + x_n{}^2 < R^2.$$

$$Ans.\quad \left(\frac{R}{2}\right)^n \frac{\varpi^{\frac{n}{2}}}{\Gamma\left(1 + \frac{n}{2}\right)}.$$

4. Prove that

$$\iiint \frac{dx\, dy\, dz}{\sqrt{1 - x^2 - y^2 - z^2}} = \frac{\pi^2}{8},$$

the integral being extended to all positive values of the variables for which the expression is real.

5. Show in general that

$$\iiint .. \frac{dx_1\, dx_2\, dx_3 .. dx_n}{\sqrt{1 - x_1{}^2 - x_2{}^2 - .. - x_n{}^2}} = \frac{\pi^{\frac{n+1}{2}}}{2^n\, \Gamma\left(\frac{n+1}{2}\right)},$$

under the same condition as in (3).

222. Transformation of Multiple Integrals.—We proceed to consider the transformation of a multiple integral to a new system of independent variables.

Suppose it be required to transform the integral

$$\iiint f(x, y, z)\, dx\, dy\, dz$$

to another system of variables, u, v, w, being given x, y, z in terms of u, v, w.

This transformation implies in general three parts— (1) the expression of $f(x, y, z)$ in terms of u, v, w; (2) the determination of the new system or systems of limits; (3) the substitution for $dx\, dy\, dz$.

The solution of the first two questions is a purely algebraical

)lem.   We here limit ourselves to the consideration of the
d question, and write the integral in the form

$$\int dx \int dy \int f(x,\, y,\, z)\, dz.$$

In the integration with respect to z, x and y are regarded
:onstant; accordingly, in order to replace z by the new
able w, we suppose z expressed, by means of the given
ations, in terms of x, y, w; and then we replace dz by

lw.   Again, to transform the integration from y to v, we
;t suppose y expressed in terms of v, w, x, and then dy
aced by $\dfrac{dy}{dv}\, dv$: we next suppose x replaced by $\dfrac{dx}{du}\, du$; and
finally replace

$$dx\ dy\ dz\ \ \text{by}\ \ \frac{dz}{dw}\,\frac{dy}{dv}\,\frac{dx}{du}\, du\ dv\ dw.$$

It should be observed that in each of the latter transfor-
ions a change in the order of integration is supposed.
By this means the transformed expression is

$$\iiint \phi\,(u,\, v,\, w)\,\frac{dz}{dw}\,\frac{dy}{dv}\,\frac{dx}{du}\, du\ dv\ dw, \qquad (8)$$

re $\phi\,(u,\, v,\, w)$ is the transformation of $f\,(x,\, y,\, z)$.
The preceding would present, in general, a problem of
·eme difficulty, especially in the investigation of the new
.ts at each change in the order of integration.   The one
ter in every case to be carefully observed is, that the trans-
ned integral or integrals must include every element
ch enters into the original expression, and no more.
Again, it may be observed that in the foregoing substitu-
s for $dx\ dy\ dz$ the order may be interchanged in any
iner.
Thus, if we commence by replacing x by u, we must
pose x expressed in terms of u, y, z ; and then replace dx
$\dfrac{lx}{lu}\, du$, &c.

As an illustration we shall consider the ordinary transformation from rectangular to polar coordinates, viz. :—

$$x = r \sin \theta \sin \phi, \quad y = r \sin \theta \cos \phi, \quad z = r \cos \theta.$$

Here we have

$$x^2 + y^2 + z^2 = r^2 ;$$

therefore

$$x^2 = r^2 - y^2 - z^2 ;$$

hence

$$\frac{dx}{dr} = \frac{r}{x} = \frac{1}{\sin \theta \sin \phi}.$$

Again

$$\frac{dz}{d\theta} = - r \sin \theta, \quad \frac{dy}{d\phi} = - r \sin \theta \sin \phi ;$$

therefore

$$\frac{dx}{dr} \frac{dz}{d\theta} \frac{dy}{d\phi} = r^2 \sin \theta ;$$

and for the element of volume $dx\, dy\, dz$ we substitute

$$r^2 \sin \theta\, dr\, d\theta\, d\phi,$$

a result which can be also readily shown from geometrical considerations.

Next, let us consider the more general transformation

$$x = r \sin \theta \sqrt{1 - m^2 \sin^2 \phi}, \quad y = r \sin \phi \sqrt{1 - n^2 \sin^2 \theta}, \quad z = r \cos \theta \cos \phi,$$

in which

$$m^2 + n^2 = 1.$$

Squaring, and adding the three equations, we get

$$x^2 + y^2 + z^2 = r^2.$$

In replacing x by r, we get, therefore,

$$\frac{dx}{dr} = \frac{r}{x} = \frac{1}{\sin \theta \sqrt{1 - m^2 \sin^2 \phi}}.$$

Next, to replace y by ϕ, we must express y in terms of r, nd z: thus

$$= r \sin \phi \sqrt{m^2 + n^2 \cos^2 \theta} = \sin \phi \sqrt{m^2 r^2 + \frac{n^2 z^2}{\cos^2 \phi}}$$

$$= \tan \phi \sqrt{m^2 r^2 \cos^2 \phi + n^2 z^2}.$$

ce

$$\frac{\cdot}{\cdot} = \sec^2 \phi \sqrt{m^2 r^2 \cos^2 \phi + n^2 z^2} - \frac{m^2 r^2 \sin^2 \phi}{\sqrt{m^2 r^2 \cos^2 \phi + n^2 z^2}}$$

$$= \frac{m^2 r^2 \cos^2 \phi + n^2 z^2 \sec^2 \phi}{\sqrt{m^2 r^2 \cos^2 \phi + n^2 z^2}} = \frac{r \left(m^2 \cos^2 \phi + n^2 \cos^2 \theta\right)}{\cos \phi \sqrt{m^2 + n^2 \cos^2 \theta}};$$

finally, $\qquad \dfrac{dz}{d\theta} = - r \sin \theta \cos \phi.$

ce for $dx\,dy\,dz$ we substitute

$$\frac{r^2 \left(m^2 \cos^2 \phi + n^2 \sin^2 \phi\right) dr\, d\theta\, d\phi}{\sqrt{1 - m^2 \sin^2 \phi}\ \sqrt{1 - n^2 \sin^2 \theta}}. \tag{9}$$

[n general (*Diff. Calc.*, Art. 325), the product $\dfrac{dz}{dw}\dfrac{dy}{dv}\dfrac{dx}{du}$ ie Jacobian of the original system of variables, x, y, z, rded as functions of the new system, u, v, w.

Accordingly, the general substitution for $dx\,dy\,dz$ is

$$\begin{vmatrix} \dfrac{dx}{du} & \dfrac{dx}{dv} & \dfrac{dx}{dw} \\[2ex] \dfrac{dy}{du} & \dfrac{dy}{dv} & \dfrac{dy}{dw} \\[2ex] \dfrac{dz}{du} & \dfrac{dz}{dv} & \dfrac{dz}{dw} \end{vmatrix} du\, dv\, dw. \tag{10}$$

223. **Transformation for Implicit Functions.**—If, ead of being given x, y, z explicitly as functions of u, v, w,

we are given equations of the form

$$F_1(x,y,z,\ u,v,w) = 0, \quad F_2(x,y,z,\ u,v,w) = 0, \quad F_3(x,y,z,\ u,v,w) = 0,$$

we have (*Diff. Calc.*, Art. 324), adopting the usual notation for Jacobians,

$$\frac{d\,(x,\ y,\ z)}{d\,(u,\ v,\ w)} = -\frac{\dfrac{d(F_1,\ F_2,\ F_3)}{d\,(u,\ v,\ w)}}{\dfrac{d\,(F_1,\ F_2,\ F_3)}{d\,(x,\ y,\ z)}}.$$

And for $dx\,dy\,dz$ we must then substitute

$$\frac{J_1}{J_2}\,du\,dv\,dw, \tag{11}$$

where J_1 is the Jacobian of the given system of equations with respect to the new variables, and J_2 their Jacobian with respect to the original system.

224. Transformation of Element of Surface.—If the equation of a surface be referred to a system of rectangular axes it is easily seen, from Art. 189, that the element of its superficial area, whose projection on the plane of xy is $dx\,dy$, is equal to

$$dx\,dy\sqrt{1 + \left(\frac{dz}{dx}\right)^2 + \left(\frac{dz}{dy}\right)^2}.$$

Accordingly the area of a surface may be represented by

$$\iint \sqrt{1 + \left(\frac{dz}{dx}\right)^2 + \left(\frac{dz}{dy}\right)^2}\,dx\,dy,$$

taken between proper limits. In this result z is regarded as a function of x and y by means of the equation of the surface.

To transform this expression to new variables u, v, we, by the preceding Article, substitute

$$\left(\frac{dx}{du}\frac{dy}{dv} - \frac{dy}{du}\frac{dx}{dv}\right)du\,dv \text{ instead of } dx\,dy.$$

$$\frac{dz}{du} = \frac{dz}{dx}\frac{dx}{du} + \frac{dz}{dy}\frac{dy}{du},$$

$$\frac{dz}{dv} = \frac{dz}{dx}\frac{dx}{dv} + \frac{dz}{dy}\frac{dy}{dv};$$

fore

$$\left.\begin{aligned}
\frac{dz}{dx} &= \frac{\dfrac{dz}{du}\dfrac{dy}{dv} - \dfrac{dy}{du}\dfrac{dz}{dv}}{\dfrac{dx}{du}\dfrac{dy}{dv} - \dfrac{dy}{du}\dfrac{dx}{dv}}, \\[2em]
\frac{dz}{dy} &= \frac{\dfrac{dz}{dv}\dfrac{dx}{du} - \dfrac{dx}{dv}\dfrac{dz}{du}}{\dfrac{dx}{du}\dfrac{dy}{dv} - \dfrac{dy}{du}\dfrac{dx}{dv}}.
\end{aligned}\right\} \qquad (12)$$

Substituting, the expression for the superficial area be-
es

$$\sqrt{\left(\frac{dx}{du}\frac{dy}{dv} - \frac{dy}{du}\frac{dx}{dv}\right)^2 + \left(\frac{dx}{dv}\frac{dz}{du} - \frac{dz}{dv}\frac{dx}{du}\right)^2 + \left(\frac{dz}{dv}\frac{dy}{du} - \frac{dy}{dv}\frac{dz}{du}\right)^2}\, du\, dv.$$

225. General Transformation for n Variables.—
transformation of Art. 223 can be readily generalized.
s, for the case of n variables, in the transformation of
multiple integral

$$\iiint \ldots V dx_1\, dx_2\, dx_3 \ldots dx_n$$

system of new variables, $y_1,\, y_2,\, \ldots y_n$, we substitute
$dx_1,\, dx_2,\, \ldots dx_n$ the Jacobian of $x_1,\, x_2,\, \ldots x_n$ regarded
inctions of $y_1,\, y_2,\, y_3 \ldots y_n$; hence

$$dx_1\, dx_2 \ldots dx_n = \frac{d\,(x_1,\, x_2,\, \ldots x_n)}{d\,(y_1,\, y_2,\, \ldots y_n)}\, dy_1\, dy_2 \ldots dy_n. \qquad (13)$$

l in the case of implicit functions, we substitute

$$\frac{J_1}{J_2}\, dy_1\, dy_2 \ldots dy_n,$$

where J_1 and J_2 are respectively the Jacobians of the system of equations with respect to the new, and to the original, system of variables (compare *Diff. Calc.*, Art 324).

226. **Green's Theorems.** — We shall conclude this Chapter with a brief notice of the very remarkable theorems given by Green ("Essay on the Application of Mathematics to Electricity and Magnetism," Nottingham, 1828, reprinted, 1871), as follows:—

If U and V be functions of x, y, z, the rectangular coordinates of a point; then, provided U and V are *finite and continuous for all points within a given closed surface S*, we have

$$\left.\begin{aligned}
&\iiint \left(\frac{dU}{dx}\frac{dV}{dx} + \frac{dU}{dy}\frac{dV}{dy} + \frac{dU}{dz}\frac{dV}{dz} \right) dx\, dy\, dz \\
&= \iint U \frac{dV}{dn} dS - \iiint U \left(\frac{d^2 V}{dx^2} + \frac{d^2 V}{dy^2} + \frac{d^2 V}{dz^2} \right) dx\, dy\, dz \\
&= \iint V \frac{dU}{dn} dS - \iiint V \left(\frac{d^2 U}{dx^2} + \frac{d^2 U}{dy^2} + \frac{d^2 U}{dz^2} \right) dx\, dy\, dz
\end{aligned}\right\},$$

where the triple integrals are extended to all points within the surface S, and the double integrals to all points on S; aud dn is the element of the normal to the surface at dS, measured *outwards*.

For, since
$$\frac{d}{dx}\left(U \frac{dV}{dx} \right) = \frac{dU}{dx}\frac{dV}{dx} + U \frac{d^2 V}{dx^2},$$
we have
$$\iiint \frac{d}{dx}\left(U \frac{dV}{dx} \right) dx\, dy\, dz = \iiint \frac{dU}{dx}\frac{dV}{dx} dx\, dy\, dz$$
$$+ \iiint U \frac{d^2 V}{dx^2} dx\, dy\, dz, \quad (14)$$

the integrals being extended to all points within S.

Again, since S is a closed surface, any intersecting right line meets it in an even number of points; consequently

$$\iiint \frac{d}{dx}\left(U \frac{dV}{dx} \right) dx\, dy\, dz = \iint dy\, dz\, \Sigma \left\{ U_2 \frac{dV_2}{dx_2} - U_1 \frac{dV_1}{dx_1} \right\},$$

re x_1, x_2, U_1, U_2, represent the values of x, U, for two
esponding points of intersection with S, made by an
finitely thin parallelepiped standing on $dy\,dz$; and Σ
tes the summation extended to all such points of inter-
ion. Now, as in Art. 192, let dS_1, dS_2, dS_3, &c., repre-
the corresponding elementary portions of the surface;
λ_1, λ_2, λ_3, &c., the angles that the *exterior* normals make
1 the positive direction of the axis of x; we shall have

$$dz = \cos\lambda_1\, dS_1 = -\cos\lambda_2\, dS_2 = \cos\lambda_3\, dS_3 = -\cos\lambda_4\, dS_4 = \&c.$$

Accordingly

$$\iiint \frac{d}{dx}\left(U\,\frac{dV}{dx}\right) dx\,dy\,dz = \iint U\,\frac{dV}{dx}\cos\lambda\,dS, \qquad (15)$$

er the same restrictions as to limits as before.
Hence, from (14), we find

$$\iint \frac{dU}{dx}\frac{dV}{dx}\,dx\,dy\,dz = \iint U\,\frac{dV}{dx}\cos\lambda\,dS - \iiint U\,\frac{d^2V}{dx^2}\,dx\,dy\,dz,$$

ig with corresponding equations for y and z.
Accordingly

$$\iiint\left(\frac{dU}{dx}\frac{dV}{dx} + \frac{dU}{dy}\frac{dV}{dy} + \frac{dU}{dz}\frac{dV}{dz}\right) dx\,dy\,dz$$

$$= \iint U\left(\frac{dV}{dx}\cos\lambda + \frac{dV}{dy}\cos\mu + \frac{dV}{dx}\cos\nu\right) dS$$

$$- \iiint U\left(\frac{d^2V}{dx^2} + \frac{d^2V}{dy^2} + \frac{d^2V}{dz^2}\right) dx\,dy\,dz.$$

Again, we obviously have

$$\cos\lambda = \frac{dx}{dn}, \quad \cos\mu = \frac{dy}{dn}, \quad \cos\nu = \frac{dz}{dn};$$

refore $\quad \dfrac{dV}{dx}\cos\lambda + \dfrac{dV}{dy}\cos\mu + \dfrac{dV}{dz}\cos\nu = \dfrac{dV}{dn}.$

Hence

$$
\iiint \left(\frac{dU}{dx}\frac{dV}{dx} + \frac{dU}{dy}\frac{dV}{dy} + \frac{dU}{dz}\frac{dV}{dz} \right) dx\,dy\,dz
$$

$$
= \iint U\frac{dV}{dn}\,dS - \iiint U\left(\frac{d^2V}{dx^2} + \frac{d^2V}{dy^2} + \frac{d^2V}{dz^2} \right) dx\,dy\,dz
$$

$$
= \iint V\frac{dU}{dn}\,dS - \iiint V\left(\frac{d^2U}{dx^2} + \frac{d^2U}{dy^2} + \frac{d^2U}{dz^2} \right) dx\,dy\,dz
$$

$$ (16) $$

The latter expression is obtained by the interchange of U and V in the preceding.

If $U = V$, we get

$$
\iiint \left\{ \left(\frac{dV}{dx}\right)^2 + \left(\frac{dV}{dy}\right)^2 + \left(\frac{dV}{dz}\right)^2 \right\} dx\,dy\,dz
$$

$$
= \iint V\frac{dV}{dn}\,dS - \iiint V\left(\frac{d^2V}{dx^2} + \frac{d^2V}{dy^2} + \frac{d^2V}{dz^2} \right) dx\,dy\,dz.
$$

We shall now determine the modification to be made when one of the functions, U for example, becomes infinite within S. Suppose this to take place at one point P only: moreover, infinitely near this point let U be sensibly equal to $\frac{1}{r}$, r being the distance from P. If we suppose an indefinitely small sphere, of radius a, described with its centre at P, it is clear that (16) is applicable to all points exterior to the sphere; also since

$$
\left(\frac{d^2}{dx^2} + \frac{d^2}{dy^2} + \frac{d^2}{dz^2} \right)\frac{1}{r} = 0,
$$

it is evident that the triple integrals may be supposed to extend through the entire enclosed space, since the part arising from points within the sphere is a small quantity of the order of a^2. Moreover, the part of $\iint U\frac{dV}{dn}\,dS$, due to the surface of the sphere is indefinitely small of the order of a. It only remains to consider the part of $\iint V\frac{dU}{dn}\,dS$ due to the spherical surɔe. Here, as V is supposed to vary continuously, we may ɔe for its value that (V') at the point P: also

$$\frac{dU}{dn} = \frac{dU}{dr} = \frac{d\left(\frac{1}{r}\right)}{dr} = -\frac{1}{r^2} = -\frac{1}{a^2};$$

ɔsequently the value of $\iint V \frac{dU}{dn} dS$, for the sphere is

$$- 4\pi V'.$$

Thus (16) becomes

$$\iint U \frac{dV}{dn} dS - \iiint U \left(\frac{d^2V}{dx^2} + \frac{d^2V}{dy^2} + \frac{d^2V}{dz^2}\right) dx\,dy\,dz$$

$$\iint V \frac{dU}{dn} dS - \iiint V \left(\frac{d^2U}{dx^2} + \frac{d^2U}{dy^2} + \frac{d^2U}{dz^2}\right) dx\,dy\,dz - 4\pi V', \tag{17}$$

ɩere, as before, the integrals extend over the whole volume ɩ over the whole exterior surface.

The same method will evidently apply however great ,y be the number of points, such as P, at which either U V becomes infinite.

EXAMPLES.

1. If
$$U = a \cos u + b \sin u \cos v + c \sin u \sin v,$$

ɾe that
$$\int_0^{2\pi} \int_0^{2\pi} f(U) \sin u \, du \, dv = 2\pi \int_{-1}^{+1} f(Aw) \, w\,dw,$$

ɾe
$$A = \sqrt{a^2 + b^2 + c^2}.$$

$$x = \cos u, \quad y = \sin u \cos v, \quad z = \sin u \sin v \, ;$$

ɩ (x, y, z) are the coordinates of a point on a sphere of unit radius, ɩ centre at the origin.
Also let $a = A\alpha$, $b = A\beta$, $c = A\gamma$; then α, β, γ is also a point on the same ɜre, and

$$a \cos u + b \sin u \cos v + c \sin u \sin v = A \cos \theta,$$

[22]

where θ is the arc joining the point a, β, γ to x, y, z. Again, the element of the surface of the sphere at the latter point may be represented by $\sin u \, du \, dv$, or by $\sin \theta \, d\theta \, d\phi$, indifferently. Consequently

$$f(a \cos u + b \sin u \cos v + c \sin u \sin v) \sin u \, du \, dv = f(A \cos \theta) \sin \theta \, d\theta \, d\phi.$$

Integrating each of these over the entire surface, we get

$$\int_0^\pi \int_0^{2\pi} f(U) \sin u \, du \, dv = \int_0^{2\pi} \int_0^\pi f(A \cos \theta) \sin \theta \, d\theta \, d\phi = 2\pi \int_0^\pi f(A \cos \theta) \sin \theta \, d\theta.$$

2. Hence, deduce the following :

$$\int_0^\pi \int_0^{2\pi} f(U) \sin u \cos u \, du \, dv = \frac{2\pi a}{A} \int_{-1}^{+1} f(Aw) \, w \, dw,$$

$$\int_0^\pi \int_0^{2\pi} f(U) \sin^2 u \cos v \, du \, dv = \frac{2\pi c}{A} \int_{-1}^{+1} f(Aw) \, w \, dw.$$

These are deduced from (1) by differentiation under the sign of integration.

3. Show that the integral

$$U = \iint f(x + y) \, x^{l-1} \, y^{m-1} \, dx \, dy,$$

supposed extended to all positive values subject to the condition $x + y < k$, can be reduced to a single definite integral, by the substitution

$$x = uv, \quad y = u(1 - v).$$

Here $x + y = u$, and $dx \, dy$ becomes $u \, dv \, dv$; also the limits for u are 0 and k, and those for v are 0 and 1 ; hence

$$U = \int_0^k \int_0^1 f(u) \, u^{l+m-1} \, v^{l-1} \, (1 - v)^{m-1} \, du \, dv$$

$$= \frac{\Gamma(l) \, \Gamma(m)}{\Gamma(l + m)} \int_0^k f(u) \, u^{l+m-1} \, du. \qquad \text{(Compare Art. 221).}$$

4. Show that the foregoing process can be extended to the integral

$$U = \iiint f(x + y + z) \, x^{l-1} \, y^{m-1} \, z^{n-1} \, dx \, dy \, dz,$$

when the variables are always positive and subject to the condition

$$x + y + z < a.$$

Substitute for x and y as in last ; then, regarding z as constant, the limits

)r v are 0 and 1, and those for u are 0 and $a - z$; hence

$$U = \frac{\Gamma(l)\,\Gamma(m)}{\Gamma(l+m)} \int_0^a \int_0^{a-z} f(u+z)\, u^{l+m-1}\, z^{n-1}\, du\, dz$$

$$= \frac{\Gamma(l)\,\Gamma(m)\,\Gamma(n)}{\Gamma(l+m+n)} \int_0^a f(u)\, u^{l+m+n-1}\, du.$$

This process is readily extended to any number of variables.

5. Find the value of the definite integral

$$\int_0^1 \frac{v^{l-1}\,(1-v)^{m-1}\,dv}{\{b\,(1-v)+av\}^{l+m}}.$$

y Art. 120 we have

$$\int_0^\infty \int_0^\infty x^{l-1}\, y^{m-1}\, e^{-ax-by}\, dx\, dy = \frac{\Gamma(l)\,\Gamma(m)}{a^l\, b^m}.$$

ransform by the substitution $x = uv$, $y = u(1-v)$, then, since the limits for
re 0 and 1, and those for u are 0 and ∞, we get

$$\frac{\Gamma(l)\,\Gamma(m)}{a^l\, b^m} = \int_0^1 \int_0^\infty u^{l+m-1}\,(1-v)^{m-1}\,v^{l-1}\, e^{-\{b(1-v)+av\}u}\, dv\, du$$

$$= \Gamma(l+m) \int_0^1 \frac{v^{l-1}\,(1-v)^{m-1}\,dv}{\{b\,(1-v)+av\}^{l+m}};$$

ıerefore
$$\int_0^1 \frac{v^{l-1}\,(1-v)^{m-1}\,dv}{\{bv\,(1-v)+av\}^{l+m}} = \frac{\Gamma(l)\,\Gamma(m)}{\Gamma(l+m)\, a^l\, b^m}.$$

6. Prove that

$$\int_{-\infty}^\infty \int_{-\infty}^\infty F(ax+by,\, a'x+b'y)\, dx\, dy = \frac{1}{k} \int_{-\infty}^\infty \int_{-\infty}^\infty F(x,\, y)\, dx\, dy,$$

here
$$k = \begin{vmatrix} a & b \\ a' & b' \end{vmatrix}.$$

7. Prove that

$$\int_0^{\frac{\pi}{2}} \int_0^{\frac{\pi}{2}} \frac{(m^2\cos^2\theta + n^2\cos^2\phi)\, d\theta\, d\phi}{\sqrt{(1-m^2\sin^2\theta)(1-n^2\sin^2\phi)}} = \frac{\pi}{2},$$

ıhen
$$m^2 + n^2 = 1.$$

This is an immediate consequence of (9), Art. 222.

8. Show that Legendre's Theorem connecting complete elliptic integrals
ıith complementary moduli follows immediately from the preceding example.

[22a]

Let $\quad F(m) = \displaystyle\int_0^{\frac{\pi}{2}} \frac{d\theta}{\sqrt{1 - m^2 \sin^2 \theta}} \quad E(m) = \displaystyle\int_0^{\frac{\pi}{2}} \sqrt{1 - m^2 \sin^2 \theta}\, d\theta,$

then the result given in Ex. 7 is easily transformed into

$$F(m)\, E(n) + E(m)\, F(n) - F(n)\, F(m) = \frac{\pi}{2}.$$

9. Prove that the area of a surface in polar coordinates is represented by

$$\iint \sqrt{\sin^2 \theta \left(r^2 + \frac{dr^2}{d\theta^2}\right) + \frac{dr^2}{d\phi^2}}\; r\, d\theta\, d\phi,$$

taken between suitable limits.

10. Show by actual integration that

$$\iiint \left(\frac{du}{dx} + \frac{dv}{dy} + \frac{dw}{dz}\right) dx\, dy\, dz = \iint (u \cos \alpha + v \cos \beta + w \cos \gamma)\, dS,$$

where the integrations, respectively, extend through the volume and over a closed surface S; α, β, γ being the direction angles of the outward drawn normal at dS.

11. Transform the multiple integral

$$\iiiint V\, dx\, dy\, dz\, dw$$

by the substitution

$$x = r \cos \theta \cos \phi, \quad y = r \cos \theta \sin \phi, \quad z = r \sin \theta \cos \psi, \quad w = r \sin \theta \sin \psi.$$

The transformed expression is

$$\iiiint V_1 r^3 \sin \theta \cos \theta\; dr\, d\theta\, d\phi\, d\psi,$$

where V_1 is the new value of V.

12. If $\quad x_1 = \dfrac{u_2 u_3}{u_1}, \quad x_2 = \dfrac{u_3 u_1}{u_2}, \quad x_3 = \dfrac{u_1 u_2}{u_3},$

prove that $\iiint V\, dx_1\, dx_2\, dx_3$ transforms into $4 \iiint V_1\, du_1\, du_2\, du_3$.

CHAPTER XII.

ON MEAN VALUE AND PROBABILITY.

227. A VERY remarkable application of the Integral Calculus is that to the solution of questions on Mean or Average Values and Probability. In this Chapter we will consider a few of the less difficult questions on these subjects, which will serve to give at least some idea of the methods employed. We will suppose the student to be already acquainted with the general fundamental principles of the theory of Probability.

Mean Values.

228. By the *Mean Value* of n quantities is meant their arithmetical mean, i.e. the nth part of their sum.

To estimate the Mean Value of a continuously varying magnitude, we take a series of n of its values, at very close intervals, n being a large number, and find the mean of these values. The larger n is taken, and consequently the smaller the intervals, the nearer is this to the required mean value.

This mean value, however, depends on the law according to which we suppose the n *representative* values to be selected, and will be different for different suppositions. Thus, for instance, if a body fall from rest till it attains the velocity v, and it be asked—What is its mean velocity during the fall? If we take the mean of the velocities at successive equal infinitesimal intervals of *time*, the answer will be $\frac{1}{2}v$; but if we consider the velocities at equal intervals of *space*, it will be $\frac{2}{3}v$. The former is the most natural supposition in this case, because it is the answer to the question —What is the velocity with which the body would move, uniformly, over the same space in the same time ?—a question which implies the former supposition. We might frame a similar question, of a less simple kind, to which the second value above would be the answer.

Again, if we wish to determine the mean value of the ordinate of a semicircle, we might take the mean of a series of ordinates equidistant from each other; or through equidistant points of the circumference; or such that the areas between each pair shall be equal: in each case the mean value will be different.

Thus we see that the Mean Value of any continuously varying magnitude is not a definite term, as might be supposed at first sight, but depends on the law assumed as to its successive values.

229. Case of One Independent Variable.—We will therefore suppose any variable magnitude y to be expressed as a function $\phi(x)$ of some quantity x on which it depends, and its mean value taken as x proceeds by equal infinitesimal increments h from the value a to the value b. Let n be the number of values, then $nh = b - a$. The mean value is

$$\frac{1}{n}\left\{\phi(a) + \phi(a + h) + \phi(a + 2h) + \ldots\right\}.$$

But (Art. 90),

$$h\left\{\phi(a) + \phi(a + h) + \phi(a + 2h) + \ldots\right\} = \int_{a}^{b}\phi(x)\,dx.$$

Hence the mean value is

$$M = \frac{1}{b - a}\int_{a}^{b}\phi(x)\,dx. \tag{1}$$

EXAMPLES.

1. To find the mean value of the ordinate of a semicircle, supposing the series taken equidistant.

$$M = \frac{1}{2r}\int_{-r}^{r}\sqrt{r^2 - x^2}\,dx = \frac{1}{4}\pi r,$$

viz., the length of an arc of 45°.

2. In the same case, let us suppose the ordinates drawn through equidistant points on the circumference.

$$M = \frac{1}{\pi}\int_{0}^{\pi}r\sin\theta\,d\theta = \frac{2}{\pi}r;$$ the ordinate of the centre of gravity of the arc.

3. Determine the mean horizontal range of a projectile *in vacuo* for different angles of elevation from $45° - \theta$ to $45° + \theta$; given the initial velocity V.

If α be the angle of elevation, the range is

$$R = \frac{V^2}{g} \sin 2\alpha.$$

Hence $\qquad M = \frac{1}{2\theta} \int \frac{V^2}{g} \sin 2\alpha \, d\alpha$, between the limits $45° \pm \theta$;

therefore $\qquad M = \frac{V^2}{g} \cdot \frac{\sin 2\theta}{2\theta}.$

The mean value for all elevations, from $0°$ to $90°$, is $\dfrac{2}{\pi} \dfrac{V^2}{g}$.

4. A number n is divided at random into two parts; to find the mean value of their product.

$$M = \frac{1}{n} \int_0^n x\,(n - x)\,dx = \frac{1}{6} n^2.$$

5. To find the mean distance of two points taken at random on the circumference of a circle.

Here we may evidently take one of the points, A, as fixed, and the other, B, to range over the whole circumference: since by altering the position of A we should only have the same series of values repeated: let θ be the angle between AB and the diameter through A: as we need only consider *one* of the two semi-circles,

$$M = \frac{2}{\pi} \int_0^{\frac{\pi}{2}} 2r \cos \theta \, d\theta = \frac{4r}{\pi}.$$

6. To find the mean values of the reciprocals of all numbers from n to $2n$, when n is large: that is, to find the mean value of the quantities

$$\frac{1}{n}, \quad \frac{1}{n} \frac{1}{1 + \frac{1}{n}}, \quad \frac{1}{n} \frac{1}{1 + \frac{2}{n}}, \quad \cdots \cdots \quad \frac{1}{n} \frac{1}{1 + \frac{n}{n}};$$

that is, the mean value of the function $\dfrac{1}{nx}$, as x goes by equal increments from to 2;

therefore $\qquad M = \int_1^2 \frac{dx}{nx} = \frac{1}{n} \log 2.$

7. To find the mean values of the two roots of the quadratic

$$x^2 - ax + b = 0,$$

the roots being known to be real, but b being unknown, except that it is positive:

That is, b is equally likely to have any value from o to $\dfrac{a^2}{4}$; hence for the greater root, a,

$$M = \frac{1}{\frac{1}{4}a^2} \int_0^{\frac{a^2}{4}} a\, db$$

$$= \frac{4}{a^2} \int_{\frac{1}{2}a}^a a(2a - a)\, da\,;$$

therefore

$$M = \frac{5}{6}\, a.$$

The mean value of the smaller root is $\dfrac{1}{6}\, a$.

The mean *squares* of the two roots are $\dfrac{17}{24}\, a^2$, $\dfrac{1}{24}a^2$. These might be deduced from the former results, since

$$M(x^2) - aM(x) + M(b) = \text{o}.$$

8. Find the mean (positive) abscissa of all points included between the axis of x and the curve

$$y = ae^{-\frac{x^2}{c^2}}.\qquad\qquad\qquad Ans.\ \ \frac{c}{\sqrt{\pi}}.$$

The mean *square* of the abscissa is $\frac{1}{2}c^2$.

230. If M be the mean of m quantities, and M' the mean of m' others of the same kind, and if μ be the mean of the whole $m + m'$ quantities, we have evidently

$$\mu = \frac{mM + m'M'}{m + m'}.\qquad\qquad (2)$$

Thus if it be required to find the mean distance of one extremity of the diameter of a semicircle from a point taken at random anywhere on the *whole* periphery of the semicircle; since the mean value when it falls on the diameter is r, and the mean value when it falls on the arc is $\dfrac{4r}{\pi}$, we have

$$\mu = \frac{2r \cdot r + \pi r \dfrac{4r}{\pi}}{2r + \pi r} = \frac{6r}{2 + \pi}.$$

231. Case of Two or More Independent Variables.
If $z = \phi(x, y)$ be any function of two independent variables,
and x, y be taken to vary by constant infinitesimal increments
h, k, between given limits of any kind, the mean value of the
function z will be

$$M = \frac{\iint z\,dx\,dy}{\iint dx\,dy}, \tag{3}$$

both integrals being taken between the given limits.

The easiest way of seeing this is to suppose x, y, z the
co-ordinates of a point; and to conceive the boundary, representing the limits, traced on the plane of xy, and then ruled with
lines parallel to x, y at intervals k, h apart. We have
thus a reticulation of infinitesimal rectangles hk; and if at
each angle an ordinate z be drawn to the surface $z = \phi(x, y)$,
as the number of ordinates will be the same as that of rectangles, we shall have

$$\text{volume } \iint z\,dx\,dy = \text{sum of ordinates} \times hk\,;$$

so the plane area $\iint dx\,dy = \text{number of ordinates} \times hk\,;$

so that dividing the sum of the ordinates by their number,
the above expression results.

It may be shown, in like manner, that for three or more
independent variables a similar expression holds.

It is evident that the above expression, viewed geometrically, gives the mean value of any function of the coordinates
of a series of points uniformly distributed over a given plane
area.

EXAMPLES.

1. Suppose a straight line a divided at random at two points, to find the
average value of the product of the three segments.

Let the distance of the two points X, Y, from one end A of the line, be
called x, y. Consider first the cases when $x > y$; the sum of the products for
these is half the whole sum; hence

$$M = \frac{2}{a^2} \int_0^a \int_0^x y\,(x - y)\,(a - x)\,dx\,dy = \frac{1}{60}a^3.$$

2. A number a is divided into three parts; to find the mean value of one
part.

Let x, y, $a - x - y$, be the parts;

$$M = \frac{\displaystyle\int_0^a \int_0^{a-x} x\, dx\, dy}{\displaystyle\int_0^a \int_0^{a-x} dx\, dy} = \frac{1}{3}a.$$

This value might be deduced, without performing the integrations, by considering that the expression is the abscissa of the centre of gravity of the triangle OAB; OA, OB being lengths taken on two rectangular axes, each $= a$.

Of course the result in this case requires no calculation; as the sum of the mean values of the three parts must be $= a$; and the three means must be equal.

The *mean square* of a part is $\frac{1}{6}a^2$.

3. A number a is divided at random into three parts: to find the mean value of the *least* of the three parts: also of the *greatest*, and of the *mean*.

Let x, y, $a - x - y$, be the greatest, mean, and least parts. The mean value of the greatest is $M = \dfrac{\iint x\, dx\, dy}{\iint dx\, dy}$: the limits of both integrations being given by

$$x > y > a - x - y > 0.$$

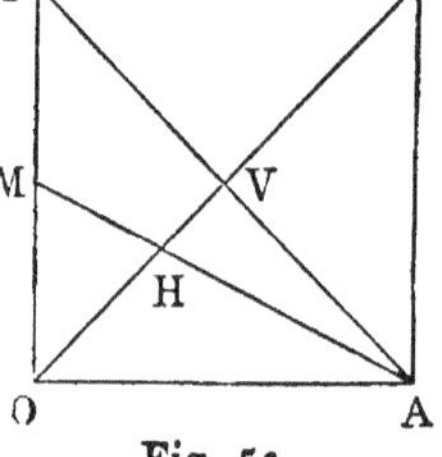

Fig. 53.

If x, y be the coordinates of a point, referred to the axes OA, OB, taking $OA = OB = a$, the above limits restrict the point to the triangle AVH (AM being drawn to bisect OB); and the above value of M is the abscissa of the centre of gravity of this triangle; i.e. $\frac{1}{3}$ of the sum of the abscissas of its angles; hence

$$M = \frac{1}{3}\left(a + \frac{1}{2}a + \frac{1}{3}a\right) = \frac{11}{18}a.$$

The *ordinate* of the same centre of gravity, viz.,

$$\frac{1}{3}\left(\frac{1}{2}a + \frac{1}{3}a\right) = \frac{5}{18}a,$$

is the mean value of the mean part; hence the mean values of the three parts required are respectively

$$\frac{11}{18}a, \quad \frac{5}{18}a, \quad \frac{1}{9}a.$$

4. To find the mean square of the distance of a point within a given square (side $= 2a$), from the centre of the square.

$$M = \frac{1}{4a^2}\int_{-a}^a \int_{-a}^a (x^2 + y^2)\, dx\, dy = \frac{2}{3}a^2.$$

is obvious that the mean square of the distance of all points on any plane
rom any fixed point in the plane is the square of the *radius of gyration* of
ea round that point.

To find the mean distance of a point on the circumference of a circle from
ints inside the circle.

aking the origin on the circumference, and the diameter for the axis, if dS
y element of the area, we have

$$M = \frac{\iint r\,dS}{\pi a^2} = \frac{1}{\pi a^2}\int_{-\frac{\pi}{2}}^{\frac{\pi}{2}}\int_0^{2a\cos\theta} r^2\,d\theta\,dr = \frac{32\,a}{9\pi}.$$

232. **Many problems on Mean Values, as well as on**
oability, **may be solved by particular artifices, which, if**
mpted **by direct calculation, lead to difficult multiple**
grals **which could hardly be dealt with.**

EXAMPLES.

To find the mean distance between two points within a given circle.

M be the required mean, the sum of the whole number of cases is repre-
d by

$$(\pi r^2)^2\,M.$$

let us consider what is the differential of this, that is, the sum of the new
introduced by giving r the increment dr. If M_0 be the mean distance of
nt on the *circumference* from a point within the circle, the new cases intro-
l by taking one of the two points A on the infinitesimal annulus $2\pi r\,dr$, are

$$\pi r^2\,M_0\;.\;2\pi r\,dr\;;$$

ing this, for the cases where the point B is taken in the annulus, we get

$$d\,.\,\{(\pi r^2)^2\,M\} = 4\pi^2 M_0 r^3\,dr.$$

ow $M_0 = \dfrac{32r}{9\pi}$ (Ex. 5, Art. 231);

fore
$$\pi^2 r^4\,M = \frac{128}{9}\,\pi\int_0^r r^4\,dr\;;$$

fore
$$M = \frac{128}{45\pi}\,r.$$

To find the mean square of the distance between two points taken on any
area Ω.

et dS, dS' be any two elements of the area, Δ their mutual distance, and
ave

$$M = \frac{1}{\Omega^2}\iiiint \Delta^2\,dS\,dS'.$$

Now, fixing the element dS, the integral of $\Delta^2 dS'$ is the moment of inertia of the area Ω round dS; so that if $K =$ radius of gyration of the area round dS,

$$M = \frac{-}{\Omega} \iint K^2 dS:$$

let $r =$ distance of dS from the centre of gravity G of the area, k the radius of gyration round G; then

$$K^2 = r^2 + k^2;$$

therefore

$$M = k^2 + \frac{1}{\Omega} \iint r^2 dS = 2k^2;$$

thus the mean square is twice the square of the radius of gyration of the area round its centre of gravity.

233. The mean distance of a point P within a given area from a fixed straight line (which does not meet the area) is evidently the distance of the centre of gravity G of the area from the line. Thus, if A, B are two fixed points on a line outside the area, the mean value of the area of the triangle $APB =$ the triangle AGB.

From this it will follow, that if X, Y, Z are three points taken at random in three given spaces on a plane (such that they cannot all be cut by any one straight line), the mean value of the area of the triangle XYZ is the triangle $GG'G''$, determined by the three centres of gravity of the spaces.

EXAMPLE.

1. A point P is taken at random within a triangle ABC, and joined with the three angles. To find the mean value of the *greatest* of the three triangles into which the whole is divided.

Let G be the centre of gravity; then if the greatest triangle stands on AB, P is restricted to the figure $CHGK$, and the mean value of APB is the same as if P were restricted to the triangle GCK; hence we have to find the area of the triangle whose vertex is the centre of gravity of GCK, and base AB;

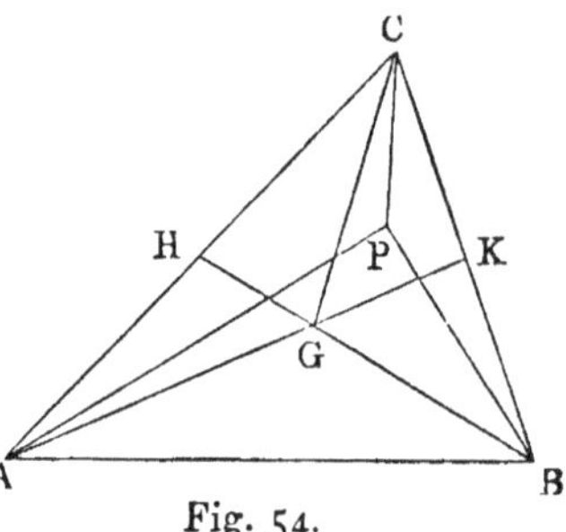

Fig. 54.

therefore

$$M = \frac{1}{3}(ACB + AKB + AGB) = \frac{1}{3}\left(1 + \frac{1}{2} + \frac{1}{3}\right) ABC;$$

hence the mean value is $\frac{11}{18}$ of the whole triangle.

The mean values of the least and mean triangles are respectively $\frac{1}{9}$ and $\frac{5}{18}$ of the whole.

This question can readily be shown to be reducible to Question 3, Art. 231.

234. If M be the mean value of any quantity depending
he positions of two points (e. g. their distance) which are
n, one in a space M, the other in a space B (external to
and if M' be the same mean when both points are taken
scriminately in the whole space $A + B$; M_A, M_B the
e mean when both points are taken in A, or both in B,
ectively; then

$$(A + B)^2 M' = 2ABM + A^2 M_A + B^2 M_B. \qquad (4)$$

If the space $A = B$,

$$4M' = 2M + M_A + M_B ;$$

lso, $M_A = M_B$,

$$2M' = M + M_A ;$$

if M be the mean distance of a point within a semi-
e from one in the opposite semicircle, M_1 that of two
ts in one semicircle, we have (Art. 232)

$$M + M_1 = \frac{256}{45\pi} r.$$

To determine M or M_1 is rather difficult, though their
is thus found. The value of M is $\dfrac{1472}{135\pi^2} r.$

Examples.

. Two points X, Y are taken at random within a triangle. What is the
area M of the triangle XYC, formed by joining them with one of the
s of the triangle ?
isect the triangle by the line CD; let M_1 be the mean value when both
s fall in the triangle ACD; M_2 the value when one falls in ACD and the
in BCD; then

$$2M = M_1 + M_2.$$

ut $M_1 = \frac{1}{2} M$; and $M_2 = GG'C$, where G, G' are the centres of gravity

CD, BCD, this being a case of the theorem in Art. 233 ; hence

$$M_2 = \frac{2}{9} ABC, \quad \text{and} \quad M = \frac{4}{27} ABC.$$

. To find the mean area of the triangle formed by joining an angle of a
re with two points anywhere within it.

By a similar method this is found to be

$$\frac{13}{108}$$ of the whole square.

3. What is the mean area of the triangle formed by joining the same two points with the centre of the square?

We may take one of the points X always in the square OA; take the whole square as unity; then if M be the mean, the sum of all the cases is

$$\frac{1}{4}\,M = \frac{1}{4^2}\,M_1 + 2\,\frac{1}{4^2}\,M_2 + \frac{1}{4^2}\,M_3,$$

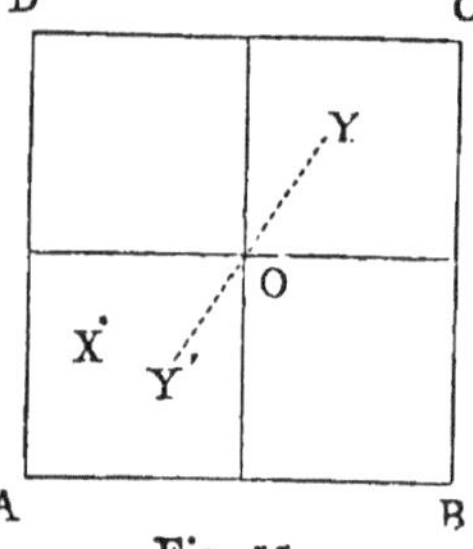

Fig. 55.

M_1, M_2, M_3 being the mean areas when the second point Y is taken respectively in OA, OB, and OC. But $M_3 = M_1$, for to any point Y in OC there corresponds one Y' in OA, which gives the area $OXY' = OXY$;

therefore $$M = \frac{1}{2}\,M_1 + \frac{1}{2}\,M_2.$$

But $M_1 = \dfrac{13}{108} \cdot \dfrac{1}{4}$, $M_2 = \dfrac{1}{16}$; hence $M = \dfrac{5}{108}$ of the whole square.*

235. If two spaces $A + C$, $B + C$ have a common part C, and M be any mean value relating to two points, one in $A + C$, the other in $B + C$; and if the whole space $A + B + C = W$, and M_W be the same mean when both points are taken indiscriminately in W; M_A when taken in A, &c., then

$$2\,(A + C)(B + C)\,M = W^2\,M_W + C^2 M_C - A^2 M_A - B^2 M_B, \qquad (5)$$

as is easily seen by dividing the whole number W^2 of cases into the different classes of cases which compose it.

---

* In such questions as the above, relating to areas determined by points taken at random in a triangle or parallelogram, we may consider the triangle as equilateral, and the parallelogram as a square. This will appear from orthogonal projection; or by deforming the triangle into a second triangle on the same base and between the same parallels, when it is easy to see that to one or more random points in the former there correspond a like set in the latter, determining the same areas. This second triangle may be made to have a side equal to a side of an equilateral triangle of the same area; and then be deformed in like manner into the equilateral triangle itself. Likewise a parallelogram may be deformed into a square.

EXAMPLE.

wo segments, AB, CD, of a straight line have a common part CB; to
the mean distance of two points taken, one in AB, the other in CD.

$$2AB \cdot CD \cdot M = AD^2 \cdot \frac{1}{3} AD + CB^2 \cdot \frac{1}{3} CB - AC^2 \cdot \frac{1}{3} AC - BD^2 \cdot \frac{1}{3} BD,$$

the mean distance of two points in any line is $\frac{1}{3}$ of the line ;

fore
$$M = \frac{AD^3 + CB^3 - AC^3 - DB^3}{6AB \cdot CD}.$$

236. The consideration of probability often may be made
assist in determining mean values. Thus, if a given
ce S is included within a given space A, the chance of a
t P, taken at random on A, falling on S, is

$$p = \frac{S}{A}.$$

t if the space S be variable, and $M(S)$ be its mean value,

$$p = \frac{M(S)}{A}. \tag{6}$$

For, if we suppose S to have n equally probable values
S_2, S_3 . . . ., the chance of any one S_1 being taken, *and* of
alling on S_1, is

$$p_1 = \frac{1}{n} \frac{S_1}{A}:$$

w the whole probability $p = p_1 + p_2 + p_3 + \ldots$; which leads
once to the above expression.

The chance of *two* points falling on S is

$$p = \frac{M(S^2)}{A^2}. \tag{7}$$

In such a case, if the probability be known, the mean value
lows, and *vice versâ*. Thus, we might find the mean value
the distance of two points X, Y taken at random in a line,

hy the consideration that if a third point Z be taken at random in the line, the chance of it falling between X and Y is $\frac{1}{3}$; as one of the three must be the middle one. Hence the mean distance is $\frac{1}{3}$ of the whole line.

Again, the mean n^{th} power of the distance is $\dfrac{2a^n}{(n+1)(n+2)}$, where a = whole line. For if p is the probability that n more points taken at random shall fall between X and Y,

$$M(XY)^n = a^n p.$$

Now the chance that out of the $n+2$ points, X shall be one of the extreme points is $\dfrac{2}{n+2}$; and if it is so, the chance that Y shall be the other extreme point is $\dfrac{1}{n+1}$.

EXAMPLES.

1. From a point X taken anywhere in a triangle, parallels are drawn to two of the sides. Find the mean value of the triangle UXV.

If a second point X' be taken at random within ABC, the chance of its falling in XUV is the same as the chance of X falling in the corresponding triangle $X'U'V'$; that is, of X' falling on the parallelogram XC. Hence the mean value of UXV = mean value of XC. But the mean value of $(UXV + XC)$ is $\frac{1}{3} ABC$; as the whole triangle can be divided into three such parts by drawing through X a parallel to AB.* Thus

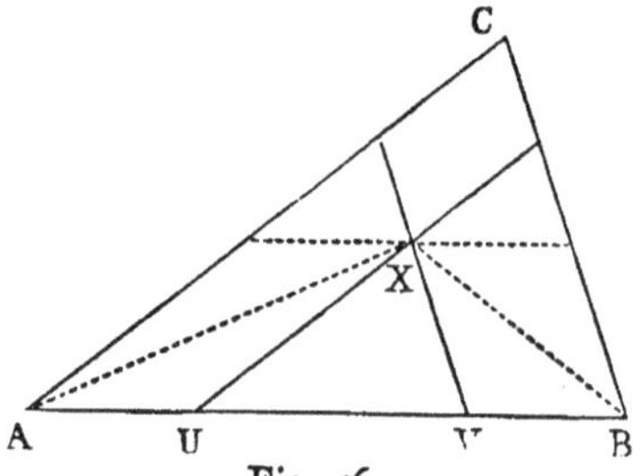

$$M(UXV) = \frac{1}{6} ABC.$$

The mean value of UV is $\frac{1}{3} AB$. For UV is the same fraction of AB that the altitude of X is of that of C: see Art. 233.

---

* The triangle may be considered equilateral: see note, Art. 234.

Cor. Hence, if p be the perpendicular from X on AB, h the altitude of angle ABC, we get

$$M(p^2) = \frac{1}{6} h^2.$$

the area ABC be taken as unity, we have, since $UXV : AXB = AXB : ABC$,

$$(AXB)^2 = UXV.$$

hus the mean square of the triangle AXB is $\frac{1}{6}$. If two other points Y, Z are ken at random in the triangle, the chance of both falling on AXB is thus the me as that of a single point falling on UXV; i. e. $\frac{1}{6}$. Hence we may easily fer the following theorem :—

If three points X, Y, Z are taken at random in a triangle, it is an even lance that Y, Z both fall on one of the triangles 'XB, AXC, BXC.

2. In a parallelogram $ABCD$ a point X is taken at ndom in the triangle ABC, and another Y in ADC. ind the chance that X is higher than Y.

Draw XH horizontal: the chance is

mean area of $AHK \div ADC$.

t $AHK = XUV$, and the mean area of $XUV = \frac{1}{6} ACB$

x. 1); hence the chance is $\frac{1}{6}$.

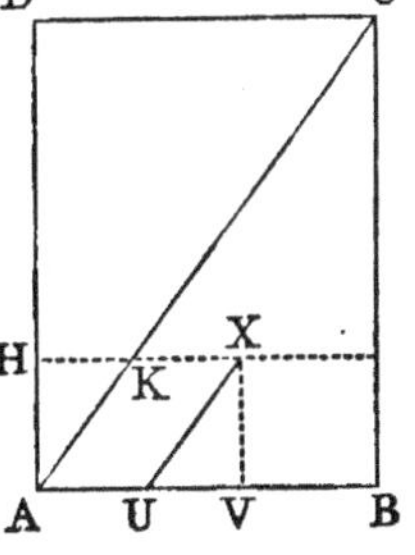

Fig. 57.

3. If O be a point taken at random on a triangle, and es be drawn through it from the angles, to find the ean value of the triangle DEF. (Mr. Miller.)

It will be sufficient to find the mean area of the triangle AEF, and subtract ree times its value from ABC. If we put α, β, γ for the triangles BOC, OC, AOB, it is easy to prove

$$AEF = \frac{\beta\gamma}{(\alpha + \beta)(\alpha + \gamma)} \cdot ABC.$$

If we put the whole area $ABC = 1$, and if be the element of the area at O,

$$M(AEF) = \iint \frac{\beta\gamma \, dS}{(1 - \beta)(1 - \gamma)},$$

e integration extending over the whole triangle.

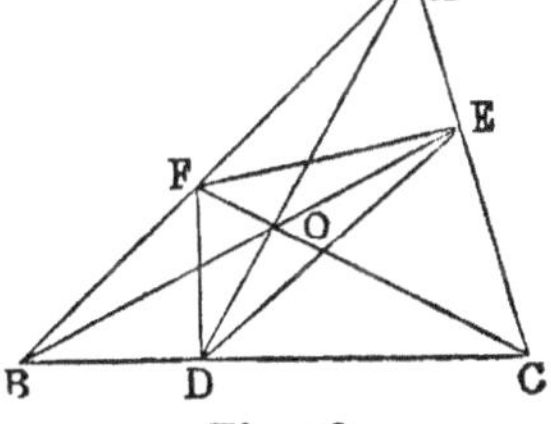

Fig. 58.

But if p, q are the perpendiculars from O on the sides b, c, it may be easily own that the element of the area is

$$dS = \frac{dp \, dq}{\sin A} = \frac{4}{bc \sin A} \, d\beta \, d\gamma = 2 d\beta \, d\gamma.$$

[23]

Thus the mean value of AEF becomes

$$M = \int_0^1 \int_0^{1-\beta} \frac{2\beta\gamma\, d\beta\, d\gamma}{(1-\beta)(1-\gamma)} = \int_0^1 (\beta - 1 - \log \beta)\, \frac{2\beta}{1-\beta}\, d\beta.$$

Again, by Art. 95, the definite integral

$$\int_0^1 \frac{\beta \log \beta}{1-\beta}\, d\beta = 1 - \frac{\pi^2}{6};$$

therefore
$$M = -1 - 2\left(1 - \frac{\pi^2}{6}\right) = \frac{\pi^2}{3} - 3.$$

Hence the mean value of the triangle DEF is

$$10 - \pi^2,$$

that of ABC being unity.

It is curious that the same value, $10 - \pi^2$, has been found by Col. Clarke to be the mean area of a triangle formed by the intersections of three lines, drawn from A, B, C to points taken at random in a, b, c respectively.

4. To find the average area of all triangles having a given perimeter $(2s)$. By this is meant that the given perimeter is divided at random in every possible way into three parts, a, b, c, and only those cases are taken in which a, b, c can form a triangle ; then the mean value of

$$A = \sqrt{s(s-a)(s-b)(s-c)}$$

has to be found.

Take $AB = 2s$, let X, Y be the two points of division, $AX = x$, $AY = y$: these are subject to the conditions

$$x < s, \quad y > s, \quad y - x < s.$$

Now
$$\frac{A}{\sqrt{s}} = \sqrt{(s-x)(y-s)(s-y+x)};$$

$$\therefore \; \frac{1}{\sqrt{s}}\, M(A) = \frac{\displaystyle\int_s^{2s} \int_{y-s}^s \sqrt{(s-x)(y-s)(s-y+x)} \cdot dy\, dx}{\displaystyle\int_s^{2s} \int_{y-s}^s dy\, dx}.$$

Again, by Art. 132, we have

$$\int_{y-s}^s \sqrt{(s-x)(s-y+x)}\, dx = \frac{\pi}{8}\, (2s - y)^2;$$

$$\therefore \; \frac{1}{\sqrt{s}}\, M(A) = \frac{1}{\frac{1}{2}s^2} \cdot \frac{\pi}{8} \int_s^{2s} (2s-y)^3 \sqrt{y-s} \cdot dy = \frac{\pi}{4s^2} \int_0^s z^{\frac{1}{2}}(s-z)^2 dz = \frac{\pi}{4} \cdot \frac{16}{105} \cdot s^{\frac{3}{2}}.$$

The result is therefore :—Mean area $= \dfrac{\pi}{105} (2s)^2.$

In the same case we should easily find
$$\text{Mean square of area} = \frac{s^4}{60}.$$

5. Three points are taken at random within a given triangle; prove that the mean area of the triangle formed by them is $\dfrac{1}{12}$ of the given triangle.

Call the area of the given triangle Δ, the required mean M: we will first prove that if M_0 be the mean area when one of the three points is restricted to a side of the given triangle,

$$M = \frac{3}{4} M_0.$$

Let Δ receive an increment of area $d\Delta$, by adding to it an infinitesimal band included between the base a and a line parallel to it; the increase produced in the sum of all the cases is found by considering one of the random points X taken in this band; the additional cases introduced will be

$$\Delta^2 d\Delta . M_0.$$

The whole increase is treble this, for we must consider also the cases when Y, Z fall in this band (the cases when *two* of the three fall on it may be negleeted, their number being proportional to the square of $d\Delta$). Now the sum of all the original cases is $\Delta^3 M$; hence

$$d(\Delta^3 M) = 3\Delta^2 M_0 d\Delta.$$

Now $\dfrac{M}{\Delta}$ is constant for all triangles (see note, Art. 234);

hence $\dfrac{M}{\Delta} d . \Delta^4 = 3\Delta^2 M_0 d\Delta$; $\therefore M = \dfrac{3}{4} M_0.$

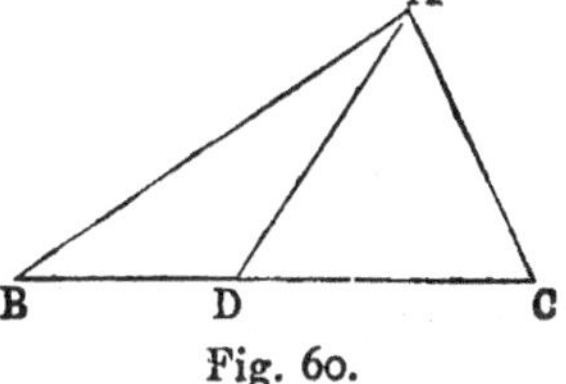

Fig. 60.

Again, to find M_0, consider the random point X fixed at a particular point of the base a, the other two points, Y, Z, ranging all over the triangle. Let M' be the mean value of DYZ; the sum of all the cases, viz., $\Delta^2 M'$, may be decomposed into three groups: (1) when Y, Z are in ABD; (2) both in ACD; (3) one in each triangle:

$$\therefore (ABC)^2 M' = (ABD)^2 . \frac{4}{27} ABD + (ACD)^2 . \frac{4}{27} ACD + 2ABD . ACD . \frac{ABC}{9},$$

by Ex. (1), Art. 234, and because in case (3) the mean value is the area of the triangle formed by joining D with the centres of gravity of ABD and ACD (Art. 233). Let $BD = x$, altitude of triangle $= p$, and we get

$$\Delta^2 M' = \frac{4}{27} \left(\frac{x}{2} p\right)^3 + \frac{4}{27} \left(\frac{a-x}{2} p\right)^3 + 2 \left(\frac{p}{2}\right)^3 x (a - x) . \frac{1}{9} a.$$

Now when the point X falls in the element dx, the sum of all the cases is

$\Delta^2 M' dx$; and hence, when X ranges from B to C, the whole sum of cases is

$$a\Delta^2 M_0 = \int_0^a \Delta^2 M' dx = (\tfrac{1}{2}p)^3 \int_0^a \left\{ \frac{4}{27} x^3 + \frac{4}{27} (a-x)^3 + \frac{2}{9} ax(a-x) \right\} dx ;$$

therefore
$$a\Delta^2 M_0 = (\tfrac{1}{2}p)^3 \frac{1}{9} a^4 = \frac{1}{9} a\Delta^3.$$

$$\text{Hence } M_0 = \frac{1}{9} \Delta ; \text{ and therefore } M = \frac{3}{4} M_0 = \frac{1}{12} \Delta.$$

Cor. Hence, if four points, A, B, C, D, are taken at random within a triangle, the chance that they determine a re-entrant quadrilateral is $\frac{1}{3}$. For the chance that D falls in ABC is the mean value of ABC divided by the whole triangle, that is $\frac{1}{12}$; and we have to add to this the chances that C falls in ABD, &c. The chance that $ABCD$ is convex is $\frac{2}{3}$.

6. The mean distance of the vertex of a triangle from all points in the area is equal to its distance from the centre of gravity, *measured along a parabolic path*, which leaves the vertex in the direction of one of its sides, and reaches the centre of gravity in a direction parallel to the other—the axis of the parabola being parallel to the base.

Let an indefinite line AP be conceived to revolve round A, from the direction AC to AB; and as it revolves, suppose that all the mass of the triangle ABC which lies to the *right* of it is transferred continuously to the vertex A. The centre of gravity of the whole mass will thus describe a curve starting from G, and ending at A. When the line is at AP let the centre of gravity be at g; and when it is in the consecutive position AP', let the centre be at g'. As the

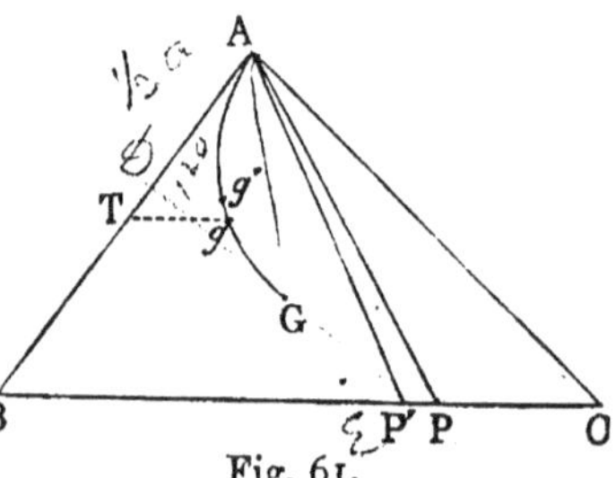

Fig. 61.

mass of the triangle APP' has been transferred to A, gg' is parallel to AP; also

$$gg' = \frac{APP'}{ABC} \cdot \frac{2}{3} AP ;$$

since $\frac{2}{3} AP$ is the distance traversed by the centre of gravity of the transferred portion of the whole mass.*

But as $\frac{2}{3} AP$ is the mean distance of all points in APP' from A, the sum of every element in APP' into its distance from $A = APP' \times \frac{2}{3} AP$. Hence the sum of all the elements gg', i.e. the whole arc $GA = $ sum of every element of ABC into its distance from A, divided by the area ABC, i.e. the mean distance required.

---

* See Rankine, *Applied Mechanics*, p. 54.

It is easy to show that if gT is drawn parallel to BC,

$$AT^2 = \frac{4}{3}\frac{c^2}{a}\, gT;$$

o that the curve is the parabola mentioned above. For A and g are in directum ith the centre of gravity of ABP; and hence, as g is the centre of gravity of BP *and* a mass at A equal to APC,

$$\frac{AT}{\frac{2}{3}\frac{A}{c}} = \frac{BP}{a}, \text{ and } \frac{BP}{2gT} = \frac{c}{AT}.$$

PROBABILITIES.

237. The calculation of Probabilities, when the number f favourable cases, as well as the whole number of cases, is nite, is not a subject for the Infinitesimal Calculus. It is when the number of cases depends on continuously varying magnitudes, and is therefore infinite, that recourse has to be made to the methods of the Integral Calculus.

The same remark applies here which we had occasion to make as to mean values (Art. 228). The value of the probability will depend on the law according to which we select the series of cases which we take as *representing* the total number—that is, it will depend on which variable (or variables) we suppose to be taken *at random*, that is, to proceed by constant infinitesimal increments ;* in other words, to be the *independent* variable (or variables). Thus, if we have to find the chance of the line, drawn from a fixed point to a given finite straight line, exceeding a given length, the results will be different if, first, we suppose a series of lines drawn to points taken at random on the given line, or, secondly, a series of lines drawn in random directions from the fixed point. In many cases, however, the problem has an obvious sense which precludes any such uncertainty.

238. Let us consider a simple question on chances. Two integers are chosen at random from o to 6 inclusive ; to find

---

* Of course a large number of values taken at random for a variable do not really form an equi-different series: but, as they must give a number of points (when measured along a straight line) of uniform *density*, they may be taken, for the purposes of calculation, as equi-different.

the chance that the greater of the two exceeds a given value, suppose 3. Here the whole number of cases, all equally probable, is easily seen to be

$$1 + 2 + 3 + 4 + 5 + 6,$$

and the number of favourable cases is

$$4 + 5 + 6,$$

so that the required chance is $\dfrac{5}{7}$.

If, however, the question is not confined to integers, but the two numbers chosen may have any arbitrary values from o to 6 ; or as we may state the question :—Two quantities are taken at random from o to a; find the chance that the greater of the two is less than a given value b :—

Let x be the greater; then for any assigned value of x the number of cases is measured by x (since the lesser may have any value from o to x); hence the number of cases when the greater falls between x and $x + dx$ is measured by $x\,dx$; the whole number of cases is therefore $\displaystyle\int_0^a x\,dx$; and the favourable cases are $\displaystyle\int_0^b x\,dx$. The required chance is therefore $p = \dfrac{b^2}{a^2}$.

This instance will serve to show how the Integral Calculus may enter into the estimation of chances. It is true that it might easily be solved otherwise ; for if the two numbers are considered as the distances of two points taken at random in a line of length a, from one end of the line, and if we measure a distance b from that end, the problem is really to find the chance that *both* points fall within b ; which chance is evidently $\dfrac{b^2}{a^2}$.

239. We proceed to give a few easy questions on probabilities : general rules can hardly be given for their solution, the number and diversity of the questions which may be proposed being so great that no attempt seems to have been made to classify or connect them into a regular theory. We will give, in particular, several on Local or Geometrical Probability.

EXAMPLES.

1. If an event B is known to have occurred in a certain century, the chance that it was not distant more than n years from the middle of the century is of course $\dfrac{2n}{100}$; but if three events, A, B, C, are known to have occurred in the century, and that A preceded B, and B preceded C, let it be proposed to find how far this amount of knowledge alters the value of the chance for B.

Let x be the time from the beginning of the century to the event B; for any assigned value of x, the number of triple cases is $x(100-x)$: hence the number of favourable cases divided by the whole number is

$$p = \frac{\displaystyle\int_{50-n}^{50+n} x(100-x)\,dx}{\displaystyle\int_{0}^{100} x(100-x)\,dx} = 3\,\frac{n}{100} - 4\left(\frac{n}{100}\right)^3.$$

2. Two numbers, x, y, are chosen at random between 0 and a: find the chance that the product xy shall be less than $\dfrac{a^2}{4}$ (its mean value).

Here

$$p = \frac{\iint dx\,dy}{a^2},$$

the integral being limited by $a > x > 0$, $a > y > 0$, and $xy < \dfrac{a^2}{4}$. We have accordingly to integrate for y from a to 0, when x is between 0 and $\dfrac{a}{4}$; and from $\dfrac{a^2}{4x}$ to 0, when x is between $\dfrac{a}{4}$ and a; thus

$$\iint dx\,dy = \int_0^{\frac{a}{4}} a\,dx + \int_{\frac{a}{4}}^{a} \frac{a^2}{4x}\,dx = \frac{a^2}{4} + \frac{a^2}{4}\log 4.$$

Hence

$$p = \frac{1}{4} + \frac{1}{2}\log 2.$$

3. Two points are taken at random in a given line a; to find the chance that their distance asunder shall exceed a given value c.

It is easy to see that the distances of two such points from one end of the line are the coordinates of a point taken at random in a square whose side is a. Thus to every case of partition of the line corresponds a point in the square—such points being uniformly distributed over its surface.

Thus, if in the above question x, y stand for the distances of the two points, from one end of the line, y being greater than x, we have to find the chance of $y - x$ exceeding c. The point P whose co-ordinates are x, y, in the square OD (side $= a$), may take all possible positions in the triangle OBD, if no condition is imposed on it. But if $y - x > c$, then if we measure $OH = c$, the favourable cases

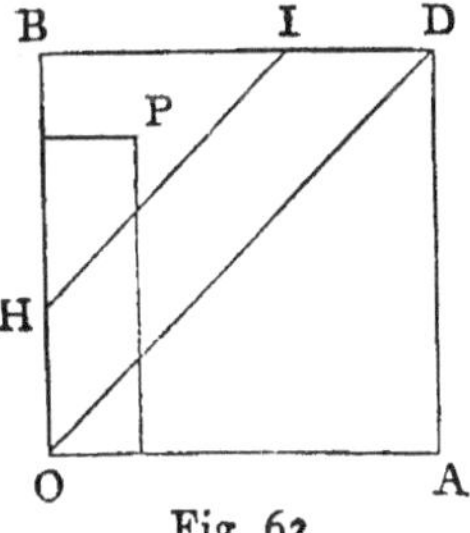

Fig. 62.

occur only when P is in the triangle BHI; hence the probability required

$$p = \frac{BHI}{OBD} = \left(\frac{a-c}{a}\right)^2.$$

In fact this is only performing the integrations in the expression

$$p = \frac{\displaystyle\int_c^a \int_0^{y-c} dx\,dy}{\displaystyle\int_0^a \int_0^y dx\,dy}.$$

4. Two points being taken at random in a line a, to find the chance that no one of the three segments shall exceed a given length c.

The segments being as before, x, $y-x$, $a-y$, $PH = x$, $PK = a - y$, $PI = y - x$. There will be *two cases* :—

(1). If $c > \frac{1}{2} a$; take $OU = BV = DZ = BN = c$;

then it is easy to see that the only favourable cases are when P falls in the hexagon $UZNMJV$;

$$p_1 = \frac{OBD - 3 \cdot UBZ}{OBD} = 1 - 3\left(\frac{a-c}{a}\right)^2.$$

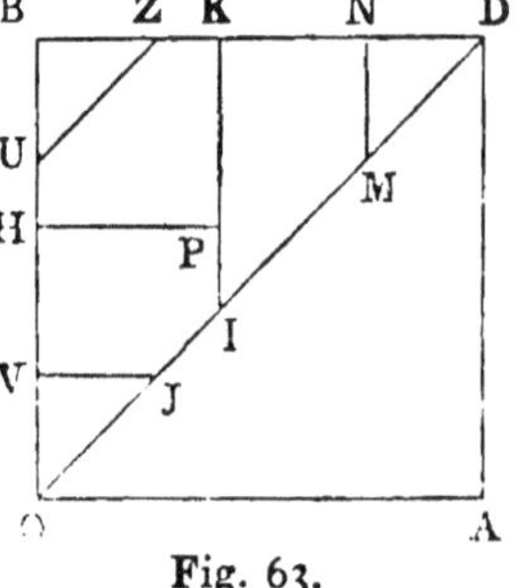

Fig. 63.

(2). If $c < \frac{1}{2} a$; take $OU = BV = c$, as before; then the only favourable cases are when P falls in the triangle RST;

therefore $$p_2 = \frac{RST}{OBD} = \left(\frac{3c-a}{a}\right)^2,$$

since $RST = \frac{1}{2} RT^2$, and $RT = VT + RH - VH = 2c - (a-c)$.

Such cases of discontinuity in the functions expressing probabilities frequently present themselves. The functions are connected by very remarkable laws. Thus, in the present question, if $p_1 = f(c)$, $p_2 = F(c)$, we have

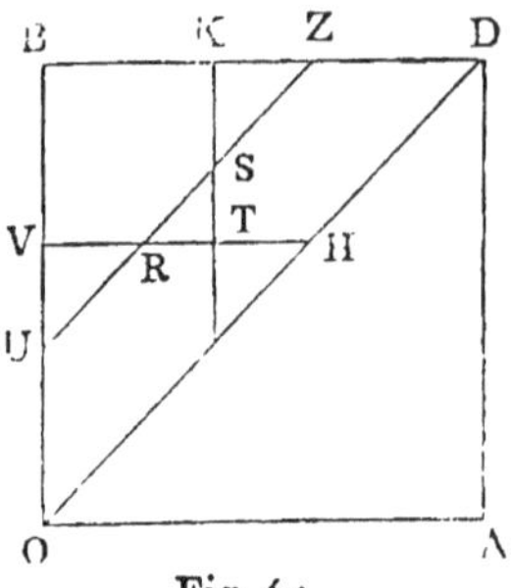

Fig. 64.

$$f(c) - f(a - c) = F(c) - F(a - c).$$

5. A floor is ruled with equidistant parallel lines; a rod, shorter than the distance between each pair, being thrown at random on the floor, to find the chance of its falling on one of the lines (*Buffon's problem*).

Let x be the distance of the centre of the rod from the nearest line, θ the inclination of the rod to a perpendicular to the parallels, $2a$ the common distance of the parallels, $2c$ the length of rod; then as all values of x and θ between their extreme limits are equally probable, the whole number of cases will be represented by

$$\int_0^a \int_{-\frac{\pi}{2}}^{\frac{\pi}{2}} dx\, d\theta = \pi a.$$

Now if the rod crosses one of the lines we must have $c > \dfrac{x}{\cos \theta}$; so that the favourable cases will be measured by

$$\int_{-\frac{\pi}{2}}^{\frac{\pi}{2}} d\theta \int_0^{c \cos \theta} dx = 2c.$$

Thus the probability required is $p = \dfrac{2c}{\pi a}$.

This question is remarkable as having been the first proposed on the subject now called Local Probability. It has been proposed, as a matter of curiosity, to determine the value of π from this result, by making a large number of trials with a rod of length $2a$: the difficulty, however, here consists in ensuring that the rod shall fall really at random. The circumstances under which it is thrown may be more favourable to certain positions of the rod than others. Though we may be unable to take account *à priori* of the causes of such a tendency, it will be found to reveal itself through the medium of repeated trials.

240. Sometimes a result depends upon a variable (or variables) all the values of which are not equally probable, but are such that the probability of a certain value for a variable depends, according to some law, on the magnitude of that value itself (and also, perhaps, on the values of other variables). Thus a point may be taken in a straight line so that all positions are not equally probable, but the probability of the distance from one end having the value x, being proportional to x itself. This would be in fact supposing the series of points in question as ranged along the line with a *density* proportional to x ; as, e. g., if they were the projections on the line of points taken at random in the space between the line and another line drawn through one of its extremities. To give an example :—

Two points are taken in a line a, with probabilities varying as the distance from one end A ; to find the chance of their distance exceeding a length c.

Let x, y, be the distances from A, and suppose $y > x$.

Here the probability of a point falling between x and $x + dx$ is not proportional to dx, but to $x\,dx$; and the result will be

$$p = \frac{\displaystyle\int_c^a y\,dy \int_0^{y-c} x\,dx}{\displaystyle\int_c^a y\,dy \int_0^y x\,dx} = \left(1 + \frac{c}{3a}\right)\left(1 - \frac{c}{a}\right)^3.$$

The mean values of the three divisions of the line, in the same case, will be found to be

$$\frac{8}{15}\,a, \qquad \frac{4}{15}\,a, \qquad \frac{1}{5}\,a.$$

The above value of p is also the value of the chance, that *the difference of the altitudes of two points within a triangle shall exceed a given fraction* $\dfrac{c}{a}$ *of the altitude of the triangle.*

Examples.

1. Two points being taken on the sides OA, OB, of a square a^2, the chance of their distance being less than a given value b is easily seen without calculation to be $\dfrac{\pi b^2}{4a^2}$, provided $b < a$; as it is the chance of a point taken at random in the square falling within a quadrant of a given circle. Suppose now that *two* points are taken on OA, and two on OB, and that we take X, Y, the two points *furthest from O* on each side, to find the chance that their distance XY is less than a given length b; ($b < a$).

Here the probability of X falling between x and $x + dx$ is proportional to $x\,dx$; likewise for y; hence

$$p = \frac{\displaystyle\iint xy\,dx\,dy}{\displaystyle\int_0^a \int_0^a xy\,dx\,dy};$$

the upper integral being limited by $x^2 + y^2 < b^2$; hence $p = \dfrac{b^4}{2a^4}$.

Thus it is an even chance that the point determined by the coordinates x, y shall fall within the quadrant $\dfrac{1}{2}\pi a^2$.

2. In a circular target of area A the area of the bull's eye is a. If a shot is heard to strike the target, the chance of its having hit the bull's eye is of course $\dfrac{a}{A}$.* If, however, *two* shots have been fired, to find the chance that the *best* of the two has hit the bull's eye.

This is easily solved by elementary considerations; as the chance of both *missing* the bull's eye is

$$p = \left(\frac{A-a}{A}\right)^2.$$

Hence the required chance of the best shot having hit it is

$$1 - p = \frac{a}{A}\left(2 - \frac{a}{A}\right).$$

3. Let it be proposed, however, to find the chance of the best of the two shots (i. e. that nearest the centre) having hit any given area a, traced out on the target.

The number of cases in which the worst shot falls on any element dS, at a distance r from the centre, is measured by $\pi r^2 dS$; hence the chance of the worst shot striking the area a is

$$p = \frac{\iint r^2 dS \text{ (over } a)}{\iint r^2 dS \text{ (over } A)} = \frac{m}{M},$$

where M, m are the moments of inertia of A, a round the centre of the target. Now, the probability of both shots missing a is

$$\left(\frac{A-a}{A}\right)^2;$$

hence that of a being hit (by one or both) is

$$1 - \left(\frac{A-a}{A}\right)^2;$$

and the chance of both hitting it is $\dfrac{a^2}{A^2}$. But the chance of a being hit is

$$\text{chance of best} + \text{chance of worst} - \text{chance of both};$$

hence if p_1 be the required chance, viz., of the best shot striking a,

$$p_1 + \frac{m}{M} - \frac{a^2}{A^2} = 1 - \left(\frac{A-a}{A}\right)^2; \quad \therefore \; p_1 = 2\frac{a}{A} - \frac{m}{M},$$

where m, M are the moments of inertia above.

Or, we might have considered the number of cases in which the best shot falls on the element dS, viz., $\pi(R^2 - r^2)dS$, where $R = $ radius of target. This would have given the required probability

$$p_1 = \frac{R^2 a - m}{R^2 A - M};$$

which is easily shown to be identical with the above value.

---

* That is, disregarding the effect of the *aim* directing it with greater probability to the centre of the target. This would be practically correct in the case of a very bad marksman, who frequently misses the target altogether.

241. Curve of Frequency.—In questions relating to a variable the probability of any value of which is a function of that value itself, it is often useful to consider what is called a *curve of frequency*. Thus, if the probability of a given value of x is proportional to $\phi(x)$, and we draw a curve $y = C\phi(x)$, then when a great number of values for x are taken, the number in any element dx is

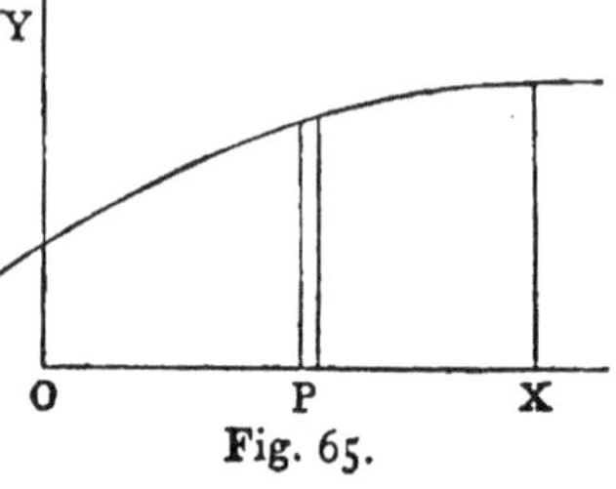

Fig. 65.

proportional to the area of the curve standing on that element ; the ordinate at any point P representing the density or frequency of the points at P: the abscissas of all points taken at random in the area of the curve are equally probable.

Thus, if two points X, Y are taken at random in a straight line AB, and X means always that nearest to A, the curve of frequency for Y will be a straight line through A; that for X a straight line through B. This will often simplify questions : e.g. suppose we have to find what is sometimes called the *most probable value* for AY, i. e. such a value AP that AY is equally likely to exceed or to fall short of it. Since the curve of frequency for Y is a line AC, we have only to find P, so that PD bisects the triangle ABC; i. e. $AP = \dfrac{AB}{\sqrt{2}}$ because as many values of AY exceed AP as fall short of it. The most probable value is not

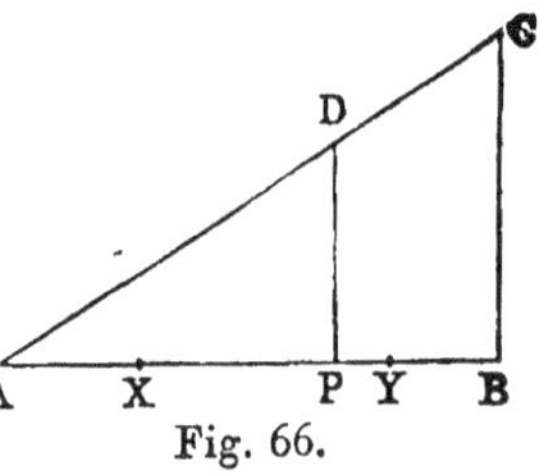

Fig. 66.

the mean value, viz., $\dfrac{2}{3} AB$, being the horizontal distance of the centre of gravity of ABC, from A.

A point Y is taken at random in a line $AB = a$, and then a point X is taken at random in AY (or a rod may be supposed broken in two at random, and one of the pieces then broken in two), to find the chance of the length of AX falling within given limits.

Let x, y, be the distances from A; for any assigned value of y, the chance of X falling between x and $x + dx$ is $\dfrac{dx}{y}$;

hence the chance of X falling between x and $x + dx$, *and* of Y falling between y and $y + dy$, is measured by

$$\frac{dx\,dy}{ay};$$

hence the whole chance of X falling between x and $x + dx$ is

$$\frac{dx}{a}\int_x^a \frac{dy}{y} = \frac{dx}{a}\log\frac{a}{x} = -\,dx\log x,$$

if for simplicity we put $a = 1$.

Thus the curve of frequency for X is a logarithmic curve BR, whose ordinate is

$$z = -\log x,$$

the frequency at A being infinitely great.

The area of this curve from 0 to x is

$$x\log\frac{e}{x};$$

and this is the probability of AX being between 0 and x; the whole area, when $x = 1$, being 1, as it ought to be, as it is certain that X falls in AB. The chance of X falling between given limits x', x'' is of course

$$x'\log\frac{e}{x'} - x''\log\frac{e}{x''}.$$

To find the *most probable* value of x we should have to solve the equation

$$x(1 - \log x) = \frac{1}{2}.$$

This gives x about one-fifth of the line AB.

The *mean* value of x is

$$M = \frac{\displaystyle\int_0^1 xz\,dx}{\displaystyle\int_0^1 z\,dx} = \text{one-fourth of } AB.$$

This last result might have been foreseen: because if we take a point at random in *each* of the segments AY, YB, the line AB is divided into four parts, the mean values of which must be the same, as each of them goes through the same series of values as the others; the sum of the mean values being AB.

EXAMPLES.

1. A line is divided at random, and one of the parts again divided at random as above, to find the chance that no one of the three parts shall exceed the sum of the other two (i.e. that a triangle might be formed by them). (*Cambridge Math. Tripos*, 1854.)

The probability that X, Y shall be taken in two assigned elements dx, dy is (taking $a = 1$),

$$\frac{dx\,dy}{y}.$$

This differential being integrated throughout any limits gives the sum of the probabilities of X, Y being found in each pair of values for dx and dy which enter into the summation:—that is, the cases being mutually exclusive, the probability that X, Y will be found in some one of those pairs.

In the present case the limits are equivalent to

$$x < \frac{1}{2} < y < 1, \quad x > y - \frac{1}{2}.$$

Hence

$$p = \int_{\frac{1}{2}}^1 \int_{y-\frac{1}{2}}^{\frac{1}{2}} \frac{dy\,dx}{y} = \log 2 - \frac{1}{2}.$$

2. An urn contains a large number of black and white balls, the proportion of each being unknown: if on drawing $m + n$ balls, m are found white and n black, to find the probability that the ratio of the numbers of each colour lies between given limits.

The question will not be altered if we suppose all the balls ranged in a line AB, the white ones on the left, the black on the right, the point X where they meet being unknown, and all positions for it in AB being *à priori* equally probable; then $m + n$ points being taken, at random in AB, m are found to fall on AX, n on XB. That is, all we know of X is, that it is the $(m + 1)^{th}$ in order,

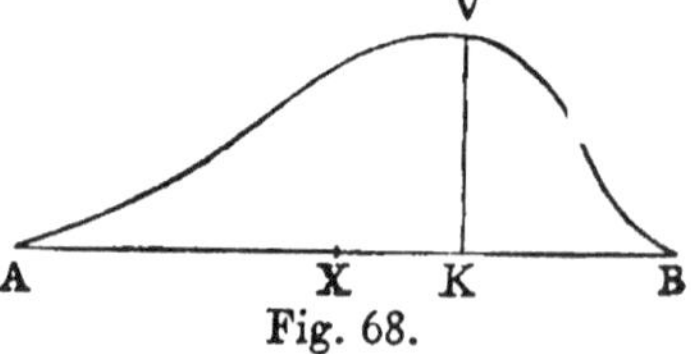

Fig. 68.

beginning from A, of $m + n + 1$ points falling at random in AB. If $AX = x$, $AB = 1$, the number of cases for X between x and $x + dx$ is measured by

$$\frac{\lfloor m + n}{\lfloor m \lfloor n} \, x^m (1 - x)^n dx.*$$

Hence the probability that the ratio of the white balls in the urn to the whole number lies between any two given limits α, β—that is, that the distance from A of the point X lies between α and β—is

$$p = \frac{\displaystyle\int_\alpha^\beta x^m (1 - x)^n \, dx}{\displaystyle\int_0^1 x^m (1 - x)^n \, dx}.$$

The *curve of frequency* for the point X will be one whose ordinate is

$$y = x^m (1 - x)^n.$$

The maximum ordinate KV occurs at a point K, dividing AB in the ratio $m : n$. This is of course what we should expect: the ratio of the numbers of black and white balls is more likely to be that of the numbers drawn of each than any other. The value for p above is simply the area of the above curve between the values α, β, of x, divided by the whole area.

Let us suppose, for instance, that 3 white and 2 black balls have been drawn; to find the chance that the proportion of white balls is between $\frac{2}{5}$ and $\frac{4}{5}$ of the whole—that is, that it differs by less than $\pm \frac{1}{5}$ from $\frac{3}{5}$, its most natural value.

$$p = \frac{\displaystyle\int_{\frac{2}{5}}^{\frac{4}{5}} x^3 (1 - x)^2 \, dx}{\displaystyle\int_0^1 x^2 (1 - x)^2 \, dx} = \frac{2256}{5^5} = \frac{18}{25}, \text{ nearly.}$$

The above results will apply to any event that must turn out in one of two ways which are mutually exclusive, this being the whole of our *à priori* knowledge with regard to it—the ratio of the black, or white balls to the whole number, meaning the real probability of either event, as would be manifested by an infinite number of trials. We will give one more example of the same kind.

3. An event has happened m times and failed n times in $m + n$ trials. To find the probability that, on $p + q$ further trials, it shall happen p times and fail q times.

---

* For a specified set of m points, out of the $m + n$, falling in AX, the number is $x^m (1 - x)^n dx$; the number of such sets is $\dfrac{\lfloor m + n}{\lfloor m \lfloor n}$.

That is, that $p + q$ more points being taken at random in AB, p shall fall in AX, and q in BX. The whole number of cases is as before

$$\frac{\lfloor\underline{m+n}}{\lfloor\underline{m}\,\lfloor\underline{n}}\,(AB)^{p+q}\int_0^1 x^m\,(1-x)^n\,dx = \frac{\lfloor\underline{m+n}}{\lfloor\underline{m}\,\lfloor\underline{n}}\int_0^1 x^m\,(1-x)^n\,dx.$$

When any *particular set* of p points, out of the $p + q$ additional trials, falls in AX, the number of favourable cases is

$$\frac{\lfloor\underline{m+n}}{\lfloor\underline{m}\,\lfloor\underline{n}}\int_0^1 x^{m+p}\,(1-x)^{n+q}\,dx.$$

But the number of different sets of p points is $\dfrac{1\cdot2\cdot3\ldots\ldots(p+q)}{1\cdot2\cdot3\ldots p\cdot1\cdot2\cdot3\ldots q}$.

Hence the probability is, putting as before $\lfloor\underline{p}$ for $1\cdot2\cdot3\ldots p$,

$$p_1 = \frac{\lfloor\underline{p+q}}{\lfloor\underline{p}\cdot\lfloor\underline{q}}\cdot\frac{\displaystyle\int_0^1 x^{m+p}\,(1-x)^{n+q}\,dx}{\displaystyle\int_0^1 x^m\,(1-x)^n\,dx}.$$

By means of the known values of these definite integrals (p. 117), we find

$$p_1 = \frac{\lfloor\underline{p+q}}{\lfloor\underline{p}\,\lfloor\underline{q}}\cdot\frac{\lfloor\underline{m+p}\,\lfloor\underline{n+q}}{\lfloor\underline{m}\,\lfloor\underline{n}}\cdot\frac{\lfloor\underline{m+n+1}}{\lfloor\underline{m+n+p+q+1}}.$$

For instance, the chance that in one further trial the event shall happen is $\dfrac{m+1}{m+n+2}$. This is easily verified, as the line AB has been divided into $m+n+2$ sections by the $m + n + 1$ points in it, including X. Now, if one more trial is made, i. e. one more point taken at random, it is equally likely to fall in any section ; and $m + 1$ sections out of the entire number are favourable.

4. Trace the curve of frequency of the ratio $\dfrac{a}{b}$; a and b being numbers taken at random within the limits ± 1.

If we measure the values of the ratio as abscissas along an axis OX, and make $OA = 1$, $OA' = -1$, $AB = A'B' = 1$; then the line whose ordinates are proportional to the frequency will be, for values of $\dfrac{a}{b}$ comprised between the limits

Y
B'
B
C'
C
A'
O
A
X

Fig 69.

± 1, the straight line BB'; but, for values beyond these limits, will consist of the arcs BC, $B'C'$ of the curve $x^2 y = 1$.

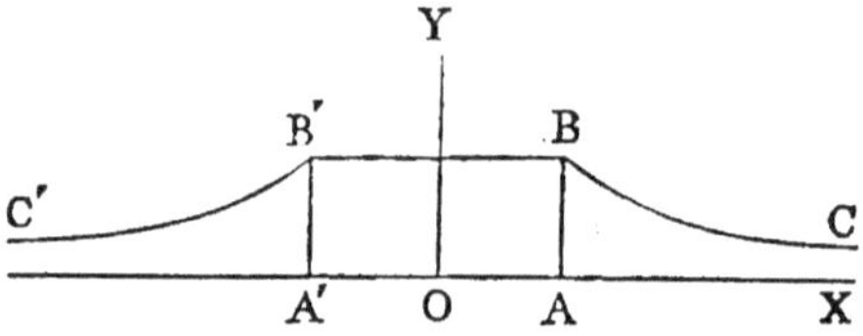

It is thus an even chance that the ratio $\dfrac{a}{b}$ lies itself between the limits ± 1 : this would also appear by a construction such as that given in the next Article.

242. **Errors of Observation.**—One of the most important, practically, as well as the most difficult, departments of the theory of Probability is that which treats of Errors of Observation. We will give here an example of the simplest description.

Two magnitudes A and B are measured ; each measurement being subject to an error, of excess or defect, which may amount to $\pm a$, all values between these limits being supposed equally probable.* To determine the probability that the error in the sum, $A + B$, of the two magnitudes, shall lie within given limits ; also its mean value.

Thus the horizontal angular distance of two objects A, C is sometimes found by measuring the angle between A and B, an intermediate object ; and afterwards that between B and C, and adding the two angles. If each measurement is liable to an error $\pm 5'$, all values being equally probable, to find the probability of the error of the result falling within assigned limits : its extreme limits being of course $\pm 10'$.

The question is more easily comprehended by means of a geometrical construction than by integration.

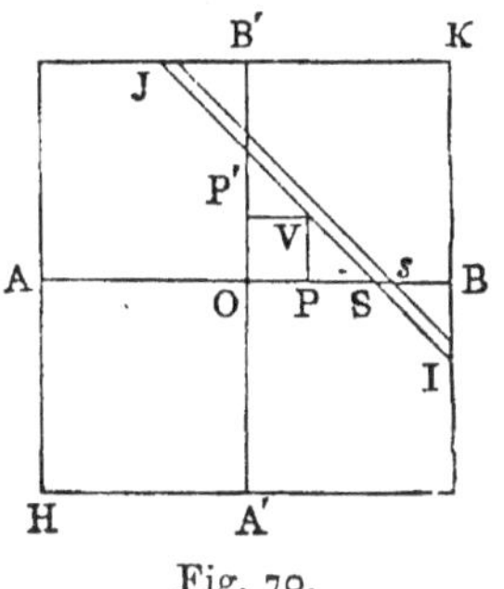

Fig. 70.

Take $AB = 2a$; then all the values of the first error are the distances from O of points P taken at random in AB ; positive when in OB ; negative when in OA. Make also $A'B' = 2a$; the values of the second error are given by points in $A'B'$. Take any values, $OP = x$ for the first, $OP' = x'$ for the second : these values taken as co-ordinates determine a point V corresponding to one case of the compound error $x + x'$; and such points V will be uniformly distributed over the square HK. The value of the compound error ε corresponding to the point V is

$$\varepsilon = x + x' = OS,$$

if VS be drawn at $45°$ to the axes. Now all values of the

---

errors x, x' which give $x + x'$ the same, give the same value for ε; hence all points on the line JI correspond to compound errors of amount OS. Take $Ss = d\varepsilon$; the number of compound errors between ε and $\varepsilon + d\varepsilon$ is the number of points between JI and a parallel to it through s. Now the area of this infinitesimal strip is evidently

$$(2a - \varepsilon)\,d\varepsilon.$$

Hence the probability of the error being between ε and $\varepsilon + d\varepsilon$ is

$$p = \frac{(2a - \varepsilon)\,d\varepsilon}{4a^2}.$$

This holds for negative values of ε, provided we only consider their arithmetical magnitude.

Thus the frequency of an error of magnitude $\varepsilon = OS$ is proportional to JI, the intercept of a line through S sloping at $45°$. The probability of the error ε falling between any two given limits OS, OS' is found by measuring these lengths (with their proper signs) from O, along AB, and dividing the area intercepted on the square by parallels through S, S' sloping at $45°$, by $4a^2$, the area of the whole square.

Thus the chance of the error falling between the limits $\pm a$ (those of the two component errors) is $\dfrac{3}{4}$.

The mean value of the error, strictly speaking, is 0; but it is evident that for this purpose we ought to consider negative errors as positive; and consequently take the mean of the arithmetical values of all the errors, which is the same as the mean of the positive errors only; hence the mean error required is

$$M(\varepsilon) = \pm \frac{2}{3}\,a.$$

The most probable value, such that it is an even chance that the error exceeds it (since the triangle JKI must be $\dfrac{1}{4}$ of the whole square, for that value of OS), is

$$\pm a\left(2 - \sqrt{2}\right) = \pm .586\,a.$$

Let it be now proposed to find the probability of a given error in the sum of A and B, assuming, according to the modern theory of errors, that the probability of an error between x and $x + dx$ in either is

$$p = \frac{1}{c\sqrt{\pi}}\, e^{-\frac{x^2}{c^2}}\, dx\,;$$

the coefficient $\dfrac{1}{c\sqrt{\pi}}$ being determined by the necessary condition that the differential, being integrated from ∞ to $-\infty$, must give unity; as the error must lie between these limits.*

Referring to the above construction, the number of values of the first error between x and $x + dx$ being proportional to

$$e^{-\frac{x^2}{c^2}}\, dx,$$

and the number of values of the second between x' and $x' + dx'$ proportional to

$$e^{-\frac{x^2}{c^2}}\, dx',$$

the corresponding number of values of the compound error is proportional to

$$e^{-\frac{x^2 + x'^2}{c^2}}\, dx\, dx'.$$

Hence the number of points, corresponding each to a case of the compound error, in any element dS of the plane at a distance r from the origin, is measured by

$$e^{-\frac{r^2}{c^2}}\, dS\,;$$

which shows that the points have the same density along any

---

* It is of course absurd to consider infinite values for an error: but the curve $y = e^{-\frac{x^2}{c^2}}$ tends so rapidly to coincide with its asymptote, the axis of x, that the cases where x has any large values are so trifling in number, that it is indifferent whether we include them or not.

[24 a]

circle whose centre is O. Now the probability of this compound error being between ε and $\varepsilon + d\varepsilon$ is proportional to the number of points between JI and the consecutive line; making, as before, $OS = \varepsilon$, $Ss = d\varepsilon$. But this number is the same as when the strip JI is turned round O through an angle of $45°$, because the points lie in concentric circles of equal density. Hence the number is proportional to

$$e^{-\frac{\varepsilon^2}{2c^2}} d \frac{\varepsilon}{\sqrt{2}} \int_{-\infty}^{\infty} e^{-\frac{x^2}{c^2}} dx = \frac{c\sqrt{\pi}}{\sqrt{2}} e^{-\frac{\varepsilon^2}{2c^2}} d\varepsilon,$$

as the perpendicular from O on JI is $\dfrac{\varepsilon}{\sqrt{2}}$.

Thus the probability of a compound error between ε and $\varepsilon + d\varepsilon$ is proportional to

$$e^{-\frac{\varepsilon^2}{2c^2}} d\varepsilon \, ;$$

and as this, when integrated between the limits $\pm \infty$, must give the probability 1, the value of p is

$$p = \frac{1}{c\sqrt{2\pi}} e^{-\frac{\varepsilon^2}{2c^2}} d\varepsilon.$$

It thus follows the same law as the two component errors, $c\sqrt{2}$ taking the place of c.

243. Various artifices have been employed for the solution of different interesting questions on Probability, which would be found extremely tedious, or impracticable, if attempted by direct integration. For example:

Two points are taken at random within a sphere of radius r; to find the chance that their distance is less than a given value c.

Let F = number of favourable cases, W = whole number; then

$$p = \frac{F}{W}; \quad W = \left(\frac{4}{3}\pi r^3\right)^2.$$

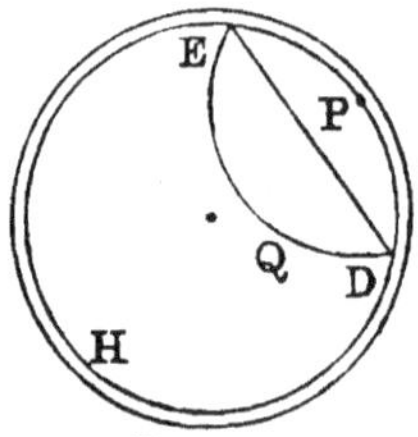

Fig. 71.

Let us consider the differential dF, or the additional favourable cases introduced by giving r the increment dr, c remaining unchanged.

If one of the points A is taken anywhere (at P) in the infinitesimal shell between the two spheres, then drawing a sphere with centre P, radius c, all positions of the second point, B, in the lens ED common to the two spheres, are favourable; let $L = $ volume ED, then the number of favourable cases when A is in the shell is

$$4\pi r^2 \, dr \cdot L :$$

doubling this, for the cases when B is in the same shell,

$$dF = 8\pi r^2 L dr.$$

Now it may be easily proved, from the value for the volume of a segment of a sphere, that

$$L = \frac{2\pi}{3} c^3 - \frac{\pi}{4} \frac{c^4}{r};$$

hence
$$F = 8\pi^2 \left(\frac{2}{9} c^3 r^3 - \frac{1}{8} c^4 r^2 + C \right);$$

C being an unknown constant; i.e. involving c, but not r;

therefore
$$p = \frac{F}{\frac{16}{9} \pi^2 r^6} = \frac{c^3}{r^3} - \frac{9}{16} \cdot \frac{c^4}{r^4} + \frac{9}{2} \frac{C}{r^6}.$$

Now the probability $= 1$ if $r = \frac{1}{2} c$;

therefore
$$1 = 8 - 9 + \frac{9}{2} \times 64 \frac{C}{c^6}; \quad \therefore \quad \frac{9}{2} C = \frac{2}{64} c^6;$$

therefore
$$p = \frac{c^3}{r^3} - \frac{9}{16} \frac{c^4}{r^4} + \frac{1}{32} \frac{c^6}{r^6}.$$

If the two points be taken within a *circle*, instead of a sphere, it may be proved by a similar process that

$$p = \frac{c^2}{r^2} + \frac{2}{\pi} \left(1 - \frac{c^2}{r^2} \right) \sin^{-1} \frac{c}{2r} - \frac{1}{4\pi} \cdot \frac{c}{r} \left(2 + \frac{c^2}{r^2} \right) \sqrt{4 - \frac{c^2}{r^2}}.$$

It is a very remarkable fact, pointed out by Mr. S. Roberts, that if we draw the chord ED, the probability is, in the case of the circle,

$$p = \frac{2 \cdot \text{segment } EQD + \text{segment } EPD}{\text{area of circle } EHD};$$

and also, in the case of the sphere,

$$p = \frac{2 \cdot \text{volume } EQD + \text{volume } EPD}{\text{volume of sphere } EHD}.$$

These results evidently suggest that there must be some manner of viewing the question which would conduct to them in a direct way.

EXAMPLES.

1. Three points being taken at random within a sphere, to find the chance that the triangle which they determine shall be acute-angled.

As the probability is independent of the radius of the sphere, it is easy to see that we may take the farthest from the centre of the three points as fixed on the surface of the sphere. For if p be the probability of an acute-angled triangle in this case, p will also be the probability of an acute-angled triangle for *each* position of the farthest point, as it travels over the whole volume of the sphere. Hence p will be the probability when no restriction is put on any of the points.

Take then A, one of the points on the surface of the sphere; two others, B, C, being taken at random within it, and let us find the chance of ABC being *obtuse-angled :* to do this, we will find separately the chance of the angles A, B, C being obtuse: the events being mutually exclusive, the probability required will be the sum of these three.

(1). To find the chance that A is obtuse, let us fix B ; then, drawing the plane AV perpendicular to AB, the chance required is

$$\frac{\text{volume of segment } AHV}{\text{volume of sphere}}.$$

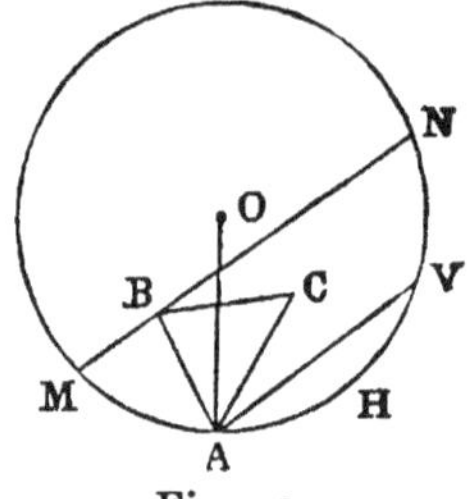

Fig. 72.

Let $r = OA$, the radius of sphere, $\rho = AB$, $\theta = \angle OAB$; then the volume of the segment AHV is

$$\tfrac{1}{3}\pi r^3 (1 - \cos\theta)^2 (2 + \cos\theta) ;$$

therefore when B is fixed the chance is

$$\tfrac{1}{4}(1 - \cos\theta)^2 (2 + \cos\theta).$$

Now let B move over the whole volume of the sphere, and we have for the probability P_A, that A is obtuse

$$P_A = \frac{1}{\text{sphere}} \iiint \frac{1}{4} (1 - \cos \theta)^2 (2 + \cos \theta)\, dV$$

$$= \frac{3}{8r^3} \int_0^{\frac{\pi}{2}} \int_0^{2r\cos\theta} (2 - 3 \cos \theta + \cos^3 \theta)\, \rho^2 \sin \theta\, d\theta\, d\rho.$$

Hence $\qquad P_A = \dfrac{3}{70}.$

(2). To find the chance, P_B, that B is obtuse. Fix B as before; then the chance that B is *acute* is

$$\frac{\text{segment } MHN}{\text{sphere}}.$$

Now, volume $MHN = \frac{1}{3}\pi r^3 \left(\dfrac{\rho}{r} + 1 - \cos \theta\right)^2 \left(2 + \cos \theta - \dfrac{\rho}{r}\right)$; so that the chance is

$$\frac{1}{4} \left\{ 2 - 3 \cos \theta + \cos^3 \theta + 3\frac{\rho}{r}(1 - \cos^2\theta) + 3\frac{\rho^2}{r^2} \cos \theta - \frac{\rho^3}{r^3} \right\}.$$

Hence the whole probability $(1 - P_B)$ that B is acute is

$$\frac{3}{8r^3} \int_0^{\frac{\pi}{2}} \int_0^{2r\cos\theta} \left\{ 2 - 3 \cos \theta + \cos^3 \theta + 3\frac{\rho}{r}(1 - \cos^2 \theta) + 3\frac{\rho^2}{r^2} \cos \theta - \frac{\rho^3}{r^3} \right\} \rho^2 \sin \theta\, d\theta\, d\rho.$$

Performing the integrations, we find $P_B = \dfrac{17}{70}.$

The probability for C is, of course, the same as for B; hence the whole probability of an obtuse-angled triangle is

$$P = P_A + P_B + P_C = \frac{3}{70} + \frac{17}{70} + \frac{17}{70} = \frac{37}{70}.$$

Hence, the chance of an *acute-angled* triangle is $\dfrac{33}{70}.$

For three points within a *circle* the chance of an acute-angled triangle is

$$\frac{4}{\pi^2} - \frac{1}{8}.$$

2. Two points, A, B, are taken at random in a triangle. If two other points, C, D, are also taken at random in the triangle, find the chance that they shall lie on opposite sides of the line AB.

The sides of the triangle ABC produced divide the whole triangle into seven spaces. Of these, the mean value of those marked (a) is the same, viz., the mean value of ABC; or, $\frac{1}{12}$ of the whole triangle, as we have shown in Art. 236; the mean value of those marked (β) being $\frac{2}{3}$ of the triangle.

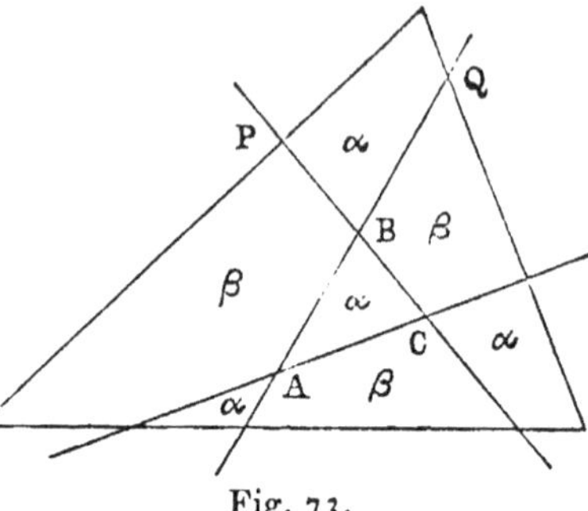

Fig. 73.

This is easily seen: for instance, if the whole area $= 1$, the mean value of the space PBQ gives the chance that if the fourth point D be taken at random, B shall fall within the triangle ADC: now the mean value of ABC gives the chance that D shall fall within ABC; but these two chances are equal.

Hence we see that if A, B, C be taken at random, the mean value of that portion of the whole triangle which lies on the same side of AB as C does is $\frac{11}{18}$ of the whole; that of the opposite portion is $\frac{7}{18}$.

Hence the chance of C and D falling on opposite sides of AB is $\frac{7}{18}$.

244. Random Straight Lines.—If an infinite number of straight lines be drawn at random in a plane, there will be as many parallel to any given direction as to any other, all directions being equally probable; also those having any given direction will be disposed with equal frequency all over the plane. Hence, if a line be determined by the *co-ordinates* p, ω, the perpendicular on it from a fixed origin O, and the inclination of that perpendicular to a fixed axis; then if p, ω be made to vary by equal infinitesimal increments, the series of lines so given will represent the entire series of random straight lines. Thus the number of lines for which p falls between p and $p + dp$, and ω between ω and $\omega + d\omega$, will be measured by $dp\,d\omega$, and the integral

$$\iint dp\,d\omega,$$

between any limits, measures the number of lines within those limits.

It is easy to show from this that *the number of random lines which meet any closed convex contour of length L is measured by L.*

For, taking O inside the contour, and integrating first for p, from 0 to p, the perpendicular on the tangent to the contour, we have $\int p\,d\omega$: taking this through four right angles for ω, we have by Legendre's theorem (p. 232), N being the measure of the number of lines,

$$N = \int_0^2 p\, d\omega = L.$$

Thus if a random line meet a given contour, of length L, the chance of its meeting another convex contour, of length l, internal to the former, is

$$p = \frac{l}{L}.$$

If the given contour be not convex, or not closed, N will evidently be the length of an endless string, drawn tight around the contour.

EXAMPLES.

1. If a random line meet a closed convex contour, of length L, the chance of it meeting another such contour, external to the former, is

$$p = \frac{X - Y}{L};$$

where X is the length of an endless band enveloping both contours, and crossing between them, and Y that of a band also enveloping both, but not crossing.

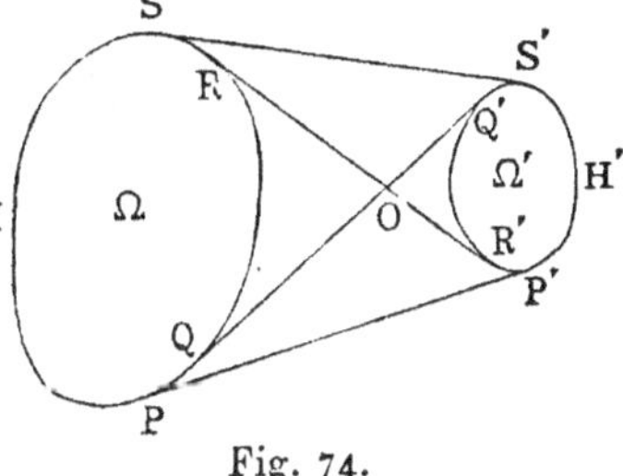

Fig. 74.

This may be shown by means of Legendre's integral above; or as follows :—

Call, for shortness, $N(A)$ the number of lines meeting an area A; $N(A, A')$ the number which meet both A and A'; then

$$N(SROQPH) + N(S'Q'OR'P'H') = N(SROQPH + S'Q'OR'P'H')$$

$$+ N(SROQPH,\ S'Q'OR'P'H'),$$

since in the first member each line meeting *both* areas is counted twice. But the number of lines meeting the non-convex figure consisting of $OQPHSR$ and $OQ'S'H'P'R'$ is equal to the band Y, and the number meeting *both* these areas is identical with that of those meeting the given areas Ω, Ω'; hence

$$X = Y + N(\Omega, \Omega').$$

Thus the number meeting both the given areas is measured by $X - Y$. Hence the theorem follows.

2. Two random chords cross a given convex boundary, of length L, and area Ω; to find the chance that their intersection falls inside the boundary.

Consider the first chord in any position: let C be its length; considering it as a closed area, the chance of the second chord meeting it is

$$\frac{2C}{L};$$

and the whole chance of its co-ordinates falling in dp, $d\omega$, and of the second chord meeting it in that position, is

$$\frac{2C}{L}\,\frac{dp\,d\omega}{\int\int dp\,d\omega} = \frac{2}{L^2}\,C\,dp\,d\omega.$$

But the whole chance is the sum of these chances for all its positions

therefore $$\text{prob.} = \frac{2}{L^2}\int\int C\,dp\,d\omega.$$

Now, for a given value of ω, the value of $\int C\,dp$ is evidently the area Ω; then taking ω from π to 0,

$$\text{required probability} = \frac{2\pi\Omega}{L^2}.$$

The *mean value* of a chord drawn at random across the boundary is

$$M = \frac{\int\int C\,dp\,d\omega}{\int\int dp\,d\omega} = \frac{\pi\Omega}{L}.$$

3. A straight band of breadth c being traced on a floor, and a circle of radius r thrown on it at random, to find the mean area of the band which is covered by the circle. (The cases are omitted where the circle falls outside the band.)*

If S be the space covered, the chance of a random point on the circle falling on the band is

$$p = \frac{M(S)}{\pi r^2}.$$

This is the same as if the circle were fixed, and the band thrown on it at random. Now let A be a position of the random point: the favourable cases are when *HK, the bisector of the band*, meets a circle, centre A, radius $\frac{1}{2}c$; and the whole number are when HK meets a circle, centre O, radius $r + \frac{1}{2}c$; hence (Art. 236) the probability is

$$p = \frac{2\pi \cdot \frac{1}{2}c}{2\pi(r + \frac{1}{2}c)} = \frac{c}{2r + c}.$$

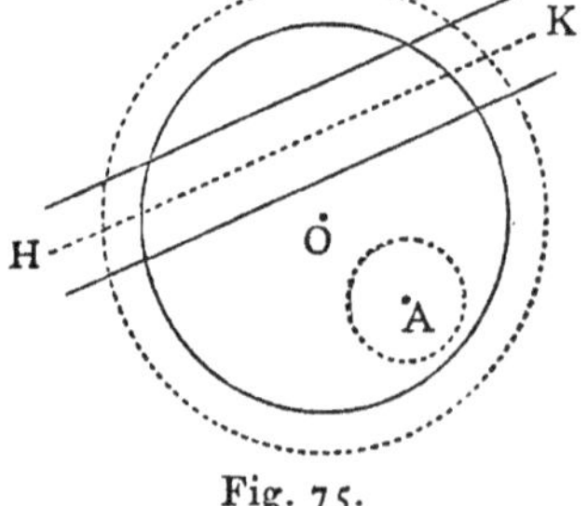
Fig. 75.

This is constant for all positions of A; hence, equating these two values of p, the

---

* Or the floor may be supposed painted with parallel bands, at a distance asunder equal to the diameter; so that the circle must fall on one.

mean area required is

$$M(S) = \frac{c}{2r + c}\,\pi r^2.$$

The mean value of the part of the *circumference* which falls on the band is the same fraction $\dfrac{c}{2r + c}$ of the whole circumference.

If *any convex area* Ω, of perimeter L, be thrown on the band, instead of a circle, the mean area covered is

$$M(S) = \frac{\pi c}{L + \pi c}\,\Omega.$$

245. **Application to Evaluation of Definite Integrals.**—The consideration of probability sometimes may be applied to determine the values of Definite Integrals. For instance, if $n + 1$ points are taken at random in a line, l, and we consider the chance that one of them, X, shall be the last, beginning from the end A of the line, the number of favourable cases, when X is the element dx, is, calling AX, x,

$$x^n\,dx.$$

Hence

$$p = \frac{\displaystyle\int_0^l x^n\,dx}{l^{n+1}};$$

but the chance must be $\dfrac{1}{n + 1}$: we thus have an independent proof that

$$\int_0^l x^n\,dx = \frac{l^{n+1}}{n + 1},$$

when n is an integer.

Again, if $m + n + 1$ points are taken, to find the chance that X shall be the $(m + 1)^{th}$ in order; the number of favourable cases, when X falls in dx, and a *particular set* of m points falls to the left of X, is

$$x^m (1 - x)^n\,dx\,; \quad \text{taking } l = 1\,;$$

hence the whole number of favourable cases is

$$\frac{\big\lfloor m + n}{\big\lfloor m \,\big\lfloor n}\int_0^1 x^m (1 - x)^n\,dx\,;$$

this is the required probability, since $l^{m+n+1} = 1$. But the value is $\dfrac{1}{m+n+1}$, as every point is equally likely to fall in the $(m+1)^{th}$ place : we thus deduce the definite integral

$$\int_0^1 x^m (1-x)^n dx = \frac{\lfloor m \ \lfloor n}{\lfloor m+n+1},$$

when m, n are integers.   (See Art. 92.)

246. To investigate the probability that the inclination of the line joining any two points in a given convex area Ω shall lie within given limits.

We give here a method of reducing this question to calculation, for the sake of an integral to which it leads, and which is not easy to deduce otherwise.

First, let one of the points, A, be fixed ; draw through it a chord $PQ = C$, at an inclination θ to some fixed line ;

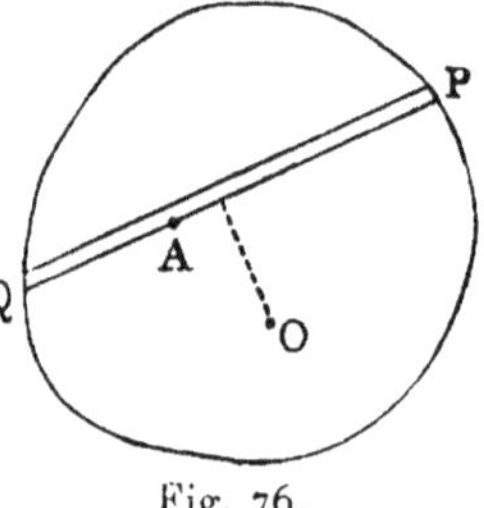

Fig. 76.

put $AP = r$, $AQ = r'$; then the number of cases for which the direction of the line joining A and B lies between θ and $\theta + d\theta$ is measured by

$$\tfrac{1}{2} \left(r^2 + r'^2 \right) d\theta.$$

Now, let A range over the space between PQ and a parallel chord distant dp from it, the number of cases for which A lies in this space, *and* the direction of AB from θ to $\theta + d\theta$, is (first considering A to lie in the element $dr\, dp$)

$$\tfrac{1}{2} dp\, d\theta \int_0^c \left(r^2 + r'^2 \right) dr = \tfrac{1}{3} C^3 dp\, d\theta.$$

Let p be the perpendicular on C from a given origin O, and let ω be the inclination of p (we may put $d\omega$ for $d\theta$), then C will be a given function of p, ω ; and integrating first for ω constant, the whole number of cases for which ω falls between given limits ω', ω'', is

$$\tfrac{1}{3} \int_{\omega'}^{\omega''} d\omega \int C^3 dp \; ;$$

the integral $\int C^3 dp$ being taken for all positions of C between two tangents to the boundary parallel to PQ. The question is thus reduced to the evaluation of this integral; which, of course, is generally difficult enough: we may, however, deduce from it a remarkable result; for if the integral

$$\tfrac{1}{3} \iint C^3 \, dp \, d\omega$$

be extended to all possible positions of C, it gives the whole number of pairs of positions of the points A, B which lie inside the area; but this number is Ω^2; hence

$$\iint C^3 \, dp \, d\omega = 3\Omega^2,$$

the integration extending to all possible positions of the chord C; its length being a given function of its co-ordinates p, ω.

Cor. Hence if L, Ω, be the perimeter and area of any closed convex contour, the mean value of the cube of a chord drawn across it at random is $\dfrac{3\Omega^2}{L}$.

It follows that if a line cross such a contour at random, the chance that *three other lines*, also drawn at random, shall meet the first *inside the contour*, is $24\,\dfrac{\Omega^2}{L^4}$.

Some other cases of definite integrals deduced from the theory of Probability are given in a Paper in the *Philosophical Transactions* for 1868, pp. 181–199. See also *Proceedings London Math. Soc.*, vol. viii.

Several Examples on Mean Values and Probability are annexed; some of them, as also some of the questions which have been explained in this Chapter, are taken from the Papers on the subject in the *Educational Times*, by the Editor, Mr. Miller, as also by Professor Sylvester, Mr. Woolhouse, Col. Clarke, Messrs. Watson, Savage, and others. Some few are rather difficult; but want of space has prevented our giving the solutions in the text.

We may refer to Todhunter's valuable *History of Probability* for an account of the more profound and difficult questions treated by the great writers on the theory of Probability.

EXAMPLES.

1. A chord is drawn joining two points taken at random on a circle : find the mean area of the lesser of the two segments into which it divides the circle.

$$Ans. \quad \frac{\pi r^2}{4} - \frac{r^2}{\pi}.$$

2. Find the mean latitude of all places north of the Equator.

$$Ans. \; 32°.704.$$

3. Find the mean square of the velocity of a projectile *in vacuo*, taken at all instants of its flight till it regains the velocity of projection.

$$Ans. \; V^2 \cos^2 a + \tfrac{1}{3} V^2 \sin^2 a :$$ where $V =$ initial velocity, and $a =$ angle of projection.

4. If x and y are two variables, each of which may take independently any value between two given limits (different for each), show that the mean value of the product xy is equal to the product of the mean values of x and y.

5. If X, Y are points taken at random in a triangle ABC, what is the chance that the quadrilateral $ABXY$ is convex ?

$$Ans. \; \frac{1}{3}.$$

For, it is easy to see that of the three quadrilaterals $ABXY$, $ACXY$, $BCXY$, one must be convex, and two re-entrant.

6. Find the mean area of the quadrilateral formed by four points taken at random on the circumference of a circle.

$$Ans. \; \frac{3}{\pi^2} \text{ (area of circle)}.$$

7. A class list at an examination is drawn up in alphabetical order ; the number of names being n. If a name be selected at random, find the chance that the candidate shall not be more than m places from his place in the order of merit.

$$Ans. \; \frac{2m + 1}{n} - \frac{m(m + 1)}{n^2}.$$ (N.B.—This is not, of course, the value of the chance *after* the selection has been made : this may easily be found.)

8. A traveller starts from a point on a straight river and travels a certain distance in a random direction. Having quite lost his way, he starts again at random the next morning, and travels the same distance as before. Find the chance of his reaching the river again in the second day's journey.

$$Ans. \; \frac{1}{4}.$$

9. Two lengths, b, b', are laid down at random in a line a, greater than either : find the chance that they shall not have a common part greater than c.

$$Ans. \; \frac{(a - b - b' + c)^2}{(a - b)(a - b')}.$$

10. A person in firing 10 shots at a mark has hit 5 times, and missed 5. Find the chance that in the next 10 shots he shall hit 5 times, and miss 5.

Ans. $\dfrac{27 \cdot 4 \cdot 7}{19 \cdot 17 \cdot 13} = \dfrac{756}{4199}$. If the first 10 shots had not been fired, so that nothing was known as to his skill, the chance would be $\dfrac{1}{11}$: if he had been found to hit the mark half the number of times out of a large number, the chance would be $\dfrac{63}{256}$.

11. If a line l be divided at random into 4 parts, the mean square of one of the parts is $\dfrac{1}{10} l^2$: but if the line be divided at random into 2 parts, and each part again divided into 2 parts, then the mean square of one of the 4 parts is $\dfrac{1}{9} l^2$.

12. Three points are taken at random in a line l. Find the mean distance of the intermediate point from the middle of the line.

$$\text{\textit{Ans.} } \frac{3}{16} l.$$

13. A certain city is situated on a river. The probability that a specified inhabitant A lives on the right bank of the river is, of course, $\frac{1}{2}$, in the absence of any further information. But if we have found that an inhabitant B lives on the right bank, find the probability that A does so also.

Ans. $\dfrac{2}{3}$. (N.B.—It is here assumed that every possible partition of the number of inhabitants into 2 parts, by the river, is equally probable *a priori*.)

14. If A, B, C, D, are four given points *in directum*, and 2 points are taken at random in AD, and one is taken in BC: find the chance that it shall fall between the former two.

$$\text{\textit{Ans.} } \frac{1}{AD^2} \left\{ \frac{1}{3} BC^2 + BC(AB + CD) + 2AB \cdot CD \right\}.$$

15. If $z = x + y$, where x may have any value from o to a, and y any value from o to b: find the probability that z is less than an assigned value c (suppose $b < a$).

$$\text{\textit{Ans.} (1) If } c < b, \qquad p_1 = \frac{c^2}{2ab}.$$

$$(2) \text{ If } a > c > b, \qquad p_2 = \frac{c - \frac{1}{2}b}{a}.$$

$$(3) \text{ If } c > a, \qquad p_3 = 1 - \frac{(a + b - c)^2}{2ab}.$$

If we denote the functions expressing the probability in the three cases by $f_1(a, b, c)$, $f_2(a, b, c)$, $f_3(a, b, c)$, we shall find the relation

$$f_1(a, b, c) + f_3(a, b, c) = f_2(a, b, c) + f_2(b, a, c).$$

16. In the cubic equation

$$x^3 + px + q = 0,$$

p and q may have any values between the limits $\pm$ 1. Find the chance that the three roots are real.

$$\text{\textit{Ans.}} \quad \frac{2}{45}\sqrt{3}.$$

17. Two observations are taken of the same magnitude, and the mean of the results is taken as the true value. If the error of each observation is assumed to lie within the limits $\pm a$, and all its values to be equally probable, show that it is an even chance that the error in the result lies between the limits $\pm$ 0.293 a.

18. A point is taken at random in each of two given plane areas. Show that the mean square of the distance between the two points is

$$k^2 + k'^2 + \Delta^2 \; ;$$

where Δ is the distance between the centres of gravity of the areas; and k, k' are the radii of gyration of each area round its centre of gravity.

19. The mean square of the area of the triangle formed by joining any three points taken in any given plane area is $\frac{3}{2} h^2 k^2$; where h, k are the radii of gyration of the area round the two principal axes of rotation in its plane.

If one of the points is fixed at the centre of gravity, the value is $\frac{1}{2} h^2 k^2$. (Mr. Woolhouse.)

20. A line is divided at random into 3 parts. Find the chance—(1) that they will form a triangle; (2) an acute-angled triangle.

$$\text{\textit{Ans.} (1). } p_1 = \tfrac{1}{4}.$$
$$\text{(2). } p_2 = 3 \log 2 - 2.$$

21. A line is divided into n parts. Find the chance that they cannot form a polygon.

$$= \quad \text{\textit{Ans.}} \quad \frac{2}{n^{n-1}}.$$

22. If two stars are taken at random in the northern hemisphere, find the chance that their distance exceeds 90°.

$$\text{\textit{Ans.}} \quad \frac{1}{\pi}.$$

23. The vertices of a spherical triangle are points taken at random on a sphere. Find the chance—(1) that all its angles are acute ; (2) that all are obtuse.

$$\text{\textit{Ans.} (1). } \frac{1}{2\pi} - \frac{1}{8}. \quad \text{(2). } \frac{3}{8} - \frac{1}{2\pi}.$$

24. Show that the mean value of $\dfrac{1}{\rho}$, where ρ is the distance of two points taken at random within a circle, is $\dfrac{16}{3\pi r}$.

25. Two equal lines of length a include an angle θ : find the chance that if two points P, Q are taken at random, one on each line, their distance PQ shall be less than a.

$$\textit{Ans. (1). When } \frac{\pi}{2} > \theta > \frac{\pi}{3}; \quad p_1 = \frac{3\theta - \pi}{2\sin\theta} + 2\cos\theta.$$

$$\text{(2). When } \theta > \frac{\pi}{2}; \quad p_2 = \frac{\pi - \theta}{2\sin\theta}.$$

Here the functions are connected by the relation $F(\theta) + F(\pi - \theta) = f(\theta) + f(\pi - \theta)$.

26. The density of a city population varies inversely as the distance from a central point. Find the chance that two inhabitants chosen at random within a radius r from the centre shall not live further than a distance r from each other.

$$\textit{Ans. } p = \frac{1}{3} - \frac{1}{4}\log 3 + \frac{2}{\pi}\left(1 - \frac{\sqrt{3}}{2}\right) + \frac{1}{2\pi}\int_0^{\frac{\pi}{2}} \frac{\theta\, d\theta}{\sin\theta} + \frac{3}{2\pi}\int_{\frac{\pi}{3}}^{\frac{\pi}{2}} \frac{\theta\, d\theta}{\sin\theta};$$

whence $p = 0.7771$. This result is easily obtained by employing the values given in Question 25.

27. Four points are taken at random within a circle or an ellipse. Show that the chance that they form a re-entrant quadrilateral is $\dfrac{35}{12\pi^2}$.

28. Find the mean distance of two points within a sphere. $\quad\textit{Ans. } \dfrac{36}{35}r.$

29. Three points A, B, C are taken within a circle, whose centre is O. Find the chance that the quadrilateral $ABCO$ is re-entrant.

$$\textit{Ans. } \frac{1}{4} + \frac{4}{3\pi^2}.$$

30. Find the chance that the distance of two points within a square shall not exceed a side of the square.

$$\textit{Ans. } p = \pi - \frac{13}{6}.$$

31. In the same case, find the chance that the distance shall not exceed an assigned value c; a being the side of the square.

$$\textit{Ans. (1). When } c < a; \quad p = \frac{c^2}{a^4}\left(\pi a^2 - \frac{8}{3}ac + \frac{1}{2}c^2\right).$$

$$\text{(2). When } c > a; \quad p = 4\frac{c^2}{a^2}\sin^{-1}\frac{a}{c} - \pi\frac{c^2}{a^2} + \frac{4}{3}\frac{2c^2 + a^2}{a^3}\sqrt{c^2 - a^2} - 2\frac{c^2}{a^2} - \frac{c^4}{2a^4} + \frac{1}{3}.$$

32. Three points are taken at random on a sphere; the chance that in the spherical triangle some one angle shall exceed the sum of the other two is $\frac{1}{2}$. Also the chance that its area shall exceed that of a great circle is $\frac{1}{6}$.

33. If a line be divided at random into 4 parts, show that it is an even chance that one of the parts is greater than half the line.

[25]

34. Prove that the mean distance of a point within a triangle from the vertex C is

$$\frac{1}{3}\left\{\frac{a+b}{2} + \frac{(a-b)(a^2-b^2)}{2c^2} - \frac{h^2}{c}\log\frac{a+b+c}{a+b-c}\right\},$$

where h is the altitude of the triangle.   (See Ex. 6, p. 347.)

35. The mean value of the distance between any two points in an equilateral triangle is

$$M = \frac{3}{5}\, a\left(\frac{1}{3} + \frac{1}{4}\log 3\right).$$

This question may be solved by proving that $M = \frac{3}{5}M_0$, where M_0 is the mean distance of an angle of the triangle from any point within it.   For, let $M_0 = \mu\Delta^{\frac{1}{2}}$, where μ is constant, and $\Delta =$ area of the triangle.   Take now any element dS of the triangle; draw from it parallels to the sides to meet the base; let δ be the area of the equilateral triangle so formed: the sum of the whole number of cases will be equal to

$$6\int\int \delta\,.\,\mu\delta^{\frac{1}{2}}\,.\,dS = M\Delta^2,$$

if dS is made to range over the whole triangle: if we call the whole triangle unity, and put $dS = 2da d\beta$ as in Ex. 3, p. 344, $\delta = a^2$, and the integral becomes $\frac{6}{10}\mu = M$.   The result then follows from 34.

36. From a tower of height h particles are projected in all directions in space with a velocity due to a fall through h.   Show that the mean value of the range is $M = 2h\displaystyle\int_0^1 \sqrt{1-x^4}\,.\,dx.$

(Prof. Wolstenholme.)

37. In n quantities $a, b, c, d \ldots$, each of which takes independently a given series of values $a_1, a_2, a_3, \ldots$; $b_1, b_2, b_3, \ldots$ &c. (the number of values is different for each), if we put

$$\Sigma a = a + b + c + d + \ldots \text{&c.,}$$

and for shortness denote "the mean value of x" by Mx, prove that

$$M\Sigma a = Ma + Mb + Mc + \ldots \text{&c.} = \Sigma Ma,$$

$$M(\Sigma a)^2 = (\Sigma Ma)^2 - \Sigma(Ma)^2 + \Sigma M(a^2).$$

38. Two points are taken at random in a triangle.   Find the mean area of the *triangular* portion which the line joining them cuts off from the whole triangle.

Ans. $\dfrac{4}{9}$ of the whole.

39. A ship at A observes another at B, whose course is unknown. Supposing their speed the same, prove that the chance of their coming within a given distance d of each other is always $\frac{2}{\pi} \sin^{-1} \frac{d}{a}$, whatever the course taken by A; provided its inclination to AB is not greater than $\cos^{-1} \frac{d}{a}$: where $AB = a$. (*Camb. Math. Tripos*, 1871. PROF. MILLER.)

40. A random straight line crosses a circle. Find the chance that two points taken at random in the circle shall lie on opposite sides of the line.

Ans. $\frac{128}{45\pi^2}$. This is deduced at once from the value of M, the mean distance of the two points; as the chance $= \frac{2M}{2\pi r}$. If *two* random lines are drawn, the chance that *both* lines shall pass between the points is $\frac{1}{\pi^2}$.

41. A point O is taken at random in a triangle. What is the probability that if three other points are taken at random, one shall lie in each of the triangles AOB, BOC, COA?

Ans. $\frac{1}{10}$. This may easily be found to depend on the integral $\iint \alpha\beta\gamma \cdot 2d\alpha\,d\beta$, where α, β, γ are the three triangles above.

42. A line crosses a circle at random; find the chance that a point taken at random in the circle shall be distant from the line by less than the radius of the circle.

$$\text{*Ans.* } 1 - \frac{2}{3\pi}.$$

43. Two points are taken on the circumference of a semicircle. Find the chance that their ordinates fall on either side of a point taken at random on the diameter.

$$\text{*Ans.* } \frac{4}{\pi^2}.$$

44. In any convex area *which has a centre* O, let an indefinite straight line revolve round O, and the locus of the centre of gravity of either half into which it divides the area be traced. Show that the mean distance of O from all points in the area is equal to $\frac{1}{4}$ the perimeter of this locus. Also, $\frac{1}{4}$ of the *area* enclosed by this locus = mean area of the triangle OXY; where X, Y are points taken at random in the given area. (CROFTON, *Proceedings*, Lond. Math. Soc., vol. viii.)

45. The probability that the distance of two points taken at random in a given convex area Ω shall exceed a given limit (a) is

$$p = \frac{1}{3\Omega^2} \iint (C^3 - 3a^2 C + 2a^3)\, dp\, d\omega,$$

where C is a chord of the area, whose co-ordinates are p, ω; the integration extending to all values of p, ω, *which give a chord* $C > a$.

[25 a]

Miscellaneous Examples.

1. If a be the sagitta of a circular segment whose base is b, prove that the area of the segment is, approximately,

$$= \frac{2}{3}\, ab + \frac{8}{15}\, \frac{a^3}{b}.$$

2. Find the area of the inverse of a hyperbola, the centre being the pole of inversion; and show that the area of the inverse of an ellipse, under the same circumstances, is an arithmetic mean between the areas of the circles described on its axes as diameters.

3. Find the integral of $\quad \dfrac{dx}{x}\sqrt{\dfrac{a^2 - x^2}{x^2 - b^2}}.$

$$Ans.\ \tan^{-1}\sqrt{\frac{a^2 - x^2}{x^2 - b^2}} + \frac{a}{b}\,\tan^{-1}\frac{b}{a}\sqrt{\frac{a^2 - x^2}{x^2 - b^2}}.$$

4. Prove that

$$\int_{x_0}^{X} f(x)\, dx = (\xi - a)\, f(\xi)\, \log\left(\frac{X - a}{x_0 - a}\right),$$

where ξ lies between X and x_0.

5. In a spiral of Archimedes, if P, Q, and P', Q' be the points of section with any two branches of the curve made by a line passing through its pole; prove that the area bounded by the right line and by the two branches is half the area of the ellipse whose semiaxes are PP' and $P'Q$.

6. Find the value of $\quad \displaystyle\int \frac{dx}{x + c}\sqrt{\frac{x + a}{x + b}}.$

7. If an ellipse roll upon a right line, show that the differential equation of the locus of its focus is

$$(y^2 + b^2)\frac{dy}{dx} = \sqrt{(2ay + y^2 + b^2)(2ay - y^2 - b^2)}.$$

8. A circle rolls from one end to the other of a curved line equal in length to the circumference of the circle, and then rolls back again on the other side of the curve: prove that, if the curvature of the curve be throughout less than that of the circle, the area contained within the closed curve traced out by the point of the circle which was first in contact with the fixed curve is six times the area of the circle. (*Camb. Math. Tripos*, 1871.)

9. In the same case show that the entire length of the path described is eight times the diameter of the circle.

10. Prove that the area of the locus formed by the points of intersection of normals to an ellipse, which cut at right angles, is $\pi (a - b)^2$.

11. Prove that the area between two focal radii of a parabola and the curve is half the area between the curve, the corresponding perpendiculars on the directrix, and the directrix.

12. Evaluate the following integrals:

$$\int \frac{dx}{\sqrt{\tan x}}, \quad \int \sqrt{\sec x - 1}\, dx, \quad \int \frac{(1+x)^4 dx}{(1+x^2)(1+x^4)}.$$

13. If $R = (x^2 + ax)^2 + bx$, and $u = \log \dfrac{x^2 + ax + \sqrt{R}}{x^2 + ax - \sqrt{R}}$, find the relation

between the integrals $\quad \displaystyle\int \frac{dx}{\sqrt{R}}, \quad \int \frac{x\,dx}{\sqrt{R}}.$

$$Ans. \quad \int \frac{x\,dx}{\sqrt{R}} = \frac{a}{3}\int \frac{dx}{\sqrt{R}} + \frac{u}{3}.$$

14. If a curve be such that the area between any portion and a fixed right line is proportional to the corresponding length of the curve, show that it is a catenary.

15. Prove that the volume of a rectangular parallelepiped is to that of its circumscribed ellipsoid as $2 : \pi\sqrt{3}$.

16. Prove that $\quad \displaystyle\int_0^a \frac{d\theta}{\sqrt{1 - \kappa^2 \sin^2\theta}} = \int_0^\beta \frac{d\theta}{\sqrt{\kappa^2 - \sin^2\theta}}$, where $\sin\beta = \kappa \sin\alpha$.

17. If any number of triangles be inscribed in one ellipse, and circumscribed to another ellipse, concentric and similar, prove that these triangles have all the same area.

18. Show that the value of the integral $\displaystyle\int_a^b \frac{dy}{\sqrt{y^m - 1}}$

may be exhibited by the following geometrical construction. Let the curve whose equation is $r^{\frac{m}{m+2}} \cos \dfrac{m}{m+2}\omega = 1$ roll on the axis of x; take the points $(x_1, y_1)\,(x_2, y_2)$ on the roulette described by the pole, such that $y_1 = a$, $y_2 = b$; then

$$\int_a^b \frac{dy}{\sqrt{y^m - 1}} = x_2 - x_1. \qquad \text{(Mr. Jellett.)}$$

19. If s be the length of the arc of a spherical curve measured to any point P, and t be the intercept on the great circle touching at P, between the point of contact and the foot of the perpendicular from the pole, prove that

$$s - t = \int \sin p \, d\omega.$$

The proof is similar to that of the corresponding theorem *in plano*. See Art. 158.

20. Prove that the volume of a polyhedron, having for bases any two polygons situated in parallel planes, and for lateral faces trapeziums, is expressed by the formula

$$\frac{H}{6}(B + B' + 4B'') \; ;$$

where H is the distance between the parallel planes, B and B' the areas of the polygonal bases, and B'' the area of the section equidistant from the two bases.

21. If S be the length of a loop of the curve $r^n = a^n \cos n\theta$, and A the area of a loop of the curve $r^{2n} = a^{2n} \cos 2n\theta$, prove that

$$A \times S = \frac{\pi a^3}{2n}.$$

22. Find approximately the area, and also the length, of a loop of the curve $r^{\frac{5}{3}} = a^{\frac{5}{3}} \cos \dfrac{5\theta}{3}$. (See *Diff. Calc.*, Art. 268.)

Ans. area $= a^2 \times 0.56616$; length $= a \times 2.72638$.

23. Show from Art. 134 that if a parabola roll on a right line, the locus of its focus is a catenary.

24. If A be the area of any oval, B that of its pedal with respect to any internal origin O, and C that of the locus of the point on the perpendicular whose distance from O is equal to the distance of the point of contact from O; prove that A, B, C are in arithmetical progression.

25. The arc of a curve is connected with the abscissa by the equation $s^2 = kx$; find the curve.

26. If the co-ordinates of a point on a curve be given by the equations

$$x = c \sin 2\theta \, (1 + \cos 2\theta), \quad y = c \cos 2\theta \, (1 - \cos 2\theta),$$

prove that the length of its arc, measured from its origin, is $\dfrac{4}{3} c \sin 3\theta$.

27. Show how to find the sum of every element of the periphery of an ellipse divided by any odd power $(2r + 1)$ of the semi-diameter conjugate to that which passes through the element, and give the result in the case of the fifth power.— (Mr. W. Roberts.)

$$\textit{Ans.} \quad \frac{4}{(ab)^{2r-1}}\int_0^{\frac{\pi}{2}} (a^2 \cos^2\theta + b^2 \sin^2\theta)^{r-1} \, d\theta.$$

This gives $\dfrac{\pi(a^2 + b^2)}{a^3 b^3}$ when $r = 2$.

28. A sphere intersects a right cylinder; prove that the entire surface of the cylinder included within the sphere is equal to the product of the diameter of the cylinder into the perimeter of an ellipse, whose axes are equal to the greatest and least intercepts made by the sphere on the edges of the cylinder.

29. Show that the equations of the involute of a circle are of the form

$$x = a \cos \phi + a\phi \sin \phi, \qquad y = a \sin \phi - a\phi \cos \phi,$$

and prove that the length of the arc of this involute, measured from $\phi = 0$, is one half of the arc of a circle which would be described by a radius equal to the arc of its evolute moving through the angle ϕ.

30. Show that the area of the cassinoid

$$r^4 - 2a^2 r^2 \cos 2\theta + a^4 = b^4$$

is expressed by aid of an elliptic arc, when $b > a$; and by a hyperbolic arc, when $a > b$.

31. A string AB, of given length, lies in contact with a plane convex curve with its end A fixed; the string is unwound, and B is made to move about A till the string is again wound on the curve, the final position of B being B'; prove that for variations of the position of A, the arc traced out by B will be a maximum or a minimum, when the tangents at B and B' are equally inclined to the tangent at A; and will be the former or the latter, according as the curvature at A is greater or less than half the sum of the curvatures at B and B'.— (*Camb. Math. Tripos*, 1871.)

32. Find the value of $\displaystyle\int_0^\infty \frac{dx}{\sqrt{x}}\, e^{-\frac{a}{x} - \beta x}.$
  Ans. $\sqrt{\dfrac{\pi}{\beta}}\, e^{-2\sqrt{a\beta}}.$

33. Find the length, and also the area, of the pedal of a cissoid, the vertex being origin.

$$Ans. \quad \frac{8a}{\sqrt{3}} \cdot \log\left(2 + \sqrt{3}\right) - 4a : \frac{\pi a^2}{24}.$$

34. Prove that the length of an arc of the lemniscate $r^2 = a^2 \cos 2\theta$ is represented by the integral

$$\frac{a}{\sqrt{2}} \int \frac{d\phi}{\sqrt{1 - \frac{1}{2}\sin^2 \phi}}.$$

35. Integrate the equation

$$\cos\theta\,(\cos\theta - \sin a \sin \phi)\, d\theta + \cos\phi\,(\cos\phi - \sin a \sin\theta)\, d\phi = 0.$$

If the arbitrary constant be determined by the condition that the equation must be satisfied by the values $(0,\ a)$ of $(\theta,\ \phi)$, show that the equation is satisfied by putting $\theta + \phi = a$.

36. Each element of the surface of an ellipsoid is divided by the area of the parallel central section of the surface; find the sum of all the elementary quotients extended through the entire ellipsoid. *Ans.* 4.

37. Hence, show that

$$\int_0^h \int_h^k \frac{(\mu^2 - \nu^2)\, d\mu\, d\nu}{\sqrt{\mu^2 - h^2}\ \sqrt{k^2 - \mu^2}\ \sqrt{h^2 - \nu^2}\ \sqrt{k^2 - \nu^2}} = \frac{\pi}{2}.$$

This depends on the expression for an element of the surface of an ellipsoid in terms of the elliptic co-ordinates of a point. See Salmon's *Geometry of Three Dimensions*, Art. 411. This proof is due to Chasles (*Liouville*, tome iii. p. 10).

38. Hence, prove the relation

$$F(m)\ E(n) + F(n)\ E(m) - F(n)\ F(m) = \frac{\pi}{2}$$

where

$$F(m) = \int_0^{\frac{\pi}{2}} \frac{d\theta}{\sqrt{1 - m^2 \sin^2\theta}}, \qquad E(m) = \int_0^{\frac{\pi}{2}} \sqrt{1 - m^2 \sin^2\theta}\, d\theta,$$

and $m^2 + n^2 = 1$.

Let $\nu = h \sin\theta$, and $\mu = \sqrt{h^2 \sin^2\phi + k^2 \cos^2\phi}$, in the preceding, and it becomes

$$\int_0^{\frac{\pi}{2}}\int_0^{\frac{\pi}{2}} \frac{h^2 \sin^2\phi + k^2 \cos^2\phi - h^2 \sin^2\theta}{\sqrt{h^2 \sin^2\phi + k^2 \cos^2\phi}\ \sqrt{k^2 - h^2 \sin^2\theta}}\, d\theta\, d\phi$$

$$= \int_0^{\frac{\pi}{2}}\int_0^{\frac{\pi}{2}} \frac{\sqrt{h^2 \sin^2\phi + k^2 \cos^2\phi}}{\sqrt{k^2 - h^2 \sin^2\theta}}\, d\theta\, d\phi \ + \int_0^{\frac{\pi}{2}}\int_0^{\frac{\pi}{2}} \frac{\sqrt{k^2 - h^2 \sin^2\theta}}{\sqrt{h^2 \sin^2\phi + k^2 \cos^2\phi}}\, d\theta\, d\phi$$

$$- \int_0^{\frac{\pi}{2}}\int_0^{\frac{\pi}{2}} \frac{k^2\, d\theta\, d\phi}{\sqrt{h^2 \sin^2\phi + k^2 \cos^2\phi}\ \sqrt{k^2 - h^2 \sin^2\theta}}.$$

This furnishes the required result on making $h = mk$.

The preceding formula, which is due to Legendre, gives a general relation between complete elliptic functions of the first and second species, with complementary moduli. (Compare Ex. 7, 8, p. 331.)

39. If three curves be described on the surface of an ellipsoid, along the first of which the perpendicular to the tangent plane makes the constant angle γ with the axis of z, along the second β with the axis of y, and along the third α with the axis of x, and if the angles be connected by the relations $\dfrac{\tan\alpha}{a} = \dfrac{\tan\beta}{b} = \dfrac{\tan\gamma}{c}$; then, if A_3, A_2, A_1, be the included portions of the ellipsoid surface, prove that

$$\frac{A_3 - A_2}{a^2} + \frac{A_1 - A_2}{b^2} + \frac{A_2 - A_1}{c^2} = 0. \qquad \text{(Mr. Jellett.)}$$

40. Show that the results given in Arts. 161 and 162 hold good for spherical conics, where the tangents are arcs of great circles on the sphere.

41. Prove that

$$\int_b^a \frac{dx}{\{(a - x)(b - x)(c - x)\}^{\frac{1}{2}}} = \int_{-\infty}^c \frac{dx}{\{(a - x)(b - x)(c - x)\}^{\frac{1}{2}}},$$

where a, b, c are in the order of magnitude.

42. If ω be an imaginary cube root of unity, show that, if

$$y = \frac{(\omega - \omega^2)\, x + \omega^2 x^3}{1 - \omega^2 (\omega - \omega^2)\, x^2}, \quad \text{then} \quad \frac{dy}{(1 - y^2)^{\frac{1}{2}} (1 + \omega y^2)^{\frac{1}{2}}} = \frac{(\omega - \omega^2)\, dx}{(1 - x^2)^{\frac{1}{2}} (1 + \omega x^2)^{\frac{1}{2}}}.$$

(Professor Cayley.)

43. Prove that the value of

$$\int_0^\infty \frac{\cos bx \sin ax}{x}\, dx \text{ is } 0, \quad \frac{\pi}{4}, \quad \text{or} \quad \frac{\pi}{2},$$

according as b is $>$, $=$, or $< a$.

44. Prove that $\displaystyle\int_0^\infty \frac{\sin bx \sin ax}{x^2}\, dx = \frac{\pi}{2}$ multiplied by the lesser of the numbers a and b.

45. If e be the eccentricity of an ellipse whose semiaxis major is unity, and E the length of its quadrant, prove that

$$\int_0^h \frac{Ee\, de}{(1 - e^2)\sqrt{h^2 - e^2}} = \frac{\pi h}{2\sqrt{1 - h^2}}. \qquad \text{(W. Roberts.)}$$

46. If S represent the length of a quadrant of the curve $r^m = a^m \cos m\theta$, and S_1 the quadrant of its first pedal, prove that

$$S \,.\, S_1 = \frac{m + 1}{2m}\, \pi a^2.$$

Here (Ex. 3, Art. 156), we have

$$S = \frac{a\sqrt{\pi}}{2m}\, \frac{\Gamma\left(\dfrac{1}{2m}\right)}{\Gamma\left(\dfrac{m + 1}{2m}\right)}.$$

Also, since the first pedal (*Diff. Calc.* Art. 268) is derived by substituting $\dfrac{m}{m + 1}$ instead of m,

$$S_1 = \frac{(m + 1)\, a\sqrt{\pi}}{2m}\, \frac{\Gamma\left(\dfrac{m + 1}{2m}\right)}{\Gamma\left(1 + \dfrac{1}{2m}\right)};$$

$$\therefore SS_1 = \frac{(m + 1)\, \pi a^2}{4m^2}\, \frac{\Gamma\left(\dfrac{1}{2m}\right)}{\Gamma\left(1 + \dfrac{1}{2m}\right)} = \frac{(m + 1)\, \pi a^2}{2m}.$$

47. In general, if S_n be the quadrant of the nth pedal of the curve in the last prove that

$$S_{n-1} S_n = \frac{mn + 1}{2m}\, \pi a^2.$$

Here it is readily seen that the nth pedal is got by substituting $\dfrac{m}{mn + 1}$ instead of m in the equation of the proposed; $\therefore$ &c. (W. Roberts, *Liouville*, 1845, p. 177.)

48. If an endless string, longer than the circumference of an ellipse, be passed round the ellipse and kept stretched by a moving pencil ; prove that the pencil will trace out a confocal ellipse.

49 If two confocal ellipses be such that a polygon can be inscribed in one and circumscribed to the other, prove that an indefinite number of such polygons can be described, and that they all have the same perimeter. (Chasles, *Comp. Rend.* 1843.)

50. To two arcs of a hyperbola whose difference is rectifiable correspond qual arcs of the lemniscate which is the pedal of the hyperbola. (*Ibid.*)

51. Prove that the tangents drawn at the extremities of two arcs of a conic, whose difference is rectifiable, form a quadrilateral whose sides all touch the same circle. (*Ibid.*)

52. In the curve

$$x^{\frac{3}{2}} + y^{\frac{3}{2}} = a^{\frac{3}{2}},$$

prove that any tangent divides that portion of the curve between two cusps into two arcs which are to each other as the segments of the portion of the tangent intercepted by the axes.

53. If two tangents to a cycloid cut at a constant angle, prove that their sum bears a constant ratio to the arc of the curve between them.

54. If AB, ab, be quadrants of two concentric circles, their radii coinciding ; show that if an arc Ab of an involute of a circle be drawn to touch the circles at A, b, the arc Ab is an arithmetical mean between the arcs AB and ab.

55. If ds represent an infinitely small superficial element of area at a point outside any closed plane curve, and t, t' the lengths of the tangents from the point to the curve, and θ the angle of intersection of these tangents : prove that the sum of the elements represented by $\dfrac{\sin \theta\, ds}{t \times t'}$, taken for all points exterior to the curve, is $2\pi^2$. (Prof. Crofton, *Phil. Trans.*, 1868.)

56. Show that, for all systems of rectangular axes drawn through a given point in a given plane area,

$$\left\{ \iint (x^2 - y^2)\, dx\, dy \right\}^{2} + 4 \left\{ \iint xy\, dx\, dy \right\}^{2},$$

taken over the whole of the area, is constant ; and that for a triangle, the point being its centre of gravity, this constant value is

$$\left(\tfrac{1}{18}\Delta\right)^{2} (a^4 + b^4 + c^4 - b^2 c^2 - c^2 a^2 - a^2 b^2).$$

Mr. J. J. Walker.)

57. If $ab = a'b'$, prove that

$$\int_0^\infty \int_0^\infty \frac{\phi\,(ax + by) - \phi\,(a'x + b'y)}{xy}\,dx\,dy$$

$$= \log\left(\frac{a}{a'}\right) \log\left(\frac{a}{b'}\right) \{\phi\,(\infty) - \phi\,(0)\},$$

provided the limits $\phi\,(0)$ and $\phi\,(\infty)$ are both definite.

(Mr. Elliott, *Proceedings*, Lond. Math. Soc., 1876.)

58. If S denote the surface, and V the volume, of the cone standing on the focal ellipse of an ellipsoid, and having its vertex at an umbilic ; prove that

$$S = \pi a\,(b^2 - c^2)^{\frac{1}{2}}, \qquad V = \tfrac{1}{3}\,\pi c\,(b^2 - c^2),$$

where a, b, c are the principal semiaxes of the ellipsoid.

59. Prove that, if p be positive and less than unity,

$$\int_0^1 (x^p + x^{-p}) \log\,(1 + x)\,\frac{dx}{x} = \frac{\pi}{p\sin p\pi} - \frac{1}{p^2}, \tag{1}$$

and

$$\int_0^1 (x^p + x^{-p}) \log\,(1 - x)\,\frac{dx}{x} = \frac{\pi}{p}\cot p\pi - \frac{1}{p^2}, \tag{2}$$

where (1) may be deduced from (2) by putting x^2 for x.

(Prof. Wolstenholme.)

60. If μ, ν be the *elliptic co-ordinates* of a point in a plane, prove that the area of any portion of the plane is represented by

$$\iint \frac{(\mu^2 - \nu^2)\,d\mu\,d\nu}{\sqrt{(\mu^2 - c^2)\,(c^2 - \nu^2)}},$$

taken between proper limits.

61. Prove that the differential equation, in elliptic co-ordinates, of any tangent to the ellipse $\mu = \mu_1$ is

$$\frac{d\mu}{\sqrt{(\mu^2 - c^2)\,(\mu^2 - \mu_1^2)}} \pm \frac{d\nu}{\sqrt{(c^2 - \nu^2)\,(\mu_1^2 - \nu^2)}} = 0.$$

62. Hence show that the preceding differential equation in μ and ν admits of an algebraic integral.

63. Prove that the differential equation of the involute of the ellipse $\mu = \mu_1$ is

$$\sqrt{\frac{\mu^2 - \mu_1^2}{\mu^2 - c^2}}\,d\mu \mp \sqrt{\frac{\mu_1^2 - \nu^2}{c^2 - \nu^2}}\,d\nu = 0.$$

64. Show that, for a homogeneous solid parallelepiped of any form and dimensions, the three principal axes at the centre of gravity coincide in direction with those of the solid inscribed ellipsoid which touches at the six centres of gravity of its six faces; and that, for each of the three coincident axes, and therefore for every axis passing through their common centre of gravity, the moment of inertia of the parallelepiped is to that of the ellipsoid in the same constant ratio, viz., that of 10 to π.—(PROF. TOWNSEND.)

65. Show that the volumes of any tetrahedron, and of the inscribed ellipsoid which touches at the centres of gravity of its four faces, have the same principal axes at their common centre of gravity; and that their moments of inertia for all planes through that point have the same constant ratio (viz. $18\sqrt{3} : \pi$).—(*Ibid.*)

66. A quantity M of matter is distributed over the surface of a sphere of radius a, so that the surface density varies inversely as the cube of the distance from a given internal point S, distant b from the centre; prove that the sum of the principal moments of inertia of M at S is equal to $2M(a^2 - b^2)$.

(Camb. Math. Tripos, 1876.)

67. If $\quad (1 - 2ax + a^2)^{-\frac{1}{2}} = 1 + aX_1 + a^2 X_2 \ldots + a^n X_n + \ldots,$ prove that

$$\int_{-1}^{+1} X_n X_m \, dx = 0, \qquad \int_{-1}^{+1} X_n^2 \, dx = \frac{2}{2n+1}.$$

68. A closed central curve revolves round an arbitrary external axis in its plane. Prove that the moments of inertia I and J, with respect to the axis of revolution and to the perpendicular plane passing through the centre of inertia, of the solid generated by the revolving area, are given respectively by the expressions

$$I = m(a^2 + 3h^2), \qquad J = m\left(k^2 - \frac{l^4}{a^2}\right);$$

where m represents the mass of the solid, a the distance of the centre of the generating area from the axis of revolution, h and k the radii of gyration of the area with respect to the parallel and perpendicular axes through its centre, and l the *arm length* of its product of inertia with respect to the same axes.

(PROF. TOWNSEND, Quarterly Journal of Mathematics, 1879.)

69. If $\quad U = \int_0^x (x - z)^{n-1} f(z) \, dz,$ find the value of $\dfrac{d^n u}{dx^n}.$ $\qquad$ *Ans.* $f(z).$

70. Prove that the superficial area of an ellipsoid is represented by

$$2\pi c^2 + 2\pi ab \int_0^1 \frac{(1 - e^2 e'^2 x^2) \, dx}{\sqrt{(1 - e^2 x^2)(1 - e'^2 x^2)}},$$

where $a^2 - b^2 = a^2 e^2, \quad b^2 - c^2 = e'^2 b^2.$

(MR. JELLETT, Hermathena, 1883.)

71. Find the mean distance of two points on opposite sides of a square whose side is unity.

Ans. $\dfrac{2 - \sqrt{2}}{3} + \log(1 + \sqrt{2}).$

72. A cube being cut at random by a plane, what is the chance that the section is a hexagon?—(Col. Clarke.)

$$\text{Ans.} \quad \frac{\sqrt{3} \cot^{-1} \sqrt{3} - \sqrt{2} \cot^{-1} \sqrt{2}}{\frac{1}{4}\pi} = .04646.$$

73. Three points are taken at random, one on each of three faces of a tetrahedron: what is the chance that the plane passing through them cuts the fourth face?—(Col. Clarke.)

$$\text{Ans.} \quad \frac{3}{4}.$$

74. Two stars are taken at random from a catalogue: what is the chance that one or both shall always be visible to an observer in a given latitude, λ?—(*Ibid.*)

$$\text{Ans.} \quad \frac{1}{2} \text{ versin } \lambda + \frac{1}{4} \sin \lambda.$$

75. Find the chance that the centre of gravity of a triangle lies inside the triangle formed by three points taken at random within the triangle.

$$\text{Ans.} \quad \frac{1}{27} \left(2 + \frac{10}{3} \log 4 \right).$$

76. Two points are taken at random in a triangle, the line joining them dividing the triangle into two portions: find the mean value of that portion which contains the centre of gravity.

$$\text{Ans.} \quad \frac{1}{3} \left(470 + \frac{82}{3} \log 4 \right) = .6967, \text{ the triangle being unity.}$$

The mean value of the *greater* of the two portions is $\frac{7}{12} + \frac{1}{6} \log 2 = .6987$.

77. Show that the mean distance M of a point in a rectangle from one angle is given by

$$3M = d + \frac{b^2}{2a} \log \frac{a+d}{b} + \frac{a^2}{2b} \log \frac{b+d}{a},$$

a and b being the sides, d the diagonal.

78. Show that the mean distance M of two points within a rectangle given by

$$15M = \frac{a^3}{b^2} + \frac{b^3}{a^2} + d \left(3 - \frac{a^2}{b^2} - \frac{b^2}{a^2} \right) + \frac{5}{2} \left(\frac{b^2}{a} \log \frac{a+d}{b} + \frac{a^2}{b} \log \frac{b+d}{a} \right).$$

This result may be deduced from the preceding; for if $\mu =$ mean distance of a point within the rectangle whose sides are x, y, from one of its angles, it is easy to see that

$$a^2 b^2 M = 4 \int_b^a \int_0^b xy\mu \, dx \, dy ; \quad \therefore \, \&c.$$

79. Show that if M be the mean distance of two points within any convex area Ω, we have

$$M = \frac{1}{\Omega^2} \int \int \Sigma\Sigma'\, dp\, d\omega,$$

where Σ, Σ' are the segments into which the area is divided by a straight line crossing it; the *co-ordinates* of the line being p, ω; and the integration extending to all positions of the line.

This may be seen by considering that if a random line crosses the area, the chance of its passing between the two points is $\dfrac{2M}{L}$, where L is the length of the boundary. Again, for any position of the line, the chance of the points lying on opposite sides of it is $\dfrac{\Sigma\Sigma'}{2\Omega^2}$; therefore the whole chance is $\dfrac{2}{\Omega^2}\, M\,(\Sigma\Sigma')$, where $M\,(\Sigma\Sigma')$ is the mean value of the product $\Sigma\Sigma'$ for all positions of the line.

80. In the same case we also have

$$M = \frac{1}{6\Omega^2} \int \int C^4\, dp\, d\omega,$$

C being the length of the intercepted chord. Hence we have the remarkable identity

$$\int\int C^4\, dp\, d\omega = 6 \int\int \Sigma\Sigma'\, dp\, d\omega.$$

(CROFTON, Proceedings, Lond. Math. Soc., vol. 8.)

81. Show that if ρ be the distance of two points taken at random in the same area,

$$M\left(\frac{1}{\rho}\right) = \frac{1}{\Omega^2} \int \int C^2\, dp\, d\omega.$$

This may be applied to the circle. (See **Ex.** 24, p. 376.)

82. Show that the mean area of the triangle determined by three points chosen at random within any convex area is

$$M = \Omega - \frac{1}{\Omega^3} \int \int C^3\, \Sigma^2\, dp\, d\omega,$$

where $\Sigma =$ either segment cut off by the chord C; but throughout the integrations, as the direction of the chord alters, Σ means always the segment on the same side of the chord as at first.

INDEX.

THE END.